Theory and Practice of Business Intelligence in Healthcare

Jiban Khuntia
University of Colorado, Denver, USA

Xue Ning
University of Colorado, Denver, USA

Mohan Tanniru
Oakland University, USA

A volume in the Advances in Healthcare Information Systems and Administration (AHISA) Book Series

IGI Global
DISSEMINATOR OF KNOWLEDGE

Published in the United States of America by
IGI Global
Medical Information Science Reference (an imprint of IGI Global)
701 E. Chocolate Avenue
Hershey PA, USA 17033
Tel: 717-533-8845
Fax: 717-533-8661
E-mail: cust@igi-global.com
Web site: http://www.igi-global.com

Library of Congress Cataloging-in-Publication Data

Names: Khuntia, Jiban, 1974- editor. | Ning, Xue, 1986- editor. | Tanniru, Mohan R., editor.
Title: Theory and practice of business intelligence in healthcare / Jiban Khuntia, Xue Ning, Mohan Tanniru, editors.
Description: Hershey, PA : Medical Information Science Reference, [2020] | Includes bibliographical references and index. | Summary: "This book introduces data mining, modeling, and analytic techniques to health and healthcare data; articulates the value of big volumes of data to health and healthcare; evaluates business intelligence tools; and explores business intelligence use and applications in healthcare" Provided by publisher.
Identifiers: LCCN 2019039514 (print) | LCCN 2019039515 (ebook) | ISBN 9781799823100 (hardcover) | ISBN 9781799823117 (ebook)
Subjects: MESH: Data Mining | Health Care Sector | Data Analysis | Big Data
Classification: LCC R859.7.D35 (print) | LCC R859.7.D35 (ebook) | NLM W 26.55.I4 | DDC 610.285--dc23
LC record available at https://lccn.loc.gov/2019039514
LC ebook record available at https://lccn.loc.gov/2019039515

This book is published in the IGI Global book series Advances in Healthcare Information Systems and Administration (AHISA) (ISSN: 2328-1243; eISSN: 2328-126X)

British Cataloguing in Publication Data
A Cataloguing in Publication record for this book is available from the British Library.

Advances in Healthcare Information Systems and Administration (AHISA) Book Series

ISSN:2328-1243
EISSN:2328-126X

Editor-in-Chief: Anastasius Moumtzoglou, Hellenic Society for Quality & Safety in Healthcare and P. & A. Kyriakou Children's Hospital, Greece

MISSION

The **Advances in Healthcare Information Systems and Administration (AHISA) Book Series** aims to provide a channel for international researchers to progress the field of study on technology and its implications on healthcare and health information systems. With the growing focus on healthcare and the importance of enhancing this industry to tend to the expanding population, the book series seeks to accelerate the awareness of technological advancements of health information systems and expand awareness and implementation.

Driven by advancing technologies and their clinical applications, the emerging field of health information systems and informatics is still searching for coherent directing frameworks to advance health care and clinical practices and research. Conducting research in these areas is both promising and challenging due to a host of factors, including rapidly evolving technologies and their application complexity. At the same time, organizational issues, including technology adoption, diffusion and acceptance as well as cost benefits and cost effectiveness of advancing health information systems and informatics applications as innovative forms of investment in healthcare are gaining attention as well. **AHISA** addresses these concepts and critical issues.

COVERAGE

- Clinical Decision Support Design, Development and Implementation
- IT security and privacy issues
- Nursing Expert Systems
- Medical Informatics
- Rehabilitative Technologies
- E-Health and M-Health
- IT Applications in Physical Therapeutic Treatments
- Virtual health technologies
- Decision Support Systems
- IS in Healthcare

IGI Global is currently accepting manuscripts for publication within this series. To submit a proposal for a volume in this series, please contact our Acquisition Editors at Acquisitions@igi-global.com or visit: http://www.igi-global.com/publish/.

The Advances in Healthcare Information Systems and Administration (AHISA) Book Series (ISSN 2328-1243) is published by IGI Global, 701 E. Chocolate Avenue, Hershey, PA 17033-1240, USA, www.igi-global.com. This series is composed of titles available for purchase individually; each title is edited to be contextually exclusive from any other title within the series. For pricing and ordering information please visit http://www.igi-global.com/book-series/advances-healthcare-information-systems-administration/37156. Postmaster: Send all address changes to above address.

Titles in this Series

For a list of additional titles in this series, please visit:
http://www.igi-global.com/book-series/advances-healthcare-information-systems-administration/37156

Smart Medical Data Sensing and IoT Systems Design in Healthcare
Chinmay Chakraborty (Birla Institute of Technoloy, India)
Medical Information Science Reference • ©2020 • 288pp • H/C (ISBN: 9781799802617) • US $275.00

Emerging Trends and Innovations in Privacy and Health Information Management
Cristina Albuquerque (University of Coimbra, Portugal)
Medical Information Science Reference • ©2019 • 376pp • H/C (ISBN: 9781522584704) • US $275.00

Mobile Health Applications for Quality Healthcare Delivery
Anastasius Moumtzoglou (P&A Kyriakou Children's Hospital, Greece)
Medical Information Science Reference • ©2019 • 327pp • H/C (ISBN: 9781522580218) • US $265.00

Intelligent Systems for Healthcare Management and Delivery
Nardjes Bouchemal (University Center of Mila, Algeria)
Medical Information Science Reference • ©2019 • 377pp • H/C (ISBN: 9781522570714) • US $245.00

Human Rights, Public Values, and Leadership in Healthcare Policy
Augustine Nduka Eneanya (University of Lagos, Nigeria)
Medical Information Science Reference • ©2019 • 311pp • H/C (ISBN: 9781522561330) • US $225.00

Contemporary Applications of Mobile Computing in Healthcare Settings
R. Rajkumar (VIT University, India)
Medical Information Science Reference • ©2018 • 259pp • H/C (ISBN: 9781522550365) • US $205.00

For an entire list of titles in this series, please visit:
http://www.igi-global.com/book-series/advances-healthcare-information-systems-administration/37156

IGI Global
DISSEMINATOR OF KNOWLEDGE

701 East Chocolate Avenue, Hershey, PA 17033, USA
Tel: 717-533-8845 x100 • Fax: 717-533-8661
E-Mail: cust@igi-global.com • www.igi-global.com

Table of Contents

Detailed Table of Contents

Business Intelligence and Analytics (BI&A) is emerging as an essential area of expertise in healthcare organizations. Healthcare organizations are trying to leverage BI&A as an integral capability to provide quality healthcare service to patients. From an organizational perspective, BI&A extends beyond an artifact or tool to include several capabilities. This chapter conceptualizes potential capabilities that BI&A can bestow to healthcare organizations. A three-category classification of BI&A healthcare capability classification is suggested: BI&A healthcare insight infrastructure capability, BI&A healthcare process capability, and BI&A healthcare integration capability. In this chapter, the authors discuss the attributes of these three BI&A healthcare capabilities to offer understandings into how these capabilities can help healthcare firms. This taxonomy will help healthcare providers and IT professionals in the healthcare industry make informed decisions on how best to adopt BI&A within their firms to provide quality healthcare service.

The relatively recent and more pervasive retention of electronic healthcare data has provided new opportunities for the advancement of analytics and business intelligence tools within healthcare. The tasks comprising the delivery process for healthcare provide numerous points for data capture, and associated analyses to improve efficiencies and quality of care. In general, healthcare data is extracted from transaction-based systems designed for billing, scheduling, and workflow. However, data characterizing medical events can be further leveraged to assist in the diagnosis and treatment of patients. In fact, healthcare information technology (HIT) to improve patient diagnosis and treatment is remarkably neglected. This chapter outlines the process flow for healthcare delivery, describes the data extracted during this process flow, details the enablers and inhibitors of HIT and accompanying analytics, presents concerns about data integrity and quality, and provides some methods for data cleansing and staging.

Value creation in healthcare calls for the design of care plans that integrate the activities of clinical and non-clinical actors of both the provider and patient ecosystems as they work towards the shared goal: ensure patient adherence outside the provider ecosystem. Given the differing institutional mechanisms that influence actor behavior, intelligence gathered through digital services has two objectives. The first objective is to use digital services to track patient adherence to care plans, so that these care plans can be adapted as needed. The second objective is to learn about the characteristics of the patient ecosystem, so that incentives can be designed to ensure that all actors are working towards the same shared goal. This chapter uses a service modeling approach to explicate the interconnected role of actors across ecosystems and develop strategies to address these two objects. Several use cases are used to illustrate this approach.

The healthcare industry has generated a huge amount of data in diverse formats. The big data in healthcare is leading the revolution in healthcare. Collecting data at the operational level is the starting point for the big data-driven healthcare revolution. By analyzing the operational level big data, healthcare organizations can gain the business intelligence for further strategy development, for example how to improve the healthcare quality, how to provide better long-term care, and how to empower the patients. This chapter discusses this process as operations-intelligence-strategy (OIS) process in healthcare. Objectives are understanding how to gain business intelligence from sensor data mining in healthcare, biomedical signal analysis, and biomedical image analysis, and exploring the applications and impacts of the OIS process, with a focus on the sensor data mining in healthcare.

Healthcare Analytics deals with patient records, effective management of hospitals, and clinical care. But the big data available is still not enough for focused research as it is complicated to find insights from complex, noisy, heterogeneous, and voluminous data, which takes time and effort, while a small clinical data will be more effective for decision making. The health care data also varies in data collection methods and their processing methods. Data generated through patient records is structured, wearable technologies generate semi structured data, and X rays and images provide unstructured data. Storing and extracting information from the structured, semi-structured, and unstructured data is a challenging task. Different machine learning techniques can simplify the process. The chapter discusses the data characteristics, identifying critical attributes, various classification and optimization algorithms for decision making purposes. The purpose of the discussion is to create a basis for selection of algorithms based on size, temporal validity, and outcomes expected.

Continual feedback to adapt to external regulatory and competitive environment is essential in today's complex healthcare landscape, and hospital leadership needs to transform its strategic planning process to reflect the market dynamic. Digital artifacts such as performance dashboard track operational data and transform these into key performance indicators (KPIs) to set organizational goals and align unit level operations. However, the velocity of change occurring in the marketplace needs a dynamic approach: a real-time aggregation of operational data into KPIs for a daily or weekly review to gain insights and respond quickly to evolving market expectations. This chapter discusses how an rtDashboard (real time dashboard) has evolved to become a key artifact that transformed the way a hospital in SE Michigan engaged in its strategic planning process.

The importance of data as the fuel of artificial intelligence is self-evident. As the degree of informatization in various industries deepens, the amount of accumulated data continues to increase; however, data processing capability lags far behind the exponential growth of data volume. To gather accurate results, more and more data should be collected. However, the more data collected, the slower the processing and analyzing of that data. The emergence of deep learning solves the problem of how to process large amounts of data quickly and precisely. With the advancement of technology, the healthcare industry has achieved a promising level of needed data. Moreover, if deep learning can be used to aid disease diagnosis, patient data can be processed efficiently, useful information can be screened, valuable diagnostic rules can be mined, and disease diagnosis results can be better formulated and treated. It is foreseeable that deep learning has the potential to improve the effectiveness and the efficiency of healthcare and relevant industries.

In the digital age, the healthcare industry is generating a huge amount of data and information. Although there are structured data such as EHRs, the major data type is unstructured data such as clinical text. The sources of health data are also diversified, including medical data, clinical data, patient-generated data, and social media data. Different methods are applied to analyze the variety of data and obtain health information. When the various types of information are generated, information retrieval and extraction techniques can be used for further decision-making. Data and information-enabled decision-making is a complex process. Many tools and methods are developed to support decision-making in healthcare. Along with the benefits of integrating business intelligence in healthcare, issues and challenges exist. This chapter discusses the health data and information and how they support decision-making in healthcare.

Information technology has enabled tertiary health care providers to improve patient access to preventive and post-discharge care transition services. When such services are supported by facilities that are under the control of the hospital, hospitals can still influence the delivery and overall quality of patient care services. However, for a variety of reasons, many hospitals rely on external care providers who operate relatively independently from the hospital to deliver these services. As such, service delivery intended to create efficiency and value to patients can become complex, challenging to deliver, and resource intensive—especially if the service delivery spans a prolonged time horizon. This chapter discusses one case of an intermediary who helps hospitals address the smoking cessation needs of patients. Using service dominant logic research, the service exchanges among three different ecosystems (healthcare providers, intermediary, and patients) are modeled and intelligence needed to align their goals using blockchain architecture is highlighted.

The healthcare system is focusing more on patient empowerment leading to patients with active health management. In this process, although some mechanisms exist, there is a need for patient empowerment to move to a new realm where the empowerment process is activated remotely from the patient's side. With the increasing importance of Internet and e-health, it is believed that patient empowerment can be facilitated in the online setting and can be more effective than traditional face-to-face setting. Facilitating patient empowerment online also paves way to data analytics as various online activities can be tracked and the emerging analytic techniques can be utilized to gain insight into the data. This chapter provides knowledge on patient empowerment, data analytics, and their relationship including the role of patient empowerment in data analytics.

Foreword

Business intelligence (BI) is the process of analyzing existing data to understand what has happened in the past, why it has happened, and what can be expected to happen in the future. BI technologies can handle large structured and unstructured healthcare data (big data) to enable healthcare managers, and analysts to conduct appropriate analysis to make informed decisions. Because of the complex nature of healthcare data and its significant impacts, it is important to understand both the theories and practices of BI in healthcare to support the decision-making process. BI in healthcare is facing both opportunities and challenges since more professionals are needed to help healthcare enterprises achieve strategic, tactical, and operational goals.

This book will aim to recognize and understand key concepts of BI relevant to healthcare, introduce data mining, modeling and analytics techniques to health and healthcare data, articulate the value of big volumes of data to health and healthcare, evaluate BI tools, generate application ideas, and explore BI use in healthcare, and critically analyze the use of BI technologies and applications in healthcare.

The target audience of this book will be students in a graduate class on the state of BI practice in the healthcare industry. Topics include the evolution of BI in healthcare, the digitization of health records and health systems integration, and the different aspects of BI in various subsets of the healthcare industry, such as hospitals and health insurance organizations. As such, it provides a key reference point for students and researchers in other relevant disciplines, such as information systems, business analytics, healthcare administration, sociology, and computer science. Moreover, it will provide insights for executives concerned with the application of BI for organizational development in the healthcare industry and other types of work communities and environments.

Jahangir Karimi
Business School, University of Colorado, Denver, USA

Foreword

Business intelligence (BI) refers to the data analyzing and information presenting process enabled by information technologies. By using different tools, techniques, and methods, various types of data from multiple resources are collected and analyzed to gain relevant information. Besides the traditional ways such as report to present information, data visualization is another efficient methodology to display analytical results for further decision-making. BI enables the decision-making process in organizations at strategic, management, and operational level.

Virtually every industry has become digitized, and, consequently, strives to use data and business intelligence to achieve their goals. Healthcare is no exception. Healthcare organizations and stakeholders use data and business intelligence tools to reach six specific clinical and business process improvement goals: (1) Improve the quality of the outcomes of care and reduce outcome disparities, (2) Lower the individual and aggregate costs of care, (3) Improve equitable and timely access to care, (4) Improve the patient and care community experience, (5) Improve the healthcare professional experience, and (6) Increase the efficiency and efficacy of medical care business processes throughout the value chain.

Healthcare business intelligence tools fall into several general categories. First, the descriptive tools are retrospective and describe what happened and when. These tools track past activities to identify trends or unwanted variations. Second, the prescriptive tools, like clinical decision support tools, are designed to help health professionals make better decisions about diagnosis and treatment. Third, the predictive tools help users identify patients at risk for disease or adverse outcomes and alert them to possible interventions to avoid premature morbidity or mortality. Moreover, computer vision tools are pattern recognition tools that are used to map features of images, like medical images, pathology slides or skin lesions that might be cancer, to improve the accuracy and efficiency of making a correct diagnosis.

Nevertheless, there are challenges to gain healthcare business intelligence. For example, the technical issues, human factors, environmental factors, and business model issues are all barriers for BI applications in the healthcare industry. However, the benefits and impacts of BI in healthcare outweigh the challenges. BI has the potential to improve the productivity of healthcare works, improve working efficiency with lower cost and fewer resources, and improve clinicians' performance and healthcare quality.

While the potential benefits are significant, winning the 4th industrial revolution in the healthcare industry will require that doctors, biomedical entrepreneurs, and patients have data and business intelligence literacy to understand its potential and avoid the inevitable unintended consequences. This book is a useful guide for graduate students and faculty to help navigate that difficult and challenging pathway.

Arlen Meyers
Society of Physician Entrepreneurs, USA & University of Colorado, USA

Preface

Healthcare is moving to be value-based care. This development is in stark contrast to the earlier episodic care management process and operations that were prevalent to shape the focus and strategy for all healthcare organizations. In the new value-based care model, clinical outcomes, not only for one episode but across the life-span of a patient or individual is the key to be considered as a success parameter. In this process, a critical enabler is the data and information, not only about to the disease and treatment process of the individual patient, but also relevant to the patient's lifestyle, choices, health and wellness activities, demographic parameters, genomic legacy and history, and broad livelihood patterns.

The time has come for healthcare to be a 'real information-driven practice' along with being an 'information-driven science.' Both practice and science will align and come together in the new healthcare paradigm, to derive value from information and communication technologies, while realizing the broader value of 'care and health' to be more realistic. In this context, the concept of 'business intelligence' is going to play an essential and unprecedented role.

This book has the objective to recognize and understand key concepts of business intelligence in healthcare. The process of data analysis and intelligence gathering is a vital process of business intelligence. Besides, technologies, strategies, and the decision-making process add value to the analysis and intelligence. Therefore, business intelligence is essential and helpful for managers in enterprises to make informed business decisions at various levels and domains.

The emerging business intelligence technologies can handle unstructured data. As widely noted, compared to the earlier structured data management process, managing unstructured data is involved. This adds to the complexity of sectoral issues, such as the complexity of information-based science and legacy practices in healthcare.

Furthermore, it is an imperative today, from both organizations and professions management prospectives, to understand the theories, concepts, and practices through which business intelligence can create value for organizations. Specific to healthcare, the realms of data-based decision making have paramount importance and often is critical to death and life. Moreover, business intelligence, if appropriately applied, can help create financial value, along with better clinical outcomes in healthcare. While broadly, business intelligence in healthcare has the promise and potential to provide tremendous support to any layer of decision making, using data, information, and analysis process; it is also emerging as a critical enabler to develop intelligence strategies while relying on data that is accrued directly and synchronized from operations. In other words, the value potential of business intelligence has emerged to be a strategic imperative than only an application or tool to manage information.

Healthcare is sitting on mines of data and is collecting volumes of data every moment. Access to data has become pervasive than before. Hospitals, providers, payers, and health systems are trying to embrace data and leverage the power of analytics and intelligence to improve patient outcomes. At the same time, payors and finance managers in healthcare are feeling the demand of data and analytics to survive the evolving policy imperative, value-based care models, and managing different strategies to be viable in the revenue-cycle process. On the other hand, clinical protocols, medicine, drugs, and pharmacy relevant information is continuously changing, adding to the real complexities of data and information management in the healthcare area. While all from practice to policy models are embracing the transformative power of information technologies and the proposed value-based models to evolve a new generation of healthcare, surviving this change for organizations and professionals is a highly enduring task.

From a career management perspective, three aspects of the healthcare revolution are driving the next generation professions in healthcare. First, data and information have evolved to be the 'core' of healthcare professions. The importance of leveraging data and information in the realm of new healthcare models is a valuable perspective to keep in mind. Second, there is a demand from all organizations and stakeholders, on professionals, to explore and find ways in which information technology can be used as business processes and models to accrue higher value and revenue. Touted as digital business models, or digital-native organizations, the newer business value propositions are emerging, relying on models that were not seen earlier—such as platforms and infomediary based models. The underlying mechanism or common denominator across these models is the way to manage data and information and provide value (and earn revenue) through innovative ways—thereby raising expectations on professionals to understand and apply business intelligence principles and applications at the workplace to create value. Finally, small and intelligence-driven business practices are emerging to be the norm in all organizations. Parallelly, developments in artificial intelligence, machine learning, and virtual technologies are driving a paradigm shift in all sectors, including that in healthcare. Professionals without an understanding of these frontiers will not be successful; while more professionals will be needed to manage different frontiers of business intelligence careers in the healthcare sector. This book is structured to be helpful and provide value in this regard and to provide guidance and path for business intelligence based careers in healthcare through learning of concepts, opportunities, and challenges.

The target audience of this book is the students in a graduate class on business intelligence in healthcare. Students will learn about different aspects of business intelligence in various subsets of the healthcare industry. The book also provides insights and support to executives concerned with the application of business intelligence and organizational development in the healthcare industry and other different types of work communities and environments.

ORGANIZATION OF THE BOOK

The book is organized into 12 chapters. A brief description of each of the chapters follows:

The introduction provides a high level view of the importance and motivation for business intelligence in healthcare and describes the structure of the book.

Chapter 1 has a focus on business intelligence and analytics as a capability in healthcare organizations. A hierarchical classification of different business intelligence capabilities is conceptualized and explained.

Chapter 2 explains the data integrity and quality, and provides some methods for data cleansing and staging, within the realm that there are enormous opportunities exist for the advancement of analytics and business intelligence in healthcare that solely relies on clean and useful data.

Chapter 3 has the objective of providing a service-modeled approach to motivate and explain the value of intelligence across the patient-provider ecosystem.

Chapter 4 articulates and explains a core concept of this book, enumerated as an operations-intelligence-strategy (OIS) process in healthcare. The chapter highlights how to gain business intelligence from sensor, signal, and image data and analysis.

Chapter 5 discusses the data characteristics, identifying critical attributes, and various classification and optimization algorithms for decision-making purposes. The purpose of the discussion is to create a basis for the selection of algorithms based on size, temporal validity, and outcomes expected—mostly for unstructured and big data in healthcare.

Chapter 6 provides a description and illustration of this process in a hospital in South East Michigan. The chapter highlights the importance of the data-analytics-insights process in the healthcare context. This chapter provides a vivid demonstration of a real time dashboard to help in strategy creation and value transformation of the hospital.

Chapter 7 provides a broad discussion of the deep learning method and how this can be used to improve healthcare effectiveness and efficiency. The evolutionary power of business intelligence can be leveraged through the application of emerging innovations and techniques. In this regard, machine and deep learning and artificial intelligence are the cutting edge directions for business intelligence to derive value.

Chapter 8 is aligned to enumerate internal-external dependencies in the data-information-intelligence process using an intermediary for smoking cessation program management, in the realm that the understanding of business intelligence and relevance to strategy and value creation in healthcare is highly contextual. Chapter 9 articulates a potential application of blockchain in healthcare that is emerging to be an application to intelligently manage some workflows both internal and external, to healthcare entities. The perspective in the chapter is to take a service-dominant logic to create efficient and value-based models for patients. An exemplary context of an intermediary working for smoking cessation needs of patients is discussed.

Chapter 10 explains the relationship of patient empowerment and data analytics and intelligence. The best potential for intelligence and analytics can be realized when it is used to move the domain of health care delivered to better care to patients –often alluded to be a patient empowered healthcare.

Chapter 11 illustrates a specific (Markov) model to help in recognition and diagnoses of behavioral changes in support of a specific context (Assistive Technologies) to motivate similar further applications and use of business intelligence. Data mined models are essential to link intelligence to value creation.

Chapter 12 uses a value-sensitive design concept to conceptualize the ethical aspect of business intelligence and investigates the sensitivity of crucial BI activities. Amongst several challenges for the use of business intelligence in healthcare, ethical concerns stand out as the prominent ones.

Acknowledgment

The primary inspiration for this book came from the students focusing on Business Intelligence and Healthcare. As an emerging professional requirement, understanding of the theories, concepts, and practices through which business intelligence can create value for organizations, is becoming critical. Many students shared a requirement for a book around concepts of the value proposition for business intelligence in the healthcare area; that was a strong motivation to edit this book.

The book has the objective to provide different aspects of business intelligence in various subsets of the healthcare industry. The book also has the objective to provide insights and support to executives concerned with the application of business intelligence and organizational development in the healthcare industry and other different types of work communities and environments.

The book would not have been feasible without the rich contributions from the authors. We appreciated all the authors for their exciting and insightful contributions to the chapters.

The quality of this book is reflected in the review process. All the chapters have gone through multiple rounds of reviews. We thank all the anonymous reviewers for constructive feedback to the authors, which helped to improve the quality immensely.

Jiban Khuntia and Xue Ning thank the Business School of at the University of Colorado Denver, including the Deans, Faculty, and Students in playing a significant role to motivate this book.

Mohan Tanniru acknowledges the support of the former executive of St Joseph Health System, Mr. Jack Wiener, and the global health initiative group at the Henry Ford Health System for sharing information on digital innovations they have developed in support of patient care.

Acknowledgment

The concepts and insights used to structure this book is a culmination of several discussions with health and information system practitioners, doctors, nurses, health administrators, and faculty in different areas. We thank all of them who have directly or indirectly contributed to shape our thoughts and insights presented in this book. Any omissions of acknowledgment and thanks are not intentional.

We thank the prospective readers and students who will use this book for their learning.

Introduction

EMERGING VALUE OF BUSINESS INTELLIGENCE IN HEALTHCARE

Recent Healthcare Advancements

Healthcare is emerging through several challenges in the United States. Quality of care is improving but at a questionable rise in the cost of care. Hospital errors and complications have been a persistent issue in healthcare. Although several innovations and technologies have helped to advance care deliveries, healthcare as a whole is still facing challenges relevant to quality, integration, and sustainable models. Indeed, recent healthcare reform and technological innovations are enabling service delivery where patients want it. Newer electronic platforms, infomediaries, and social communities are emerging as alternate and effective models to empower patients. These developments and advancements need patients to view and analyze information at their end, to make decisions both on the expenses and quality cares.

Information technology is being used to addresses some of the challenges in healthcare. The role of health information systems and their impact on healthcare is well documented (Ritu Agarwal, Gao, DesRoches, & Jha, 2010; Khuntia, Tanniru, Fregoli, & Nawrocki, 2016). Digitization of data is almost completed in all aspects of healthcare that started in the last decade as a policy and practice move to leverage the transformational power of information technology. Sharing, exchange, analysis, and use of the digitized data for better information and decision is being planned; for instance, health information exchanges are emerging as the frontiers of providing value to patients through exchange and availability of critical information needed for care, beyond locational boundaries (Khuntia, Mithas, & Agarwal, 2017). Similarly, a new development in the United States healthcare is the move to be value-based care. With the consensus from policy to practice on this move, there is a huge demand for the value of care, not only in terms of episodic clinical outcomes, but that can extend to the wellness and life-span of a patient is becoming important. It is beyond doubt that in this process, a critical enabler is the data and information, not only about to the disease and treatment process of the individual patient, but also relevant to the patient's lifestyle, choices, health and wellness activities, demographic parameters, genomic legacy and history, and broad livelihood patterns. The concept of virtual hospitals and care, although it is limited in applications today, are emerging to be next-generation models for health service delivery (Kahn, 2015). The medical community, as a whole, is trying to experiment with alternative payment models and big data management tools. Broadly, the technological, digital, and application combined advancements will lead to significant changes in healthcare, from delivery to cost management to enable access for care.

On one side of this development is the move towards big data. Almost all organizations in healthcare today have started leveraging from big data in some way, albeit it may be minimal. However, the implementation of big data and relevant applications to derive any business value proposition remains a widely accepted challenge (Wang, Kung, & Byrd, 2018). The move from relational and static databased to highly flexible or fluid non-relational databases to merge patient information from many sources so that actionable outcomes and decisions can be derived—is perceived as a crucial attribute for emerging health systems, that are hoping to transform the care using the transformational power of information technologies. As we know, the traditional relational databases that have been used to store and access patient information have challenges to efficiently manage unstructured data and information sourced from different operational aspects of healthcare. For example, doctor notes, patient conversation transcripts, and bedside remarks are often not stored in the traditional relational databases (Wang et al., 2018). These challenges lead to the paradigm change to foster and leverage from non-relational databases.

Non-relational databases use data modeling approaches other than the tabular relations used in relational databases. Amongst other aspects, the simplicity in design, so that one does not have to deal with the widely discussed impedance mismatch between the object-oriented approach to writing applications and the schema-based tables and rows of a relational database is an excellent motivation for non-relational databases (James & Asagba, 2017). For example, storing all the patient information in one document is quite beneficial, in comparison to the earlier relational method of joining tables and accessing information using queries. The non-relational data acquisition, storing, and management processes involve less code to write, debug, and maintain; and, therefore, are touted to be lean and efficient to manage. Similarly, scaling approaches, control over data, capturing all kinds of data with higher speed, and lower cost are further benefits of the non-relational databases, which undoubtedly are underlying reasons for non-relational databases to gain prominence in several business applications and sectors.

The healthcare sector realizes the value of emerging big data and non-relational database application relevant advancements. Although this realization is at the forefront of most significant and financially capable health organizations, others are trying to transit from relational to non-relational databases at a snail pace, with some efforts. Nevertheless, these developments are helping both patients and care providers in moving to the much-awaited era of 'integrated healthcare,' while using information as the base for this integration (Haun et al., 2015). Care providers recognize that information integration--both internal and external—help organizations to enable efficient and effective care while containing the cost aspect. Examples would include: remote yet real-time care decisions and deliver real-time medical product use monitoring, and discovery of solutions for current patients using the information on the flow. Healthcare has already realized the informational power of 'static and relational' databases in providing several insights. For example, data-driven insights have helped to shape call-bell implementations for an efficient and effective response within patient rooms and hospital wards (Khuntia et al., 2016); or informing which services are essential to achieve higher patient satisfaction in emergency units (Tanniru & Khuntia, 2017).

Beyond the role of information and analysis for decision making, the intelligence enabled through different portals and infomediaries can drive next-generation healthcare. For instance, several health infomediaries have emerged that differ from purely online health communities by the objective in bringing doctors, caregivers, and medical professionals to participate in one platform; trying to reduce the information asymmetry in healthcare systems, and bringing provider-patients together in an online platform (Agarwal et al., 2010; Kallinikos & Tempini, 2014; Lefebvre & Bornkessel, 2013; Nambisan, 2011). Several of these infomediaries, such as patientslikeme.com, realself.com, webmd.com, drugs.com, healthline.com have thousands of visitors and pageviews on a daily basis. These infomediaries are important; as currently, disease- and treatment-specific knowledge is restricted to professionals within structural confines of a health system, i.e., information is available to patients only through a physician's office, clinic, or hospital. Inquiries remain unanswered due to the lack of trained professionals and resources, which leads to uninformed and disengaged patients. Irrespective of the realization that information availability and access will help in early diagnosis, adequate care, better health, and wellness, information asymmetry prevails. Information asymmetry is explicitly concerning risky, uncertain and voluntary medical procedures for which patients are left on their own to seek diagnosis and treatment in the current healthcare systems. Driven by intelligence, data and real-time communications enabled by internet, these health infomediaries provide user-contributed first-hand knowledge and experience, from patients who have undergone treatments or procedures, and drive the next generation healthcare to be an 'empowering' one for patients, by delivering both knowledge and care at their ends, in a seamless, integrated and real-time manner (Khuntia, Yim, Tanniru, & Lim, 2017; Permwonguswa, Khuntia, Yim, & Gregg, 2017; Permwonguswa, Khuntia, Yim, Gregg, & Kathuria, 2018; Yim, Khuntia, Lim, & Duan, 2017).

Business Intelligence to Foster Value From Information Integration

Business intelligence (BI) is a holistic term referring to several aspects of the process of data analysis and information integration. However, the vital aspect of business intelligence is the alignment of information and strategies to derive business value (Wang et al., 2018). Business intelligence has emerged as an essential strategic imperative in many other sectors, from finance to retail to logistics. Noteworthy to mention that BI helps managers to make informed decisions, at various levels and domains, while keeping the value accrual process to be aligned to the goals and objectives of the enterprise. On the outset or at the ground level, business intelligence is nothing but managing big or large data, both structured and non-structured, in a seamless and integrated manner, to derive informed decisions and subsequent value.

The value proposition of business intelligence in medicine and healthcare comes from the widely discussed 'informational' based dependency on health care. Healthcare, by itself, is a 'knowledge or information-based science.' Beyond that, the aspirations and progress towards just-in-time and just-in-place care delivery models are driving the higher demands for information integration and business intelligence in healthcare (Sagalowsky, Wynter, Auerbach, Pusic, & Kessler, 2016). Much healthcare has been in the forefronts of applying data and analytics in many areas, such as evidence-based science, clinical trials, and disease surveillance. Still, top organizational level strategic decisions based on business intelligence is a niche area in medicine and healthcare. Some entities have moved towards this frontier, in various subsets of the healthcare sector, such as large hospitals and a few health insurance organizations, but for many others, business intelligence and analytics remain as a nascent scope.

Modern developments in information technology tools and applications have provided a plethora of data collection opportunities. The continually increasing number of data sources and the complexity of data generated within healthcare organizations demand the data be used for better decision making. This is where the need for advanced analytics and intelligence enabled decision-making capabilities is growing than before. As articulated well earlier, the role of data, information and design of appropriate systems to derive information, both from the providers and from the patients' side, will influence better consumer-oriented care, by improving management of health, wellness and personal health information management avenues (Agarwal & Khuntia, 2009). Business intelligence tools such as predictive modeling, data visualization, and dashboards can inform hospitals and other healthcare organizations regarding patient care, workforce distribution, clinical operations, daily practices of physicians and nurses, and administration and management. The most notable outcomes may be improvements in patient satisfaction through improved care while keeping the cost intact (Ivan & Velicanu, 2015).

Undoubtedly, healthcare administrators and managers are challenged with the issues related to systems, operations, equipment, facilities, diagnostics, patient, and clinical care. Efficient coordination among different units in healthcare entities and workplaces is a crucial issue for the practices to deliver care (Yeoh & Popovič, 2016). In this space, with the support of business intelligence, healthcare entities can navigate the complexities of healthcare governance. Advanced analytical capabilities can provide breakthroughs to solve challenges relevant to patient, clinical, and operational connections and deriving insights. At the outset, business intelligence applications can help administrators to track performance indicators to collect, analyze, and manage performance-aligned information.

Moreover, connecting varied data sources can help in patient-relevant insights that will enable elevated and effective care. Furthermore, streamlined, simple, and efficient business intelligence for healthcare dashboards is also vital to facilitate decision making at the apex C-levels. Interestingly, as the public infrastructure and cities are moving to smart technologies and smart ecosystems, the scope of health management need to rely on many of these smart systems, and leverage from the real-time business intelligence; more so, integrating through the public-private partnerships around the smart-ecosystem developments (Ning & Khuntia, 2019).

Healthcare context and healthcare data - both are complex. Decisions taken in this context have one simple objective, i.e., to provide better care. However, a strategy to leverage data for better care remains a significant shortcoming in healthcare. As much as healthcare is increasingly adopting digital technologies to support operations and workflow, the business intelligence for healthcare would provide the critical avenues to manage the massive amounts of both structured and unstructured data, and the healthcare organizational deal daily. Embedding intelligence tools in the daily practices of physicians, administrators, and other personnel in healthcare will enable them to make more informed decisions—that, in turn, will help in effective patient care (Spruit & Lytras, 2018).

A widely known issue in healthcare is the cost conundrum, i.e., highly increasing cost against the moderate quality and efficiency issues. Business intelligence platforms can allow and help healthcare organizations to make sense of data, and use analytics capabilities to aid cost management (Wang & Hajli, 2017). For instance, predictive analytical capabilities can show patient-relevant costs and benefits, with success probabilities for options available for treatments at the time of admission. Information derived from such capabilities can provide effective, yet cost-efficient, operational, financial, and clinical practices. Indeed, when professionals in healthcare derive and apply information-based insights to address risks, forecast future events, and answer care-, management- and operations- relevant questions, the outcomes will be better (Khalifa, 2018). Providing better patient and clinical care, improving personnel distribution, decreasing readmissions, and managing expenses require the smart application of business intelligence in healthcare. Based on well-analyzed data, healthcare organizations can derive insights from BI tools to provide the best level of care for patients. Besides, using BI applications is not only part of a learning and emerging healthcare industry, but a movement towards sharing and establishing evidence-based best practices across all elements of care and management.

A significant segment of the United States healthcare is moving to the 'information integration' advancements, deploying non-relational databases and relevant applications, along with collaborations with different entities to enable value proposition from the integrated information. Several challenges remain for appropriate value accrual in this process. Sharing of information remains a matter of realms of privacy barriers to add to the emerging concerns around the misuse of data and information in the internet age (Yüksel, Küpçü, & Özkasap, 2017). Questions arise on the qualms of providing information to drug manufacturers or similar third parties, with vested interests to misuse the data. Perhaps much work has to be done in this space, to create awareness, build trust, and limit misuse—without which the value that can be derived from information integration may not be viable. For example, information sharing may reduce the cost of drug advancements, or free information flow can help providers to plan for personalized services. Once all concerned understand these benefits, the concerns regarding information sharing will be mitigated, and willingness to share data will be higher—leading to more comprehensive information integration in healthcare.

To reiterate the scope of business intelligence in healthcare, five motivations are emerging to be the center of discussion from policy to practice levels: (1) the influence of business intelligence tools and applications on the decision-making process. (2) Application of different mining, modeling, and analytic techniques to health and healthcare data to obtain insightful information. (3) The articulation that the value of big data to health is helpful for the discovery process. (4) Cultivate business intelligence tools and applications for different areas of healthcare, starting from quality management to patient empowerment to population health. (5) Development of an intelligent workforce to both use and leverage business intelligence.

Today, it is critical that every healthcare professional should understand the role of business intelligence in healthcare (Wang, Kung, Ting, & Byrd, 2015). Business intelligence is a complex domain by itself, and correctly applied to the healthcare context, the complexities are multifold. The process of data, information, analysis, and decision making is not only essential but also is a need of the hour for healthcare professionals. Along with, operational data that is created at every moment in healthcare workflows, need to be analyzed, more or less synchronously to aid intelligent decision making. All these then can help in strategy for healthcare entities and move organizations in a better direction. The possible benefit of business intelligence spans from effective outcomes such as patient safety, readmissions, patient satisfaction, wait times, scheduling issues, hospital stays, cost management, to informed strategic planning and managing population health (Wang et al., 2018).

As the information age is moving towards an information-based-intelligence age, the importance of business intelligence is emerging to be central to developments in several sectors, along with healthcare. Current use and applications of business intelligence in healthcare, maybe lagged with several challenges but have tremendous opportunities to move forward. Nonetheless, the established and emerging usage of business intelligence in other sectors should motivate the healthcare sector to be proactive towards the assimilation of business intelligence and look forward to future trends with an open mindset.

Importance of This Book to Learn Concepts Around Business Intelligence in Healthcare

This book has the objective of providing different aspects of value creation from business intelligence in healthcare. Several resources are available to learn the tools, applications, and methods used in business intelligence. However, articulation of concepts that can be helpful in using all the artifacts for business intelligence, and use them in the healthcare context to derive value is the crucial aspect that is fulfilled by this book.

This book structure follows a three-module approach to discuss business intelligence in healthcare.

Module 1: Broader Aspects of the Business Intelligence-Value Creation Process

The introduction and the first three chapters, i.e., Chapters 1 to 3 are focused on the business intelligence to value creation aspect while informing about the data-information-decision process for business intelligence. The introduction provides a high-level view of the importance and motivation for business intelligence in healthcare and describes the structure of the book. The first chapter highlights business intelligence and analytics as a capability in healthcare organizations and explains a hierarchical classification of different business intelligence capabilities. The second chapter explains the data integrity and quality and provides some methods for data cleansing and staging. It indicates that there are enormous opportunities exist for the advancement of analytics and business intelligence in healthcare that solely relies on clean and useful data. Finally, the third chapter explains a service-modeled approach to motivate and gain the value of intelligence across the patient-provider ecosystem.

Module 2: The Operations-Information-Strategy Aspect of Business Intelligence

Chapters 4 to 7 highlight the core aspect of the book in terms of explaining the operations-information-strategy aspect of business intelligence. Chapter 4 articulates the operations-intelligence-strategy (OIS) process and highlights how to gain business intelligence from sensor, signal, and image data and analysis. Chapter 5 discusses the data characteristics, identifying critical attributes, and various classification and optimization algorithms for decision-making purposes. The purpose of the discussion is to create a basis for the selection of algorithms based on size, temporal validity, and outcomes expected—mostly for unstructured and big data in healthcare. Chapter 6 provides a vivid demonstration of a real-time dashboard to help in strategy creation and value transformation of the hospital. Finally, Chapter 7 provides a broad discussion of the deep learning method and how this can be used to improve healthcare effectiveness and efficiency.

Module 3: Levels of Influence of Business Intelligence in Healthcare

The last five chapters illustrate how the integration of information and business intelligence creates value within the challenges at different levels, from operations to policy. Chapter 8 is aligned to enumerate internal-external dependencies relevant to business intelligence use and implementation, in the context of using an intermediary for smoking cessation program management. Chapter 9 explains the relationship of patient empowerment and data analytics and intelligence. Chapter 10 discusses emerging business intelligence tools such as blockchains to manage patient services, with an example of an intermediary working for smoking cessation for patients. Chapter 11 illustrates the use of the Markov model to help in diagnoses of behavioral changes in support of an assistive context. Finally, some challenges, including ethical concerns are discussed using a value-sensitive design concept through Chapter 12.

In summary, it is perceived that the practice and science will align and come together in the new healthcare paradigm, to derive value from information and communication technologies, while realizing the more value through 'intelligent healthcare.' The details of the intelligent healthcare need to be planned, executed and implemented by current and future professionals and leaders in the healthcare sector. Existing examples and best cases demonstrate that the leaders need to be knowledgeable while taking an approach that is practical, both incremental and radical in different implementations, and rely on the technology-business alignments, are able to leverage from the transformative power of information technologies better (Tanniru, Khuntia, & Weiner, 2018). Thus, there is a need to train the next generation leaders to leverage from the emerging "intelligence-driven healthcare". This book is scoped to fulfill the objective to train the next generation leaders in healthcare and information systems.

Thus, this book is planned to be highly useful to learn different aspects of business intelligence concepts, especially in the healthcare context. This book informs about the process from data and information to decision making and the operations-information-strategy aspect of business intelligence. Cases and examples illustrate how the integration of information and business intelligence creates value at different levels. This book is expected to be influential in sharpening the readers' learning and knowledge around business intelligence concepts and critical thinking about business intelligence applications in healthcare.

Jiban Khuntia
University of Colorado, Denver, USA

REFERENCES

Agarwal, R., Gao, G., DesRoches, C., & Jha, A. K. (2010). Research commentary--the digital transformation of healthcare: current status and the road ahead. *Information Systems Research*, *21*(4), 796–809. doi:10.1287/isrc.1100.0327

Agarwal, R., & Khuntia, J. (2009). *Personal health information and the design of consumer health information technology: Background report.* AHRQ Publication.

Haun, J. N., Patel, N. R., French, D. D., Campbell, R. R., Bradham, D. D., & Lapcevic, W. A. (2015). Association between health literacy and medical care costs in an integrated healthcare system: A regional population based study. *BMC Health Services Research*, *15*(1), 249. doi:10.118612913-015-0887-z PMID:26113118

Ivan, M., & Velicanu, M. (2015). Healthcare industry improvement with business intelligence. *Informações Econômicas*, *19*(2), 81.

James, B. E., & Asagba, P. (2017). Hybrid database system for big data storage and management. *International Journal of Computer Science Engineering and Applications*, *7*(3/4), 15–27.

Kahn, J. M. (2015). Virtual visits—Confronting the challenges of telemedicine. *The New England Journal of Medicine*, *372*(18), 1684–1685. doi:10.1056/NEJMp1500533 PMID:25923547

Kallinikos, J., & Tempini, N. (2014). Patient data as medical facts: Social media practices as a foundation for medical knowledge creation. *Information Systems Research*, *25*(4), 817–833. doi:10.1287/isre.2014.0544

Khalifa, M. (2018). *Health analytics types, functions and levels: a review of literature.* Paper presented at the ICIMTH.

Khuntia, J., Mithas, S., & Agarwal, R. (2017). How service offerings and operational maturity influence the viability of health information exchanges. *Production and Operations Management*, *26*(11), 1989–2005. doi:10.1111/poms.12735

Khuntia, J., Tanniru, M., Fregoli, F., & Nawrocki, M. (2016). Information systems impact on nurse call response–role of velocity and uncertainty. *Pacific Asia Journal of the Association for Information Systems, 8*(1).

Khuntia, J., Yim, D., Tanniru, M., & Lim, S. (2017). Patient empowerment and engagement with a health infomediary. *Health Policy and Technology*, *6*(1), 40–50. doi:10.1016/j.hlpt.2016.11.003

Lefebvre, R. C., & Bornkessel, A. S. (2013). Digital social networks and health. *Circulation*, *127*(17), 1829–1836. doi:10.1161/CIRCULATIONAHA.112.000897 PMID:23630086

Nambisan, P. (2011). Evaluating patient experience in online health communities: Implications for health care organizations. *Health Care Management Review*, *36*(2), 124–133. doi:10.1097/HMR.0b013e3182099f82 PMID:21317657

Ning, X., & Khuntia, J. (2019). *Citizen-government ecosystem for smart technology enabled city performance*. Academic Press.

Permwonguswa, S., Khuntia, J., Yim, D., & Gregg, D. (2017). *Empowerment and knowledge sharing in health infomediary: empirical evidence from reconstructive surgery patients.* Academic Press.

Permwonguswa, S., Khuntia, J., Yim, D., Gregg, D., & Kathuria, A. (2018). Knowledge sharing in a health infomediary: Role of self-concept, emotional empowerment, and self-esteem. *Health Systems (Basingstoke, England)*, *7*(3), 181–194. doi:10.1080/20476965.2017.1405875 PMID:31214347

Sagalowsky, S. T., Wynter, S.-A., Auerbach, M., Pusic, M. V., & Kessler, D. O. (2016). Simulation-based procedural skills training in pediatric emergency medicine. *Clinical Pediatric Emergency Medicine*, *17*(3), 169–178. doi:10.1016/j.cpem.2016.05.007

Spruit, M., & Lytras, M. (2018). *Applied data science in patient-centric healthcare: Adaptive analytic systems for empowering physicians and patients*. Elsevier.

Tanniru, M., & Khuntia, J. (2017). Dimensions of patient experience and overall satisfaction in emergency departments. *Journal of Patient Experience, 4*(3), 95-100.

Tanniru, M., Khuntia, J., & Weiner, J. (2018). Hospital leadership in support of digital transformation. *Pacific Asia Journal of the Association for Information Systems, 10*(3).

Wang, Y., & Hajli, N. (2017). Exploring the path to big data analytics success in healthcare. *Journal of Business Research, 70*, 287–299. doi:10.1016/j.jbusres.2016.08.002

Wang, Y., Kung, L., & Byrd, T. A. (2018). Big data analytics: Understanding its capabilities and potential benefits for healthcare organizations. *Technological Forecasting and Social Change, 126*, 3–13. doi:10.1016/j.techfore.2015.12.019

Wang, Y., Kung, L., Ting, C., & Byrd, T. A. (2015). Beyond a technical perspective: understanding big data capabilities in health care. *Proceedings of the 2015 48th Hawaii International Conference on System Sciences.* 10.1109/HICSS.2015.368

Yeoh, W., & Popovič, A. (2016). Extending the understanding of critical success factors for implementing business intelligence systems. *Journal of the Association for Information Science and Technology, 67*(1), 134–147. doi:10.1002/asi.23366

Yim, D., Khuntia, J., Lim, S., & Duan, W. (2017). *To ask or not to ask? An investigation of user engagement and doctor-seeking decision in online health infomediary*. Academic Press.

Yüksel, B., Küpçü, A., & Özkasap, Ö. (2017). Research issues for privacy and security of electronic health services. *Future Generation Computer Systems, 68*, 1–13. doi:10.1016/j.future.2016.08.011

Chapter 1
Business Intelligence and Analytics (BI&A) Capabilities in Healthcare

Thiagarajan Ramakrishnan
Prairie View A&M University, USA

Abhishek Kathuria
Indian School of Business, India

Terence J. V. Saldanha
University of Georgia, USA

ABSTRACT

Business Intelligence and Analytics (BI&A) is emerging as an essential area of expertise in healthcare organizations. Healthcare organizations are trying to leverage BI&A as an integral capability to provide quality healthcare service to patients. From an organizational perspective, BI&A extends beyond an artifact or tool to include several capabilities. This chapter conceptualizes potential capabilities that BI&A can bestow to healthcare organizations. A three-category classification of BI&A healthcare capability classification is suggested: BI&A healthcare insight infrastructure capability, BI&A healthcare process capability, and BI&A healthcare integration capability. In this chapter, the authors discuss the attributes of these three BI&A healthcare capabilities to offer understandings into how these capabilities can help healthcare firms. This taxonomy will help healthcare providers and IT professionals in the healthcare industry make informed decisions on how best to adopt BI&A within their firms to provide quality healthcare service.

DOI: 10.4018/978-1-7998-2310-0.ch001

INTRODUCTION

The healthcare sector has long used information technologies and systems for improving the efficiency, effectiveness, and quality of healthcare services. To provide quality health care services, as well as to improve several business outcomes, health care organizations require accurate information at the right time, and available to the right person. Information systems have contributed to making the economic activities within the healthcare sector transparent and in making the information available in real time (Mettler and Vimurlund, 2009). Prior studies have shown a strong relationship between the adoption of IS and the productivity and the financial wellbeing of healthcare organizations (Fonkych and Taylor, 2005; Permwonguswa et al., 2018). Hospitals that have adopted integrated information technologies and systems have higher operating margins and total profits as compared to healthcare organizations that do not have enough health information technologies (Parente and Dunbar, 2001). However, due to the sheer amount of ever-expanding knowledge in the healthcare sector, providing the right information in the right format at the right time is becoming a very difficult challenge (Stroemann and Aisenbrey, 2012). Healthcare organizations are turning their attention to Business Intelligence and Analytics (BI&A) to meet this challenge of collecting, storing, manipulating, analyzing, and providing the right information for making better decisions (Bonney, 2013). For example, four hospitals in Paris, France that are a part of the Assistance Publique-Hopitaux de Paris use BI&A to analyze ten years worth of hospital records data from internal and external sources to predict the daily and the hourly number of patients expected at each hospital (Marr, 2016). Another example of the use of BI&A in healthcare is in the Cancer Moonshot program launched by Federal Government Initiative towards curing cancer. Medical researchers can view how cancer proteins and mutations react with different treatments by examining large amounts of data on recovery rates of cancer patients that are linked to data on treatment plans to find trends that can lead to better patient outcomes (Lebied, 2018).

One overarching theme that has surfaced in the area of BI&A is regarding its business value to the various organizations; how well the BI&A fits the organization and how can firms leverage their BI&A to improve their performance. Further, studies suggest that BI&A capabilities can be an essential strategy for organizations in a competitive landscape (Thamir and Poulis, 2015). However, the focus of BI&A capabilities research has been towards generic industries and organizations. For example, Isik et al. (2013) examine Technological BI capability and Organizational BI capability that can influence BI success in generic organizations. Similarly, Ramakrishnan et al. (2018) study how BI Innovation Infrastructure capability, BI process capability, and BI Integration capability can improve the performance firms from multiple industries. Along the same lines, Torres et al. (2018) investigated BI&A

management capability, BI&A sensing capability, BI&A seizing capability, and BI&A process change capability that can impact firm performance. The focus of all these studies is generic and they do not explicitly focus on healthcare organizations. Healthcare organizations differ from generic organizations in a crucial manner. In addition to the traditional business process and support process that comprises of activities suggested by Porter, healthcare organizations also need these processes to be integrated with their medical processes. Medical processes include activities within the healthcare organization that apply to the health services delivery such as nursing, medical treatment, and so on (Mettler and Vimarlund, 2009). Thus, in order to successfully implement and utilize BI&A in healthcare organizations, it is critical to understand the BI&A capabilities that these organizations need to leverage to support decision-making using BI&A.

The goal of this chapter is to highlight a typology of BI&A capabilities in healthcare organizations. This chapter will start with the introduction of BI&A and its importance for healthcare organizations. This chapter will then go on to provide categories of classification for BI&A capabilities necessary for healthcare organizations. Finally, this chapter will conclude with suggestions on how to use this classification and discuss the managerial and research implications.

WHAT IS BI&A?

From an Information Systems perspective, Business Intelligence and Analytics (BI&A) is an umbrella term that encompasses data processing, analytical applications, technologies, systems, business-centric techniques, practices, and methodologies that transform massive amounts of data from different sources into meaningful information to help an organization understand its business and support effective decision-making (Ramakrishnan et al., 2018). Business Intelligence and Analytics Capability refers to the ability of an organization to collect, retain, and consolidate knowledge through BI&A. This has developed as an essential area of study for both researchers and practitioners, which reflects the effect and scale of data-related problems present in current business enterprises (Kao et al., 2016).

More recently, the term BI&A has been suggested to highlight the growing importance of analytics component in the BI system (Torres et al., 2018). Depending on the different perspectives, several definitions have emerged for BI&A. For example, examining BI&A through an organizational perspective, Olszak and Ziemba (2003) define BI&A as "a set of concepts, method, and processes that aim at not only improving business decisions but also at supporting the realization of an enterprises' strategy." Similarly, focusing on the technological perspective, Moss and Atre (2007) define BI&A as "architecture and a collection of integrated operational as well as decision support applications and databases that provide the business community easy access to business data."

Based on these definitions, it is clear that BI&A assists in supporting intelligent decision-making by providing meaningful information to decision-makers from a large amount of data present in disparate data sources and as such is considered to be among the top priorities for the organizations in almost all industry sectors (Isik et al., 2013). The ability of BI&A to support decision-making and to provide relevant and timely information to decision makers is what makes BI&A effective in the organization (Ramakrishnan et al., 2012). These prospects associated with BI&A in various industry sectors have helped develop a substantial interest in BI&A. However, previous literature has shown that the adoption of BI&A within healthcare organizations is relatively low in comparison with other industry sectors (Mettler and Vimarlund, 2009; O'Riain and Helfert, 2005; Parente, 2000). One of the reasons for this could be that there is no clear framework that can help highlight the BI&A capabilities that need to be developed in order to successfully adapt and use BI&A in healthcare organizations. Thus, an overarching view of the capabilities that BI&A endows in healthcare organizations is still a gap in BI&A literature. This chapter tries to fill in this gap.

CLASSIFICATION OF BI&A HEALTHCARE CAPABILITIES

Drawing on prior work related to BI literature and IT capability, in this chapter, the authors propose BI&A healthcare capabilities that can help orient healthcare organizations' ability to develop, integrate, and reconfigure internal and external proficiencies to address rapidly fluctuating environments by using BI&A as an artifact, tool, and process level integrative capabilities. The resource-based view of a firm, which suggests that firms acquire competitive advantage through applying a combination of resources that are economically valuable, scarce, non-substitutable, and difficult to imitate (Barney, 1991), forms the theoretical basis of the notion of IT capability. IT capability is defined as a firms' "ability to mobilize and deploy IT-based resources in combination or co-present with other resources and capabilities," (Bharadwaj, 2000, p. 171). Initial work on IT capability examined a single dimension either in terms of managerial IT capability (Sambhamurthy and Zmud, 1997) or technological IT capability (Sabherwal and Kris, 1994) and since then has evolved to contain three dimensions including organizational, technological, and human dimensions (Schaefferling, 2013; Kim et al., 2011). The organizational dimension of IT capabilities looks into how IT/business partnerships and organizational resources can offer a competitive advantage to firms. Similarly, the technological dimension of IT capability examines how hardware, software, networking, and other

IT applications can offer firms a competitive edge. Along the same lines, the focus of human dimension of IT capabilities is more into the skill sets and the knowledge of IT workers in leveraging IT for gaining competitive advantage within the organization (Rockmann et al., 2014; Bhatt and Grover, 2005; Melville et al., 2004).

BI&A is a capability warrants operational or process capability that helps support and integrate different processes within an organization (Isik et al., 2013; Ramakrishnan et al., 2018). Thus, drawing on previous work to conceptualize BI&A healthcare capabilities as an overall culmination of different operational capabilities or processes (Kathuria et al., 2016) within the healthcare organization, this chapter, provides a conceptualization that incorporates an additional layer of integrative capability in the healthcare organization. Hence, BI&A healthcare capability in healthcare organizations is established through the three underlying dimensions: (1) to provide the infrastructure for using appropriate BI&A healthcare tools through cultural, structural, and technological improvements, (2) to use BI&A to improve the different processes such as clinical, financial, and operational process within the healthcare organization, and (3) to integrate BI&A within the healthcare organization. These three dimensions translate into the three BI&A healthcare capabilities: BI&A healthcare insight infrastructure capability (BI&A HIIC), BI&A healthcare process capability (BI&A HPC), and BI&A healthcare integration capability (BI&A HInC). These three dimensions are further elaborated in the subsequent sub-sections.

BI&A Healthcare Insight Infrastructure Capability (BI&A HIIC)

BI&A Healthcare Insight Infrastructure Capability is the ability to seamlessly support and incorporate, within the healthcare organization, the different tools, and techniques for understanding past events and making predictions and thereby facilitating effective and efficient decision-making through cultural, structural, and technological improvements. A mechanism to provide fast and reliable answers is critical in complex domains such as healthcare, where, quick reflexes warrants fast decisions based on information from multiple and diverse sources (Ashrafi et al. 2014). In order to support BI&A technology, the right data collection strategy and proper infrastructure are required (Ramakrishnan et al., 2016). It is further essential to have a suitable organizational structure that can enable collaboration and sharing to leverage this BI&A technology in the healthcare industry. Further, within the healthcare firms, culture plays a crucial role in the collaboration and sharing of information generated by BI&A technology.

Thus, BI&A healthcare insight infrastructure capability consists of cultural, structural, and technological elements. The cultural element of BI&A HIIC deals with the shared values and beliefs of the healthcare workers in the use of BI&A technology for gathering, sharing, and leveraging healthcare related information

(Pearlson and Saunders, 2013). BI&A culture enhances the firms' ability to manage data, intelligence, and knowledge; and advocates collaboration between individuals and groups as the basis of efficient use of information for effective decision-making. The structural aspect of BI&A HIIC refers to the modular organizational design that enables the technical architecture and subsequent functions related to BI&A in healthcare organizations. The technological element of the BI&A HIIC refers to the readiness of the firm to adopt different BI&A tools within the healthcare organization. This dimension may include technologies such as data warehouse that is a key element of BI&A, different analytical tools and techniques that are used to mine the vast amount of data, collaboration and information sharing related tools as well as tools and techniques related to security and privacy of data and information.

Cultural, Structural, and Technological features associated with BI&A HIIC provide the healthcare organizations with the abilities required to manage data, intelligence, and knowledge through entrenched processes and routines of the firm. BI&A culture facilitates engagements between individuals and groups as a basis of effective use of information. Therefore, a more collaborative and interactive culture is a forerunner for transforming fact-based tacit healthcare information into explicit actionable intelligence and to further move it from an individual to an organizational level. Employees operating in such a cultural environment within the healthcare organization can develop the ability to self-organize their practices and knowledge to provide solutions and novel insight into existing or new problems and facilitate effective decision-making.

While BI&A technological element provides the foundation for the effective use of BI&A technology, the BI&A structural element associated with BI&A HIIC provides the readiness and organizational framework to use this foundation. The structural aspect of BI&A HIIC looks into the dissemination of tasks, the synchronization among the employees, the information flow, and the decision-making rights within the healthcare organization (Pugh, 1990). Healthcare firms that follow a rigid structure may fall prey to the inadvertent effect of ineffective sharing of knowledge and information across the different units within the company, rather than facilitating collaboration and communication (Gold et al., 2001). Thus, in order to effectively use BI&A healthcare technologies, it is imperative to have BI&A healthcare structure in place that facilitates the easy dissemination of intelligence and information. Instead of individualistic expertise, healthcare firms have to encourage collective intelligence. Healthcare organizations have to encourage the exchange of intelligence across the various units within the organization. Therefore, BI&A healthcare structure plays a crucial role in providing support to BI&A healthcare technology, and thus, is a significant element in the BI&A healthcare capabilities classification.

Finally, as mentioned in the previous paragraph, BI&A healthcare technology plays a significant role in the structural dimension required to capture, stock, and analyze data in the healthcare organization. Proper utilization of BI&A technology such as data warehouse can play an essential role in integrating information from diverse and multiple systems used in healthcare organizations. These systems include information related to health surveys, administrative enrollment, billing records, and medical records utilized by several entities, including physicians and different hospitals (Ashrafi et al., 2014). Further, electronic medical records systems (EMR) from different hospitals can also provide information to the data warehouse making it easy to access these individual records by authorized healthcare organizations within the electronic network (Hillestad et al., 2005). Further, BI&A technologies such as artificial intelligence (AI) can be leveraged by pharmaceutical companies for developing drugs in treating fast-moving diseases. For example, the pharmaceutical company Atomwise did a virtual search and analyzed around 7000 drugs that can be restructured to combat the Ebola virus. They found two drugs that their company's technology predicted that can significantly lessen Ebola ineffectively. This analysis was completed in less than a day, which otherwise would have taken months or even a year (Atomwise, 2015; Mesko, 2017). Other BI&A technologies also include real-time decision support systems and data mining tools that can enable creating insights by building predictive models and providing in-depth analysis of data related to healthcare (Koh and Tan, 2011). For example, Duke University Health System (DUHS) efficiently leveraged their BI&A HIIC to provide timely vaccination to combat swine flu virus. In Spring 2009, when World Health Organization (WHO) declared a pandemic of swine flu, DUHS was faced with the problem of either ordering less vaccine that can lead to a shortage or ordering more vaccines that can lead to waste and shortage at other locations. DUHS used a data warehouse and analyzed the data warehouse based on the CDC vaccination priority eligibility criteria to estimate the number of patients likely to need vaccination (Ferranti et al., 2010). Thus, BI&A allowed targeted distribution of vaccines to high volume hospitals.

Therefore, with proper BI&A structure, and empowered BI&A culture, various BI&A technologies including data warehouses, predictive analytical tools, artificial intelligence technologies, and communication systems can be linked in an organization to assimilate the disjointed flow of information and data. These linkages can eliminate the barrier to communication between the different units within the healthcare organization thereby providing better insights and enabling better decision-making to offer better service to healthcare customers.

BI&A Healthcare Process Capability (BI&A HPC)

The processes within the healthcare firms' necessitates the collaboration of different medical disciplines and organizational units (Lenz & Reicher, 2007). BI&A healthcare process capability refers to the ability of BI&A to support the healthcare firms' different processes. This capability examines the functionalities of BI&A that can sustain the medical processes, business processes, and the support processes that form an integral part of a healthcare firm's process. BI&A helps healthcare organizations by supporting the different processes that improve the performance of the firms and gives them a competitive edge.

Mettler & Vimarlund (2009) define medical processes as "those activities and work practices within a healthcare organization which are mainly focused on the health services delivery (e.g., nursing, medical treatment)" (p. 257). The medical processes are more patient specific. For example, planning medical procedures for patients such as lab tests, scheduling appointments with different service providers, transporting patients and arranging physicians from other departments, generating and evaluating patient reports are all part of the medical process (Lenz & Reicher, 2007). Further, based on the continuous evolution of medical knowledge, the discovery of new diseases, the unpredictability of patients and treatments, and a large amount of data that needs to be exchanged, medical processes become highly complex and dynamic (Rebuge and Ferreira, 2012). Business process, on the other hand, is not sector specific, and within the healthcare organizations, focus on the activities required to run the healthcare firm effectively. This process involves activities related to financial accounting, monitoring and controlling, organizational development, compliance and risk management, and so on (Mettler & Vimarlund, 2009). Finally, the support process includes all the activities that support both the medical process and the business process. The support process involves activities related to human resources, communication, the supply of materials, etc (Mettler & Vimarlund, 2009).

Thus, healthcare firm processes are not autonomous and involve multiple orientations. Therefore, in this chapter, BI&A HPC is conceptualized as a multi-dimensional construct consisting of two dimensions; BI&A administrative process capability and BI&A clinical process capability. BI&A administrative process capability is concerned with the way BI&A is oriented towards supporting the business process and activities of the support process related to the business process. BI&A administrative process capability consists of exploiting BI&A to improve clinical and operational efficiencies, reduce cost, continually improve their business process to allow the firms to be profitable while maintaining high-quality care at low costs (Spruit et al., 2014; Kao et al., 2016). For example, Zorgprisma Publiek, a Dutch company, uses IBM Watson to mine invoice data of insurance companies and hospitals to see whether repetitive mistakes are being made by clinics, doctors, or hospitals in treating certain types of conditions. This helps improve patient care and hospital services and prevents unnecessary hospitalization of patients (Mesko, 2017). Similarly, one of the pilot hospitals of UniPoint Health in Iowa used leveraged their BI&A capabilities to reduce their patients' readmission rate by 40% over the course of three years (Miliard, 2017). Another example of effectively leveraging the BI&A administrative capability is by Washington State Health Care Authority. They made it easy to identify patients who frequently visited the ER department in hospitals by integrating patient data across the ER departments through the implementation of BI&A. This led to an overall decrease in frequent ER visits by 10% (Lebied, 2017). Thus, leveraging BI&A administrate process capability can lead to healthcare institutions being more effective and efficient and can provide better service to patients. BI&A clinical process capability focuses on the way BI&A is oriented towards supporting medical process and activities of support process related to the medical process. For instance, BI&A clinical process capability consists of leveraging BI&A to meet the patients' needs and serve them. Capabilities that can utilize information from BI&A to provide better surgery services, emergency room services, inpatient care, lab services, diagnostics imaging services, and pharmacy services among others (Foshay and Kuziemsky, 2014). This capability further can facilitate the use of BI&A to absorb data and information from different clinical data sources and provide healthcare providers the resources to make real-time decisions and support evidence-based practices for improving patient healthcare (Bonney, 2013). For example, IBM developed a program called Medical Sieve for assisting in clinical decision-making in cardiology and radiology. This program with a range of clinical knowledge and analytical reasoning capability can analyze radiology images and detect problems faster and reliably (Mesko, 2017). Similarly, Moorfield's eye hospital has partnered with Google's DeepMind Health program and have shared with them a set of anonymized one million eye scans and anonymous information about eye conditions and disease management. Using this information, Moorefield's eye hospital can better serve the patients through earlier discovery and treatment that can remove cases of avoidable eye disease (Mesko, 2017; Moorfields eye hospital, 2016). Thus, hospitals and healthcare providers can leverage BI&A clinical process capabilities to provide effective and improved services to patients that can lead to better patient outcomes. Together, BI&A healthcare process capabilities offer the healthcare organizations with the capacity to derive analytical insights into its medical and business processes, which in turn improves the healthcare firms' organizational effectiveness and improved and efficient services for their patients.

BI&A Healthcare Integration Capability (BI&A HInC)

BI&A integration plays a crucial role in successfully using BI&A (Isik et al., 2013). Healthcare organizations chiefly include three different sources of data; viz. Administrative data sources, Clinical data sources, and External data sources (Mettler and Vimurland, 2009). Administrative data sources include personal data and financial data, which are data related to business that is needed for managing the healthcare organization. Clinical data sources contain patients' medical data such as their medical records, laboratory results, etc, that are required to offer health service delivery to patients. External data sources may contain administrative data and clinical data from external providers such as insurance companies, hospitals, or any other governing body (Mettler and Vimurland, 2009). The ability to integrate data from these various sources is critical for healthcare organizations to deliver healthcare services efficiently and at a lower cost (Ashrafi et al., 2014). Healthcare firms need to develop mechanisms to collect, integrate, and transform information from these disparate sources into actionable business intelligence towards improving their performance.

BI&A healthcare integration capability has two dimensions that can contribute towards improving the healthcare firms' performance. First, the BI&A healthcare capability concerned with gathering data from the above-mentioned different types of healthcare data sources. Apart from collecting healthcare data from different sources, healthcare firms must also develop BI&A healthcare acquisition capability that can collect and integrate patients' past data with current real-time content (Ashrafi et al., 2014). Data collected from these different sources needs to be cleaned and standardized in order for it to be used by healthcare professionals without errors (Ramakrishnan et al., 2012). Second, the BI&A healthcare capability that can transform these collected and standardized data into useful information by applying descriptive and predictive models and provide useful insight to healthcare professionals. Therefore, BI&A healthcare integration entails the acquisition of data followed by the transformation of these data into useful information that can help healthcare professionals in providing quality patient service.

Thus, along with the acquisition capabilities of BI&A for collecting and integrating data from different disparate sources, the results of this acquisition and transformation through integration helps healthcare firms improve their performance. For example, the healthcare organization NorthShore University Health System leveraged their BI&A HInC to use Information Systems for successfully tackling health issues related to hypertension (Degaspari, 2013). First, with EMR, they acquired data regarding patients' who were undiagnosed or at risk of hypertension. Second, they converted this data into useful information by developing algorithms to decide which patients they need to contact for additional follow-up. More than 500 patients who were previously undiagnosed for hypertension were identified using this system (Degaspari, 2013). Thus, BI&A HInC can facilitate the collecting of data from different sources and transform them into actionable information for the healthcare providers making the BI&A more effective.

USING THE BI&A HEALTHCARE CAPABILITIES TAXONOMY

Organizations are turning their attention towards BI&A for deriving value from the massive amount of data and for providing the right information to the decision makers within the organization (Sidorova et al., 2018). However, BI&A is just recently emerging as an essential area of expertise in healthcare organizations for improving their performance and providing excellent health care services. There are a lot of different perspectives regarding the applications, concepts, and definitions of BI&A and different viewpoints regarding the best practice for utilizing BI&A vary across different firms. This could be one of the reasons for the slow assimilation of BI&A tools and techniques by healthcare organizations. Understanding the capabilities required to implement and use BI&A in healthcare firms successfully can alleviate any misconception surrounding the use of BI&A by healthcare firms. The objective of this chapter is to offer a general view regarding BI&A in healthcare organizations from a capabilities perspective. Taking the capabilities perspective helps showcase the fact that creating an environment for the successful use of BI&A in healthcare firms is very important rather than the tool or technology itself. The theoretical concepts developed in this chapter are focused on providing an understanding of the different BI&A healthcare capabilities and their importance in the successful use of BI&A in healthcare organizations.

Typologies and taxonomies play a critical role in research (e.g., Kathuria et al. 2018a). The classification schema developed in this chapter can also be helpful in future research. One line of research that can be pursued is examining the causality or hierarchy of BI&A healthcare capabilities, akin to other capability pathways demonstrated for other information systems (e.g. cloud computing by Kathuria et al., 2018b). For instance, one can examine whether higher BI&A healthcare insight infrastructure capability can lead to a higher BI&A healthcare process capability, which in turn can lead to a higher BI&A healthcare integration capability as suggested in our conceptual diagram (Figure 1). Other research can explore the relationship between these capabilities and effectiveness of BI&A in healthcare firms. Another research can investigate the impact of these capabilities on the performance of healthcare firms.

Figure 1. Suggested relationship model between BI&A healthcare capabilities

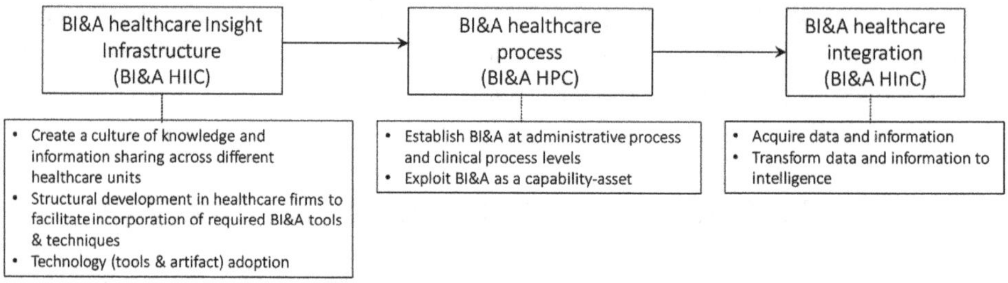

The BI&A healthcare integrative model and dimensions conceptualized in this chapter offer three theoretical contributions. First, although existing literature in BI&A suggests that BI&A can help in improving traditional organizational decision-making, there are not many studies that examine how BI&A can be used in healthcare organizations. This chapter provides a theoretical understanding of the capabilities required to effectively utilize BI&A in healthcare firms based on the processes generic to healthcare firms. Second, it is advocated in this chapter that in order to use BI&A effectively in healthcare organizations, apart from the appropriate BI&A tools and techniques, healthcare firms have to cultivate a culture that encourages collaboration and sharing of data and information amongst the different elements of healthcare providers. Finally, in this chapter, it is suggested that BI&A is not just a unilateral perspective that can help in siloed decision-making; rather it has to be examined in terms of a process-integrative organization-wide framework that can improve the quality of healthcare providers and patients.

The integrative model has implications for healthcare providers practice also. This model provides stepwise direction from acquisition to transformation and process integration for BI&A application and tools. Furthermore, this chapter suggests that developing capabilities is very important for successfully leveraging the BI&A tools and application in healthcare firms. Thus, healthcare providers should focus on developing capabilities rather than only trying to acquire off the shelf BI&A products for improving their firms' performance.

In conclusion, this chapter takes an integrative approach to BI&A. The central tenet of this chapter focuses on three dimensions of BI&A capability related to organizations in the healthcare industry. The concepts proposed here are expected to provide an integrated capability framework for effective usage of BI&A applications and motivate healthcare providers to see BI&A through a holistic view of infrastructure, process, and integration for providing high-quality healthcare services.

REFERENCES

Ashrafi, N., Kelleher, L., & Kuilboer, J. P. (2014). The impact of business intelligence on healthcare delivery in the USA. *Interdisciplinary Journal of Information, Knowledge, and Management,* (9), 117-130.

Atomwise. (2015). *Atomwise finds first evidence towards new ebola treatment.* Retrieved from http://www.atomwise.com/2015/03/24/atomwise-finds-first-evidence-towards-new-ebola-treatments/

Barney, J. (1991). Firms resources and sustained competitive advantage. *Journal of Management, 17*(1), 99–120. doi:10.1177/014920639101700108

Bharadwaj, A. S. (2000). A resource-based perspective on information technology capability and firm performance: an empirical investigation. *Management Information Systems Quarterly, 24*(1), 169–196. doi:10.2307/3250983

Bhatt, G. D., & Grover, V. (2005). Types of information technology capabilities and their role in competitive advantage: an empirical study. *Journal of Management Information Systems, 22*(2), 253–277. doi:10.1080/07421222.2005.11045844

Bonney, W. (2013). Applicability of business intelligence in electronic health record. In *Proceedings of the 2nd International Conference on Integrated Information.* 10.1016/j.sbspro.2013.02.050

Degaspari, J. (2013). NorthShore University Health System. *Healthcare Informatics, 29*(1), 12–16. PMID:23505944

Ferranti, J. M., Langman, M. K., Tanaka, D., McCall, J., & Ahmad, A. (2010). Bridging the gap: leveraging business intelligence tools in support of patient safety and financial effectiveness. *Journal of the American Medical Informatics Association, 17*(2), 136–143. doi:10.1136/jamia.2009.002220 PMID:20190055

Fonkych, K., & Taylor, R. (2005). *The state and pattern of health information technology adoption.* Santa Monica, CA: RAND Corporation.

Foshay, N., & Kuziemsky, C. (2014). Towards an implementation framework for business intelligence in healthcare. *International Journal of Information Management, 34*(1), 20–27. doi:10.1016/j.ijinfomgt.2013.09.003

Gold, A. H., Malhotra, A., & Segars, A. H. (2001). Knowledge management: an organizational capabilities perspective. *Journal of Management Information Systems, 18*(1), 185–214. doi:10.1080/07421222.2001.11045669

Hillestad, R., Bigelow, J., Bower, A., Girosi, F., Meili, R., Scoville, R., & Taylor, R. (2005). Can electronic medical record systems transform health care? potential health benefits, savings, and costs. *Health Affairs*, *24*(4), 1103–1117. doi:10.1377/hlthaff.24.5.1103 PMID:16162551

Isik, O., Jones, M. C., & Sidorova, A. (2013). Business intelligence success: the role of BI capabilities and decision environment. *Information & Management*, *50*(1), 13–23. doi:10.1016/j.im.2012.12.001

Kao, H.-Y., Yu, M.-C., Masud, M., Wu, W.-H., Chen, L.-J., & Wu, Y.-C. J. (2016). Design and evaluation of hospital-based business intelligence system (HBIS): a foundation for design science research methodology. *Computers in Human Behavior*, *62*, 495–505. doi:10.1016/j.chb.2016.04.021

Kathuria, A., Mann, A., Khuntia, J., Saldanha, T. J., & Kauffman, R. J. (2018b). A strategic value appropriation path for cloud computing. *Journal of Management Information Systems*, *35*(3), 740–775. doi:10.1080/07421222.2018.1481635

Kathuria, A., Saldanha, T. J. V., Khuntia, J., & Andrade Rojas, M. G. (2016). How information management capability affects innovation capability and firm performance under turbulence: evidence from India. In *Proceedings of the Thirty Seventh International Conference on Information Systems*, Dublin.

Kathuria, R., Kathuria, N. N., & Kathuria, A. (2018a). Mutually supportive or trade-offs: An analysis of competitive priorities in the emerging economy of India. *The Journal of High Technology Management Research*, *29*(2), 227–236. doi:10.1016/j.hitech.2018.09.003

Kim, G., Shin, B., Kim, K. K., & Lee, H. G. (2011). IT capabilities, process-oriented dynamic capabilities, and firm financial performance. *Journal of AIS*, *12*(7), 487–517.

Koh, H. C., & Tan, G. (2011). Data mining applications in healthcare. *Journal of Healthcare Information Management*, *19*(2), 64–72. PMID:15869215

Lebied, M. (2017). Business intelligence in healthcare: improving patient care and expenses. *Business Intelligence*, Retrieved from https://www.datapine.com/blog/business-intelligence-in-healthcare/

Lebied, M. (2018). 12 examples of big data analytics in healthcare that can save people. *Business Intelligence*. Retrieved from https://www.datapine.com/blog/big-data-examples-in-healthcare/

Lenz, R., & Reichert, M. (2007). IT support for healthcare processes, premises, challenges, perspectives. *Data & Knowledge Engineering*, *61*(1), 39–58. doi:10.1016/j.datak.2006.04.007

Marr, B. (2016). Big data in healthcare: Paris hospitals predict admission rates using machine learning. *Forbes*. Retrieved from https://www.forbes.com/sites/bernardmarr/2016/12/13/big-data-in-healthcare-paris-hospitals-predict-admission-rates-using-machine-learning/#1215710e79a2

Melville, N., Kraemer, K., & Gurubaxani, V. (2004). Information technology and organizational performance: an integrative model of IT business value. *Management Information Systems Quarterly*, *28*(2), 283–322. doi:10.2307/25148636

Mesko, B. (2017). The role of artificial intelligence in precision medicine. *Expert Review of Precision Medicine and Drug Development*, *2*(5), 239–241. doi:10.1080/23808993.2017.1380516

Mettler, T., & Vimarlund, V. (2009). Understanding business intelligence in the context of healthcare. *Health Informatics Journal*, *15*(3), 254–264. doi:10.1177/1460458209337446 PMID:19713399

Miliard, M. (2017). How predictive analytics helped reduce readmission at UnityPoint Health. *HealthcareITNews*. Retrieved from https://www.healthcareitnews.com/news/how-predictive-analytics-helped-reduce-readmissions-unitypoint-health

Moorfields Eye Hospital. (2016). *Moorfields Announces Research Partnership*. Retrieved from https://www.moorfields.nhs.uk/news/moorfields-announces-research-partnership

Moss, L. T., & Atre, S. (2007). *Business Intelligence Roadmap*. Boston, MA: Pearson Education.

O'Riain, C., & Hlefert, M. (2005). Analysis healthcare information strategies in Europe. In *UKAIS 2005, 10th Annual Conference*, Newcastle, UK.

Olszak, C. M., & Ziemba, E. (2003). Business intelligence as a key to management of an enterprise. In Proceedings of Informing Science and IT Education, Santa Rosa, CA. doi:10.28945/2672

Parente, S. T. (2000). Beyond the hype: a taxonomy of e-health business models. *Health Affairs*, *19*(6), 89–102. doi:10.1377/hlthaff.19.6.89 PMID:11192424

Parente, S. T., & Dunbar, J. L. (2001). Is health information technology investment related to the financial performance of US hospitals? an exploratory analysis. *International Journal of Healthcare Technology and Management, 3*(1), 48–58. doi:10.1504/IJHTM.2001.001104

Pearlson, K. E., & Saunders, C. S. (2013). *Managing & using information systems: a strategic approach*. Johnson Wiley & Sons.

Permwonguswa, S., Khuntia, J., Yim, D., Gregg, D., & Kathuria, A. (2018). Knowledge sharing in a health infomediary: role of self-concept, emotional empowerment, and self-esteem. *Health Systems (Basingstoke, England), 7*(3), 181–194. doi:10.1080/20476965.2017.1405875 PMID:31214347

Pugh, D. S. (1990). *Organization theory: selected readings*. Harmondsworth, UK: Penguin.

Ramakrishnan, T., Jones, M. C., & Sidorova, A. (2012). Factors influencing business intelligence (BI) data collection strategies: an empirical investigation. *Decision Support Systems*, (52): 729–739.

Ramakrishnan, T., Khuntia, J., Kathuria, A., & Saldanha, J. V. (2018). Business intelligence capabilities. In A. Deokar, A. Gupta, L. Iyer, & M. Jones (Eds.), *Analytics and data science. Annals of information systems*. Cham, Switzerland: Springer. doi:10.1007/978-3-319-58097-5_3

Ramakrishnan, T., Khuntia, J., Kathuria, A., & Saldanha, T. (2016). Business intelligence capabilities and effectiveness: an integrative model. In *Proceedings of the 49th Hawaii International Conference on System Sciences*, Kuai, HI. 10.1109/HICSS.2016.623

Rebuge, A., & Ferreira, D. (2012). Business process analysis in healthcare environments: a methodology based on process mining. *Information Systems, 37*(2), 99–116. doi:10.1016/j.is.2011.01.003

Rockmann, R., Weeger, A., & Gewald, H. (2014). Identifying organizational capabilities for the enterprise-wide usage of cloud computing. In *Proceedings of the Pacific Asia Conference on Information Systems*.

Sabherwal, R., & Kris, P. (1994). The alignment between organizational critical success factors and information technology capability in academic institutions. *Decision Sciences, 25*(2), 301–330. doi:10.1111/j.1540-5915.1994.tb01844.x

Sambamurthy, V., & Zmud, R. (1997). At the heart of success: organizational wide management competencies. In C. Sauer, P. Yetton, & L. Alexander (Eds.), *Steps to the future: fresh thinking on the management of IT-based organizational information* (pp. 143–163). San Francisco, CA: Jossey-Bass.

Schaefferling, A. (2013). Determinants and consequences of IT capability: review and synthesis of the literature. In *Proceedings of the 19th American Conference on Information Systems*, Chicago, IL.

Sidorova, A., Gupta, B., & Dinter, B. (2018). Introduction: research and research-in-progress. In A. Deokar, A. Gupta, L. Iyer, & M. Jones (Eds.), *Analytics and data science. annals of information systems*. Cham, Switzerland: Springer. doi:10.1007/978-3-319-58097-5_2

Spruit, M., Vroon, R., & Batenburg, R. (2014). Towards healthcare business intelligence in long-term care: an explorative case study in the Netherlands. *Computers in Human Behavior*, *30*, 698–707. doi:10.1016/j.chb.2013.07.038

Stroetmann, B., & Aisenbrey, A. (2012). Medical knowledge management in healthcare industry. *International Journal of Social, Behavioral, Educational, Economic, Business and Industrial Engineering*, *6*(4), 531–536.

Thamir, A., & Poulis, E. (2015). Business intelligence capabilities and implementation strategies. *International Journal of Global Business*, *8*(1), 34–45.

Torres, R., Sidorova, A., & Jones, M. C. (2018). Enabling firm performance through business intelligence and analytics: a dynamic capabilities perspective. *Information & Management*, *55*(7), 822–839. doi:10.1016/j.im.2018.03.010

Chapter 2
Billing and Review Perspectives in Healthcare

Joel Fredrickson
University of Colorado, Denver, USA

ABSTRACT

The relatively recent and more pervasive retention of electronic healthcare data has provided new opportunities for the advancement of analytics and business intelligence tools within healthcare. The tasks comprising the delivery process for healthcare provide numerous points for data capture, and associated analyses to improve efficiencies and quality of care. In general, healthcare data is extracted from transaction-based systems designed for billing, scheduling, and workflow. However, data characterizing medical events can be further leveraged to assist in the diagnosis and treatment of patients. In fact, healthcare information technology (HIT) to improve patient diagnosis and treatment is remarkably neglected. This chapter outlines the process flow for healthcare delivery, describes the data extracted during this process flow, details the enablers and inhibitors of HIT and accompanying analytics, presents concerns about data integrity and quality, and provides some methods for data cleansing and staging.

INTRODUCTION

The relatively recent and more pervasive retention of electronic healthcare data has provided new opportunities for the advancement of analytics and business intelligence tools within healthcare. The tasks comprising the delivery process for healthcare provide numerous points for data capture, and associated analyses to improve efficiencies and quality of care. In general, healthcare data is extracted

DOI: 10.4018/978-1-7998-2310-0.ch002

from transaction-based systems designed for billing, scheduling, and workflow. However, data characterizing medical events can be further leveraged to assist in the diagnosis and treatment of patients. In fact, healthcare information technology (HIT) to improve patient diagnosis and treatment is remarkably neglected. This chapter outlines the process flow for healthcare delivery, describes the data extracted during this process flow, details the enablers and inhibitors of HIT and accompanying analytics, presents concerns about data integrity and quality, and provides some methods for data cleansing and staging.

HEALTHCARE PROCESS OVERVIEW

Revenue Cycle Management

The healthcare delivery process is structured according to a "revenue cycle" and related management systems. The revenue cycle entails all facets of a patient's account, from its inception to payment. It integrates every aspect of a healthcare provider's clinical and financial operations. Specifically, healthcare revenue cycle management is the financial process used by providers to administer functions associated with patient care, from scheduling and account creation to billing and final payment. Figure 1 shows the primary process steps in the healthcare "revenue cycle".

Stakeholders

The process of healthcare delivery consists of numerous stakeholders. The behavior of each stakeholder impacts other stakeholders, and the efficiency and outcomes of the revenue cycle. Roughly, there are four major groups of stakeholders in the healthcare delivery process. They are policy makers, patients, providers/facilities and payers. Each of these stakeholders is described below.

Policy Makers

Policy makers establish the framework for the provision of healthcare. Essentially, the environment under which the other stakeholders operate is determined by policy maker actions. For example, the coding practices for characterizing medical events, in terms of code sets and data transmission protocols, are established by policy makers such as the Centers for Medicaid and Medicare Services (CMS). CMS also incents healthcare providers to appropriately use and maintain electronic health records (EHR). An important function of policy makers is the collection of aggregate data from patients, providers, and payors to develop population-level metrics. These

Figure 1. Healthcare revenue cycle management

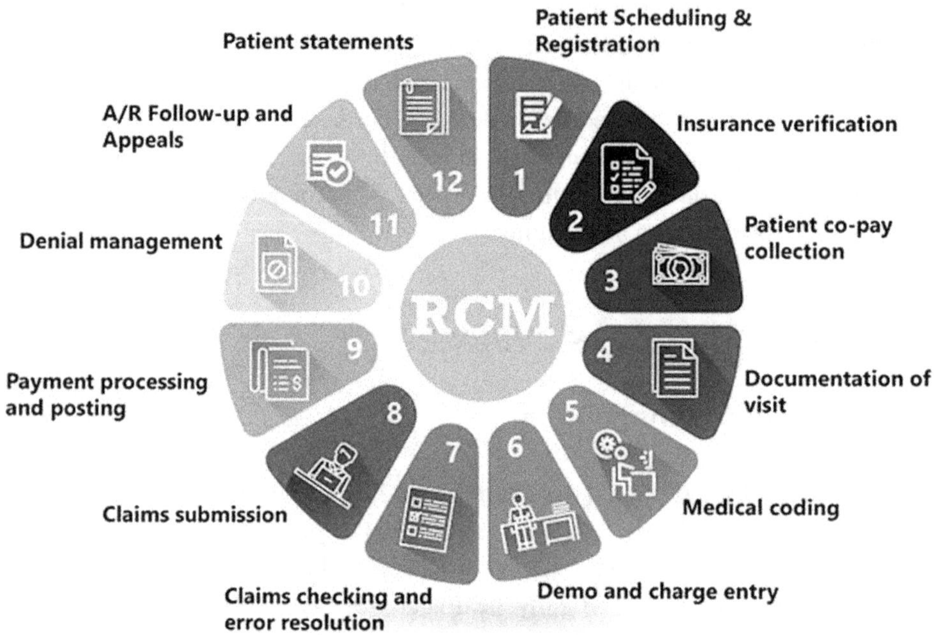

metrics inform health and health economic policies. Examples of such metrics are those comprising the Healthcare Effectiveness Data and Information Set (HEDIS). This is a commonly used set of performance measures used by managed care and maintained by the National Committee for Quality Assurance serving as the policy maker. It allows the comparison of health plan performance to other plans, and to established benchmarks. Additionally, results are helpful in tracking year-to-year performance.

Patients

Patients receive healthcare services from providers and are the recipient customers of financial benefits from payors. Policy makers have a fiduciary duty to patients, and the healthcare policy framework is intended to benefit patients. The patient experience includes all of the interactions that a patient has with the healthcare system, including their care from health plans, and from doctors, nurses, and staff in hospitals, physician practices, and other healthcare facilities, along with all payer interactions. A patient's greater engagement in their healthcare contributes to improved health outcomes, and information technologies can support these increased levels of engagement. Patients wish to be engaged in the clinical decision-making process, and those who are, tend to be healthier and have better outcomes.

Providers

Providers deliver healthcare services to patients and are responsible for maintaining health information about them. Providers should also be involved with the coordination of patient care among other providers and care facilities. Many providers are independent businesses managing their own operations and finances. Following are the major categories of healthcare providers:

Primary Care

A primary care provider is a person you normally see first for checkups and health problems. They help manage patient's overall health and serve as the conduit to other healthcare services including those provided by specialists and ancillary care providers. Some major categories of primary care providers are:

- Generalist: Medical doctors and doctors of osteopathic medicine specializing in internal medicine, family practice, or pediatrics.
- Obstetrician/Gynecologists: Doctors specializing in obstetrics and gynecology, including women's healthcare, wellness, and prenatal care.
- Nurse Practitioners: Nurses with graduate training. They can serve as a primary care provider in family medicine, pediatrics, adult care, or geriatrics. Others are trained to address women's healthcare and family planning. This type of provider can also prescribe medicines.
- Physician Assistant: Individuals providing a range of services in collaboration with a generalist.

Nursing Care

There are many forms of nursing care available to patients. These forms of care are normally accessed by patients based on primary care provider recommendations. Some forms of nursing care are:

- Licensed Practical Nurses: State-licensed caregivers.
- Registered Nurses: Graduated from a nursing program, have passed a state board examination, and are licensed by the state.
- Advanced Practice Nurses: Education and experience beyond the basic training and licensing required of all RNs.

- Clinical Nurse Specialists: Trained in a field such as cardiac, psychiatric, or community health.
- Certified Nurse Midwives: Trained in women's healthcare needs, including prenatal care, labor and delivery, and the care of a woman who has given birth.
- Certified Registered Nurse Anesthetists: Trained in the field of anesthesia.

Drug Therapy

These healthcare providers are licensed pharmacists that have graduate training from a college of pharmacy. A pharmacist prepares and processes drug prescriptions normally written by your primary or specialty care provider. Pharmacists provide information to people about medicines and also consult with providers about dosages, interactions, and side effects of medicines. Your pharmacist may also follow your progress to check that you are using your medicine safely and effectively.

Specialty Care

Your primary care provider may refer you to professionals in various specialties when necessary. These specialties include:

- Allergy and asthma
- Anesthesiology --general anesthesia or spinal block for surgeries and some forms of pain control
- Cardiology -- heart disorders
- Dermatology -- skin disorders
- Endocrinology -- hormonal and metabolic disorders, including diabetes
- Gastroenterology -- digestive system disorders
- General surgery -- common surgeries involving any part of the body
- Hematology -- blood disorders
- Immunology -- disorders of the immune system
- Infectious disease -- infections affecting the tissues of any part of the body
- Nephrology -- kidney disorders
- Neurology -- nervous system disorders
- Obstetrics/gynecology -- pregnancy and women's reproductive disorders
- Oncology -- cancer treatment
- Ophthalmology -- eye disorders and surgery
- Orthopedics -- bone and connective tissue disorders
- Otorhinolaryngology -- ear, nose, and throat disorders
- Physical therapy and rehabilitative medicine -- for disorders such as low back injury, spinal cord injuries, and stroke

- Psychiatry -- emotional or mental disorders
- Pulmonary (lung) -- respiratory tract disorders
- Radiology -- x-rays and related procedures (such as ultrasound, CT, and MRI)
- Rheumatology -- pain and other symptoms related to joints and other parts of the musculoskeletal system
- Urology -- disorders of the male reproductive system and urinary tract and the female urinary tract
- Nurse practitioners and physician assistants may also provide care in association with most types of specialists.

Facilities

With the increasing complexity of the healthcare system, patients now have numerous and varied choices for receiving healthcare. This includes options for selecting the type of healthcare facility they wish to utilize. Understanding the differences between the various types of facilities is crucial to patients when trying to make an informed decision about their medical care. The main healthcare facilities are listed below.

Hospital

A hospital's primary task is to provide short-term care for people with severe health issues resulting from injury, disease or genetic anomaly. Hospitals bring together physicians in assorted specialties, a highly skilled nursing staff, various medical technicians, healthcare administrators and specialized equipment to deliver care to people with acute and chronic health conditions. Many hospitals offer a wide range of services, including emergency care, scheduled surgeries, labor and delivery services, diagnostic testing, lab work, and patient education. Depending on their health situation, patients may receive inpatient or outpatient care from a hospital.

Ambulatory Surgical Center

Some procedures are too complex to be done safely in a doctor's office, but simple enough that patients may not require hospital care. Ambulatory surgical centers are designed to provide these types of procedures. Also referred to as outpatient or same day surgery centers, these facilities offer a safe environment for the surgery and basic monitoring during the initial post-operation hours. Ambulatory surgical centers are often a less expensive option than a hospital. Studies have shown that procedures generally cost significantly less when performed at an ambulatory surgical center instead of a hospital.

Doctor's Office

A doctor's office is a medical facility where one or more doctors provide treatment to patients. Doctor's offices may focus on one type of medicine; the health providers operating there are either general practitioners or practice a common specialty. Doctor's offices provide routine care as well as treatment for acute conditions that do not require immediate intervention. While these facilities are traditionally called a doctor's office, the doctor is rarely the only medical professional on staff. In many cases, physician assistants and nurses contribute to the delivery of patient care.

Urgent Care Clinic

When patients are unable to get to their doctor's office or want basic medical care without an appointment, an urgent care clinic is an option. Sometimes called walk-in clinics, these facilities offer outpatient care immediately. Importantly, an urgent care clinic is not the same as a hospital's emergency room. If the issue is something that you would normally see your doctor for like a stomach virus or a sprained ankle, then an urgent care clinic is appropriate. If you have a more complex health situation or your issue is a medical emergency like chest pain, breathing difficulties, broken bones or an extremely high fever, a hospital's emergency room is the choice.

Nursing Home

A nursing home is designed for patients who require constant care but do not need to be hospitalized and cannot be cared for at home. Often associated with seniors who require custodial care in a residential facility, it can actually serve patients of all ages who require this level of care. Nursing homes have medical personal onsite 24 hours a day. A physician, skilled nurses and therapists are on staff to oversee and provide medical care, assistance with medications, and services like physical, speech and occupational therapy. In addition, the nursing home's staff offers help with basic tasks that can be challenging for individuals with health issues, including feeding, bathing and dressing.

Payors

Payors operationalize the financial elements of the policy framework. Payors enroll patients as beneficiaries. They procure care services from the providers on behalf of their patient beneficiaries and reimburse providers for services delivered. They also perform the actuarial task of ensuring the financial sustainability of the care program and assume reporting tasks outlined by policy makers. Third-party payers are insurance carriers, including public, private, managed care and preferred provider networks, that reimburse fully or partially the cost of healthcare provider services. Many types of healthcare insurance are available to patients either by employer-provided plans or commercial plans. Currently, the largest health payer is United Health Group which provides networks for care and is a commercial and employer-based insurance company. Public options include Medicare for adults over 65, TRICARE established by the Department of Defense, and Medicaid, which is a joint plan funded by states and the federal government for those with low income. Third-party payers often do not pay all of a patient's bill. Deductibles are the portion of the bill the patient pays before the insurance company becomes responsible.

Here are a few more payer options that are available:

- Managed Care Organizations or Health Management Organizations (HMO) combine healthcare providers with insurance companies to keep costs down.
- Preferred Provider Organizations (PPO) are networks that include healthcare providers and insurance that does not require the patient to use a certain provider, but the patient incurs more expense if they go outside the network.
- Health Insurance Exchanges (HIE) offer an opportunity to purchase insurance that is not employer-provided or for patients that are self-employed.
- High-deductible health plans provide a big incentive to stay healthy for those that need less expensive insurance.

Medical Coding

Medical events are described through the use of various claims forms submitted by healthcare providers for payment purposes. These forms incorporate a number of "code sets" specific to various categories of healthcare service. For example, diagnoses are characterized by the International Classification of Diseases (ICD) code set. Excluding specialized types of claims such as vision and dental, almost all claims relating to medical events are prepared using standardized code sets. The more prominent code sets relate to services and procedure, condition diagnoses and pharmaceuticals. First, Current Procedural Terminology (CPT) codes are procedural codes used by providers to describe services and procedures. CPT codes are maintained by the American Medical Association through the CPT Editorial Panel. Specifically, the CPT code set describes medical, surgical, and diagnostic services and is designed to communicate standardized information about medical services and procedures among healthcare stakeholders for administrative, financial, and analytical purposes. Next, the International Classification of Diseases (ICD) code set is maintained by the World Health Organization. The ICD is designed as a healthcare classification system, providing a system of diagnostic codes for classifying diseases. This includes more detailed classifications of a wide variety

Figure 2. Key healthcare stakeholders

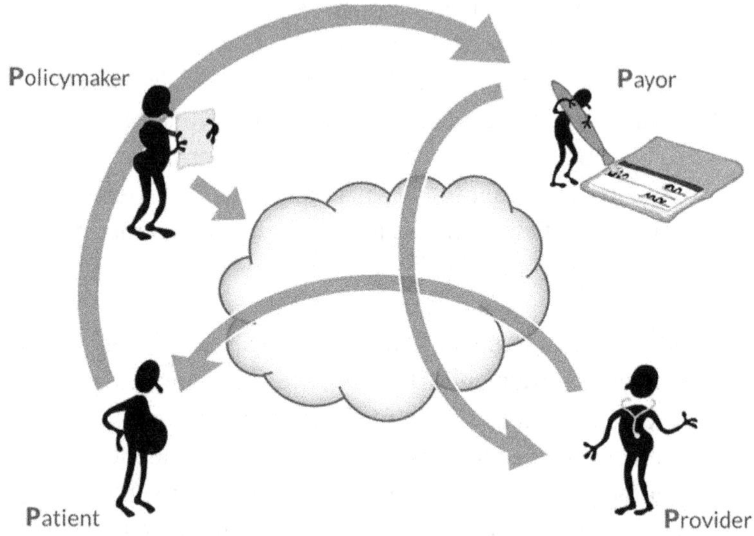

of signs, symptoms, abnormal findings, complaints, social circumstances, and external causes of injury or disease. Finally, the National Drug Code is a unique product identifier used in the United States for drugs intended for human use. The Drug Listing Act of 1972 requires registered drug establishments to provide the Food and Drug Administration (FDA) with a current list of all drugs manufactured, prepared, propagated, compounded, or processed by it for commercial distribution. Drug products are identified and reported using the National Drug Code.

Abstraction

With accessible and pervasive healthcare data, there is a need to insure consistent and meaningful information is "abstracted" from electronic health records. "Abstraction" in the context of healthcare, research is simply the process of transforming a patient's medical record, as prepared by a physician or healthcare provider, into a form compatible with coded EHRs or medical claims. This transformation is achieved through the implementation of code sets for condition diagnoses, treatment procedures or tests, and pharmaceuticals. The use of standardized codes represents only a simplified synopsis of information extracted from a health record, therefore this kind of coding is referred to as abstraction. It is important to note that abstraction is a somewhat subjective process and, therefore, affects the reliability of healthcare information and resulting analytics procured in that way.

Figure 3. Medical coding abstraction

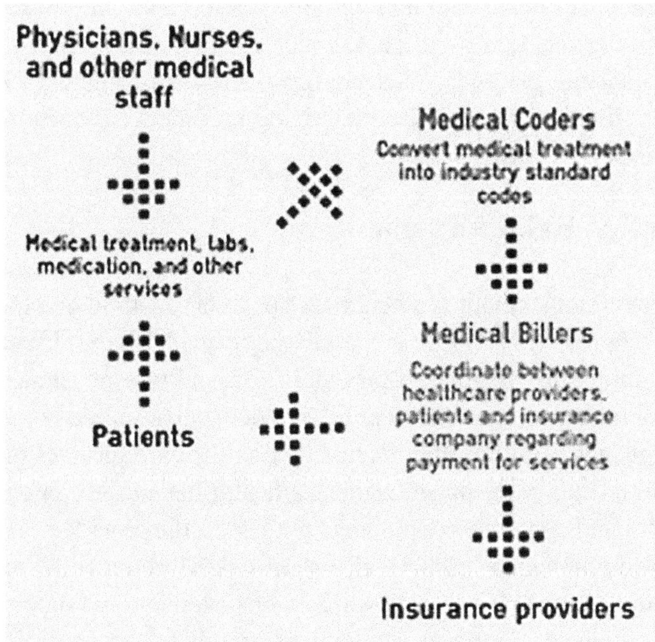

Reimbursement Methods

There are many variants of physician reimbursement methods. As such, this overview of provider reimbursement focuses on their major features, rather than the details of each reimbursement variant. Essentially, reimbursement methods for healthcare services have three characteristics: the unit of payment, the time orientation, and the extent of financial risk for each stakeholder. First, the unit of payment refers to the cost associated healthcare item and may, for example, be as specific as an individual procedure, or as broad as an entire population. Second, the time orientation can be retrospective or prospective. Retrospective reimbursement methods entail cost determination and reimbursement after services are provided. For prospective reimbursement methods, the payment levels for healthcare services are determined prior to the services being rendered. Financial risk shifts with the time orientation of the reimbursement. With retrospective methods, the financial risk is more incurred by the payer (insurer) given the uncertainty of their future, "service-incurred" reimbursements to providers. In contrast, the provider incurs the majority of financial risk with prospective methods, as they must work within preset financial constraints to deliver appropriate levels of care. Importantly, the more significant determinant of care quality, in terms of provider reimbursement approaches, is the unit of payment. That is, provider incentives change dramatically when being paid for their volume of services, common with fee-for-service reimbursement, instead of patient outcomes and quality of care, which are more associated with episode-of-care reimbursement methods. As such, this overview is organized according to these two major units of payment characterizing provider reimbursement: fee-for-service and episode-of-care.

Fee-for-Service Reimbursement

Fee-for-service reimbursement is a healthcare payment method in which providers receive payment retrospectively for each service performed. It is the oldest and simplest method for reimbursing healthcare providers. Basically, a physician, healthcare organization, or other provider bills for each service that has already been provided. This is accomplished by submitting a claim listing the care services provided. The claim is sent to a third-party payer, usually a health insurance company or health agency. In traditional retrospective payment processes, the providers are reimbursed a pre-established amount for each service rendered. More recently, managed care methods afford payers more control over cost management and outcomes of care. In managed care plans, the payer implements conditions to control the costs of healthcare while maintaining appropriate levels of quality.

Episode-of-Care Reimbursement

Episode-of-care reimbursement is a healthcare payment method in which providers receive one lump sum for services comprising an "episode of care" often related to a condition or disease. For this payment method, the unit of payment is the episode, not each individual health service. Therefore, the episode-of-care payment method eliminates individual fees or charges. The episode-of-care payment method is an attempt to correct perceived faults in the fee-for-service reimbursement method. Thus, the episode-of-care reimbursement method controls costs on a grand or systematic scale. An episode of care comprises the health services that a patient receives for a particular health condition or illness, or during a period of relatively continuous care from a provider. In the episode of care, one amount is set for all the care services and materials associated with the condition or illness. Forms of episode-of-care reimbursement are capitation, global payment, and prospective payment.

Capitated Payment Method

Capitation is a method of payment for health services in which a third-party payer reimburses providers a fixed amount for a given period or medical event. A common phrase in capitated contracts is "per member per month". This is the amount of money paid each month for each individual enrolled in the health insurance plan. Capitation is characteristic of health maintenance organizations. In capitation, the actual volume or intensity of services provided to each patient has no effect on the payment. More services do not increase the payment, nor do fewer services decrease the payment. If the provider contracts with a third-party payer to provide services to a group of workers for a capitated rate, the provider receives the payments for each member of the group regardless of whether all the members receive the provider's services. There are no adjustments for the complexity or extent of the health services.

Global Payment Method

In the global payment method, a third-party payer makes one combined payment to cover the services of multiple providers who are treating a single episode of care. Thus, this payment method consolidates payments. A "block grant" is a fixed amount of money given or allocated for a specific purpose. For example, in a block grant there is a transfer of governmental funds to cover health services. In the global payment method, there is no additional payment for higher volumes of services or more expensive or complex services. Less comprehensive versions of the global payment method exist. For example, some global payment methods include only ambulatory costs, inpatient costs, or some other costs related to a specific category of service.

Prospective Payment Methods

In the prospective payment method, payment rates for healthcare services are established in advance for a specific time period. The predetermined rates are based on average levels of resource use for certain types of healthcare. The prospective risk or cost of the covered population is often "scored" to appropriately allocate reimbursement funds. It is important to note that prospective payment methods are based upon averages. On individual patients, providers can lose money or make money, but, over time, providers should come out even given they are using appropriate risk assessment tools. Payment is determined by the needs of the average patient in the covered population for a (a) set period of time or (b) given set of conditions or diseases. Prospective payment methods representing these two situations are per-diem payment and case-based payment, respectively, and are explained below.

Per-Diem Payment

Per diem or per day (daily rate) is a limited type of prospective payment method. The third-party payer reimburses the provider a fixed rate for each day a covered member is treated. Although not common, some supplemental health insurance plans use per-diem methods. Traditionally, the per diem payment method has been used to reimburse providers for inpatient hospital services.

Case-Based Payment

In the case-based payment method, providers receive a fixed, preestablished payment for each case. Cases are patients, residents, or clients who receive health services for a condition or disease. Third party payers reimburse providers for each case rather than for each service (fee-for-service or FFS) or per diem. An example of the case-based payment system built on categories of cases is Medicare's method of payment for inpatient hospital services (prospective payment system; PPS). This method of payment is based on categories of payment called "diagnosis related groups" (DRG). Each DRG categorizes patients who are homogeneous in terms of clinical profiles and requisite resources. Therefore, patients classified to the same group should have similar diagnoses and treatments, consumption of resources, and lengths of stay. Each DRG has a payment rate called a "weight." Weights are relative to one another. Higher weights are associated with groups in which patients require more resources for care and treatment. Higher resource consumption is related to higher intensity of services due to the severity of illness or the types of services needed for care and treatment, such as expensive equipment or medications. Higher weights translate into higher payments.

Value-Based Payment Programs

Recently, CMS has implemented several value-based payment programs to help reward healthcare providers with incentive payments for the quality of care they provide to Medicare patients. In 2015, the Medicare Access and CHIP Reauthorization Act was signed into law. Among other things, this law outlines a timetable for the implementation of a merit-based incentive payment system to replace other value-based payment programs. This payment system will use a set of performance measures, divided into categories, to calculate a score (between 0 and 100) for eligible professionals. Healthcare providers meeting an established threshold score will receive no adjustment to payment; those scoring below will receive a negative adjustment, and those above, a positive adjustment.

HEALTHCARE DATA ADMINISTRATION

Government Programs Impacting HIT

Passage of significant healthcare reform legislation has brought dramatic change to the healthcare sector, including formal efforts to promote HIT. Legislation to bring about "healthcare reform" is, in effect, an attempt to achieve the simultaneous "triple aims" for the healthcare delivery system: improve the patient experience of care, improve the health of populations, and reduce per capita cost of healthcare. Achievement of these goals is often difficult within a healthcare delivery system managed by the diverse stakeholders described above and whose goals are frequently misaligned. Some of the more important legislative efforts and their impact on HIT are described below.

Health Insurance Portability and Accountability Act (1996)

The Health Insurance Portability and Accountability Act (HIPAA) was enacted by the United States Congress and signed by President Bill Clinton in 1996. It was created primarily to streamline the flow of healthcare information through standardized code sets and transfer protocols, establish methods concerning Protected Health Information, and address outstanding issues with healthcare insurance coverage. The Act consists of five Titles. Title I protects health insurance coverage when workers change or lose their jobs. Title II establishes national standards for electronic healthcare transactions and national identifiers for providers, health insurance plans, and employers. Title III sets guidelines for pre-tax medical spending accounts. Title IV sets operating guidelines for group health plans. And, Title V governs company-owned life insurance policies. HIPAA was part of a larger healthcare reform effort and expanded federal interest in HIT for purposes beyond reimbursement. HIPAA also brought national attention to the issues surrounding the use of personal health information in electronic form. Leveraging Internet functionality, HIPAA revolutionized the way that consumers, providers, and healthcare organizations accessed health information, communicated with each other, and conducted business. This greatly streamlined many healthcare processes including billing and reimbursement, but created new risks related to patient privacy and security.

Medicare Modernization Act (2003)

The Medicare Prescription Drug, Improvement, and Modernization Act, also called the Medicare Modernization Act, is a federal law enacted in 2003. It resulted in the largest renovation of Medicare in the public health program's then 38-year history. The federal government was responding to quality of care concerns through improved healthcare transparency and furthering the adoption of HIT. Specifically, this legislation expanded the program to include prescription drugs and required the use of electronic prescribing (e-prescribing) among health plans providing prescription drug coverage to Medicare beneficiaries. A year later, the government further focused on the expanded use of HIT, and emphasized widespread adoption of EHR systems within the decade to improve efficiency, reduce medical errors, and improve quality of care. By 2006, an executive order was signed directing federal agencies administering health insurance programs to make information about prices paid to healthcare providers for procedures, and information on the quality of services, publicly available. This executive order also encouraged adoption of HIT standards to enable the rapid exchange of health information.

Health Information Technology for Economic and Clinical Health Act (2009)

The Health Information Technology for Economic and Clinical Health Act (HITECH) was enacted under Title XIII of the American Recovery and Reinvestment Act of 2009. Under HITECH, the United States Department of Health and Human Services is intending to expand the adoption of health information technology. Specifically, it promotes the adoption and "meaningful use" of information technology within the healthcare industry. HITECH establishes a system of incentive payments to healthcare providers for the demonstrated and "meaningful use" of EMRs. The act states "that, as of 2011 [and until 2015], healthcare providers will be offered financial incentives for demonstrating meaningful use of electronic health records" (healthcareitnews.com 2014). After 2015, however, penalties may be incurred for not demonstrating such use. Additionally, grants for training centers are funded through HITECH for personnel required to support a healthcare IT infrastructure.

The requirements for "meaningful use" of information technology by healthcare providers were established by the Centers for Medicare and Medicaid Services (cms.gov). To qualify for incentive payments and to avoid future penalties, healthcare providers in the form of eligible professionals, eligible hospitals, and critical access hospitals must meet "measurement thresholds [for EHR use] that range from recording patient information as structured data to exchanging summary care records" (healthit.

gov 2014). The CMS incentive programs have three stages with each stage having more extensive requirements for indication of appropriate IT usage.

Patient Protection and Affordable Care Act (2010)

The Patient Protection and Affordable Care Act, often shortened to the Affordable Care Act, and nicknamed Obamacare, was signed into law by President Barack Obama on March 23, 2010. Together with the Healthcare and Education Reconciliation Act of 2010 amendment, it represents the most significant regulatory overhaul and expansion of healthcare coverage since the passage of Medicare and Medicaid in 1965. The major provisions of this legislation came into force in 2014. By 2016, the uninsured share of the population had roughly halved, with estimates ranging from 20 to 24 million additional people covered during 2016. The increased coverage was due, roughly equally, to an expansion of Medicaid eligibility and to major changes to individual insurance markets. Both involved new spending, funded through a combination of new taxes and cuts to Medicare provider rates and Medicare Advantage. The law also included delivery system reforms intended to constrain healthcare costs and improve quality.

Along with mandating that individuals have health insurance and expanding Medicaid programs, the Affordable Care Act created the structure for health insurance exchanges, including a greater role for states, and imposed changes to private insurance, such as prohibiting health plans from placing lifetime limits on the dollar value of coverage and prohibiting preexisting condition exclusions. Numerous changes were to be made to the Medicare program, including continued reductions in Medicare payments to certain hospitals for hospital-acquired conditions and excessive preventable hospital readmissions. Additionally, CMS established an innovation center to test, evaluate, and expand different payment structures and methodologies to reduce program expenditures while maintaining or improving quality of care. Through the innovation center and other means, CMS has been aggressively pursuing implementation of value-based payment methods

Code Sets

The revenue cycle in healthcare relies almost solely on "code sets" for capturing descriptive information about medical services. Essentially, a medical event is characterized, billed, and reimbursed through standardized code sets mandated in part by the government programs mentioned above. The more significant codes, explained below, are utilized during the complete care cycle, from diagnosis through clinical pathway.

CPT

Current Procedural Terminology (CPT) codes are procedural codes used by providers to describe services and procedures. This well accepted code set is maintained by the American Medical Association, and it, along with ICD, is an important method to abstract meaning from medical incidents for analytic purposes. Specifically, CPT codes describe tests, surgeries, evaluations, and other medical procedures. This code set is extremely large and includes codes for thousands of medical procedures. CPT codes serve two fundamental purposes. Chiefly, CPT codes are an essential part of the billing process. CPT codes submitted by the healthcare provider tell the payer the procedures requiring reimbursement. As well, CPT codes are used to monitor health measure performance and efficiency. For example, government agencies use CPT codes to track the prevalence and value of certain procedures, and hospitals can use CPT codes to evaluate the performance of individuals or divisions within their facility.

ICD

International Classification of Diseases (ICD) are diagnosis codes used to describe what condition is being identified and subsequently treated. ICD is the "archetypal coding system for medical record abstraction" and is essentially a hierarchical coding algorithm that consists of a core classification of three-digit codes" (Cimino 1996). ICD codes have been used extensively in healthcare research and "play a key role in reporting medical statistics to government organizations" (Yan et. al 2010). The most recent version of the ICD code set is called the International Statistical Classification of Diseases and Related Health Problems 10th Revision (ICD-10). Specifically, it is a code set of "diseases, signs and symptoms, abnormal findings, complaints, social circumstances and external causes of injury or diseases" classified by the World Health Organization (medicaid.gov 2016). ICD-10 is an updated version of the ICD-9 code sets. The United States, through the National Center for Health Statistics, has developed the ICD-10-CM (or Clinical Modification) version of the code set for use in the US. CMS has created a new code set, ICD-10-PCS (or Procedure Coding System). These code sets are considered classification code sets and provide greater granularity than some other medical code sets like the Systematized Nomenclature of Medicine, which is used by federal government systems for the electronic exchange of clinical health information.

NDC

The NDC, or National Drug Code, is a unique 10-digit, 3-segment number. It is a universal product identifier for human drugs in the United States. The code is present on all nonprescription and prescription medication packages and inserts in the US. The 3 segments of the NDC identify the labeler, the product, and the commercial package size. The first set of numbers in the NDC identifies the labeler (manufacturer, repackager, or distributer). The second set of numbers is the product code, which identifies the specific strength, dosage form (i.e, capsule, tablet, liquid) and formulation of a drug for a specific manufacturer. Finally, the third set is the package code, which identifies package sizes and types. The labeler code is assigned by the FDA, while the product and package code are assigned by the labeler. Resembling ICD codes, a hierarchical coding scheme has been developed by First Data Bank for pharmaceutical data. Specifically, the Hierarchical Ingredient Code (HIC) is used by the First Data Bank as a drug classifier. HIC is a 6-character code that identifies each drug. However, because the coding is hierarchical, part of the HIC may be used to group drugs together. For example, the specific therapeutic class or HIC3 consists of the first 3 characters of the Hierarchical Ingredient Code and this drug grouper may prove useful to a similarity measure.

HCPCS

HCPCS stands for Healthcare Common Procedure Coding System. Technically CPT codes are part of the HCPCS code set and are officially designated as Level I HCPCS codes. The regulation that CMS published on August 17, 2000 (45 CFR 162.10002) to implement the HIPAA requirement for standardized coding systems established the HCPCS level II codes as the standardized coding system for healthcare equipment and supplies that are not identified by the HCPCS level I, CPT codes. The HCPCS level II coding system was selected as the standardized coding system because of its wide acceptance among both public and private insurers. Level II HCPCS are primarily used to identify products, supplies, and services not included in the CPT codes. The code set is made up of five-character, alpha-numeric codes mainly representing medical supplies, durable medical goods, non-physician services, and services not represented in the Level I code set (CPT). HCPCS Level II includes services such as ambulance, durable medical equipment, prosthetics, orthotics and supplies, when used outside a physician's office. This coding system is also used as an official code set for outpatient hospital care, chemotherapy drugs, Medicaid, and other services.

Revenue

Revenue (REV) codes are used by hospitals and other facilities to bill for services that were provided by the institution to a patient. They can represent either inpatient or outpatient services and are typically billed on a different claim form. Revenue codes are three-digit codes that affect reimbursement and represent the services provided by a given facility for a payer. HCPCS or CPT codes may be required in addition to specific revenue codes to describe the services rendered. For each line item charge listed on the claim, there must be an associated revenue code listed. However, not all charges on the claim will have an associated CPT code.

Groupers

A claim can include any combination of codes from the code sets described previously. The "typical" codes used to represent medical services number over 35,000. Interestingly, considering only two code combinations, there are over 1.2 billion possible permutations. One cannot analyze that many combinations with sufficient accuracy, while preserving a reasonable sample size. Because of the large number of codes and code combinations, algorithms have been created to logically group the many codes into different buckets that share certain characteristics. This approach makes the data more viewable, understandable, and comparable. Additionally, because you have a much smaller number of possibilities, the analysis of a given group is not only easier, but will provide higher statistical validity and probability of representing reality. As a reference, some of the more common code set classifiers (groupers) that already exist are shown in Table 1.

DRG

A common grouper developed at Yale University on behalf of CMS is called Diagnosis Related Groups (DRG). It was intended to aggregate hospital services into buckets that could be risk adjusted and drive prospective payment systems for planned hospital services. DRGs were designed to describe homogeneous units of hospital activity to which binding prices could be attached. They were also intended to enable hospital administrators to alter the behavior of the physicians and surgeons comprising their medical staffs through practice pattern information. Given the initial results of a pilot program, it was decided in 1983 to implement DRGs in hospitals nationwide. Since then, the focus of all Medicare DRG modifications has primarily been the elderly population. As a result, DRG's are extremely weak in the areas of obstetrics, gynecology, and pediatrics. The 3M corporation has done all of the maintenance for the DRG grouper for CMS since 1983.

Table 1. Common medical coding groupers

Diagnosis Related Groups (DRG)
This classification scheme was developed by researchers at Yale University in the 1970's on behalf of Medicare. Basically, it is a means of aggregating hospital services into buckets that could be risk adjusted and form the basis for a prospective payment system for hospital services.
Adjusted Clinical Groupings (ACG)
ACG's (Adjusted Clinical Groups) were developed by researchers at the Johns Hopkins School of Medicine. Their concentration was on combinations of services and conditions that ended up having similar resource consumption.
Episode Treatment Groups (ETG)
ETG's (Episode Treatment Groups) were developed by Symmetry Health Data Systems. The ETG methodology is similar to DRG, but it incorporates all claims (medical, pharmacy, and hospital) data. The objective is to define homogeneous groupings of conditions having similar resource utilization and clinical patterns.
Diagnostic Clinical Groups (DCG)
DCG's (Diagnostic Cost Groups) were developed by DxCG; primarily by actuaries and statisticians. They are intended to categorize resource usage and clinical similarity and predict relative risk. Methodology results in a "relative risk score" at the patient level and quantifies the financial implications of the patient's "illness burden" or morbidity.
Med-STAT Grouper or Medical Episode Grouper (MEG)
MEG (Medstat Episode Grouper or Medical Episode Grouper) methodology is similar to the way ETGs classify inpatient, outpatient, and pharmaceutical claims into clinically homogeneous units of analysis called "episodes" that describe a patient's complete course of care for a single illness or condition. The Medstat grouper classifies medical/pharmacy claims into one of 555 disease categories that are further stratified by severity level.

APR-DRG

Pediatric researchers, through the National Association of Children's Hospitals and Affiliated Institutions developed a more pediatric focused version of DRG. This was intended to make up for the absence of pediatric emphasis in the Medicare version. This extended DRG version is called Pediatric Modified DRG (PM-DRG). In 1987, when the State of New York mandated that hospitalizations for all payers move to DRG payment systems, the New York Department of Health employed 3M to come up with a combined DRG methodology. That contract resulted in the All-Payer DRG (AP-DRG). Eventually DRG groupings were being used for many purposes beyond the original establishment of a prospective payment system. Although the original DRG and AP-DRG systems focused purely on resource consumption, 3M extended their use and also incorporated patient attributes for severity of illness and risk of mortality. The resulting grouper became known as All Payer Refined DRG (APR-DRG).

MS-DRG

The latest iteration of DRG grouper methodology again represents work done on behalf of CMS by 3M. It is often called the CMS Grouper or, more accurately, the Medicare Severity Diagnosis Related Groups (MS-DRG). It incorporates features from both the original DRG and the modifications of the APR-DRG. The original 538 DRG classifications were replaced with 745 MS-DRG classifications. The DRG's were first collapsed into 335 base MS-DRG's. Of these 106 were split into two subgroups, and 152 were split into three subgroups. This resulted in 745 total MS-DRGs. The subgroups are based on the presence of complications or comorbidities. Reimbursements are adjusted to reflect the relative severity compared to the old system. MS-DRG's are now only available from the National Technical Information Service. What began as a relatively straightforward approach to classifying resource utilization, has grown into a sophisticated analytical tool to not only look at similar utilization amongst clinically homogeneous events, but also to account for differences in severity and risk of mortality.

ACG

Adjusted Clinical Groups (ACG) were developed at the Johns Hopkins School of Medicine. Their original name was ambulatory care groupings and they were developed to help predict which children leaving the pediatric intensive care unit would require expensive and high utilization services. They focused on combining services and conditions having similar resource consumption. This grouper has evolved to include hospital services and pharmaceuticals. ACGs are the first grouper used to risk-adjust capitation services, and they probably remain the most common grouper used for that purpose. The ACG "Case-Mix System" classifies all ICD codes to one of 32 diagnosis groups, known as Adjusted Diagnosis Groups (ADG). Diseases are placed in a diagnosis group (ADG) based on five clinical dimensions: duration (acute, recurrent or chronic), severity (minor/stable versus major/unstable), diagnostic certainty (symptoms versus diseases), etiology (infectious, injury or other), and specialty care (medical, surgical, obstetric, hematology, etc). Because most management applications require that patients be grouped into mutually exclusive categories, the ACG Case-Mix System uses a branching algorithm to place people into one of 93 discrete ACG categories. An individual is assigned to an ACG based on his or her particular combination of ADGs, as well as his or her age and gender. As such, individuals within a given ACG have experienced a similar pattern of morbidity and resource consumption over the course of a given year. ACGs are also calibrated for a given type of population (Commercial, Medicaid and Medicare). This grouper is less clinically based than other groupers and this impacts their understanding by physicians. There is risk adjustment included with the tool and there is a predictive model (both medical and pharmacy based and pharmacy only based) tool that is also available with them.

ETG

Episode Treatment Groups (ETG) were developed by Symmetry Health Data Systems. The founders of Symmetry worked on the original DRG grouping methodology. Accordingly, the ETG methodology is similar to that used by the DRG grouper. However, ETG differs in that they incorporate all claim types (medical, pharmacy and hospital), as well as enrollment data, and the classifications are clinically based. The goal of ETG is to create unique and clinically homogeneous groupings of conditions with both similar resource utilization and clinical patterns. They are designed around episodes of care and allow analysis of utilization and cost patterns across groups and over time. ETGs are a patented illness classification and episode-building grouping technology, are one of the most commercially successful groupers, and serve as a reference standard in healthcare. The grouping concept is similar to DRG, except ETG classifies all relevant medical and pharmacy services, regardless of place of service. Using claims information as input, ETG grouping captures data on the relevant services and prescriptions provided during a patient's treatment and "groups" claims information into meaningful episodes of care. ETGs combine inpatient, outpatient, ancillary and pharmacy claims to build a comprehensive treatment episode from onset of care until treatment is complete. The duration of each episode is based on a continuous time period in which there is an absence of treatment, called a "clean period". When analyzing claims data, the ETG grouper evaluates each expense line, the services performed and the provider who billed for them, then assigns them to the most appropriate episode. Each ETG belongs to a specific Major Practice Category (MPC), with each MPC representing a body system and physician specialty. There are approximately 600 clinically similar groups containing patients with similar conditions. The approach uses common medical terms and is more easily understood by healthcare providers.

DCG

Diagnostic Cost Groups (DCG) were developed by DxCG. Unlike other groupers, DCG was built primarily by actuaries and statisticians. They were designed specifically as a risk adjustment methodology and incorporate both resource usage and clinical similarity. DxCG predictive models are built from two basic classification systems: DCG for diagnoses and RxGroups® for pharmacy data. DxCG models work by classifying administrative data into clinical groupings to create an aggregated, empirically valid measure of expected resource use. The measure, called a "relative risk score," is calculated at the patient level and quantifies the financial implications of the patient's "illness burden" or morbidity. DCG assigns ICD codes to homogeneous groups called DX Groups. These are not unique at a member level and most members (patients) fall into more than one of these groups. These Dx Groups are then compressed into Condition Categories (CC) having similar resource usage patterns. Each Dx Group maps to only one CC. A hierarchy is then imposed on the CC groups, and these groups are compressed and ordered into Hierarchical Condition Categories (HCC). These clinical hierarchies provide the costliest manifestation of each disease. A member is assigned the highest CC in each hierarchy and will often appear in multiple HCC groups. The DCG relative risk score is built by aggregating the individual component scores for the HCC assignments for each patient. DCGs have been well accepted as a predictive model, risk adjuster, and the basis for capitation methodologies. DCGs cannot simply be applied against any population and you must calibrate the tool based upon the population of interest. As such, separate models are normally available for Commercial, Medicaid, or Medicare populations, with the HCC weights differing from population to population.

MEG

The Medstat Episode Grouper or Medical Episode Grouper (MEG) was developed by Medstat, an organization performing data management services along with statistical analysis and modeling. They were originally known for their statistics expertise while being viewed as less proficient clinically. MEG methodology is similar to ETG with their episodes of care having similarities to the those used by ETGs. MEG software groups inpatient, outpatient, and pharmaceutical claims into clinically homogeneous units called "episodes", describing a patient's complete course of care for a single condition. Medstat algorithms classify medical and pharmacy claims into one of numerous disease categories that are further stratified by severity level. Additionally, Medstat uses the DCG methodology from DxCG to perform predictive modeling and risk scoring for risk adjustment, and to evaluate the relative complexity of patients and populations.

Interoperability

Interoperability of healthcare information is an extremely important concern of researchers and industry stakeholders. Interoperability that enables HIT has much more breadth than simply the sharing of EHRs across healthcare systems. The burgeoning realm of devices both capturing and retaining personal healthcare data challenge comprehensive "interoperability" affording optimum patient care.

Additionally, telehealth is advancing, and large healthcare databases are being established at state and national levels. True interoperability must integrate any electronic source having information needed to provide the best possible healthcare. Notable efforts toward HIT interoperability include those most recently initiated under the direction of the Office of the National Coordinator for Health Information Technology (ONC). In 2015, ONC published "Connecting Health and Care for the Nation: A Shared Nationwide Interoperability Roadmap," a ten-year plan for achieving HIT interoperability in the United States. This document defines interoperability as "the ability of a system to exchange electronic health information with and use electronic health information from other systems without special effort on the part of the user". Essentially, ONC proposes that "all individuals, their families and healthcare providers should be able to send, receive, find and use electronic health information in a manner that is appropriate, secure, timely and reliable to support the health and wellness of individuals through informed, shared decision-making". The availability of the right information at the right time, enables individuals and caregivers to be active participants in healthcare delivery. Importantly for analytics, interoperability supports data aggregation and accessibility for research, which can lead to improved clinical guidelines and practices and eventually, patient outcomes. From a HIT perspective, data exchange architectures and standards allow relevant patient information to be shared effectively and securely across the complete spectrum of care, from all applicable platforms, and with relevant stakeholders. Ideally, interoperability enables integration across systems, regardless of data origin or destination or the source application, and ensures data usability and accessibility without additional intervention by users. Interoperability requires not only technical standards but also an effective governing system. Most experts agree that technology is not the barrier to interoperability, but the misalignment of incentives for achieving interoperability.

Despite ongoing efforts initiated at the inception of digitized patient records, complete interoperability among HIT systems has proved difficult to achieve. However, a number of initiatives are in place to advance the interoperability of healthcare data. For example, Health Level Seven International (HL7), a nonprofit standards-developing organization, is focused on technical standards for HIE. In fact, the HL7 Fast Healthcare Interoperability Resources standards were introduced in 2012 to improve the exchange of EHR data. Additionally, Healtheway, currently the Sequoia Project, is another nonprofit organization to "advance the implementation of secure, interoperable nationwide health information exchange". The Sequoia Project supports several initiatives, including the eHealth Exchange, a group of government and nongovernment organizations devoted to improving patient care through "interoperable health information exchange". Unlike HL7, which focuses on technical standards, eHealth Exchange's primary focus is on the legal and policy barriers associated with nationwide interoperability. A third interoperability endeavor, Commonwell Health Alliance, is a conglomerate of HIT organizations committed to achieving interoperability. Commonwell began in 2013 with six EHR vendors. In 2015, their membership had expanded to 70 percent of hospitals. Provider members of Commonwell register patients to facilitate information exchange with other member providers. These enterprises address the fact that interoperability requires not only technical standards, but also a health information infrastructure and effective governance systems. This need for governance comes from the misalignment of incentives for stakeholders key to achieving interoperability. Once more, experts agree that technology is not the most significant barrier to interoperability, but the lack of governance and alignment of agendas among disparate healthcare organizations.

ENABLERS OF HIT

Pervasive and Standardized Data Capture and Retention

Significant developments are evident within the healthcare industry in terms of pervasive capture, retention and use of medical event information. The positive news for healthcare researchers is the focus on widespread use of electronic healthcare data by providers, and standardized coding algorithms for information abstraction. Encouragingly, IT trends in healthcare are enabling the application of business intelligence techniques to ever-growing sources of clinical data.

To reiterate information provided previously, the healthcare industry formally directed its attention to increased application of IT to capture and leverage patient information with the mandates of HIPAA. Fundamental to HIPAA is the institution of "code sets" and transmission protocols to capture and share data describing medical events. Since the enactment of HIPAA, the government has placed increasing emphasis on the need to adopt technology within healthcare, culminating with HITECH. A central focus of this legislation is the "meaningful use" of EHRs by healthcare providers. Specific to electronic health or medical records, HITECH establishes a system of incentive payments to healthcare providers for the "meaningful use" of EHRs. The act states "that, as of 2011 [and until 2015], healthcare providers will be offered financial incentives for demonstrating meaningful use of electronic health records" (healthcareitnews.com 2014). The requirements for "meaningful use" of IT by healthcare providers are administered by the Centers for Medicare and Medicaid Services (cms.gov). To qualify for incentive payments, and to avoid future penalties, healthcare providers in the form of eligible professionals, eligible hospitals, and critical access hospitals must meet "measurement thresholds [for EHR use] that range from recording patient information as structured data to exchanging summary care records" (healthit.gov 2014). The CMS incentive programs have three stages, and each stage requires additional evidence of IT usage.

Research Data Sources

This section describes some of the more common and accessible "data stores" of healthcare information available for research purposes. This is an abbreviated list and the number of research enabling sources of healthcare data is expanding at a rapid pace. As such, the establishment of a comprehensive reference for healthcare research data is becoming an important requirement.

Observational Medical Outcomes Partnership (OMOP)

In the presence of every-expanding stores of EHRs, their collaborative use for research requires an enabling common data model (CDM) and associated standards. The federal government first realized the enabling power of a CDM having a common format for disparate data sources with the FDA Amendments Act of 2007. Specifically, this act mandated that "the FDA collaborate with public, academic, and private entities to access disparate data sources and to validate ways to link and analyze safety data from multiple sources for medical product safety surveillance" (Stang et al. 2010). As a result, the Observational Medical Outcomes Partnership (OMOP) (http://omop.fnih.org), a partnership among the FDA, academia, data owners, and the pharmaceutical industry, was initially created to identify needs and test scientific methods and data infrastructure of an "active drug safety surveillance system". While this first effort at building a facilitating healthcare data source for collaborative research was restricted to "maximizing the benefit and minimizing the risk of pharmaceuticals"', its potential for other categories of healthcare service quickly became apparent (Stang et al. 2010). Given the obvious value of a standardized data resource for collaborative healthcare research, the OMOP stakeholders, upon the conclusion of their project, initiated the Observational Health Data Sciences and Informatics (OHDSI) initiative (Hripcsak 2015). OHDSI strives "to bring out the value of observational health data through large-scale analytics" (https://ohdsi.org/who-we-are/). Integral to the OHDSI initiative is the establishment of a CDM for abstracted healthcare data and the development of associated ETL methods and informatic applications.

A CDM for healthcare data responds to the fundamental premise that healthcare data varies greatly among organizations. This is due to (1) the capture of information for different purposes and through different means, and (2) the use of "abstracted" and varied code sets to represent medical events. First, healthcare data may be retained for a variety of purposes including reimbursement, research and analytics, or patient care. Each of these purposes involves different code sets, forms, and retention methods. Second, numerous code sets exist to capture medical events, including code sets for diagnoses, procedures, clinical tests, and drugs. Furthermore, a code must be "abstracted" to represent a medical event, and this process involves a great deal of subjectivity and human error. Obviously, given these factors, the variance among "observational" data stores can be significant. The OMOP CDM is a concerted effort to convert disparate data into a common format enabling systematic analysis. Accordingly, Overhage et al. (2011) argue that "translating the data from these idiosyncratic data models to a common data model (CDM) could facilitate both the analysts' understanding and the suitability for large-scale systematic analysis". The OMOP CDM provisions standardized healthcare data from diverse sources as furnished by an open network of observational data holders. Each element in a participant's database must be mapped to the approved CDM vocabulary and subsequently placed in the data schema. Once the OMOP CDM data store exists, it affords researchers the opportunity to utilize numerous data exploration and analytics tools.

OHDSI asserts that OMOP CDM enables improved and accessible analytics. As such, it allows participants to "perform systematic analyses using a library of standard analytic routines that have been written based on the common format" (https://ohdsi.org/data-standardization/). A couple of examples of such enhanced analytics are the open-source package ACHILLES and a study for temporal pattern discovery in longitudinal electronic patient records. First, ACHILLES (Automated Characterization of Health Information at Large-scale Longitudinal Exploration System) provides a graphical representation of healthcare information found in the OMOP CDM. Basically, this application is a visualization tool for reviewing clinical content based on summary statistics derived from OMOP CDM content. The second example of an application leveraging OMOP CDM is more relevant to the temporal pattern of medical events. In this example, Noren et al. (2010) demonstrate the use of enhanced graphics to portray drug prescription and medical event sequences and evaluate expected and observed medical event frequencies for drug combinations. Overall, this study shows the value of a summarized data store of MESs (such as OMOP CDM) when used in conjunction with sophisticated analytical tools.

CMS

Data Entrepreneurs' Synthetic Public Use File (DE-SynPUF)

CMS provides real claims data intended "for data entrepreneurs, for software and application development, and for research training purposes" (cms.gov). This data source provides inpatient, outpatient, carrier, and prescription drug claims for randomly selected Medicare beneficiaries. The files are synthesized in the sense that "a unique unidentifiable ID, DESYNPUF_ID…is provided on each file to link synthetic claims to a synthetic beneficiary" (cms.gov). The DE-SynPUF was created with the goal of providing a realistic set of claims data in the public domain while protecting Medicare beneficiaries' protected health information. The data structure of the Medicare DE-SynPUF is very similar to the CMS Limited Data Sets, but with a smaller number of variables. The DE-SynPUF has limited value for inferential research about Medicare beneficiaries because of the synthetic processes used to create the files. However, the Medicare DE-SynPUF extracts increase access to realistic Medicare claims data in a timely and less expensive manner.

Limited Data Sets

CMS also makes Limited Data Set (LDS) files available to researchers and entrepreneurs. LDS files contain beneficiary-level health information and are considered "identifiable" files, although they do not contain specific direct identifiers according to HIPAA privacy rules. Acquisition of LDS files requires a signed LDS Data Use Agreement between CMS and the data recipient. LDS requestors are required to provide a research purpose as part of their request. The research purpose must relate to projects that could improve the U.S. healthcare delivery system. This includes projects related to improving the quality of life for CMS beneficiaries or improving the administration of CMS programs. In addition, these research projects must contribute to "generalizable knowledge". Of note concerning this information is the capability to attach patient record attributes to medical "events", thus enabling more inferential research that is problematic with the Medicare DE-SynPUF information.

National Trauma Data Bank

Hospital-based trauma registries provide a foundation for much research about improving care of injured patients. Research has been limited by the lack of consistent, quality data received from disparate hospitals, regions, and states. To address this limitation, the American College of Surgeons developed the National Trauma Data

Standard (NTDS) to standardize core variables across hospitals. A wide variety of trauma centers contribute to the National Trauma Data Bank (NTDB), a large aggregation of trauma data conforming to the NTDS.

INHIBITORS OF HIT

Usability

Traditionally, technology theories have broadly focused on "ease of use" and "usefulness" as important determinants of adoption. For HIT, while these factors remain important, there are other determinants specific to healthcare and impacting technology adoption. One such determinant of overriding importance is the "usability" of technology. Healthcare providers must be able to trust the systems informing their clinical decisions and work with these systems to efficiently provide quality care. Poor usability of systems contributes to provider frustration with HIT, and can also lead to errors and patient safety concerns. Specifically, usability refers to "the effectiveness, efficiency, and satisfaction with which the intended users can achieve their tasks in the intended context of produce use" (Bevan, 2001). The American Medical Informatics Association provided some recommendations related to critical issues affecting patient safety and the quality of care. The recommendations fall into four categories:

1. Usability and human factors research
2. Policy recommendations
3. Industry recommendations
4. Clinical end user recommendations

Based on these categories, usability is clearly a multi-dimensional issue requiring appropriate research, standardization and interoperability, helpful user interfaces, best practice guidelines, and a cyclical process for improvement. In summary, analytics and associated HIT tools must demonstrate to physicians that patient outcomes could improve, and professional autonomy maintained, with their use.

Financial Considerations

Financial considerations are a strong determinant of the meaningful use of EHRs by healthcare providers. Providers face varied and significant costs during EHR implementation and upkeep, and they also encounter challenges unique to the healthcare industry when funding technology. Primary consideration was given in earlier research to the "initial costs" of acquiring and installing an EHR system. Miller and Sim (2004) have this initial cost focus when speaking of "high initial financial costs, slow and uncertain financial payoffs, and high initial physician time costs". Similar treatment of the initial costs for EHR systems is found in research by Ford et al. (2006) saying that a cost "physicians in small practices have had to internalize is the system's initial purchase" and by Boonstra and Broekhuis (2010) defining initial EHR costs to "include all the expenditure needed to get an EHR system working in the physician's practice, such as the purchase of hardware and software, selecting and contracting costs and installation expenses". Another initial cost identified by Vishwanath and Scamurra (2007) is the direct "cost of the current legacy system in place". The initial cost barrier concerns both the source of funds and eventual financial benefit (ROI) for HIT adoption. Accordingly, Gans et al. (2005) highlight the "lack of capital resources to invest in an EHR" as a top five barrier to HIT adoption and Hennington and Janz (2007) address this issue in the form of two questions that each physician must ask: "1) What is the likelihood of seeing a positive return on the investment? [and] 2) Are there financial means available to purchase and maintain the system?". Hennington and Janz (2007) apply these two questions to the Unified Theory of Acceptance and Use of Technology (UTAUT) model in terms of UTAUT constructs where EHR ROI is related to "physicians' performance expectancy" and the availability of funds "addresses whether or not facilitating conditions exist".

As healthcare providers have become more experienced in the use of HIT, the financial determinant of "meaningful use" has shifted in its focus somewhat to include worries about the ongoing costs for EHR maintenance and support. Ford et al. (2006) describes this financial component as "ongoing operational costs" and limits it to a discussion about EHR vendor transience and risk. Other researchers, including Randaree (2007), expand this discussion and find that physicians face other often unexpected ongoing EHR costs including those "associated with the customizability of their system", expensive "maintenance agreements" and "technology obsolescence". The general impression from the research about financial determinants of HIT adoption is that (a) initial and ongoing costs remain underrepresented and (b) there is a great deal of uncertainty concerning the availability of incentive payments and effective reimbursement mechanisms from payers to fund EHR meaningful use. Miller and Sim (2004) feel that these barriers are even more significant in the context of smaller physician practices, saying "these barriers were most acute for physicians in solo/small-group practice, a mode in which a substantial majority of U.S. physicians practice".

Technical Limitations

The technical determinant of EHR meaningful use can be considered using the two components of the classic Technology Acceptance Model (TAM): perceived "ease of use" and perceived "usefulness". First, in terms of EHR "ease of use", a significant amount of research points to the distinctive resistance to technology within the healthcare industry and lack of technical expertise found in physician's practices, both by the physicians themselves and their support staff. Smaller practices do not have the necessary background, training or time to learn and deploy often complex EHR systems. Randaree (2007) describes this phenomenon by saying that "smaller practices do not have the capacity to implement the software while dealing with issues of care and reimbursement" and "medical schools and residency programs do not currently employ or train future physicians in the use of EHR" leaving them unequipped to properly select and deploy EHRs. Terry et al. (2009) expand upon this by stating EHR "barriers included level of computer literacy, training, and time" with the initial transition period being especially challenging in its time burden upon poorly trained staff and doctors. Boonstra and Broekhuis (2010) also note that "physicians struggle to get appropriate technical training and support for the systems from the vendor". Terry et al. (2009) suggest the need for an "in-house problem-solver" to "serve a key role in helping novice users move forward to achieve … EHR adoption". An additional factor of EHR "ease of use" is system complexity with Miller and Sim (2004) finding "even highly regarded, industry-leading EHRs to be challenging to use because of the multiplicity of screens, options, and navigational aids". Randaree (2007) elaborates saying a "recent study showed that at least 264 EHR software programs are in use; on average, the percentage of respondents with the same EHR software was 0.4%". Obviously, this issue is aggravated by the lack of technical skills possessed by most healthcare providers and staff. The need for EHR customizability is another factor of EHR perceived "ease of use". Nambisan (2014) describes how "adopters of new innovations often learn by using the innovation or reinvent the technology to adapt it to their own context" and how this is "invaluable during the adoption of new technologies such as EHR", but may not be possible given the knowledge and time limitations for physicians. One final consideration has to do with the interoperability of the EHR system to other internal and external IT systems and existing physician office processes. This is described as an inability of the EHR system to "interconnect with other devices that "complement" the EHR system" and EHRs that "are not compatible with the existing practice systems" (Boonstra and Broekhuis 2010). Establishment of data standards is key to this interoperability and repeatedly surfaces as a concern healthcare providers have with EHRs.

The second component of TAM deals with the perceived usefulness of a prospective technology. Physicians are told of great possible utility for EHRs, including enhanced quality of patient outcomes, better compliance with various reporting and healthcare mandates, and improved process efficiencies. However, most healthcare providers are skeptical of EHR capability to deliver these benefits, and they are also not provided compelling incentives to improve clinical performance. Hennington and Janz (2007) describe an environment where the "system does not compensate physicians based upon the quality of the care they provide, and thus does not reward them for investing in systems designed to improve quality of care". Finally, effective knowledge management helps mitigate technical obstacles for EHR meaningful use, but "barriers to establishing a learning culture in healthcare organizations" are more problematic than those found in other industries (Nambisan 2014).

Time

The time determinant for EHR meaningful use is noteworthy where a "key obstacle in this path to quality [of care] is the extra time it takes physicians to learn to use the EHR effectively for their daily tasks" (Miller and Sim 2004). Time spent to install and maintain an EHR system comes at the detriment of patient-doctor relationships. This is an extremely important issue given most healthcare providers are principally driven to provide the best patient care possible. Along these lines, Miller and Sim (2004) find "that most physicians using EHRs spent more time per patient for a period of months or even years after EHR implementation. The increased time costs resulted in longer workdays or fewer patients seen, or both, during that initial period". Research points to especially frustrating and unexpected time investments for process redundancy caused by duplicating medical records and functionality during EHR transition, software maintenance and upgrades, vendor management and dedicated EHR training. Unexpected amounts of time are predominantly incurred during the initial transition period between a paper based and electronic medical records system. Gans et al. (2005) discover that "concern about loss of productivity during transition to an EHR system" is among the top five barriers to HIT adoption for practices. Other research also points to this surprising investment of time during EHR implementation. For example, Randaree (2007) argues that during EHR transition; "Expect staffing changes and lots of training. Slow your implementation expectations. Create redundant systems until errors are eliminated. Whatever your timetable and budget (double it)." Relating to this time and effort outlay, Hennington and Janz (2007) believe "the time required to enter information into EHR systems is one of the greatest challenges to EHR adoption".

Psychological Factors

The psychological determinant of HIT adoption is especially significant within the unique environment of healthcare and to its behaviorally unique physicians. Nambisan (2014) feels that the psychological determinant does not receive appropriate attention arguing that "innovation adoption is situated in a social (cultural) context and implies that the norms and values of the individual, the larger community of the individual, and the organization that the individual belongs to, all can influence adoption". To best understand the psychological barriers to HIT adoption, an understanding of the socio-cultural and psychological context of healthcare is important. Significantly, physicians in smaller practices have control and authority over both clinical and business processes. As such, without their full support, HIT adoption is extremely difficult to realize. Miller and Sim (2004) support this view saying "nonchampion [unsupportive] physicians tended to be less positive toward EHRs and more easily discouraged by usability problems... without exhortation and support from physician champions, these physicians tended to remain as lower-level EHR users." The issue primarily seems to be one of process control that is particularly evident with older physicians stubbornly retaining old paper-based systems. Randaree (2007) explains that "older physicians were reluctant to transition to the EHR while the younger ones were driving the adoption". This issue of control is better explained by Vishwanath and Scamurra (2007) as "the loss of control of patient information, the loss of control over business processes, systems tend not to be very easy to use, negative perceptions among administrative staff, and problems in understanding the vernacular". Control is related to "professional autonomy" defined as "professionals having control over the conditions, processes, procedures, or content of their work" (Walter 2008). Accordingly, "physicians' perceptions of the threat to their professional autonomy are very important in their reaction to EHR adoption" (Boonstra and Broekhuis 2010). In addition to a perceived lack of control, many physicians are skeptical about the capability of EHRs to improve patient outcomes or quality of care. In fact, "more than half (58.1%) of the physicians without an EHR doubt that EHRs can improve patient care or clinical outcomes" (Boonstra and Broekhuis 2010). Finally, an important facet of the psychological determinant is the need for support and empathy from fellow adopters of EHR systems. Nambisan (2014) applies Social Cohesion Theory to highlight the importance of "empathetic communication between the adopter and the laggard". In the context of HIT adoption, the "higher chance of adoption of the innovation by the laggard" is realized through an appropriate level of social cohesion (Nambisan 2014).

Social Factors

Because healthcare providers cannot function in isolation, their network of relationships is a key determinant of HIT adoption. Boonstra and Broekhuis (2010) highlight some of the relationships impacting physician behavior saying "physicians in medical practices work together and cooperate with other parties in the healthcare industry, such as vendors, subsidizers, insurance companies, patients, administrative staff, and managers". The influence of these relationships has been shown to be of greater importance than was originally thought in HER adoption research. Vishwanath and Scamurra (2007) point to the unexpected breadth of social related determinants found in more recent research that professes social determinants to be "more expansive and complex and include the lack of community level participation, the lack of involvement of major players such as hospitals, the lack of involvement of major players such as insurance companies, the lack of organizational support, the lack of knowledge/awareness of current or local success stories, and the fact that others do not use or recommend EHRs". Along these lines, Hennington and Janz (2007) draw from more current technology adoption models, including the Model of PC Utilization, to include social factors for "the individual's internalization of the reference group's subjective culture, and specific interpersonal agreements that the individual has made with others, in specific social situations". More recent research into the social determinant looks to understand the underlying causes for the unique healthcare culture and resulting social interactions. Accordingly, Nambisan (2014) believes much of the social determinant is explained by the communication style prevalent in healthcare settings, finding that an "important factor that affects learning is the mode of communication in the healthcare organization". Specifically, Nambisan (2014) argues that "face-to-face or phone [communication prevalent in healthcare facilities] has been found to be highly interruptive and is a leading cause of errors". The specific reason for the ineffectiveness of this communication style is that "communication among employees in a hospital environment often leads to interruption-driven work contexts, where miscommunication or ineffective communication is the norm" (Coiera and Tombs 1998). Obviously, knowledge sharing facilitating EHR meaningful use is a challenge to achieve when constrained by this type of communication environment.

Safety and Legal Considerations

The legal determinant of HIT adoption relates to (a) the electronic storage and transfer of confidential healthcare information and (b) the various reporting requirements for compliance with healthcare agency mandates. Interestingly, in earlier research, concerns over the privacy of patient information were rated lowest for those practices with EHRs (Gans et al. 2005). Initial concern over the security of EHR information may have been lessened by the lack of enforcement measures provided with the Health Insurance Portability and Accountability Act of 1996 that was intended to help protect confidential healthcare information. In fact, "HIPAA enforcement and compliance changed in a dramatic way after 2009. As part of the American Recovery and Reinvestment Act, HITECH greatly strengthened HIPAA by dramatically increasing the penalties for HIPAA violations—up to $1.5 million for a violation in certain circumstances" (library.ahima.org 2014). Research describes two concerns for physicians over the privacy of patient information in the context of EHR usage. First is providing adequate protection to safeguard a patient's confidential medical information in compliance with HIPAA regulations. Second is the need to maintain access to and usability of this information for proper patient care. Often these two concerns conflict as heightened information security may result in reduced information access. Randaree (2007) explains this by saying "Medical data availability has to be balanced between access and privacy…Maximum controls may inhibit physicians from performing their job; minimal controls could leave patient information vulnerable to theft and misuse". The increased focus in the healthcare industry on protection of patient privacy and the more stringent regulations along those lines has heightened the significance of this determinant for physicians. Again, Randaree (2007) argues "patient record management is not new to the medical industry, information technology (IT) solutions using EHRs have special considerations relating to the security of patient information (HIPAA, privacy, firewalls, virus protection, transmission) and performance issues (reliability of services, service levels, customization) as well as long term impacts (storage, computer upgrades, data efficacy)". Ironically, Boonstra and Broekhuis (2010) find that physicians are more concerned than patients with the security of patient information saying, "physicians are more concerned about this issue than the patients themselves…among the physicians who do use EHRs, most believe that there are more security and confidentiality risks involved with EHRs than with paper records". Another determinant of HIT use is the anticipated benefit from EHR systems based on compliance with federal and healthcare agency programs. Ford et al. (2006) state that "The policy mechanism most commonly discussed for increasing EHR's external influence coefficient in the United States is the introduction of clinical reporting mandates…. As reporting requirements increase, the only feasible mechanism for gathering such data will be the EHR. While this may initially be viewed as having a positive impact on EHR meaningful use, Ford et al. (2006) caution "while such programs may be of some use, they may not advance the goal of full HIT adoption significantly, because U.S. providers tend to respond negatively to such mandated-use policies". An example of a healthcare program requiring enhanced reporting capabilities is National Center for Quality Assurance accreditation. This program is claimed to be "the most comprehensive evaluation in the industry, and the only assessment that bases results of clinical performance (i.e., HEDIS measures) and consumer experience (i.e., CAHPS measures)" (ncqa.org 2014). Accreditation is becoming a necessity for competitive healthcare facilities and EHRs are believed to ease the reporting burdens from this program. Obviously, the "meaningful use" requirements under HITECH necessitate similar enhanced reporting capabilities available through EHR systems. Care should be taken when evaluating the reporting component of this determinant as many of the physicians experienced with EHR usage have not experienced anticipated reporting benefits. Randaree (2007) indicates that customizable and enhanced reporting was not there for many practices requiring physicians to incorporate "new [and] redundant workflows" for reporting purposes.

Organizational Culture

Facets of the organizational culture determinant of HIT adoption include (a) facility characteristics for size, clinic type or scope of services (inpatient, outpatient, ambulatory, etc.), and specialty (psychiatry, pediatrics, orthopedics, etc.), (b) extent of separation, both socially and professionally, between physicians and staff and (c) the organizational structure in terms of horizontal or vertical orientation. First, the most consistent organizational determinant is practice size, measured either by the number of physicians or patients. Gans et al. (2005) corroborates saying "the percentage of practices with EHRs differs greatly by size of practice". Specifically, practice size impacts HIT adoption because "larger practices could spread the sizeable fixed cost of purchase and implementation over more physicians" (Burt and Sisk 2005). Burt and Sisk (2005) contend that ownership type (physician or physician group; health maintenance organization (HMO); and all other healthcare organizations) is what really drives HIT adoption, arguing "Physician owned practices have low probabilities of using EHRs no matter what the size." Therefore, Burt and Sisk (2005) maintain that smaller practices lag larger practices in HIT adoption due to their inability to fund EHRs, rather than some other intrinsic property of smaller practices. Boonstra and Broekhuis (2010) confirm this saying "physicians who are employed by or contracted to a medical practice are more likely to use EHRs than those who own their own practices". Burt and Sisk (2005) also propose that the unique scope of services provided by practices impacts HIT adoption where "scope of services may also influence adoption, to the extent that EHRs offer the potential for practices with a wider range of services to achieve greater efficiencies". However, this hypothesis was later disproven by Burt and Sisk (2005) because "neither the scope of services, as measured by single versus multispecialty practice, nor broadly defined categories of specialty, as measured by primary care, medical, or surgical, were significantly associated with use". They did find "use varied by specific physician specialty, however, with psychiatrists and dermatologists least likely and orthopedic surgeons and cardiovascular disease specialists most likely to use EHRs" (Burt and Sisk 2005). The second component of the organizational determinant deals with the debilitating effect, in many practices, of the wide social and professional gulf between physicians and support staff. Research indicates that support staff often is more receptive to HIT adoption to improve process efficiency and reduce paperwork. In fact, adoption interventions often have a greater effect when geared toward support staff instead of physicians. For example, Vishwanath and Scamurra (2007) explain that "intervention aimed at alleviating integration issues is better off training support staff". In the same vein, a hierarchical organization structure reinforcing the separation of physicians and support staff is especially detrimental to HIT adoption, and necessitates effective networking and "a more open and less hierarchical environment for peer to peer interactions and knowledge transfer" (Nambisan 2014). The role of an effective organizational structure is further highlighted by Hennington and Janz (2007) when claiming HIT adoption requires "existence of both "an organizational and technical infrastructure" that would support actual usage". A more collaborative relationship between physicians and support staff, unencumbered by a formal hierarchical structure, is necessary because the "ability to share such user innovations and experiences are invaluable during the adoption of new technologies such as EHR" (Nambisan 2014).

Change Process

Reluctance to change involves not only the social determinant of physician "lack of control" discussed earlier, but also physician inadequacies in managing the change process required for HIT adoption. Boonstra and Broekhuis (2010) frame the argument as "EHRs in medical practices amounts to a major change for physicians who tend to have their own unique working styles that they have developed over years". As such, healthcare providers anticipate difficulties managing the EHR change process without a facilitating organizational culture, effective incentives, individual and local support, community level participation, and leadership. The magnitude of the change process is determined by the extent of alignment between existing business processes and the functionality of the chosen (and possibly customized) EHR system. Given the mindset of most physicians described previously; "physician concerns surrounding

EHR adoption center more on integrating EHRs into existing clinical processes than on the need to fundamentally alter those processes" (Hennington and Janz 2007). This approach to make EHRs fit existing processes, results in significant frustration for healthcare providers, patients and support staff, and is compounded by EHR system designers unfamiliar with procedures unique to the healthcare industry. An example of an EHR system poorly equipped to match existing healthcare processes is described by Hennington and Janz (2007) when they "cited EHR designers' poor understanding of clinical workflows as one reason for low HIT adoption rates among chest physicians, noting system designers' failure to recognize the role of group interaction in the clinical process". The consequence of poorly designed or incompatible EHR systems is costly and time-consuming customization. Miller and Sim (2004) maintain that many times "EHR hardware and software cannot simply be used "out of the box." Instead, physician practices must carry out many complex, costly, and time-consuming activities to "complement" an EHR product, hence, customization. The need for EHR customization is compounded by the lack of physician and support staff expertise and time as described earlier. Most physicians in smaller practices find they have insufficient resources to "customize the system and make it do what I want it to do, and potential inability to customize the software, reports, and outputs to my satisfaction" and are thus reluctant to proceed with HIT adoption (Vishwanath and Scamurra 2007).

Reimbursement

The reimbursement determinant of HIT adoption mainly concerns the unique payment models under which physicians function. To summarize a previous discussion, physicians reimbursement is performed using one of two approaches. First, is the more traditional "Fee for Service" (FFS) model where healthcare services are unbundled and "doctors and other healthcare providers receive a fee for each service such as an office visit, test, procedure, or other healthcare service" (opm.gov 2014). The second payment model is "outcomes based", and accounts for the quality of care afforded the patient. Essentially this is a new payment model where "Medicare and Medicaid, as well as private insurance plans, are shifting payment to what is referred to as "accountable care" where physicians are paid for quality rather than the quantity of care delivered" (creators.com 2012). Clearly, reimbursement based on the first approach tracking service volume de-incents the efficiencies promised with EHRs. The environmental determinant further includes the technical factors external to practices and impacting HIT adoption. These technical factors include interoperability standards, open-source EHR systems and single patient EHR accessibility for multiple providers.

Third Party Intervention

Another usage determinant concerns the impact of intervening third parties on HIT adoption. Previously, the impacts of several "third parties" have been touched upon by other determinants (e.g. government intervention with the legal determinant and third-party vendor relationships with the change process determinant). The overall conclusion from these analyses being that a physician's anticipated effort in dealing with all the third-party interventions associated with HIT adoption is consequential. It is important to note that IT efforts especially, including complex system installations, are onerous to most physicians, and often necessitate extensive third-party involvement for training, technological support, or additional reasons. Managing these and other third-party relationships is obviously an area of concern to physicians without the time or expertise to effectively perform vendor management tasks.

QUALITY, DATA CAPTURE AND ABSTRACTION INTEGRITY

There are a number of causes for the variability in EHR data quality. For example, Brown et al. (2013) argues that "idiosyncratic data quality issues in multi-site environments can arise from variation in data capture, differences and changes in medical coding terminologies and coding practices, local business-rules regarding data adjudication, clinical workflows, and delivery system differences such as formularies, provider contracts, and payment contracts." Additionally, data abstraction quality is dependent upon the diagnoses or treatments being recorded where conditions with more "clear diagnostic features such as diabetes have higher quality recording than conditions with more subjective criteria such as asthma" (Jordan et al. 2004) Furthermore, there is a great deal of subjectivity with the abstraction of information describing medical incidents, and often the "completeness and correctness of data entry may rely on the enthusiasm of practices and of individual GPs. GPs may have personal preferences for certain codes which may not always be appropriate." (Jordan et al. 2004) Finally, the unique technical specifications of the facilities EHR system impacts the accuracy and consistency of information and "semantic representational variations among data collected by different EHR systems are typical in many healthcare organizations." (Botsis 2010) Table 2 lists many concerns regarding the use of "administrative" medical information for research purposes.

On the positive side, extensive efforts are underway to more effectively measure the quality of clinical data being mined and devise solutions to help improve the credibility of data driving healthcare research. For example, original studies pointed to "the three common measurements of data quality: Incompleteness – missing information; Inconsistency – information mismatch between various or within the

Table 2. Data issues with operational health records

Type	Description	Example
Diagnostic uncertainty	Diagnosis may *be* recorded when there is only a suspicion of disease	Patient with suspected diabetes mellitus before diagnosis confirmed by laboratory testing
	Some overlapping clinical conditions are difficult to distinguish reliably	Various forms of upper respiratory and related infections, e.g., sinusitis, pharyngitis, bronchitis, rhinitis, etc.
	Patients may only partially fit diagnostic criteria	Patients with non-diagnostic gastrointestinal symptoms may partially fit diagnostic criteria for one or multiple diseases
	Patients in whom diagnostic testing is done but is negative are still more likely to have disease	Patients undergoing echocardiography for shortness of breath and edema who are found to have normal left ventricular function are different from asymptomatic patients with normal left ventricular function
Diagnostic timing	Repeated diagnosis codes over time may represent a new event or a follow up to a prior event	Two hospitalizations with a primary diagnosis of MI are likely two events, but a code for myocardial infarction in outpatient setting is more likely a follow up to an inpatient MI
	First diagnosis in a database is not necessarily an incident case of disease	· A new patient in the system with diabetes may have had diabetes for many years prior to presentation
	Chronic diseases may vary in severity over time	Patient with congestive heart failure with waxing and waning of symptoms
Treatment choice and timing	Many conditions do not require immediate drug or other treatment	Hyperlipidemia or hypertension may have a trial of lifestyle changes before initiation of drug therapy
	Patient co-morbidities may affect timing and choice of treatment	Patient with hypertension may have related diagnoses that were not recorded before initiation of treatment, but may be recorded later to indicate the compelling reason for a treatment choice, such as the use of ACE inhibitors in hypertensive patients with heat failure
Treatment decisions	Treatment decisions not randomized	Physician choosing treatment based on personal views or biases regarding efficacy
	Some treatment decisions are remote to the patient provider interaction	Restrictions by patient insurance or institutional drug formulary
	Some treatments not reliably recorded	Medications available over the counter and not requiring a prescription may not be recorded, e.g. aspirin, proton pump inhibitors
Treatment follow-up	Some treatments confounded by clinical factors unrelated to condition being treated	Patient with multiple co-morbidities may be seen more frequently and have conditions treated faster, e.g. hyperlipidemia in otherwise healthy person versus patient with diabetes and its complications
	Non-clinical factors impact availability of data	Patient access to resources in order to follow treatment recommendations may *be* limited due to travel, payor systems, or other non-clinical factors

same EHR data source; and Inaccuracy – non-specific, non-standards-based, inexact, incorrect, or imprecise information." (Botsis 2010). This work has been expanded to now propose five dimensions of data quality: completeness, correctness, concordance, plausibility, and currency" (Hersh et al. 2013). Along these lines, research is now addressing the constructs having greatest impact on these quality metrics. For example, Botsis (2010) conducted a study with the conclusion being "to reduce the health data that is unavailable, inaccessible or incomputable, new technology for storage (e.g. for radiology data) and new methods for natural language processing (e.g. for symptoms or signs recorded on free-text formats) are needed." Botsis (2010) points to the health information exchange impacts on data quality saying that the "incompleteness caused by information fragmentation of the healthcare systems (i.e., patients moving between multiple healthcare entities for special referrals or emergency healthcare, with each entity holding partial health records for the patients) could be mitigated using health information exchange methods that support information federation across multiple healthcare entities." Overall, the advent of personal health records relying on patient input, is perceived to improve medical data credibility, because they are "a new form of health records for engaging individual patients to control access to their own health information." (Botsis 2010)

DATA CLEANSING, ETL, AND STAGING

Data quality is fundamental to the validity of conclusions drawn from healthcare analytics. As described previously, the methods for "abstracting" digitized data about medical events are prone to error and human subjectivity. Accordingly, the functions related to data cleansing, ETL (extract, transform and load), and data staging, will emerge as focal points in process evaluations to insure the credibility of information driving healthcare analytics. Van den Broeck (2005) defines data cleansing to be "the process of detecting and correcting (or removing) corrupt or inaccurate records from a record set, table, or database and refers to identifying incomplete, incorrect, inaccurate or irrelevant parts of the data and then replacing, modifying, or deleting the dirty or coarse data". In healthcare analytics, issues with data can result in erroneous results and conclusions, despite a valid study design. Because of the relative infancy of many healthcare data sources, cleansing techniques pursuant to healthcare data often lack rigor and appropriate institutionalization. However, there is a vast amount of research related to data quality and associated data cleansing techniques in other fields. Broadly, data cleansing may be thought of as a three-step process: screening, diagnosis and treatment. First, screening helps identify certain data anomalies: lack or excess of data, outliers, unusual patterns, and unexpected analysis outcomes. Screening methods are often not rigorous or algorithm-based, but may be subjective in terms of perceived nonconformity with prior expectations, alignment with experience, use of pilot studies, evidence in referential literature, or common sense. Second, the diagnostic phase quantifies the extent of abnormality through pattern recognition and statistics. Possible diagnoses for each data point may adhere to a preset spectrum for issue severity, such as erroneous, true extreme, true normal, or idiopathic. Finally, the treatment phase applies methods dealing with problematic observations. In general, one may correct, delete, or leave unchanged data points perceived erroneous. A final and important step is the documentation of actions taken to discover and correct data issues, and then the recording of the actual issues identified and associated corrective measures.

REFERENCES

Angst, C. M., & Agarwal, R. (2009). Adoption of electronic health records in the presence of privacy concerns: The elaboration likelihood model and individual persuasion. *Management Information Systems Quarterly*, *33*(2), 339–370. doi:10.2307/20650295

Bevan, N. (2001). International standards for HCI and usability. *International Journal of Human-Computer Studies*, *55*(4), 533–552. doi:10.1006/ijhc.2001.0483

Birman-Deych, E., Waterman, A. D., Yan, Y., Nilasena, D. S., Radford, M. J., & Gage, B. F. (2005). Accuracy of ICD-9-CM codes for identifying cardiovascular and stroke risk factors. *Medical Care*, *43*(5), 480–485. doi:10.1097/01.mlr.0000160417.39497.a9 PMID:15838413

Blumenthal, D. (2010). Launching hitech. *The New England Journal of Medicine*, *362*(5), 382–385. doi:10.1056/NEJMp0912825 PMID:20042745

Boonstra, A., & Broekhuis, M. (2010). Barriers to the acceptance of electronic medical records by physicians from systematic review to taxonomy and interventions. *BMC Health Services Research*, *10*(1), 231. doi:10.1186/1472-6963-10-231 PMID:20691097

Botsis, T., Hartvigsen, G., Chen, F., & Weng, C. (2010). Secondary use of EHR: Data quality issues and informatics opportunities. *Summit on Translational Bioinformatics*, *2010*, 1. PMID:21347133

Brown, J., Kahn, M., & Toh, S. (2013). Data quality assessment for comparative effectiveness research in distributed data networks. Medical care, 51(8 0 3), S22.

Burt, C. W., & Sisk, J. E. (2005). Which physicians and practices are using electronic medical records? *Health Affairs, 24*(5), 1334–1343. doi:10.1377/hlthaff.24.5.1334 PMID:16162581

Campbell, H., Hotchkiss, R., Bradshaw, N., & Porteous, M. (1998). Integrated care pathways. *BMJ: British Medical Journal, 316*(7125), 133–137. doi:10.1136/bmj.316.7125.133 PMID:9462322

cdc.gov. 2014. Meaningful use. Retrieved from http://www.cdc.gov/ehrmeaningfuluse/

Chismar, W. G., & Wiley-Patton, S. (2003, January). Does the extended technology acceptance model apply to physicians. In *Proceedings of the 36th Annual Hawaii International Conference on System Sciences,* 2003. (pp. 8-pp). IEEE. 10.1109/HICSS.2003.1174354

Cimino, J. J. (2006). "Coding systems in healthcare." Methods of information in medicine 35 (1996): 273-284.

Clark, D. E., & Ahmad, S. (n.d.). Estimating injury severity using the Barell matrix. Injury Prevention, 12(2), 111–116. *PubMed.*

cms.gov. (2014). EHR incentive programs. Retrieved from http://www.cms.gov/Regulations-and-Guidance/Legislation/EHRIncentivePrograms/index.html?redirect=/EHRIncentivePrograms/

Coiera, E., & Tombs, V. (1998). Communication behaviours in a hospital setting: An observational study. *BMJ (Clinical Research Ed.), 316*(7132), 673–676. doi:10.1136/bmj.316.7132.673 PMID:9522794

Coyte, P. C., & Holmes, D. (2007). Healthcare technology adoption and diffusion in a social context. *Policy, Politics, & Nursing Practice, 8*(1), 47–54. doi:10.1177/1527154407299646 PMID:17470771

Davis, F. D. (1989). Perceived usefulness, perceived ease of use, and user acceptance of information technology. *Management Information Systems Quarterly, 13*(3), 319–340. doi:10.2307/249008

De Bleser, L., Depreitere, R., Waele, K. D., Vanhaecht, K., Vlayen, J., & Sermeus, W. (2006). Defining pathways. *Journal of Nursing Management, 14*(7), 553–563. doi:10.1111/j.1365-2934.2006.00702.x PMID:17004966

De Coster, C., Quan, H., Finlayson, A., Gao, M., Halfon, P., Humphries, K. H., ... Romano, P. S. (2006). Identifying priorities in methodological research using ICD-9-CM and ICD-10 administrative data: Report from an international consortium. *BMC Health Services Research, 6*(1), 77. doi:10.1186/1472-6963-6-77 PMID:16776836

Devaraj, S., Sharma, S. K., Fausto, D. J., Viernes, S., & Kharrazi, H. (2014). Barriers and facilitators to clinical decision support systems adoption: A systematic review. *Journal of Business Administration Research*, *3*(2), 36. doi:10.5430/jbar.v3n2p36

Farmer, K. C. (1999). Methods for measuring and monitoring medication regimen adherence in clinical trials and clinical practice. *Clinical Therapeutics*, *21*(6), 1074–1090. doi:10.1016/S0149-2918(99)80026-5 PMID:10440628

Ford, E. W., Menachemi, N., & Phillips, M. T. (2006). Predicting the adoption of electronic health records by physicians: When will healthcare be paperless? *Journal of the American Medical Informatics Association*, *13*(1), 106–112. doi:10.1197/jamia.M1913 PMID:16221936

Ganova-Iolovska, M., & Geraedts, M. (2009). Clinical pathways–the Bulgarian approach. *Journal of Public Health*, *17*(3), 225–230. doi:10.100710389-008-0239-0

Gans, D., Kralewski, J., Hammons, T., & Dowd, B. (2005). Medical groups' adoption of electronic health records and information systems. *Health Affairs*, *24*(5), 1323 1333. doi:10.1377/hlthaff.24.5.1323 PMID:16162580

Garg, A. X., Adhikari, N. K., McDonald, H., Rosas-Arellano, M. P., Devereaux, P. J., Beyene, J., ... Haynes, R. B. (2005). Effects of computerized clinical decision support systems on practitioner performance and patient outcomes: A systematic review. *Journal of the American Medical Association*, *293*(10), 1223–1238. doi:10.1001/jama.293.10.1223 PMID:15755945

Goldzweig, C. L., Towfigh, A., Maglione, M., & Shekelle, P. G. (2009). Costs and benefits of health information technology: New trends from the literature. *Health Affairs*, *28*(2Supplement 2), w282–w293. doi:10.1377/hlthaff.28.2.w282 PMID:19174390

Hedegaard, H. B., Johnson, R. L., & Ballesteros, M. F. (2017). Proposed ICD-10-CM surveillance case definitions for injury hospitalizations and emergency department visits. *National Health Statistics Reports*, (100): 1–8. PMID:28135183

Henderson, R., & Divett, M. J. (2003). Perceived usefulness, ease of use and electronic supermarket use. *International Journal of Human-Computer Studies*, *59*(3), 383–395. doi:10.1016/S1071-5819(03)00079-X

Henderson, T., Shepheard, J., & Sundararajan, V. (2006). Quality of diagnosis and procedure coding in ICD-10 administrative data. *Medical Care*, *44*(11), 1011 1019. doi:10.1097/01.mlr.0000228018.48783.34 PMID:17063133

Hennington, A., & Janz, B. D. (2007). Information systems and healthcare XVI: physician adoption of electronic medical records: applying the UTAUT model in a healthcare context. *Communications of the Association for Information Systems, 19*(1), 5.

Hersh, W. R., Weiner, M. G., Embi, P. J., Logan, J. R., Payne, P. R., Bernstam, E. V., ... Saltz, J. H. (2013). Caveats for the use of operational electronic health record data in comparative effectiveness research. *Medical care, 51*(8 0 3), S30.

Hripcsak, G., Duke, J. D., Shah, N. H., Reich, C. G., Huser, V., Schuemie, M. J., ... Van Der Lei, J. (2015). Observational health data sciences and informatics (OHDSI): Opportunities for observational researchers. *Studies in Health Technology and Informatics, 216*, 574. PMID:26262116

https://jln1.pressbooks.com/chapter/3-introducing-the-key-stakeholders-patients-providers-payors-and-policymakers-the-four-ps/

https://www.cms.gov/Research-Statistics-Data-and-Systems/Downloadable-Public-Use-Files/SynPUFs/DE_Syn_PUF.htmlCMS Linkable 2008–2010 medicare data entrepreneurs' synthetic public use file (DE-SynPUF) –

Jordan, K., Porcheret, M., & Croft, P. (2004). Quality of morbidity coding in general practice computerized medical records: A systematic review. *Family Practice, 21*(4), 396–412. doi:10.1093/fampra/cmh409 PMID:15249528

Khosla, V. (2014). 20-percent doctor included: Speculations & musings of a technology optimist.

Kinsman, L., Rotter, T., James, E., Snow, P., & Willis, J. (2010). What is a clinical pathway? Development of a definition to inform the debate. *BMC Medicine, 8*(1), 31. doi:10.1186/1741-7015-8-31 PMID:20507550

Liberati, E. G., Ruggiero, F., Galuppo, L., Gorli, M., González-Lorenzo, M., Maraldi, M., ... Vespignani, R. (2017). What hinders the uptake of computerized decision support systems in hospitals? A qualitative study and framework for implementation. *Implementation Science; IS, 12*(1), 113. doi:10.118613012-017-0644-2 PMID:28915822

Löhr, H., Sadeghi, A. R., & Winandy, M. (2010, November). Securing the e-health cloud. In *Proceedings of the 1st ACM International Health Informatics Symposium* (pp. 220-229). ACM.

Manjunath, T. N., Hegadi, R. S., & Ravikumar, G. K. (2010). Analysis of data quality aspects in datawarehouse systems. *International Journal of Computer Science and Information Technologies*, *2*(1), 477–485.

Miller, R. H., & Sim, I. (2004). Physicians' use of electronic medical records: Barriers and solutions. *Health Affairs*, *23*(2), 116–126. doi:10.1377/hlthaff.23.2.116 PMID:15046136

Morton, M. E., & Wiedenbeck, S. (2009). A framework for predicting EHR adoption attitudes: a physician survey. Perspectives in health information management/AHIMA, American Health Information Management Association, 6(Fall).

Nambisan, P. (2014, January). EMR adoption among office-based physicians and practices: Impact of peer-to-peer interactions, peer support and online forums. In *Proceedings 2014 47th Hawaii International Conference on System Sciences (HICSS),* (pp. 2733-2740). IEEE.

Norén, G. N., Hopstadius, J., Bate, A., Star, K., & Edwards, I. R. (2010). Temporal pattern discovery in longitudinal electronic patient records. *Data Mining and Knowledge Discovery*, *20*(3), 361–387. doi:10.100710618-009-0152-3

Painter, M. W., & Jha, A. K. (2015). *Health information technology in the United States, 2015: Transition to a post-HITECH world (Executive summary) (No. 03f5b8d79339485f90149d875ac0b40b).* Mathematica Policy Research.

Plaisant, C., Mushlin, R., Snyder, A., Li, J., Heller, D., & Shneiderman, B. (2003). LifeLines: using visualization to enhance navigation and analysis of patient records. In The craft of information visualization (pp. 308-312). doi:10.1016/B978-155860915-0/50038-X

Plaisant, C., Shneiderman, B., & Mushlin, R. (1998). An information architecture to support the visualization of personal histories. *Information Processing & Management*, *34*(5), 581–597. doi:10.1016/S0306-4573(98)00024-7

Posnack, S. (2015). Connecting health and care for the nation: a shared nationwide interoperability roadmap.

Quan, H., Li, B., Duncan Saunders, L., Parsons, G. A., Nilsson, C. I., Alibhai, A., & Ghali, W. A. (2008). Assessing validity of ICD-9-CM and ICD-10 administrative data in recording clinical conditions in a unique dually coded database. *Health Services Research*, *43*(4), 1424–1441. doi:10.1111/j.1475-6773.2007.00822.x PMID:18756617

Quan, H., Parsons, G. A., & Ghali, W. A. (2002). Validity of information on comorbidity derived from ICD-9-CCM administrative data. *Medical Care*, *40*(8), 675–685. doi:10.1097/00005650-200208000-00007 PMID:12187181

Quan, H., Sundararajan, V., Halfon, P., Fong, A., Burnand, B., Luthi, J. C., ... Ghali, W. A. (2005). Coding algorithms for defining comorbidities in ICD-9-CM and ICD-10 administrative data. *Medical Care*, *43*(11), 1130–1139. doi:10.1097/01.mlr.0000182534.19832.83 PMID:16224307

Randeree, E. (2007). Exploring physician adoption of EMRs: A multi-case analysis. *Journal of Medical Systems*, *31*(6), 489–496. doi:10.100710916-007-9089-5 PMID:18041282

Sanders, D., Burton, D. A., & Protti, D. (2013). The healthcare analytics adoption model: a framework and roadmap.

Skinner, R. I. (2003). The value of information technology in healthcare/reply. *Frontiers of Health Services Management*, *19*(3), 3–15. doi:10.1097/01974520-200301000-00002 PMID:12645778

Sox, H., McNeil, B., Wheatley, B., & Eden, J. (Eds.). (2008). *Knowing what works in healthcare: a roadmap for the nation*. National Academies Press.

Terry, A. L., Giles, G., Brown, J. B., Thind, A., & Stewart, M. (2009). Adoption of electronic medical records in family practice: The providers' perspective. *Family Medicine*, *41*(7), 508. PMID:19582637

van de Klundert, J., Gorissen, P., & Zeemering, S. (2010). Measuring clinical pathway adherence. *Journal of Biomedical Informatics*, *43*(6), 861–872. doi:10.1016/j.jbi.2010.08.002 PMID:20696277

Van den Broeck, J., Cunningham, S. A., Eeckels, R., & Herbst, K. (2005). Data cleaning: Detecting, diagnosing, and editing data abnormalities. *PLoS Medicine*, *2*(10), e267. doi:10.1371/journal.pmed.0020267 PMID:16138788

Vanhaecht, K., Witte, K. D., Depreitere, R., & Sermeus, W. (2006). Clinical pathway audit tools: A systematic review. *Journal of Nursing Management*, *14*(7), 529–537. doi:10.1111/j.1365-2934.2006.00705.x PMID:17004963

Varshney, U. (2007). Pervasive healthcare and wireless health monitoring. *Mobile Networks and Applications*, *12*(2-3), 113–127. doi:10.100711036-007-0017-1

Venkatesh, V., Zhang, X., & Sykes, T. A. (2011). "Doctors do too little technology": A longitudinal field study of an electronic healthcare system implementation. *Information Systems Research*, *22*(3), 523–546. doi:10.1287/isre.1110.0383

Vishwanath, A., & Scamurra, S. D. (2007). Barriers to the adoption of electronic health records: Using concept mapping to develop a comprehensive empirical model. *Health Informatics Journal*, *13*(2), 119–134. doi:10.1177/1460458207076468 PMID:17510224

Walter, Z., & Lopez, M. S. (2008). Physician acceptance of information technologies: Role of perceived threat to professional autonomy. *Decision Support Systems*, *46*(1), 206–215. doi:10.1016/j.dss.2008.06.004

Wu, J. H., Wang, S. C., & Lin, L. M. (2007). Mobile computing acceptance factors in the healthcare industry: A structural equation model. *International Journal of Medical Informatics*, *76*(1), 66–77. doi:10.1016/j.ijmedinf.2006.06.006 PMID:16901749

Wu, L., Li, J. Y., & Fu, C. Y. (2011). The adoption of mobile healthcare by hospital's professionals: An integrative perspective. *Decision Support Systems*, *51*(3), 587–596. doi:10.1016/j.dss.2011.03.003

Yan, Y., Fung, G., Dy, J. G., & Rosales, R. (2010, July). Medical coding classification by leveraging inter-code relationships. In *Proceedings of the 16th ACM SIGKDD international conference on Knowledge discovery and data mining* (pp. 193-202). ACM. 10.1145/1835804.1835831

Yao, W., & Kumar, A. (2013). Conflexflow: Integrating flexible clinical pathways into clinical decision support systems using context and rules. *Decision Support Systems*, *55*(2), 499–515. doi:10.1016/j.dss.2012.10.008

Yoo, S., Cho, M., Kim, S., Kim, E., Park, S. M., Kim, K., ... Song, M. (2015). Conformance analysis of clinical pathway using electronic health record data. *Healthcare Informatics Research*, *21*(3), 161–166. doi:10.4258/hir.2015.21.3.161 PMID:26279952

KEY TERMS AND DEFINITIONS

ACA: Affordable Care Act.

ACG: Adjusted Clinical Groups.

ACHILLES: Automated Characterization of Health Information at Large-scale Longitudinal Exploration System.

ADG: Adjusted Diagnosis Groups.

AMA: American Medical Association.

ANP: Adult Care.

ANSI: American National Standards Institute.

AP-DRG: All-Payer DRG.
APR-DRG: All Payer Refined DRG.
ARRA: American Recovery and Reinvestment Act.
CAH: Critical Access Hospitals.
CC: Condition Categories.
CDM: Common Data Model.
CMS: Centers for Medicaid and Medicare Services.
CNM: Certified Nurse Midwife.
CNS: Clinical Nurse Specialists.
CPT: Current Procedural Terminology.
CRNA: Certified Registered Nurse Anesthetists.
DCG: Diagnostic Cost Groups.
DMEPOS: Durable Medical Equipment, Prosthetics, Orthotics and Supplies.
DO: Doctor of Osteopathic Medicine.
DRG: Diagnosis Related Group.
EMR: Electronic Medical Record.
ETG: Episode Treatment Groups.
FDA: Food and Drug Administration.
FFS: Fee For Service.
FHIR: Fast Healthcare Interoperability Resources.
FNP: Primary Care Provider in Family Medicine.
GNP: Geriatrics.
HCC: Hierarchical Condition Category.
HCPCS: Healthcare Common Procedure Coding System.
HEDIS: Healthcare Effectiveness Data and Information Set.
HER: Electronic Health Record.
HIC: Hierarchical Ingredient Code.
HIE: Health Insurance Exchange.
HIPAA: Health Insurance Portability and Accountability Act.
HIT: Health Information Technology.
HITECH: Health Information Technology for Economic and Clinical Health Act.
HL7: Health Level Seven International.
HMO: Health Maintenance Organization.
HMO: Managed Care (Health Maintenance Organizations).
ICD: International Classification of Diseases.
LPN: Licensed Practical Nurse.
MACRA: Medicare Access and CHIP Reauthorization Act.
MD: Medical Doctor.
MEG: Medstat Episode Grouper or Medical Episode Grouper.
MIPS: Merit-Based Incentive Payment System.

MMA: Medicare Modernization Act.

MPC: Major Practice Category.

MS-DRG: Medicare Severity Diagnosis Related Group.

NAHCRI: National Association of Children's Hospitals and Affiliated Institutions.

NCHSR: National Center for Health Services Research and Healthcare Technology Assessment.

NCQA: National Committee for Quality Assurance.

NDC: National Drug Code.

NP: Nurse Practitioner.

NTIS: National Technical Information Service.

OB/GYN: Obstetrician/Gynecologists.

OHDSI: Observational Health Data Sciences and Informatics.

OMOP: Observational Medical Outcomes Partnership.

ONC: Office of the National Coordinator for Health Information Technology.

PA: Physician Assistant.

PCP: Primary Care Provider.

PHI: Protected Health Information.

PM-DRG: Pediatric Modified DRG.

PMPM: Per Member Per Month.

PNP: Pediatrics.

PPACA: Patient Protection and Affordable Care Act.

PPO: Preferred Provider Organizations.

PPS: Prospective Payment System.

RCM: Revenue Cycle Management.

RN: Registered Nurses.

SNOMED: Systematized Nomenclature of Medicine.

TAM: Technology Acceptance Model.

UTAUT: Unified Theory of Acceptance and Use of Technology.

WHO: World Health Organization.

Chapter 3
Leveraging Intelligence in Value Creation Across Provider Patient Ecosystems

Mohan Tanniru
https://orcid.org/0000-0002-9584-0090
College of Public Health, University of Arizona, USA

ABSTRACT

Value creation in healthcare calls for the design of care plans that integrate the activities of clinical and non-clinical actors of both the provider and patient ecosystems as they work towards the shared goal: ensure patient adherence outside the provider ecosystem. Given the differing institutional mechanisms that influence actor behavior, intelligence gathered through digital services has two objectives. The first objective is to use digital services to track patient adherence to care plans, so that these care plans can be adapted as needed. The second objective is to learn about the characteristics of the patient ecosystem, so that incentives can be designed to ensure that all actors are working towards the same shared goal. This chapter uses a service modeling approach to explicate the interconnected role of actors across ecosystems and develop strategies to address these two objects. Several use cases are used to illustrate this approach.

DOI: 10.4018/978-1-7998-2310-0.ch003

INTRODUCTION

Organizations have been developing services not only to create value that addresses customer needs but also to gain intelligence about customer use behavior post-purchase to sustain the value created (Vargo and Lusch 2008). In fact, rapidly developing new service innovations using a mix of internal and external resources to create and sustain value is one of the basic tenets of service dominant logic (Lusch and Nambisan 2015). The gap between the value created and the value perceived by the customer, i.e. value-in-use or value-in-context, often forms the basis for successive instances of value creation and allows service systems to adapt to changing customer expectations.

Healthcare organizations (referred to here as hospitals or provider ecosystems) have an interesting challenge and an opportunity to create value for patients through care plans and to track patient use behavior (i.e. patient adherence to the care plans) to develop new instances of value creation. Like business organizations, provider ecosystems use a number of technologies to gain intelligence on patient adherence within the patient ecosystem and to analyze it before they adapt their care plans (Herzig et al. 2016). The challenge, however, is that hospitals rely on many external actors, clinical and non-clinical, in the patient ecosystem to both track patient adherence and potentially influence it. This is different from businesses that can use shared incentives as a part of their business models to ensure that all external partners are working towards the shared goal of customer value creation. Many clinical actors outside the provider ecosystem, such as pharmacies, testing labs, counseling and rehab centers, and primary care facilities, have different incentive mechanisms and are paid by different institutions. They are not all centrally controlled and coordinated by the provider ecosystem. Also, the provider ecosystems rely on non-clinical actors, such as social, community, and public health agencies, to support diverse populations with varying levels of support within the patient ecosystem. Incentives are needed to align the goals of these actors with those of the provider and the patient. Therefore, it is a major challenge to understand the role multiple actors play outside the provider ecosystem and influence their activities through incentives towards the shared goal of patient adherence to care plans.

Unlike other businesses, hospitals do have an opportunity to learn about the actors who can influence patient behavior within the patient ecosystem. Patients spend time in the provider ecosystem as patients and providers co-create value as they diagnose medical condition and design treatment plans for patients to adhere to when they leave the hospitals. While this time is often spent in addressing the clinical needs of patients, providers can use some of this time to learn about the patient ecosystem and potentially develop strategies to ensure patient adherence to these care plans. With hospitals becoming increasingly responsible for patient care outside the hospital due to changing reimbursement guidelines (e.g. bundled payments and penalties for unanticipated patient readmissions and low patient satisfaction scores), gaining intelligence about the patient ecosystem while patients are under provider care is becoming very important (Koh et al. 2016). While there are currently many digital strategies used by providers to influence care plan adherence in patient ecosystems, there is no systematic way to tailor these to the individual patient context (Health Affairs, 2013). We propose a service modeling approach to analyze the service exchanges needed to create value and develop strategies to track adherence and/or align goals of actors across ecosystems.

The chapter is organized as follows. The second section develops a service modeling approach to explicate the role of service exchanges between patients and providers for tracking patient adherence and seeking goal alignment. The third section uses the modeling approach to illustrate several use cases outside a hospital and highlight the role of digital services in addressing some of the challenges. The fourth section illustrates the opportunities providers have to learn about patient ecosystems and potentially incorporate this knowledge in digital service design. The last section provides some concluding comments and opportunities for future research.

SERVICE EXCHANGES FOR VALUE CREATION AND GOAL ALIGNMENT

Adaptive systems continually use service innovations to compare value created to value-in-use to learn about changing customer expectations and create a new instances of value creation. In today's fast changing business environment, organizations rely on digital services to track value-in-use and use a mix of internal and external resources to address quickly changing customer expectations. Business models are used to align the goals of multiple stakeholders such as customers and partners, including providing incentives to customers in value creation such as LEGO making its customers design toys and Marriott allowing some lead customers to provide event information.

In healthcare, providers use clinical diagnosis to co-create value with patients by designing care treatment plans so that patients can recover from an illness. Once the value is created, providers design service innovations, such as external interventions, and they leverage technology when appropriate to track value-in-use, i.e. patient adherence to treatment plan. Several intervention strategies are discussed in the literature to influence patient adherence to care plans as part of care transition to improve patient engagement and satisfaction as well as reduce hospital readmissions (Dreyer 2014). However, these initiatives tend to be tailored to specific patients with severe or chronic conditions.

Figure 1. Care service model of mental health patient

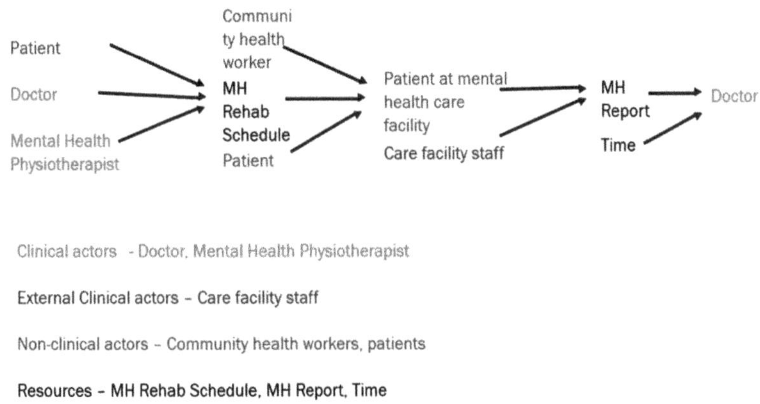

Service Exchanges in Value Creation

Let us look at one simple example of a patient visiting a provider clinic for mental health issues, as shown in Figure 1. Based on the patient condition, a physician might recommend a mental health rehabilitation counseling service at scheduled intervals using an external care provider such as a rehab center. However, based on an understanding of both the provider and patient ecosystems, the hospital used two types of service innovations (one clinical and one non-clinical) to create value and improve patient adherence or use behavior. The clinical innovation included the use of a mental health psychotherapist (MHP) who supports a physician (D) in the provider ecosystem in the development of a care plan. The non-clinical innovation is the use of an actor, community health worker (CHW), from the patient ecosystem to help the patient visit the rehab facilities (an external care provider) at periodic intervals (Plum et al. 2019). The rehab facility prepares reports that are sent to the doctor for evaluation and change in the care plans.

There are four service exchanges used here. Some are to share information or resources and others are to track adherence. The first exchange leads to a resource shared with the patient (a rehab schedule) and aligns the goals of the doctor and the patient in creating value using an expert MHP. The second exchange provides a resource (access to a CHW) to the patient, so that the patient can visit the rehab facility. It is designed as an incentive to align the goals of the patient, who wants to visit but is not mentally or physically capable of acting on his own, and the provider, who seeks to create value. The third exchange leads the generation of a resource (MH report), which tracks patient progress in these sessions. The last exchange leads to providing this feedback to the doctor for evaluation and care adaptation. The service model and the two interventions are designed to align the goals of the patient and provider, and the service exchanges are designed to share resources to fulfill these goals and track patient adherence.

There are three actors besides the patient and doctor. These are the rehab facility, CHW, and MHP. They all operate within their own ecosystem (unless MHP works for the provider), and they need to share in the same goals as those of the patient and provider, or they need incentives to participate in this effort. In this particular case, the hospital pays for MHP and CHW, and payers cover for the services provided by the rehab facility. Even when incentives are designed to motivate all to work towards shared goals, intelligence is still needed to assess the effectiveness with which these shared goals are met.

For example, intelligence gathered may be used for the following analysis:

- *Alignment of goals between providers who create value and patients receiving value.* Variations in patient conditions may trigger changing the nature of intervention supporting value creation. For example, an early stage in the mental health condition of a patient, who has support from family members, may require a different type of care related intervention compared to a patient with a deteriorating mental health condition who may need to spend some time at a counseling facility. In other words, tracking patient condition or adherence may inform how value is created and supported.
- *Assessing effectiveness before creating new value through revised interventions.* For example, how long should the intervention last before an assessment can be made on its effectiveness? This may depend on the nature of the medical condition or patient behavior captured by the number of visits the patient made to the rehab center. Lack of visits independent of ecosystem actor support or information from reports created by rehab staff may require a reassessment of the effectiveness of the intervention.
- *Number of patients using the intervention to assess its relevance.* Creating an intervention to support adherence may not imply that all patients need such intervention. Some patients who visited the facility may do so as per schedule without using the support of CHW, as they like to have the option and will only use it if absolutely needed. Therefore, measuring the effectiveness of the intervention based on how many patients use it can be misleading, as the loss of this option may influence patient capacity or comfort level to seek the care.

Incentives to Seek Alignment of Goals

Incentives discussed in the previous section, such as providing CHW to help a patient get to a rehab facility and MHP to support a doctor provide quality treatment, may not always be effective if patients are not motivated towards a shared goal for any number of reasons. American Psychological Association (APA 2015) defines "incentive" as an external stimulus, such as a condition or an object, that enhances or serves as a motive to influence behavior. An incentive system in an organizational setting is defined by a set of rules and rewards, dictated by the environment within which the value of the rewards to influence behavior is perceived. Relevance, as seen by the individual, is often the key in motivating people to change and it can act as an incentive.

Research proposed several ways to influence behavioral change such as informing on the need for change (content theories) and value of change (process theories) and identifying the motivational drivers that contribute to change (contemporary change) (Saif et al. 2012). Facilitating communication among actors across from multiple ecosystems and sharing resources to address patient adherence to care has become feasible with the use of advanced technologies and tracking such adherence (i.e. Justify the *need for change* in the way information is shared by reducing barriers for such communication). Lack of immediate action when there are gaps in patient adherence can lead to complications to all involved. and lack of payment for clinical and non-clinical actors if patients are not engaged in activities related to adherence can be used to explain the *value of change*. However, motivational drivers for change can vary depending on the degree of impact it has on actors within their own ecosystem. For example, drivers that motivate MHP, CHW and rehab facility or even the patient to change their behavior are influenced by their ecosystems. For example, do patients with a supportive ecosystem vis-à-vis patients in economically or socially challenging environments have the same motivation to seek mental health services in the manner they are provided, and do the incentives provided to CHW or MHP sufficient to align their goals with that of the provider?

In summary, human beings need incentives (external factors) to change their behavior and motivation (internal factors) to sustain behavioral change. Gaining intelligence from service exchanges on patient adherence and actors involved can help tailor digital services to influence change behaviors needed on both patient adherence and goal alignment. The next section looks at several use cases outside a provider ecosystem using the service modeling approach discussed in this section.

Figure 2. Service model for providing therapy guidelines

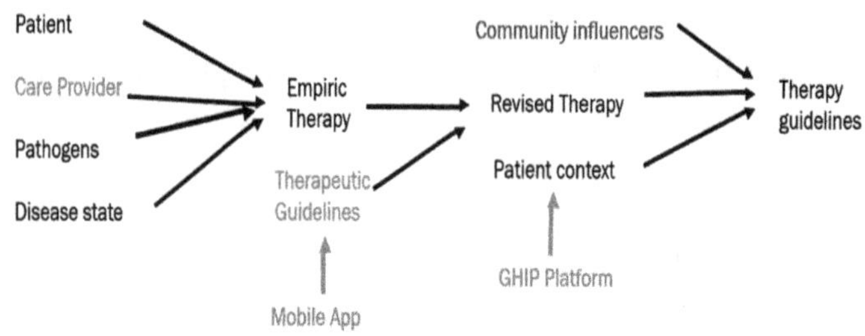

MODELING OF SERVICE IN CARE OUTSIDE A PROVIDER ECOSYSTEM

Modeling service exchanges among actors across ecosystems to create value and align their goals vary depending on the context of how care is delivered and the role various intermediaries play in connecting providers and patients. For example, service exchanges between a provider and patient in the case of a critically ill patient at home or nursing home is different from service exchanges used by the provider of care in a public health setting. Such layering of actors and the institutional characteristics of the ecosystems these actors are a part of will influence how one might develop digital strategies to share resources, track adherence and align goals of all involved. We will illustrate this using four different uses cases in this section.

Public Health Use Case

Public health officials' role is to create value by developing services to prevent illnesses caused by contaminated food, reduce spread of viruses or develop treatment options to address complications caused by infections. Since the patient ecosystem is highly diverse, with varying social, cultural and economic differences, public health agencies often rely on intermediaries and broader types of messaging to create value and influence patient behavior. For example, a hospital has used service exchanges between the public health officials and clinical care providers in the US and around the globe to share best practices, so they can be contextualized and used to special patient populations as shown in Figure 2. In order to make needed resources available to patients, the hospital needed to align the goals of public health officials and clinical care providers. A part of this alignment is to make the therapeutic guidelines available quickly to care providers and have these contextualized to their population context. A platform is designed to share this knowledge under different contexts and when information is incomplete and make such knowledge available using technologies such as smart phone apps.

Figure 3. An illustration of an app providing guidelines on therapy recommendations

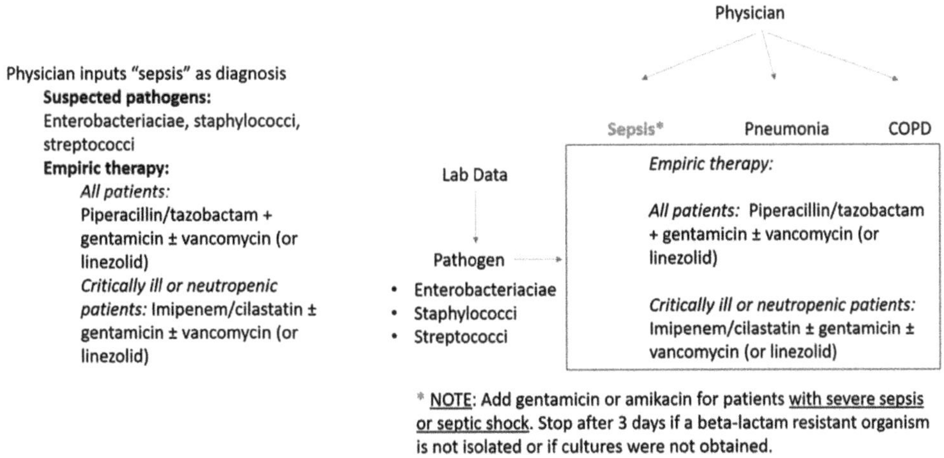

In order to make the recommendation generic and yet customized to reflect different contexts, the organization developed a template strategy shown in Figure 3 to create guidelines based on information on pathogens from patient lab data.

While the use of digital services is still under development, the following questions are being asked to assess the effectiveness of the guidelines and the value of the platform created to support the clinical care providers.

- Which disease states are complex enough to need global consultation?
- How accurate should the collected pathogen data be to make the guidelines effective?
- How reliable is the technology provided to support consultation?
- What is the role of other actors, besides clinical care providers, in the global context to ensure patient engagement?
- What dimensions of patient ecosystem are critical to best practices?

This case illustrates how intelligence gathered from the utilization of the platform can be used to not only see how goals are aligned as well as effectiveness of the data tracked. Similar strategies may be employed for situations such as smoking cessation and diabetes interventions (ASHLine, GDAHC). In summary, there is no difference between businesses who use distributors or retailers to bring products to consumers, and public health professionals who need to analyze and disseminate information to public through intermediate care providers, public health institutions, community leaders and general broadcast of information. One need not look too far to see the role of Jewish rabbis in NY in the recent measles outbreak as they, as

Figure 4. Three service models of patient engagement

Patient at Pharmacy

PatientAtDoctor*Doctor***PPrescription**
Patient*TransportStaff***PatientAtPharmacy**
Patient*Pprescription*PharmacyStaff***PrescriptionFilled**
TransportStaff*CareProvider***Transportfee**

Patient at Rehab Facility

PatientAtDoctor*Doctor***PRehabPlan**
Time*PRehabPlan*ChildCareStaff***PatientNeedingRehab**
PatientAtRehab*FacilityStaff***RehabReport**
ChildCareStaff*SocialServicesOrganization***ChildCareFee**

Lab Test Service Exchange

PatientAtDoctor*Doctor***BloodTestPlan**
Time*PatientAlert***PatientAtLab**
PatientAtLab*LabStaff***PatientTests**
PatientTests*LabAnalysis***LabResultstoDoctor**

local community leaders, have influence on certain populations and their need to change behavior.

Primary Care Use Case

Providers use several digital health strategies (e.g. patient portals, text alerts, or tele-health consultations, etc.) to engage patients as a part of post-discharge follow-up. Many of these are initiated by care providers to reduce readmissions or prevent admissions to hospitals through preventive care. These digital health strategies need to consider the capacity of the patients to seek and engage with the provider. As discussed earlier, social, cultural, economic, and other dimensions can inhibit patient capacity to seek information and manage their health conditions. Even when they have the capacity, they need reminders or fewer work related disruptions. A few examples of service exchanges between providers in primary care are shown in Figure 4, where each service exchange is shown separately with the output shown with bold lettering.

Digital services can be developed for each service exchange to either track intelligence on actor engagement or seek goal alignment or both. For example, in lab test service exchange, the second line is a mobile app used to send reminders to let patients know they need to visit the lab. If needed, based on the patient goals, digital service supporting this exchange can be altered such as use of phone calls to be picked up by someone at schedule time. Similarly, for visiting a pharmacy, patients may be given an opportunity to receive a text message from transport staff,

Figure 5. Actors and resources interacting across ecosystems

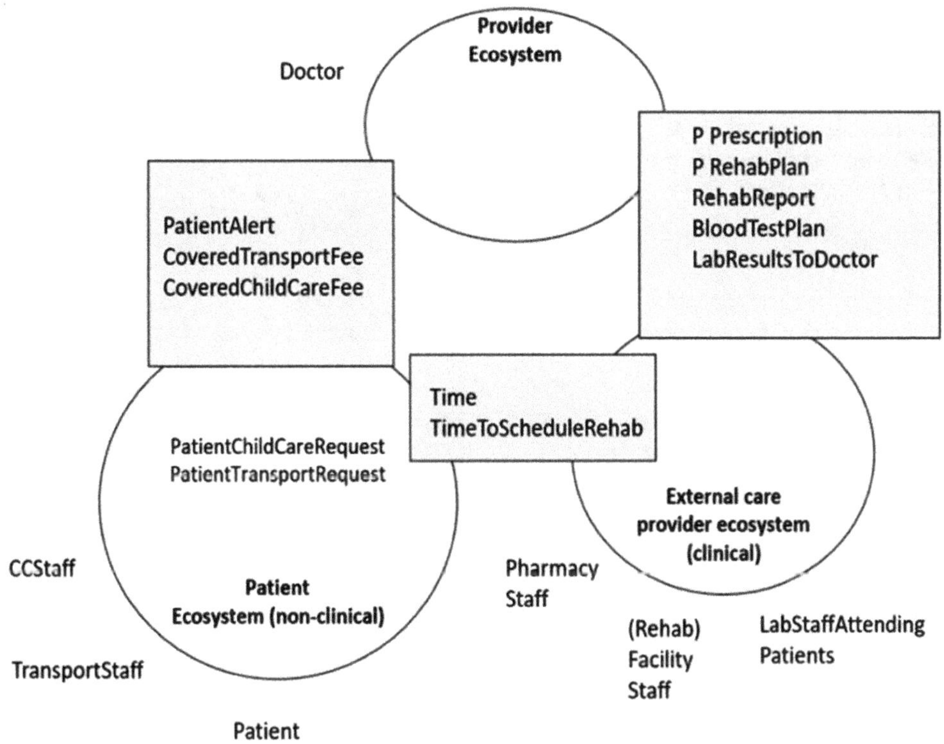

and care providers such as rehab facilities may be provided alternatives to share their reports (e.g. link to provider ERM, faxing data, etc.).

The actor/resource engagement in service exchanges across multiple ecosystems as shown in Figure 5. Intelligence gathered from these service exchanges can be used to track patient use behavior, look for opportunities to enhance patient adherence by innovative interventions, leveraging technology to speed up communication and coordination, or tailor the digital services as and when appropriate to ensures goals of all actors are aligned. Some questions that guide intelligence gathering and value creation include:

Figure 6. ANP as a connector across multiple ecosystems

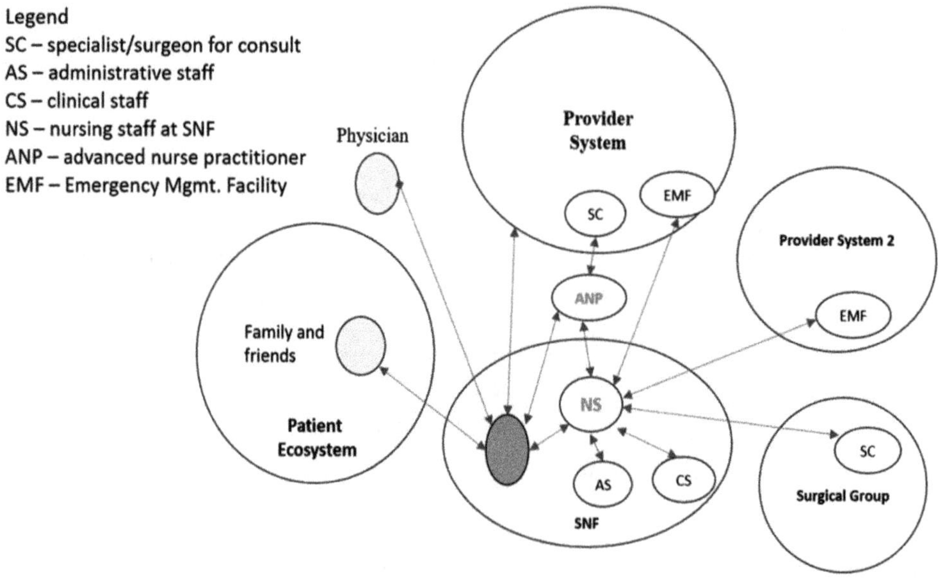

- Which patients are leveraging non-clinical resources to support medication adherence by visiting pharmacies?
- Where are patients geographically located, and how are they using various social services such as transportation or childcare?
- Which non-clinical actors are patients choosing most often – brand named pharmacies like Walmart and CVS or those that reside in grocery stores? This can help identify patient preferences so that complementary care services such as flu vaccines or glucose monitoring for diabetics can be provided to the patients at these locations to reduce time and costs.

In summary, in either primary care that is designed to address health maintenance or care transition post-discharge from a hospital to continue care plan designed, physicians can interact directly with patients as opposed to intermediate care providers as in public health. Yet, such patient interaction needs the support of many clinical and non-clinical actors of the patient ecosystem and they collectively need to communicate and coordinate their activities to influence patient adherence.

Skilled Nursing Home Use Case

Patients discharged from a hospital to a skilled nursing facility (SNF) form a different type of care transition. Similar to public health case, SNFs act as a health intermediary between provider and patient in support of care transition and care plan adherence. Given the diverse patient populations SNFs have to work with, many SNFs need to partner with other care providers such as specialists and these can come from multiple provider systems. Figure 6 illustrates how a SNF used a mix of internal resources and special consults, as well as another intermediary (advanced nurse practitioner -ANP) to support a patient's care transition. With care providers supporting patients outside a provider ecosystem, use of a ANP provides a single point of contact (or case agent) for addressing patient needs and potentially align the goals of all involved. It also helps SNF improve its capacity to handle a large number of patients with diverse complications (Tanniru et al. 2019).

To track the success of SNFs in care transitions, a hospital analyzed its readmitted patients from multiple locations they are discharged to. Using the Length of Stay (LOS) of Sepsis patients readmitted, it found that patients discharged to some skilled nursing facilities (SNF) have double the average LOS compared to others and this led to look more deeply to identify ways to improve cross-training of nursing staff, thus enhancing its care related capacity. A different strategy was used by a group of hospitals to create value to patients by increasing the capacity of the SNFs by having them share best practices and engage in frequent interactions for shared knowledge (Craft 2017).

In summary, with more healthcare intermediaries playing a role in post-discharge care transition such as home care centers, independent living facilities, rehabilitation centers along with SNFs, hospitals need to explore opportunities to improve the capacity of these external care facilities and help them look for partners resources, including hospitals, to support patient care.

All four use cases illustrate different ways to bring resources other than the provider to track patient adherence and improve capacity of patient ecosystem actors by distributing responsibility and align the goals of all involved. Next section will explore the role of service exchanges between patients and providers within a provider ecosystem and how it can influence the digital strategy development when patients leave the hospital.

Figure 7. ER patient flow analysis with several patient touch points

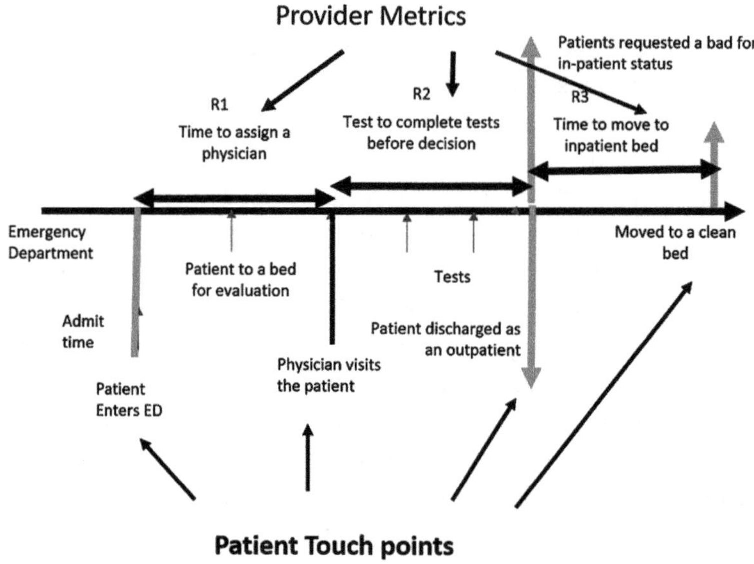

VALUE CREATION IN THE PROVIDER ECOSYSTEM

Healthcare systems have used digital health strategies to improve their productivity and support clinical and administrative needs, and these strategies will continue with advances in digital technologies such as robotics, the Internet of Things, and AI/ machine learning. While these digital health strategies, on the surface, can create value for patients over time with improved responsiveness and better clinical care quality, the focus of these digital strategies tends to be provider centric and clinically focused. However, care delivery systems within a hospital do have touchpoints with patients, which can provide opportunities for hospitals to influence patient behavior while they are within the provider ecosystem and potentially align it with the provider goals. In fact, many hospitals are looking to use their patient touch points to change the nature of care they provide. For example, hospitals want to reduce emergency room (ER) admissions by shifting some care to other care facilities, better prepare a patient for operating room (OR) surgeries to reduce un-necessary costs and scheduling conflicts, and educate and engage patients in patient rooms (PR) to reduce readmissions. Let us use three use cases to illustrate these opportunities.

ER Operations

Figure 7 depicts the flow of patients through multiple stages in the ER. Each of these stages is a touchpoint between a patient and a provider. While optimizing patient flow can help reduce costs and improved resource utilization for the hospital, as well as reduce the time spent by the patient in the ER, the service exchanges between patients and actors can also be used to influence patient engagement on what is needed post-discharge. Given that many patients that come to ER have with them their family members, these actors can be used in future patient engagement or patient decision making as opposed to have them left in the waiting room wondering what is happening to the patient. We worked with a firm that managed multiple ER facilities as they wanted to track patients' use behavior (perceive value created by the ER). Using text mining of patient comments as well as quantitative analysis of patient sentiments (Khuntia et al. 2017), several key issues came to light. Patients' assessment of value is influenced by positive and negative experiences they have with nursing staff, communications that occur between patients and providers, and the ER infrastructure. In addition, the analysis of another ER facility led to these following observations:

- Most patients have 4-6 orders for tests each.
- The minimum average time linearly increases with the number of orders for tests.
- "ECG Lead Tracking" has the highest time required for patients to get into the room
- Most of the orders are placed on weekdays and Thursday, especially.

Information such as this, while useful to align resources within the provider ecosystem to improve patient flow, can also provide useful information to patients while they are waiting for care within ER. For example, by providing patients with an iPad and a visual map of the ER facility, along with estimated times for different tests based on historical data and physician schedules, patient expectations can be better managed. During waiting times, patient may be educated on symptoms they can monitor at home and visit other facilities such as urgent care or even mini-clinics rather than wait till things get worse and seek care within ER.

In summary, the goal of ER is to inform and educate patients on ways to reduce the need to visit ER and using today's technologies such as wearables or portals, patients will have more resources to track their conditions and look for alternatives in care related access than an ER visit.

Figure 8. Several technologies supporting patient services

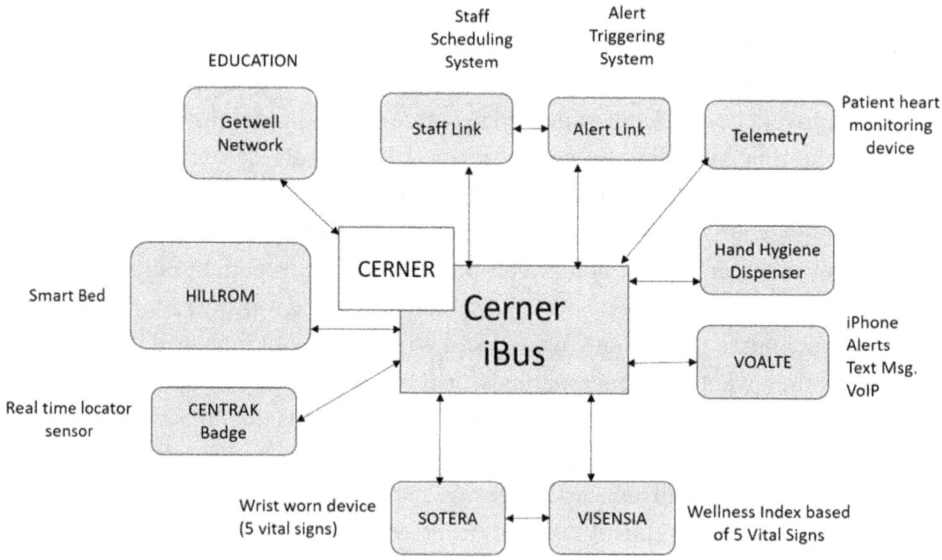

Operating Rooms

The ecosystem of an OR is complex because of both the surgical process and the number of people involved (e.g. surgeons, nurses, and anesthesiologists as well as other specialists). Hospitals are using several digital strategies to schedule OR rooms based on prior utilization and robotics and AI to help improve non-invasive surgical interventions and improve clinical diagnosis, as well as creating buffer space in the OR to accommodate surgical delays and provide block time for operating rooms for physicians to trade off among each other. One area that patients can play a role in reducing surgical delays and costs while improving their surgical success (i.e. align the goals of all involved) is during pre-op, where patients are prepared for surgery by PACUs (pre-anesthesiology care units).

Patient health condition is stabilized for glucose levels, blood pressure, etc. and they may need to visit multiple sites for test data (x-rays, blood tests, etc.), which is gathered by the peri-operative team to decide when to administer anesthesiology and what medications to provide prior to the surgical procedure. Improved coordination of actors outside the hospital (e.g. patients, primary care physician, surgeon performing the procedure, and various test facilities), using technology as appropriate, can help PACUs track patient conditions and stabilize these prior to their coming to a hospital. Such a coordination aligns the goals of hospitals, surgeons as well as patients, who often have to spend time and money by traveling to a hospital, sometimes far from their home.

In summary, patient education and engagement is not only needed in the surgery planned for a medical condition but also for assistance in the pre-operative care planning. Similar engagement is also useful in the clinical decision itself (where the surgery is to be done and when) as well as what post-operative care will lead to fastest recovery from the surgery.

Patient Rooms (PRs)

Patient rooms are undergoing significant transformations ever since a number of technologies—such as smart beds, wrist worn devices, PillowTalk that connects patients and nursing staff, RFID technologies that track care staff's adherence to washing of hands, etc. have started to transform services in patient rooms (PRs). These are often introduced to improve service to patients as well as to reduce costs (e.g. hospital acquired infections, patient falls, patient mortality, etc.) and improve patient satisfaction. Each of these services is digitized to track hospital performance on multiple metrics and Figure 8 illustrates several of the technologies introduced in a hospital in SE Michigan (Khuntia et al. 2015).

While digital services are designed to create value to providers at various patient touch points and patient conditions are tracked to assess their impact, the same touch points can be used to gain insight on patient's capacity to participate and engage in their care transition post-discharge. For example, PillowTalk is used to speed up the staff responsiveness to patient calls and improve patient satisfaction. It uses three different buttons (bathroom visit, general information or pain call) to seek the support of different care related staff. It also has escalation protocols, so calls can be sent to others when the primary nurse is busy. Similarly, a smart bed is used to track a fall risk patient's movement from bed and send alerts to multiple nurses before a patient falls and injures himself. This contributed to significant stress on staff and led to some un-even response for calls made on different floors: surgical, cardiac, oncology or neurology (Khuntia et al. 2016). Lastly, patients were visited by an inter-disciplinary team to ask questions at periodic intervals to improve patient care.

Tracking of smart bed data revealed some interesting insights that could have been used to educate patients to align both provider and patient goals. For example, patients needing to go to bathroom could call a nurse using PillowTalk as opposed to getting out of bed, thus aligning the goals of provider (reduced stress on staff) and faster response by a designed staff for such requests (patient need). A patient needing to move from the bed to a chair could have used PillowTalk for general support, again reducing stress on staff and improving staff response. By engaging patients as actors within the provider ecosystem, they become an important source of information for the provider and increases patients' perceived capacity to take action with a broader knowledge of the services. Similarly, when hospital discovered that the inter-disciplinary team doing rounding is intimidating to patients, they reduced the number of people involved in the rounding. But, in the process, they discovered a few goals of patients and introduced both an incident report to quickly act on some patient requests and provided them a care plan folder when they are admitted to the PR, so patients can track their care plan progress and even ask questions (Fowler et al. 2018).

In summary, while provider ecosystems can be complex and not all patients are equally competent to engaging in decision making, educating and engaging patients and their family members to the extent possible can not only improve their self-worth but also enhance their capacity to self-manage their condition post-discharge by seeking needed resources. In fact, several patients expressed an interest in taking wearable technology home and the hospital provided these for some critical care patients for both remote monitoring as well as gave them an iPad to record their weights and consult with staff. This pilot project has shown success and the hospital expanded the effort to another region (Tanniru et al. 2019).

Each of the cases discussed in the provider ecosystem illustrates how patients can be viewed as an actor within a provider ecosystem and can be leveraged to play an important role in support of healthcare strategies of the provider. With hospitals needing to reduce the number of unnecessary ER visits, preparing patients for surgical success in OR and engaging patients in PR so they can carry over this engagement post discharge to reduce readmissions, providers need to exhibit leadership to address dual goals – enhancing their capacity to leverage technology to address clinical goals, and improving patient capacity by allowing patients to leverage resources and actors within their ecosystem to self-manage their health (Weiner et al. 2016).

CONCLUSION

Co-creation of value between a provider and patient requires the integration of actors and resources from several provider and patient ecosystems if clinical care treatment plans are to be effectively adhered to. Such co-creation can occur not only by tracking patient adherence behavior outside a hospital through digital services, but also by aligning the goals of all actors involved in the patient ecosystem. In this chapter, multiple use cases outside a hospital were used to illustrate the challenge of tracking patient adherence and goal alignment of actors involved in the patient ecosystem. Opportunities to use digital services to address these were highlighted. Then a few use cases were used to illustrate the opportunities providers have to understand the patient ecosystem while they are in the hospital. Specifically, patient touchpoints inside a hospital were used to illustrate how they can improve patients' capacity to manage their health conditions by leveraging resources within their ecosystem.

DIRECTIONS FOR FUTURE RESEARCH

In today's evolving competitive landscape, with changing customer expectations and technology changes, digital transformation is calling for improved organizational capability to leverage a mix of internal and external resources to quickly react to create and sustain value. This is no different for an individual consumer, who needs to improve their capability to use a mix of internal and external resources within their ecosystem to create value that will advance their own utility or professional growth. This is more significant when it comes to the healthcare consumer. The healthcare domain is complex, with evolving technologies that monitor health and the growing number of resources, clinical and non-clinical, available with insufficient credibility and evidence based support. Making intelligent decisions in this environment, when patient capacity to make such decisions is often clouded by emotional and personal judgment, is not always easy unless they can leverage a mix of their own resources and those who they can partner with. Providers need to recognize the varying capacity of patients and decide how best to improve their own capacity so value creation can be matched with effective value-in-use behavior.

Social diagnosis research suggests that an individual's capacity to manage their medical conditions may depend on the role patients play in their ecosystem (e.g. parent, educator, single mom, visible member of a community, etc.), the resources they have access to (e.g. financial, emotional, cultural, etc.), the reaction they have to the disease condition (e.g. fear, stress, feeling of helplessness, etc.), and the relationships they have with people within their ecosystem (e.g. how connected they are with members of their family, friends, and other community members). Some of these social determinants may be critical for hospitals to consider as they seek intelligence from multiple patient touchpoints and develop digital services to improve patient access to resources needed to self-manage their health.

While the focus of this chapter was not on the policies and politics involved in addressing the shared responsibility of many in patient or provider capacity building, it is clear that communication and coordination is critical among those who not only provide clinical care but also provide resources to support a healthcare consumer or patients' ability to seek the needed resources. Hospitals and other healthcare organizations can help understand the role of actors who play a major role in supporting patients, and working with these actors within the patient ecosystem so they can become an integral part of care plan design for preventive as well as care transition post-discharge. Currently, work is underway in addressing care delivery models for underserved served populations, categorized along geographical regions: urban and rural and Midwest to Southwest in the US as well as economic continuum (high income vis-à-vis low to middle income countries) and disease conditions (obesity, mental health, etc.).

REFERENCES

ASHLine. (n.d.). Retrieved from https://uahs.arizona.edu/arizona-smokers-helpline-ashline

Craft, S. (2017). A collaborative blueprint for reducing SNF readmissions: Driving results with quality reporting and performance metrics. *Health Intelligence Network*, July. Retrieved from www.hin.com

Dreyer, T. (2014). Care transitions: Best practices and evidence-based programs. *Home Healthcare Nurse*, *32*(5), 309–316. doi:10.1097/NHH.0000000000000069 PMID:24802602

Fowler, B. L. J., Johns, J., Tanniru, M. R., Ballijepally, V., Roumani, Y. F., Bobryk, D., & Mitchell, K. (2018). Engaging patients through multi-disciplinary rounding – The case study at a Michigan hospital. *Journal of Hospital Administration*, *7*(5), 17–26. doi:10.5430/jha.v7n5p17

GDAHC. (n.d.). Retrieved from http://www.gdahc.org/

Herzig, S. J., Schnipper, J. L., Doctoroff, L., Kim, C. S., Flanders, S. A., Robinson, E. J., ... Williams, M. V. (2016). Physician perspectives on factors contributing to readmissions and potential prevention strategies: a multicenter survey. *Journal of General Internal Medicine*, *31*(11), 1287–1293. doi:10.100711606-016-3764-5 PMID:27282857

Khuntia, J., Tanniru, M., Fragoli, F., & Nawrocki, M. (2016). Mindfulness differences in hospital unit operations: analysis of response to nurse call systems [PAJAIS]. *Pacific Asia Journal of the Association for Information Systems*, *8*(1), 33–64. doi:10.17705/1pais.08102

Khuntia, J., Tanniru, M., & Weiner, J. (2015). Juggling digitization and technostress: the case of alert fatigues due to intelligent care system implementation at a hospital. *Health Policy and Technology*, *4*, 364–377. doi:10.1016/j.hlpt.2015.08.005

Khuntia, J., Tanniru, M., & Weiner, J. (2017). Dimensions of patient experience and overall satisfaction in emergency units. *Journal of Patient Satisfaction, SAGE Publications*, *4*(3), 95–100.

Koh, K. W., Wang, W., Richards, A. M., Chan, M. Y., & Cheng, K. F. (2016). Effectiveness of advanced practice nurse-led telehealth on readmissions and health-related outcomes among patients with post-acute myocardial infarction: ALTRA Study Protocol. *Journal of Advanced Nursing*, *72*(6), 1357–1367. doi:10.1111/jan.12933 PMID:26915719

Lusch, R. F., & Nambisan, S. (2015). Service innovation: a service-dominant logic perspective. *Management Information Systems Quarterly*, *39*(1), 155–175. doi:10.25300/MISQ/2015/39.1.07

Medicare Hospital Readmissions Reduction Program. (2013, Nov. 12). Health Affairs. Retrieved from http://www.healthaffairs.org/healthpolicybriefs/brief.php?brief_id=102

Plum, A., Tanniru, M, & Khuntia, J. (2019, January) *An innovation platform for diffusing public health practices across a global network, HICSS-2019,* Hawaii. APA Dictionary of Psychology, 2015.

Saif, K. F., Nawaz, A., Jan, A., & Khan, M. I. (2012). Synthesizing the theories of job-satisfaction across the cultural/attitudinal dimensions. *Interdisciplinary Journal of Contemporary Research in Business*, 1382–1396.

Tanniru, M., Jones, J., Kazziha, S., & Hornberger, M. (2019). Strategies to address care transition - a methodology and a case study. *Journal of Hospital Administration*, *8*(3). doi:10.5430/jha.v8n3p38

Tanniru, M. (2019) Engagement leading to empowerment—digital innovation strategies for patient care continuity, Forthcoming in *Journal of Hospital Management and Health Policy*

Vargo, S. L., & Lusch, R. F. (2008). Service-dominant logic: continuing the evolution. *Journal of the Academy of Marketing Science*, *36*(1), 1–10. doi:10.100711747-007-0069-6

Weiner, J., Tanniru, M., Khuntia, J., Bobryk, D., Naik, M., & Page, K. L. (2016). Digital leadership in action in a hospital through a real time dashboard system implementation and experience. *Journal of Hospital Administration*, (May), 2016.

Chapter 4
Operations-Intelligence-Strategy (OIS) Process in Healthcare

Xue Ning
University of Colorado, Denver, USA

ABSTRACT

The healthcare industry has generated a huge amount of data in diverse formats. The big data in healthcare is leading the revolution in healthcare. Collecting data at the operational level is the starting point for the big data-driven healthcare revolution. By analyzing the operational level big data, healthcare organizations can gain the business intelligence for further strategy development, for example how to improve the healthcare quality, how to provide better long-term care, and how to empower the patients. This chapter discusses this process as operations-intelligence-strategy (OIS) process in healthcare. Objectives are understanding how to gain business intelligence from sensor data mining in healthcare, biomedical signal analysis, and biomedical image analysis, and exploring the applications and impacts of the OIS process, with a focus on the sensor data mining in healthcare.

INTRODUCTION

Big data refers to a collection of large, complex data sets, including structured and unstructured data, which cannot be analyzed using traditional database methods and tools (Baltzan, 2012). Big data has 5-Vs as its common characteristics: volume, velocity, variety, value, and veracity (White, 2012). Volume refers to the scale of data and the name-big data itself indicates the enormous volume; velocity is about

DOI: 10.4018/978-1-7998-2310-0.ch004

the analysis of streaming data as it travels around the Internet; variety indicates the different forms of structured and unstructured data; value suggests the potential values of big data; veracity concerns the uncertainty of data, including biases, noise, and abnormalities.

In the healthcare industry, data is captured from sensors, various signals, medical equipment, digital pictures, etc. The volume of data in healthcare is huge while its forms are diversified (variety). For example, healthcare data can be clinical data from clinical decision support systems, patient data in Electronic Health Records (EHRs), machine-generated data, and patient-generated contents. These different types of data travel via multiple channels such as social media and networks. However, not all healthcare data is clean and trustworthy. When using big data in healthcare, filtering noisy data is always important. Nevertheless, big data in healthcare is creating values. It is a source of innovation in healthcare and is transforming the healthcare industry by improving healthcare quality, long-term care, and patient empowerment (Chen, Chiang, & Storey, 2012).

The focus of this chapter is data collected from the operational level, more specifically, the sensor data, biomedical signals, and biomedical images. The mining and analysis techniques of the operational level data are discussed, from which, users are able to derive business intelligence. Furthermore, examples of the application and impacts of sensor data mining in healthcare demonstrate the OIS process.

SENSOR DATA MINING IN HEALTHCARE

Sensor refers to a device, module, or subsystem that is used to detect changes in its environment and then send the information to other processing devices or cloud platforms (Dargie & Poellabauer, 2010). Examples of common sensors in daily life include breath analyzer, CO2 sensor, CO detector, smoke detector and etc. Sensor-based monitoring is applied for data collection purposes as sensors provide immense amounts of data. In healthcare, it is critical to use sensors to monitor some cases at the time of treatments. There are different types of sensors are used in medical informatics. They can be categorized into four groups: physiological sensors, wearable activity sensors, human sensors, and contextual sensors (Sow, Turaga, & Schmidt, 2013). Physiological sensors such as ECG sensors, SpO2, temperature sensors in the intensive care unit (ICU) measure patient vital signs or physiological statistics. Wearable activity sensors measure attributes of gross user activity, different from narrowly focused vital sign sensors. Today, there are various wearable devices such as cell phones. Human sensors refer to human bodies for physicians examination, self-reporting, social media sharing. Examples of these sensors are care-provider notes, entries in the Electronic Medical Records (EMRs). Contextual sensors are embedded in the environment around the user to measure different contextual properties. For example, radio frequency identification (RFID) sensors linked with care providers, video and cameras.

Using data collected by sensors has various benefits for healthcare (Darwish & Hassanien, 2011). It facilitates the design of sophisticated clinical decision support systems capable of better observing patients' physiological signals, helps provide situational awareness to the bedside, and promotes insight on the inefficiencies in the healthcare system that may be the root cause of surging costs. The rich sensor-generated data provides foundation for medical informatics that improves healthcare by acquiring and transmitting knowledge for application. Many sensor data mining techniques are applied in healthcare to gain business intelligence for further decision making.

Medical informatics contributes to the improvement of healthcare by acquiring and transmitting knowledge for application. By adopting a proactive way instead of a reactive approach, sensor data can be used for monitoring and understanding of patients. For example, many wearable technologies are used to track and analyze users' health status (Darwish & Hassanien, 2011). However, with tremendous sensor data, there is data overload problem, which needs data mining and analytics technologies. Sensor data mining technologies have been applied in both clinical and nonclinical (e.g., smart environments) contexts.

In general, data mining procedures include data acquisition, data preprocessing, data transformation, modeling, and evaluation (Mariscal, Marban, & Fernandez, 2010). Data acquisition is the process of collecting external sensor data. Data preprocessing refers to filtering noisy data with sampling, interpolation, and summarization. Data transformation converts the normalized and cleaned input data to a representation for the extraction in the mining process. This procedure can be linear and nonlinear transformations from unstructured data to numeric data, dimensionality reduction and de-correlation techniques for summarization, choice of transformation and representation for the features. Modeling is a process of pattern identification by using algorithms. There are different types of models such as clustering models, classification models, regression models, and summarization models. Once the data mining is completed, evaluation is the last step to evaluate and interpret the results. However, users should be aware of the challenges of sensor data mining in healthcare.

Challenges of Sensor Data Mining in Healthcare

Numerous challenges are along with the sensor data mining procedures (Sow et al., 2013). First, because of the different types of sensor data and lack of standards and protocols, it is challenging to acquire and integrate data with heterogeneity. The interoperability across multiple data sources is little too. There are also privacy concerns, especially in the healthcare context, in the data acquisition process. Second, there are reprocessing challenges. Heterogeneity and standards issues always exist as nature of processing multiple data types, because of which, data is hard to be aligned and synchronized syntactically. Also, sensor reporting rates are different for both structured data and unstructured data. Semantic normalization is another issue as the sensing processes are different. For example, a blood pressure measure can be a daily average value or an absolute value for a specific time. These values should be normalized before further comparison and interpretation to get a meaningful conclusion. Third, there are many options such as Fourier Transform, Wavelet Transform, text extraction, and principal component analysis in the data transformation process. It is essential to have in-depth understanding of the healthcare problem for the appropriate choice. To have such in-depth understanding, domain experts' input is needed for appropriate interpretation. However, we also need to note that the inputs from physicians or nurses can be biased by their experiences and other factors (Hall et al., 2015).

The process of modeling shares common modeling challenges and specific challenges in healthcare sensor data mining. Time series nature of data requires complex sequential mining algorithms while there is limited application to capture the dynamic nature of the data (Varatharajan, Manogaran, Priyan, & Sundarasekar, 2018). Furthermore, because of communication and computational costs, sharing restrictions for patient privacy, there is inherent distributed nature of applications; thus, complex distributed mining algorithms are needed. Although modeling process optimization is problematic in distributed data mining, data availability issue in remote settings requires distribution of analytic approaches. In the cases that need training data, the input data can either be very noisy or be biased because the historical datasets are sparse (Nie et al., 2015). The data mining results need to be interpreted by domain experts, but most domain experts are not data mining experts. Furthermore, the model output needs to be validated with the metadata supported by existing medical knowledge. The validated results also need further evaluation. These are challenges in the evaluation process.

Besides these procedure-specific challenges, there are generic systems challenges. For example, as we are living in the big data era, the huge amount of data that can overwhelm a relational database system needs innovative management that beyond conventional data management. In most cases, the sensors data is unstructured, which makes it more difficult for a real-time system to operate sensor mining applications (Raghupathi & Raghupathi, 2014). Some other sensor data mining challenges include it needs integrating stream processing system technology to cope with large amounts of real-time data for both structured and unstructured sensor data analysis. Besides the general sensor data, biomedical signals and biomedical images are two specific types of operational level data in healthcare.

BIOMEDICAL SIGNAL ANALYSIS

Biomedical Signals

Biomedical signals refer to signals of physiological activities of organisms, such Electroneurogram (ENG), Electromyogram (EMG), Electrocardiogram (ECG), Electroencephalogram (EEG), Electrogastrogram (EGG), Phonocardiogram (PCG) and other biomedical signals (Kaçar & Sakoğlu, 2016).

When stimulated by an electrical current, there is a series of electrical responses that occur in the cell because of the mechanical contraction of a single cell. Electroneurogram (ENG) is an electrical signal that is observed when the nerve is stimulated. Electromyogram (EMG) is electrical activity of muscle. Each skeletal muscle is composed of many motor units (Ibrahim, Gannapathy, Chong, & Isa, 2016). Spatio-temporal summation of the motor unit action potentials of all the active motor units gives rise to an EMG of the muscle, which can be recorded by placing needle electrodes on the surface of the body. Electrocardiogram (ECG) is a consequence of electrical activity of the heart. ECG is used to diagnose and monitor various cardiac conditions, including arrhythmias (irregularities of cardiac rhythm) and myocardial damage such as myocardial infarction. Typically, 12 electrodes are placed at well-defined locations to measure the heart's conduction system (Zhang et al., 2018). Electroencephalogram (EEG) is electrical activity recorded at the surface of the brain. The main parts of the brain are the cerebrum, the cerebellum, the spinal cord, and the limbic system. The main generators of the EEG are the postsynaptic potentials in the dendrites of large pyramidal neurons (Cohen, 2014). Electrogastrogram (EGG) reflects the electrical control activity and the electrical response activity of the stomach. By using cutaneous electrodes placed on the anterior abdominal wall, the gastric myoelectrical activity is recorded. Phonocardiogram (PCG) is recorded by placing a transducer (microphone) on the thorax. It is measurement of a vibration or sound signal produced by the contractile activity of the heart and blood together. Some other biomedical signals include carotid pulse (CP), the speech signals, signals recorded using catheter-tip sensors such as left ventricular pressure, right atrial pressure, aortic pressure, and vibration signals that accompany EMG (i.e., vibromyogram).

Biomedical Signal Analysis

We first use ECG signal analysis as an example to illustrate the biomedical signal analysis. ECG waveform is complex and has different waves (PQRST waves). This complex nature of ECG waveform encompasses features such as cardiac rate, rhythm, PR interval, QRS duration, ST segment, QT interval, and T waves (Benatar, 2017). To extract these features, noises that affect the ECG signals should be addressed. For example, power line interference, electrode contact noise, motion artifacts, muscle contraction, baseline drift and ECG amplitude modulation with respiration, instrumentation noise generated during signal acquisition, electrosurgical noises, and many other less significant noises. A process of noise filtering that can deal with these noises is needed before the QRS detection.

Furthermore, the denoising of signals aims to improve measurement accuracy and reproducibility. The approach for denoising of signals can be statistical such as principal component analysis (PCA), nonstationary such as wavelet, and optimum such as wavelet Wiener filtering (Kaur & Rajni, 2017). The PCA approach has been used in many cases, including classification, data reduction, feature extraction, and signal separation. PCA-based denoising can be used for both single-channel and multi-channel ECG signals. The rationale of this method is to concentrate the low-noisy and robust ECG signals. An alternative of the PCA method is denoising using truncated singular value decomposition.

Wavelet filtering is based on the discrete wavelet transform, which distributes larger coefficients to the original signal and smaller coefficients to the noise. Setting a proper threshold value is critical for this method. Wavelet wiener filtering is the combination of wavelet filtering and wiener filtering theory (Kaur & Rajni, 2017). It can set hybrid thresholding. The pilot estimation method is used to connect the wavelet filtering block and wiener filtering block.

There are also numerous advanced techniques for biomedical signal analysis. Multivariate analysis is used for the non-linear combination of signals and random vectors (Yong, Ward, & Birch, 2008). Cross-correlation analysis is applied for comparison of two biomedical signals by quantifying their underlying relationship. This method can detect a deterministic signal in a noisy environment. More specifically, Pearson's correlation coefficient is an example of methods to study connectivity. With the growing availability and access of biomedical data, including structured and robust time-series data as well as unstructured and disparate time-series data, it's possible to study the dynamics of networks (Cohen, 2014). Through compressive sensing and dimensionality reduction, some analytical techniques can be used for signal processing on graphs by learning from very large matrix and graph data, by addressing the imputation, scalability, convergence, and complexity issues, and by improving robustness to outliers and missing data.

For example, for the EEG signal analyses, the time-frequency domains analyses based on discrete-time Fourier transform, power and phase analyses, and PCA are the popular techniques. Also, there are various connectivity analyses methods, including phase-based connectivity, power-based connectivity, and Granger prediction (Cohen, 2014). Researchers also suggested models such as the multivariate autoregressive (MAR) model and the Hidden Markov model (HMM) as method to analyze the EEG data (Vidaurre et al., 2016). The MAR model is useful for time series data while the HMM is used to model each time series as a sequence of states.

BIOMEDICAL IMAGE ANALYSIS

Biomedical Images

Biomedical images are images of a biological specimen such as human body or animal anatomy (Shen, Wu, & Suk, 2017). These specimens are usually very small and cannot be viewed with the naked eye. Biomedical image analysis refers to acquiring images inside of the body without harming the body and analyzing the biological structure, function, and processes based on the images (Schindelin, Rueden, Hiner, & Eliceiri, 2015).

Biomedical imaging modalities are techniques used to visualize the biomedical images of the human body, either in 2D or 3D manner. For example, magnetic resonance imaging (MRI), computed tomography (CT), positron emission tomography (PET), ultrasound (U/S), electron microscopy, etc (Sharma & Kumar, 2017). CT creates 2D axial cross-section images of the body by collecting several 1-dimensional projections of conventional X-ray data using an X-ray source on one side and a detector on the other side. PET is a nuclear imaging modality that uses radioactively labeled tracers to create activity maps inside the body based on uptake of a compound based on metabolic function. MRI refers to a high resolution, high contrast, and noninvasive imaging modality. This technique can provide extremely rich and versatile contrast mechanisms that make it the modality of choice for looking at soft-tissue contrast. Ultrasound is one of the most ubiquitous imaging modalities because of its low cost and completely noninvasive nature. This modality transmits high-frequency sound waves using specialized ultrasound transducers, and then collects the reflected ultrasound waves from the body using specialized probes. Microscopy uses the microscope to examine the biological samples such as tissues obtained from biopsy specimens for evidence of pathology.

Various standards and systems are developed for the biomedical imaging analysis. The most widely used ones are digital imaging and communications in medicine (DICOM), HL7, and picture archiving and communications system (PACS) (Pilliouras, Suss, & Yu, 2015). The differences between these three standards and systems are DICOM classifies medical images based on communications protocol, HL7 is a more general standard not only for medical imaging data but also for general electronic healthcare data, and PACS is a specialized system that stores and manages medical imaging data.

Biomedical Images Analysis

Object detection, image segmentation, image registration, registration transforms, similarity and distance metrics, registration optimizers, feature extraction, feature selection and dimensionality reduction, and PCA are the exemplary techniques for biomedical images analysis (Padfield, Mendonça, & Gupta, 2015).

Object detection is a process through which regions of potential interest such as anatomical structures or localized pathological areas are identified. There are different approaches to realize object detection, including template matching, model-based detection, and data-driven detection methods (Riegler, Urschler, Ruther, Bischof, & Stern, 2015). Template matching refers to the method that selects a representative template and applies some variant of template matching to find similar regions in the image of interest. One example is the normalized cross-correlation (NCC) that measures the similarity between two signals (Hisham, Yaakob, Raof, Nazren, & Embedded, 2015). Model-based detection is a generalization of template matching. It replaces the template and the NCC function with arbitrary models and figures of merit for the matching between the model and the data. Applications of this method include lung-nodule detection and colonic-polyp detection. However, model-based methods need expert knowledge, algorithm, and explicit models. As a complementary method, data-driven detection applies machine learning techniques to automatically extract features and models relevant to the detection problem from labeled data. Data-driven methods can be used to construct more common models of normal regions. Especially, with the unsupervised learning method, it's easier to detect abnormal features. One application example of data-driven methods is detection of carotid plaques.

Image segmentation aims to divide a digital image into separate parts or regions that have strong correlations with the real-world objects or areas contained in the image (Abdel-Khalek, Ishak, Omer, & Obada, 2017). This type of technique is used to locate objects and boundaries in images. The categories of image segmentation are thresholding, watershed, region-growing, classification, wavelets, and level-sets. Thresholding is the most simple and intuitive segmentation approach. It separates an image into foreground or background using a cutoff value through a simple loop-based on image histogram. For example, the Otsu algorithm can exhaustively search the histogram for a threshold that maximizes the between-class variance (Senthilkumaran & Vaithegi, 2016). Thresholding is a simple and speedy method for image segmentation, but it is mostly used only for simple appearance. Watershed transform is an algorithm and solution framework that is very commonly used for image segmentation and for binary shape separation (Lobo & Guruprasad, 2018). The term watershed refers to the phenomenon that valleys flood progressively higher and eventually merge together as rainfalls. Similarly, through watershed transform, all of the work goes together to create an appropriate speed image. Generally, segment based on image edges and segment based on shape are the two ways of watershed transform for segmentation. For the image edges, when there is over-segmentation, it creates noises. Then certain watershed is developed to correct over-segmentation. For the shape method, distance transform is conducted by computing the distance map. Watershed transform is based on quick, easy, and flexible computation. On the other hand, users should concern the over-segmentation and effectiveness issues when using this method.

Region growing is another technique for image segmentation (Hore et al., 2016). It first locates an initial seeded region and gradually expands the region with some constraints that define the region of interest to obtain more accurate region boundaries. In most cases, the constraint is a range of threshold that has a lower threshold and an upper threshold, based on which the region grows. Thus, the most important and difficult part of applying this method is to determine the lower and upper thresholds. Users need a great deal of testing to figure out a proper threshold range. The difference between this method and thresholding is that regions that have a path to seed are included in the segmentation. The use of region growing algorithm depends on whether the pixel is considered or not (Hore et al., 2016). When the pixel is considered, a confidence connected algorithm is used to compute the mean and standard deviation of the pixel values that labeled as foreground. Then a new internal is defined by multiplying the obtained standard deviation and a chosen factor.

Often, the classification methods have two groups: supervised classification and unsupervised classification. Supervised classification requires training of classifier where the algorithm is fed some cases along with the labeled ground truth corresponding to those cases. Then apply to unseen test data where labels are not known to the classifier. In contrast, unsupervised classification automatically finds patterns and clusters in the data, and it does not require a training step (Li, Xu, Tan, & Piechocki, 2017). The tradeoff of no need for training is the result is not very accurate. Wavelet transform is also used for biomedical image analysis. It is an effective tool for decomposing an image in the frequency and spatial domain.

Image registration is the process of aligning or bringing into the spatial correspondence of two different images or volumes (Prabhu & Khan, 2017). It is used for motion correction or motion estimation, multimodality registration, and inter-subject comparisons. In a mathematical sense, image registration can be considered as an optimization problem of finding a change of the moving image from the fixed image. The outcome is a transformed image that maximizes some similarity metric or minimizes a distance metric regarding the original true fixed image (García et al., 2017).

Registration transforms incorporate rigid body transform, similarity transform, affine transform, and B-spline deformable transform (Avants et al., 2011). Rigid body transform is comprised of image translation and rotation. Similarity transform consists of an isotropic scaling factor in addition to the rigid body transformation of rotation and translation. An affine transform is a general linear transform in which straight lines remain straight lines after transformation, but distances and angles may not be preserved, while ratios of distances between points are preserved. B-spline deformable transform is used for solving deformable registration problems where the image undergoes local deformations, and different parts of the image do not all obey the same transformation.

Similarity and distance metrics are used to define the goodness of registration. The most popular metrics are mean squares metric, which computes the mean-squared pixel-wise difference between two images; normalized cross-correlation (NCC) metric, which computes the pixel-wise cross-correlation of images and normalizes it using the autocorrelation of the two images; and mutual information metric that measures how much intensity information in one image informs the intensity information of the second image (Russakoff, Tomasi, Rohlfing, & Maurer, 2004).

Registration optimizers can be used for both registration that is considered as an optimization problem and the similarity/distance metric, which is maximized/minimized using an iterative optimization method (Pirpinia et al., 2017). Registration optimizer method selection depends on several factors, including computational efficiency, robustness to local minima, initialization, and automated registration method or semi-automated, user- guidance-based method.

A feature is a number that describes some aspect of an object such as its shape, size, brightness, and texture. *Feature extraction* is a process of summarizing or converting raw image data into expressive representations that are more informative or show better association with an underlying biological phenomenon (Mitra & Shankar, 2015). Since the most relevant elements of the data are not known beforehand, methods such as deep learning can reduce the burden of having to carefully design features and learn the most appropriate features for a given task from labeled data. In order to compute object features, a definition of an object must first be determined.

Feature selection is used to solve the problem of how many features should be used, considering the countless features of an object that can be measured (Bron, Smits, Niessen, & Klein, 2015). A good feature has some merits, including discriminatory, information rich, easy to compute, and statistically independent. Another way to determine the features is *dimensionality reduction*. It uses an exhaustive approach such as top-down, bottom-up, stepwise approach that considers all subsets of features and picks the best features (Shi, Jiang, Zhang, Huang, & Li, 2015). In biomedical image analysis, *principal component analysis* (PCA) approach is used to represent the underlying structure and variance of the data with as few dimensions as possible (Cohen, 2014; Kaur & Rajni, 2017).

OPERATIONS-INTELLIGENCE-STRATEGY (OIS) PROCESS IN HEALTHCARE

Applications and Impacts of Sensor Data Mining in Healthcare

With the big data and intelligence gained through the data analysis, users in healthcare industry can make decisions and plan to improve healthcare quality, reduce healthcare cost, and empower patients. One example is the value creation by sensor data mining in healthcare.

Sensors are devices that detect physical, chemical-related to body function signals. These signals can be measured and recorded physical properties such as sound level, temperature, weight, pressure and more. Sensors are playing important role in many industries, providing the mechanical "vision" used for counting, sorting, reading. Sensors can detect specific chemical pressures and fluid levels. Sensor technology will move the place at which health care is delivered in the future, changing the roles of hospitals, outpatient sites, homes, and ambulatory programmed outside the home. In the near future, biosensors will cause changes in positions of care and the arrangement of delivery systems (Ngoepe et al., 2013). In several cases the excellence of care will be upgraded, and patients can manage in their homes. Hospitals will run differently, besides more carefully and efficiently. We have many sensors that can detect our heart rate, blood pressure, oxygen saturation, number of steps, sleep rate, sleep stages (light and deep), calories burned, food and liquids intake, running, climbing, respiratory rate, distance traveled, oxygen consumption.

Sensors are important components of the Internet of Things (IoT), which refers to the network of devices that are connected through software for better data exchange and information extraction. Sensors are used widely in healthcare industry with the aim to enhance healthcare quality, reduce costs, and improve access by patients (Yang et al., 2015). For example, sensors can be used to increase the intelligence of medical equipment, enhance the bedside and remote monitoring quality, and deliver data of vital signs and health factors, such as heart rate and parameters that fall outside of normal level. Especially, with the growth of aging population, the needs and demands of medical equipment with multiple sensors are increasing (Hu, Chen, Fan, & Wang, 2017). This medical equipment allows efficient monitoring for both inpatient and outpatient, thus enable reliable, real-time diagnostic results. Furthermore, this medical equipment can be used for monitoring chronic disease, postoperative care, and other cases that need ongoing followups such as asthmatics. A sensor-based product is developed to study conditions that may trigger an individual's asthma. The sensor is connected with a patient's rescue inhaler, and once the patient uses the inhaler, the sensor can send the location information based on GPS signals (Su et al., 2016).

Health IoT is a new field which is being explored. This is a new domain in which more updated or important information can be obtained for a refining analysis. It is increasingly becoming a part of home automation. For example, multiple sensors can be placed at multiple locations in the house which helps to determine the mood of the individual in the house. There is also a thing that the individual who keeps listening to a particular type of music will undergo some type of mental state which might be either good or bad (Boonstra et al., 2018). All of the devices which are part of the home can be connected using a common application which helps in posting and sharing the issues at home. It also helps in monitoring individuals who are rather depressed or affected by any mental disorders. Smart water bottles help in monitoring the levels of the water content in the body and help the individual in monitoring any issues.

Sensors are also used in analyzing eye movements for diagnosis of balance disorders by measuring physiological parameters during cardiopulmonary resuscitation. Some devices with sensors can keep tracking of insulin dosages and transmits the information to user's mobile phone application, eliminating the need for the patient to record it manually and helps in optimal diabetes management (Heintzman, 2016). Some other application examples include: sensors are used in examining the degree of tremor caused by certain diseases, electrical activity of the brain, early detection of breast tumors. They are helpful in chronic disease management by storing the data or readings in the cloud which are accessed by medical personnel, in cancer detection and monitoring.

Many wearable devices also consist of various sensors for healthcare purpose. For example, Apple's HealthKit can collect data from connected devices, and the Apple watch is used as a fitness device to automate the recording of medical metrics. Fitbit Aria can track users' weight and body fat percentage and upload the information to a cloud-based account (Inupakutika et al., 2018). Fitbit watches can gather health data a step further by detecting cancers or other illness signals and reporting the data. Hexoskin Biometric Shirt can monitor heart rate, respiratory rate, number of steps, distance traveled, pace, maximal oxygen consumption, and calories burned (Al Sayed, Vinches, & Hallé, 2017). The heath recording is transferred to the device by Bluetooth.

AT&T partnered with Clairvoyant networks in order to produce wearables regarding healthcare that can greatly benefit people suffering from cognitive diseases such as Alzheimer[1]. Theora Care is a smartwatch device developed by caregivers who know the fears of taking care of Alzheimer's patients. This device fitted with sensors when used sends the patient data over a secured AT&T network connection to the caregiver. If the patient strays outside the designated safe zone, this device can alert the caregiver and will allow for two way audio communications for patient care. The caregiver can have the peace of mind with the help of this device while allowing the patients to stay home as opposed to nursing homes or assisted living communities.

With all these applications and many more, sensor technology could prove to be the best way for making healthcare more affordable and accessible to everyone as these devices are giving patients more control over their health and knowledge about their diseases and symptoms thereby reducing the amount of time spent on medical procedures (Zhao et al., 2017). The medical experts can also have access to their patient's real-time information allowing them to provide care more efficiently. To sum up, for patients, it reduces the time and cost to get detailed tests results, and for hospitals, it improves the healthcare quality and efficiency.

CONCLUSION

With the increasing trend of healthcare big data, it is significant to collect and analyze the operational healthcare data for further implications. This chapter discusses sensor data, biomedical signals, and biomedical images as three types of healthcare data that can be collected from operations. It then describes various data mining and data analysis techniques to gain intelligence from these operational-level data. With a focus on the applications and impacts of sensor data mining in healthcare, this chapter shows the last step of the operations-intelligence-strategy (OIS) process, revealing the impact of big data in healthcare. The detailed information and summary in this chapter will facilitate readers' understanding of sensor data, biomedical signals, biomedical images and the analyses techniques of these types of data. By illustrating the OIS process in healthcare (see Figure 1), this chapter also provides practical implications for the big data-enabled value creation pathway in healthcare industry.

Figure 1. OIS process in healthcare

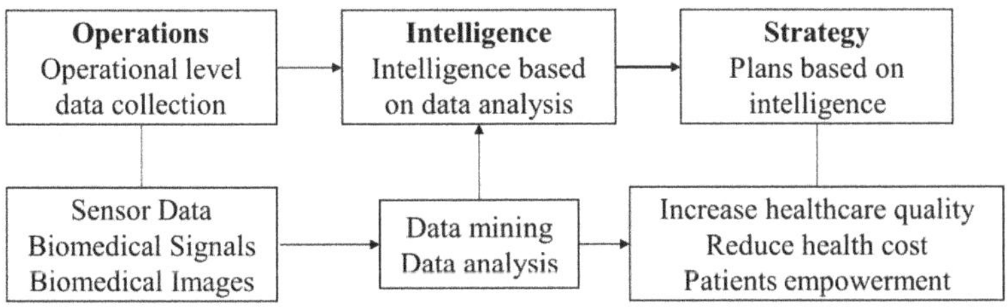

REFERENCES

Abdel-Khalek, S., Ishak, A. B., Omer, O. A., & Obada, A.-S. (2017). A two-dimensional image segmentation method based on genetic algorithm and entropy. *Optik (Stuttgart)*, *131*, 414–422. doi:10.1016/j.ijleo.2016.11.039

Al Sayed, C., Vinches, L., & Hallé, S. (2017). Validation of a wearable biometric system's ability to monitor heart rate in two different climate conditions under variable physical activities. *E-Health Telecommunication Systems and Networks*, *6*(02), 19–30. doi:10.4236/etsn.2017.62002

Avants, B. B., Tustison, N. J., Song, G., Cook, P. A., Klein, A., & Gee, J. C. (2011). A reproducible evaluation of ANTs similarity metric performance in brain image registration. *NeuroImage*, *54*(3), 2033–2044. doi:10.1016/j.neuroimage.2010.09.025 PMID:20851191

Baltzan, P. (2012). *Business driven technology*. McGraw-Hill/Irwin.

Benatar, A. (2017). The pediatric electrocardiogram. *Ann Cardiol Cardiovasc Dis*, *2*(1), 1009.

Boonstra, T. W., Nicholas, J., Wong, Q. J., Shaw, F., Townsend, S., & Christensen, H. (2018). Using mobile phone sensor technology for mental health research: Integrated analysis to identify hidden challenges and potential solutions. *Journal of Medical Internet Research*, *20*(7). doi:10.2196/10131 PMID:30061092

Bron, E. E., Smits, M., Niessen, W. J., & Klein, S. (2015). Feature selection based on the SVM weight vector for classification of dementia. *IEEE Journal of Biomedical and Health Informatics*, *19*(5), 1617–1626. doi:10.1109/JBHI.2015.2432832 PMID:25974958

Chen, H., Chiang, R. H., & Storey, V. C. (2012). Business intelligence and analytics: From big data to big impact. *Management Information Systems Quarterly*, *36*(4), 1165. doi:10.2307/41703503

Cohen, M. X. (2014). *Analyzing neural time series data: theory and practice*. Cambridge, MA: MIT Press. doi:10.7551/mitpress/9609.001.0001

Dargie, W., & Poellabauer, C. (2010). *Fundamentals of wireless sensor networks: theory and practice*. John Wiley & Sons. doi:10.1002/9780470666388

Darwish, A., & Hassanien, A. E. (2011). Wearable and implantable wireless sensor network solutions for healthcare monitoring. *Sensors (Basel)*, *11*(6), 5561–5595. doi:10.3390110605561 PMID:22163914

García, E., Oliver, A., Diez, Y., Diaz, O., Lladó, X., Martí, R., & Martí, J. (2017). Similarity metrics for intensity-based registration using breast density maps. In *Proceedings Iberian Conference on Pattern Recognition and Image Analysis*. 10.1007/978-3-319-58838-4_24

Hall, W. J., Chapman, M. V., Lee, K. M., Merino, Y. M., Thomas, T. W., Payne, B. K., ... Coyne-Beasley, T. (2015). Implicit racial/ethnic bias among health care professionals and its influence on health care outcomes: A systematic review. *American Journal of Public Health*, *105*(12), e60–e76. doi:10.2105/AJPH.2015.302903 PMID:26469668

Heintzman, N. D. (2016). A digital ecosystem of diabetes data and technology: Services, systems, and tools enabled by wearables, sensors, and apps. *Journal of Diabetes Science and Technology*, *10*(1), 35–41. doi:10.1177/1932296815622453 PMID:26685994

Hisham, M., Yaakob, S. N., Raof, R. A., Nazren, A. A., & Embedded, N. W. (2015). Template matching using sum of squared difference and normalized cross correlation. In *Proceedings 2015 IEEE Student Conference on Research and Development (SCOReD)*. 10.1109/SCORED.2015.7449303

Hore, S., Chakraborty, S., Chatterjee, S., Dey, N., Ashour, A. S., Van Chung, L., & Le, D.-N. (2016). An integrated interactive technique for image segmentation using stack based seeded region growing and thresholding. *International Journal of Electrical & Computer Engineering (2088-8708)*, *6*(6).

Hu, J.-X., Chen, C.-L., Fan, C.-L., & Wang, K.-H. (2017). An intelligent and secure health monitoring scheme using IoT sensor based on cloud computing. *Journal of Sensors*, 2017.

Ibrahim, A., Gannapathy, V., Chong, L., & Isa, I. (2016). Analysis of electromyography (EMG) signal for human arm muscle: A review. In Advanced Computer and Communication Engineering Technology (pp. 567-575): Springer.

Inupakutika, D., Natarajan, G. V., Kaghyan, S., Akopian, D., Evans, M., Zenong, Y., & Parra-Medina, D. (2018). An integration of health tracking sensor applications and elearning environments for cloud-based health promotion campaigns. *Electronic Imaging, 2018*(6), 1-8.

Kaçar, S., & Sakoğlu, Ü. (2016). Design of a novel biomedical signal processing and analysis tool for functional neuroimaging. *Computer Methods and Programs in Biomedicine, 125*, 46–57. doi:10.1016/j.cmpb.2015.11.011 PMID:26679001

Kaur, H., & Rajni, R. (2017). Electrocardiogram signal analysis for R-peak detection and denoising with hybrid linearization and principal component analysis. *Turkish Journal of Electrical Engineering and Computer Sciences, 25*(3), 2163–2175. doi:10.3906/elk-1604-84

Li, W., Xu, Y., Tan, B., & Piechocki, R. J. (2017). Passive wireless sensing for unsupervised human activity recognition in healthcare. In *Proceedings 2017 13th International Wireless Communications and Mobile Computing Conference (IWCMC)*. 10.1109/IWCMC.2017.7986511

Lobo, P., & Guruprasad, S. (2018). Classification and segmentation techniques for detection of lung cancer from CT images. In *Proceedings 2018 International Conference on Inventive Research in Computing Applications (ICIRCA)*. 10.1109/ICIRCA.2018.8597273

Mariscal, G., Marban, O., & Fernandez, C. (2010). A survey of data mining and knowledge discovery process models and methodologies. *The Knowledge Engineering Review, 25*(2), 137–166. doi:10.1017/S0269888910000032

Mitra, S., & Shankar, B. U. (2015). Medical image analysis for cancer management in natural computing framework. *Information Sciences, 306*, 111–131. doi:10.1016/j.ins.2015.02.015

Ngoepe, M., Choonara, Y., Tyagi, C., Tomar, L., Du Toit, L., Kumar, P., ... Pillay, V. (2013). Integration of biosensors and drug delivery technologies for early detection and chronic management of illness. *Sensors (Basel), 13*(6), 7680–7713. doi:10.3390130607680 PMID:23771157

Nie, L., Wang, M., Zhang, L., Yan, S., Zhang, B., & Chua, T. S. (2015). Disease inference from health-related questions via sparse deep learning. *IEEE Transactions on Knowledge and Data Engineering, 27*(8), 2107–2119. doi:10.1109/TKDE.2015.2399298

Padfield, D. R., Mendonça, P. R., & Gupta, S. (2015). *Biomedical image analysis.*

Piliouras, T. C., Suss, R. J., & Yu, P. L. (2015). Digital imaging & electronic health record systems: Implementation and regulatory challenges faced by healthcare providers. In *Proceedings 2015 Long Island Systems, Applications and Technology*. 10.1109/LISAT.2015.7160179

Pirpinia, K., Bosman, P. A., Loo, C. E., Winter-Warnars, G., Janssen, N. N., Scholten, A. N., ... Alderliesten, T. (2017). The feasibility of manual parameter tuning for deformable breast MR image registration from a multi-objective optimization perspective. *Physics in Medicine and Biology*, *62*(14), 5723–5743. doi:10.1088/1361-6560/aa6edc PMID:28436922

Prabhu, R., & Khan, A. (2017). *A study of bio-medical image registration algorithms.*

Raghupathi, W., & Raghupathi, V. (2014). Big data analytics in healthcare: promise and potential. *Health information science and systems, 2*(1), 3.

Riegler, G., Urschler, M., Ruther, M., Bischof, H., & Stern, D. (2015). Anatomical landmark detection in medical applications driven by synthetic data. In *Proceedings of the IEEE International Conference on Computer Vision Workshops*. 10.1109/ICCVW.2015.21

Russakoff, D. B., Tomasi, C., Rohlfing, T., & Maurer, C. R. (2004). Image similarity using mutual information of regions. In *Proceedings European Conference on Computer Vision*. 10.1007/978-3-540-24672-5_47

Schindelin, J., Rueden, C. T., Hiner, M. C., & Eliceiri, K. W. (2015). The ImageJ ecosystem: An open platform for biomedical image analysis. *Molecular Reproduction and Development*, *82*(7-8), 518–529. doi:10.1002/mrd.22489 PMID:26153368

Senthilkumaran, N., & Vaithegi, S. (2016). Image segmentation by using thresholding techniques for medical images. *Computer Science & Engineering: An International Journal*, *6*(1), 1–13.

Sharma, G., & Kumar, K. (2017). Acceleration of images via software and hardware using proprietary tools & open sources for healthcare industry. *International Journal of Image, Graphics, and Signal Processing*, *9*(7), 10–22. doi:10.5815/ijigsp.2017.07.02

Shen, D., Wu, G., & Suk, H.-I. (2017). Deep learning in medical image analysis. *Annual Review of Biomedical Engineering*, *19*(1), 221–248. doi:10.1146/annurev-bioeng-071516-044442 PMID:28301734

Shi, J., Jiang, Q., Zhang, Q., Huang, Q., & Li, X. (2015). Sparse kernel entropy component analysis for dimensionality reduction of biomedical data. *Neurocomputing*, *168*, 930–940. doi:10.1016/j.neucom.2015.05.032

Sow, D., Turaga, D. S., & Schmidt, M. (2013). Mining of sensor data in healthcare: A survey. In *Managing and mining sensor data* (pp. 459–504). Springer. doi:10.1007/978-1-4614-6309-2_14

Su, J. G., Barrett, M. A., Henderson, K., Humblet, O., Smith, T., Sublett, J. W., ... Sublett, J. L. (2016). Feasibility of deploying inhaler sensors to identify the impacts of environmental triggers and built environment factors on asthma short-acting bronchodilator use. *Environmental Health Perspectives*, *125*(2), 254–261. doi:10.1289/EHP266 PMID:27340894

Varatharajan, R., Manogaran, G., Priyan, M. K., & Sundarasekar, R. (2018). Wearable sensor devices for early detection of Alzheimer disease using dynamic time warping algorithm. *Cluster Computing*, *21*(1), 681–690. doi:10.100710586-017-0977-2

Vidaurre, D., Quinn, A. J., Baker, A. P., Dupret, D., Tejero-Cantero, A., & Woolrich, M. W. (2016). Spectrally resolved fast transient brain states in electrophysiological data. *NeuroImage*, *126*, 81–95. doi:10.1016/j.neuroimage.2015.11.047 PMID:26631815

White, M. (2012). Digital workplaces: Vision and reality. *Business Information Review*, *29*(4), 205–214. doi:10.1177/0266382112470412

Yang, J.-J., Li, J., Mulder, J., Wang, Y., Chen, S., Wu, H., ... Pan, H. (2015). Emerging information technologies for enhanced healthcare. *Computers in Industry*, *69*, 3–11. doi:10.1016/j.compind.2015.01.012

Yong, X., Ward, R. K., & Birch, G. E. (2008). *Robust common spatial patterns for EEG signal preprocessing*. Paper presented at the 2008 30th Annual International Conference of the IEEE Engineering in Medicine and Biology Society.

Zhang, S., Breitner, S., Cascio, W. E., Devlin, R. B., Neas, L. M., Diaz-Sanchez, D., ... Peters, A. (2018). Short-term effects of fine particulate matter and ozone on the cardiac conduction system in patients undergoing cardiac catheterization. *Particle and Fibre Toxicology*, *15*(1), 38. doi:10.118612989-018-0275-z PMID:30305173

Zhao, Y., Parvinzamir, F., Wilson, S., Wei, H., Deng, Z., Portokallidis, N., ... Dong, F. (2017). Integrated visualisation of wearable sensor data and risk models for individualised health monitoring and risk assessment to promote patient empowerment. *Journal of Visualization / the Visualization Society of Japan*, *20*(2), 405–413. doi:10.100712650-016-0402-6

ENDNOTE

1 https://theoracare.com/clairvoyant-teams-with-att-on-new-wearable-for-alzheimers/

Chapter 5
Generation and Management of Data for Healthcare and Health Diagnostics

Ramalatha Marimuthu
Kumaraguru College of Technology, India

Shivappriya S. N.
Kumaraguru College of Technology, India

Saroja M. N.
Kumaraguru College of Technology, India

ABSTRACT

Healthcare Analytics deals with patient records, effective management of hospitals, and clinical care. But the big data available is still not enough for focused research as it is complicated to find insights from complex, noisy, heterogeneous, and voluminous data, which takes time and effort, while a small clinical data will be more effective for decision making. The health care data also varies in data collection methods and their processing methods. Data generated through patient records is structured, wearable technologies generate semi structured data, and X rays and images provide unstructured data. Storing and extracting information from the structured, semi-structured, and unstructured data is a challenging task. Different machine learning techniques can simplify the process. The chapter discusses the data characteristics, identifying critical attributes, various classification and optimization algorithms for decision making purposes. The purpose of the discussion is to create a basis for selection of algorithms based on size, temporal validity, and outcomes expected.

DOI: 10.4018/978-1-7998-2310-0.ch005

INTRODUCTION

Healthcare has become an important and interesting field of study in recent years with introducing "Big Data". Despite the money paid on healthcare, the number of health-related mortalities is still at an alarming high-level and steadily increasing. The exponential increase in the number and variety of health care centers equals the rate of increase in the exploding population. From small one man clinics to a vast chain of hospitals and nursing homes, the increase in these establishments shows an increase in the number of issues in healthcare. Diseases and Disorders are increasing recently and created a booming business for hospitals. Changes in the way of living, lack of alimentary food, environmental degradation, diagnosis and consumption of medicines while not steering are major reasons for this increase. But nature and the huge unfold of the causes across disciplines produce an outsized quantity of data. Studying these data becomes difficult owing to the complexity, volume as well as the variety of the data.

Healthcare expenses are the highest ever in developed economies like the USA. Around 95% of the money spent is for personal direct medical care services and only a meager amount goes to mass approaches for health care improvement. This shows the attention the health care improvement is drawing from the society. Increasing the lifetime of an individual is important for healthcare. Here,history is an important source since it helps us to see the present and future. Healthcare data helps in predicting epidemics or issues with lifestyle changes.

The healthcare industry has experienced a drastic shift with developing technology. Also, there is a pattern shift in the healthcare industry from knowledge-based care to value-based care. Adapting the technology changes does not happen as the changes occur often than learning. According to Tom Burton, the President of Professional Services, USA, the healthcare industry is people-oriented rather than process-oriented. This led in the working style of the cottage industry. Healthcare quality relies on location and individuals and not technological progress. But to provide systematic and standardized healthcare, it is often necessary to strengthen the knowledge base and the training methods of the healthcare personnel. Clinical effectiveness is not the only issue, but to provide value-based care, it is necessary to reduce the waste and patient safety bringing us to the importance of the data analytics. With these variants, healthcare analytics have taken many forms, shapes, and sizes, thus complicating the issue more. The various methods of data analysis will require various forms of data as discussed by John Haughaom et .al (2014) and Russ Staheli (2014).

Data Analytics in Healthcare plays a major role in finding out diseases, predicting epidemics, spreading awareness as well as finding new cures. According to a 2014 IDC (International Data Corporation) report, the volume of healthcare data in 2013 was 153 exabytes -- one exabyte equals a billion gigabytes. That number is projected to skyrocket to 2,314 exabytes by 2020. Research Studies evident that the big data available is still not enough for focused research. Learning by generating data from small groups is required. The conclusion is Big data alone is not enough, a small clinical data will be more effective for decision making. The most wanted decisions right now in healthcare involve providing personalized health care through the right intervention to the right patient at the right time.

The data produced through healthcare, not only helps in proper diagnosis but also helps in managing hospitals, the insurance field and pharmacy where Business Intelligence comes into play. The healthcare data can be used to ensure doctor's availability, scheduling the admission time for patients, patient record maintenance and report generation. Healthcare Prediction deals with preventing disease at an earlier stage thereby reducing the medical cost which will benefit the insurance sector. Analytics on Healthcare data from sensors helps in the accurate diagnosis of diseases. E-healthcare applications and mobile applications are used for collecting real-time information from patients.

Healthcare data is either in the form of sensor data (small data) and Electronics -Health Record data (Big Data). Recently, wearable technologies generate a wide range of semi-structured data. Apart from the clinical data collected from the patients, modern technologies help in collecting real-time data through sensors and wearables. The wearable gadgets improve the enthusiastic connection between the system and individuals. Accurate results are gathered using those gadgets. Data formed through patient records are structured and it can be stored easily. Storing unstructured data such as x-ray images, MRI and CT scans is difficult. Processing it is more complex. Sensors and wearable gadgets create semi-structured data. Storing and Extracting information from the available structured, semi-structured and unstructured data is a challenging task.

A Business Intelligence system has to decide the way of organization of data and managing the enormous amount of it. Interpreting and adapting the two major types of Big and small data, and hybridization of those data is classified as diagnosis data. Intervention data is a combination of diagnosis data and patient history. The patient's vital signs and the precise medical reason for the disease can be recognized and linked using various extraction features and selection methods. Optimization methods are used to define the main characteristics of the dataset based on the nature of the information either derivative or derivative-free. The advanced optimization approaches like stochastic programming, evolutionary algorithms such as genetic algorithm, bio-inspired algorithms such as swarm intelligence are used to map the exact symptom of the disease. The healthcare expert system uses the intervention data formed through sensors. The Expert System identifies the insights of the regular and common illnesses and the prerequisite of medication. Distinct machine learning techniques like supervised, unsupervised, reinforcement and regression algorithms relates patient's therapeutic features with their illnesses. At first, preparing the expert system with the huge information will progress the classification and prediction accuracy.

Linear Regression, Logistic Regression, Linear Discriminant Analysis, Classification and Regression Tree, Naive Bayes, K-Nearest Neighbors, Learning Vector Quantization, Support Vector Machines are a few of the prediction techniques utilized in both big as well as small data. These methods can be used to foresee patient's essential signs and their diseases, which forms the educational data. Doctors can use this information in connecting the therapeutic records with the right illness. This will raise the expert system's accuracy and reduce the number of false alarms.

The Business Intelligence system comprising of data analytics and Machine learning (DA & ML) will provide accurate detection of disease and integrate the relationship of symptoms with the disease. This will be helpful for the physicians to relate the patient symptoms to diagnose the unpredictable diseases with the proposed DA & ML techniques. This chapter brings in an overall view of the big data, their characteristics, pertaining to generation and storage methods, identifying critical attributes for decision-making purposes, analysing the various data characteristics, comparing the big data and small data and discusses the various algorithms and tools used for analysing them.

DATA COLLECTION AND PREPROCESSING

The health care data can be classified into various types like diagnosis data, intervention data, and educational data. Laboratory, Radiology and Electronic record data from patients form the diagnosis data. This will provide the details on symptoms of the ailments, parameters like vital signs of the patients and previous treatments undergone. The physicist can use it to decide the real state of the patients, the degree to which they are influenced and the medications to be given.

The treatments given and the treatments already experienced by the patient, and the general vaccination welfare systems will form the intervention data.This will provide a comprehensive chart of the interventions effective for both common and seasonal diseases. The data from different patients need to be organized and integrated to map the diseases and interventions.

Figure 1. General classification of the healthcare data

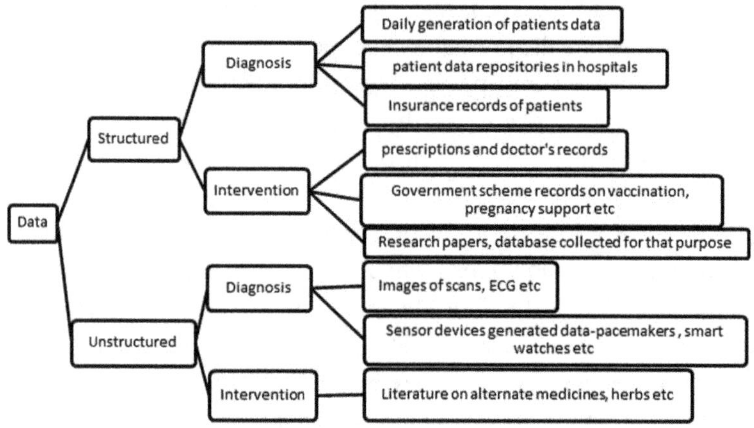

The organized data gained from the diagnosis and intervention provide the researchers with educational data for discovering new interventions and drugs. The results that can be pictured for the examination that expands upon this composed information can be to discover the nearness of illness, both existing and new, deciding how genuine it is and whether an enormous level intercession is required or not. The outcome of the educational database is to help in disease predictions and identify the non-treatable disease.This will help in seasonal epidemics preparation with resource improvement. This will also enable to improve research in health care by identifying new challenges and opportunities.

Figure 1 shows the broad classification of possible healthcare data. It is obvious structured data is available for the analysts to utilize. But the data is in the form of raw data and not having a uniform structure. So data mining steps need to be performed before we go in for analytical solutions. Transforming raw data into information involves three steps-data capture, information supply, and data analytics.

Data Capture

Data that is to be captured will be impacted by the people, processes, and devices that generate data. The sources of the data are not always digitized making the collection and storage of data in the desired format difficult. This also creates a multitude of issues like redundancy, lack of appropriateness, difficulty in extraction which will filter out to the next stages and renders the analytics solutions inefficient. The data are coming from various sources, which leads to much ambiguity in the decision-making system. To overcome this, pre-processing has to be well planned so that the subsequent steps will be error-free (Lee et al., 2017)

The digitized data can be broadly classified as EMR records and sensor data. Further, EMR data can be classified based on data attributes, source of data, age of the data and purpose of the data. For example, the EMR records for the diagnosis will contain the patient's medical history, present ailment, diagnosis details, observation period and the treatments taken. The patient's billing records will contain the prescriptions given and the dosages administered along with the period of observation. Although this will contain the prescriptions and dosages, the exact treatment given will not be available, however the data overlaps with the diagnostic records, such as observation period and expert visits.The age of the data is important when finding out best practices for treating certain diseases is going on. The updated data along with the periodical data will provide a basis for educational data.

However, EMR data are often unstructured data converted into structured ones since the major part of the data is manually entered. The attributes of the data will be varied and often incomplete since the data is collected over a long period of time. This also gives rise to the problem of high dimension with a large number of features increasing the probability of noise and complexity. These EMR information will be better suited as a knowledge repository for education and research. But the main difficulties are to identify the particular characteristics necessary for a health problem and to interpret the information to provide a customized solution. So, this data should be treated as a collection from which, for specific end goals, the needed partial data can be removed. The various analytical steps such as cleaning, storage and interpretation can be performed to provide an end-to-end solution.For example, a physician who wishes to get a solution for a current epidemic of seasonal ailments can take out the data for that purpose alone. But if a large scale end to end solution is required for the hospital to find out the need for additional infrastructure, a long term data study on the utilization of the current infrastructure, patient's feedback on the status of the infrastructure and suggestions for improvements will help provide the directions to the decision-makers.

On the other hand, sensor data indicates the technological advancement in the field of healthcare data analytics. The data capturing from sensors vary in structure and functionality since the sources vary from independent devices to IoT based devices, wearables to large immovable equipment and computer connected to mobile devices. The advantage of the sensor data is that it is structured, captured in real-time and does not require much human interference for capturing. By its own heterogeneity, it has become an important and valuable source for expanding healthcare in various platforms like remote monitoring, instant emergency handling, and even remote healthcare. For example, smartwatches can measure the vital signs of the patients and can transfer the real-time data to the healthcare provider through the cloud instantaneously. This will help chronic patients to get advice from their healthcare provider based on real-time data. Many emergency situations can be prevented by monitoring a patient's vital signs and proposing alternatives without requiring the patient's physical presence to save many retrospectively life and money (Reddy & Aggarwal, 2015).

Although data analytics in healthcare is increasing unprecedently, there is still a non-negligible gap to bridge if we are to realize its real potential. A simple look at the healthcare costs of the developed countries can offer the feeling that although the healthcare system has improved significantly, it has also failed to deliver the expected return on investment. And growth in healthcare spending is impacting the spending on other categories like education and infrastructure development for the country.

One solution to reduce the inefficiency is to create a data warehouse for healthcare. Both structured as well as unstructured data can be appropriately stored and checked for the above issues periodically. Many hospitals and healthcare centres are digitizing their data moving towards effective health analytics solutions. The daily generation of patient data is therefore recorded in a structured format. Insurance records will contain valuable data that will be separately available. Since the data is structured, the only requirement for the analyst is to capture and map the data, and create the data warehouse.

Apart from these methods of data capture, various researchers capture data on a focused basis pertaining to their area of research. The most important method is the survey conducted with the stakeholders to collect data required for their research. The data collected will be organized and processed according to their requirements but the data set may contain relevant data for the already collected records of a patient or a disease. For example, a hospital can keep records of hundreds of pregnant women with and without health complications, but they may not be sufficient for a researcher exploring complications during labor, as this will involve both personal and clinical data. Hospitals usually store the clinical data but when it comes to personal data with respect to the factors affecting the health of the woman, like her family relationships, her career-related anxiety, financial anxiety, etc, it is usually not available. These can be collected from women who are attending the hospitals but it is also challenging in the sense that women usually do not want to disclose such information. So a one to one interview and personal surveys would be more effective. This database is usually ignored but as per the case study has given later, this is more effective.

Data Provisioning

Data provisioning or arrangement is the next step which requires multiple source data to be collected, arranged, modified and manipulated according to the outcomes expected. For various needs and requirements, the analysts arrange the available data into a meaningful format and extract the outcome. Aggregating the data from various sources into one location is a mammoth process since the fidelity of the data has to be ensured while the expense has to be reduced. The cost of the data varies with the number of sources from which it is accumulated and the lifetime of the data. Multiple sources include sensor data, survey data, clinical observation data, billing data, and patient satisfaction data. The goal is to provide access to the analysts to build, break, rebuild and test the data according to the outcomes required. More details are discussed about the Data Provisioning later in the chapter.

Data Analytics

Before we invest in an analytics solution, the goal of the analytics solution should be clearly defined - to improve the quality of healthcare and reduce the cost. All further problems and pitfalls that may set in are to be addressed by the analyst before the solution is developed. This will reduce the waste and the inefficiencies that may set in after a period of usage (Wadsworth, 2017).

Often it has been seen that the data analytics process developed in an organization to serve a certain purpose will not sustain the period intended since the requirements of the customers change during the time and the process will need enhancements. Even if the enhancements are implemented on the base software, the software will withstand the enhancements only up to a limit. After that, the software has to be scrapped and new software put in. More often than not, the lack of vision on the management is the major drawback for this sad state of affairs. Having a long term strategic plan with concrete goals in mind will help.

One more consideration is the training on the technology developed to be deployed to the end-user. Many organizations think that creating a good software tool for analytics is the only step that is most important. But if the staff who will be using the tool are not properly trained to use it, the tool will not be incorporated into the organisation that will impact the longevity of the use of the tool.Frequent feedback on the positive and negative aspects of the tool should also be communicated to the designer to optimize the workflow.

Optimization of the Data

Despite the inherent issues and complexities found in the usage of big data in healthcare, it is evident that outcome-based analytics will save a lot of money in the sector. For that, the data captured should be tested and kept updated. It is often found that data quality is a big issue with big data. The reason is that the data has multiple sources and they lack the format to be mapped directly. It is a time consuming and error-prone task to integrate them. But the population oriented health management

Table 1. SWOT Analysis

S.No	Data Resources	Strengths	Weaknesses	Opportunities	Threats
1.	EMR data	Electronic data Real-time values Patient-wise record Can be used to study a pattern of the diseases	Unstructured Interpretation can vary Collation of data may be difficult	Can be collected to provide structured data A potential research area in treatment and interpretation	Expensive to interpret Less accuracy Availability of previous records
2.	Sensor data	Electronic data Real-Time values Record of a particular attribute Can be used to monitor a particular patient	Needs continuous internet and power connectivity Needs continuous proximity to the patients Failure of sensors results in discontinuity. A very high volume of data	Can be used to identify similarities between symptoms Potential big data resource for research	Reliability on continuity of data is less The high percentage of redundancy
3.	Prescription, insurance, and billing data	Can provide information on ongoing trend in diagnosis, medication, and treatment Can provide collective information on the patient's health history	A large amount of data may not be used Manual entering is required Error-prone system A large amount of peripheral data	Can be used to analyze requirements in infrastructure Can provide a direction on cost trend of healthcare	May be used in creating unethical practices Too many unreliable sources make verification of data difficult
4.	Data collection through survey and feedback	First-hand data on best practices Voice of the customer for data collection and decision making	Mostly unstructured Interpretation can vary Collation of data may be difficult	Can be used for improvements and research Focused data collection making analysis simple	May be used in creating unethical practices Contradiction with previous data and practices possible
5.	Research data collected through various means	Focused on the particular issue making interpretation easy First hand and real-time data	A weak questionnaire or interviewer may generate wrong data Narrow database with the possibility of missed data	Best practices across the world on the particular issue available Can act as a base for further research to solve a related bigger issue	Manipulation and unethical practices possible Contradictions may provide confusion which may create dangerous practices

system needs to know how to optimize the big data where the essential requirements are met and the analysts are able to pull out the required data quickly (Staheli, 2016).

Hence it is obvious that before utilizing the big data in health care, a SWOT analysis can provide better insights into the challenges and suggest solutions. The following Table 1 explains some of the strengths, weaknesses, opportunities, and threats of using the data from various resources for healthcare analytics.

The SWOT analysis takes only the type of data for the analysis but can be extended to the collection methods, processing, etc. From the above, it is possible for the technologists to find ways of eliminating the threats and weaknesses and enhancing the strengths before building the model.

COLLECTION AND PREPROCESSING OF DATA

While developing a prediction model, many issues and factors need to be addressed to keep quality and norms as life is at stake here. Even for an issue that is not so extreme and life-threatening, the faulty prediction can lead to new complications and problems that can permanently affect the patient's health. This shows the importance of quality in building a predictive healthcare model. The first stage is to guarantee the patient data collected is correct and can be used for prediction.

But ensuring the data collected is correct and in the usable form poses many challenges and some are addressed here. The Challenges involved are

1. How to collect all the necessary data from the patients and store it?
2. How to handle the missing data in the Electronic Health Record (EHR)?
3. Selection of features from the EHR
4. How to deal with unstructured data?
5. How to pre-process images?
6. Gathering and manipulating sensor data
7. Finally, how to integrate all the available data for model building

Let us address the challenges one by one.

Collecting and Storing Data From Patients

Russ Staheli, MPH (2016), addresses the various issues associated with collecting data for healthcare is depicted in Figure 2. Jing Lu, Alan Hales, David Rew, Malcolm Keech (2016), discussed the issues and data mining techniques for preprocessing the clinical data. Hospitals used to collect the patients' detail during admission. The medication data can be collected through billing. Specialists will be suggested in multi-specialty hospitals based on the symptoms pointed out by the individuals. There is no standard method to collect data. A single man clinic will collect only minimal data when compared with multi-specialty hospital data. In both, medical records will be in different for mats. Report maintenance will be different. Insurance providers will need some other data. To match all this stuff, it is important to standardize data gathering to make the information useful for global healthcare studies.

The second important thing for data collection is the person, from whom the data is collected. The data on symptoms and ailment will be collected from the patient. But, he is not a medical expert to provide the information in technical terms. If the same is collected from the caregiver (the person who is accompanying the patient and again may not be a medical expert), it may not be precise. The caregiver never knows about the patient's comfort. So exact data will not be available with both the cases. When a medical practitioner observes, the reasons behind the symptoms will be given from a medical perspective and recorded. Not all the above said data will match accurately not will they be very comprehensive and complete.

The third thing is how much data is being collected? Is it continuous? Is the quantity of data small or big? A small group of patient data needs to be analyzed for personalized medicine whereas big data needs to be analyzed for generalized medicine.

The fourth thing is the repetition of data. Collecting the same personal details everytime from patients will irritate them. A proper mechanism should be followed for storing, searching and retrieval of data.

The last thing is collecting data through sensors. Wearables are created to monitor chronic patients or elderly people on a regular basis. Data is being collected from sensors present in the wearables all day and stored. Analyzing which data needs to be stored is another issue that will be dealt with later in this section.

Besides all these issues, patients must be truthful in exchanging all the necessary information with medical personnel and professionals. Sometimes, the patients hide some of the conditions or symptoms which may lead to complications later. Data collected through these mechanisms from patients form the diagnosis data. Besides the diagnosis data, the treatments given to the patients are recorded which form the intervention data.

Once the data needed from patients is collected, how to store it? Each organization will have its own server or mechanism to store data. But it that enough? It is important to have a common platform to store so that it can be accessed for diagnosis easily. Data produced from EHR, CT and MRI scans, x-rays, sensors are in different forms. Also, the amount of data generated by the world population is enormous. To support all, it is important to store data in the cloud as the growth of data is exponential. The cloud server also offers safety so patient's privacy is not affected. To make

Figure 2. Issues to be considered for data collection

the data usable, it is important to use artificial intelligence and machine learning techniques to retrieve the data.

Handling Missing Data in EHR

The major reason behind missing data in EHR is the inefficiency in the data conversion. Patients may not be able to clearly articulate their symptoms and may not be aware of the medical terminologies. Staff getting information from such people must be patient enough to gather information. Another reason is the hesitation to provide symptoms by the patients for privacy reasons. While collecting data from surveys, people may not fill the optional attributes. We cannot avoid such situations. Providing mandatory fields may make the survey more effective but too many questions may lessen the inclination to take the survey.

Marina Soley, (2013) shows the various methods for handling missing data. Complete case analysis and mutation methods are suitable for handling missing data. Complete case analysis is the method of removing the tuple with missing data and keeping all other tuples. This may not be suitable, as every person will hide some information and so, there is a possibility of having missing data in all tuples.

Available case analysis handles missing data by generating different models with the available subset of values. By supplying weights to the available data based on their importance, a weighted model for replacing missing values can be done. Imputation methods are also available for retaining the data.

As healthcare data is very sensitive, common techniques such as replacing the missing data with backfill and forward fill methods will not be suitable as patients and their symptoms may differ. Filling with mean, median and mode values is also not suitable. The best approach is to replace the most probable value. But how do we find the most probable value? The first method is to select the similar cases and replace the missing value from them. The second method is to predict the missing value using the regression algorithm. The latter approach is most suited for healthcare data

Selection of Features From EHR

Different approaches such as feature selection, feature reduction and extraction techniques for selecting data from a specific dataset are available. Electronic Health Record (EHR) consists of wide variety of patient information such as patient name, gender, age, lab test records, patient characteristics, etc. Not all the information will be required for predicting disease. Feature selection selects only the relevant features and not all the features. This will also reduce the dimensionality of the healthcare data. Feature Selection uses both filter and wrapper methods, but the simplest is the filter method. Shreyal Gajare et al discussed feature selection from EHR data in which only the needed features are chosen.

Only a small distinction in feature values will predict the disease in medical information, i.e. attributes that occur together are necessary for prediction. Association mining is one of the appropriate techniques for selecting the important features from healthcare data.

For predicting dipredicting women, which is caused by insulin deficiency the following attributes have been considered in the PIMA dataset. (Smith et al., 1988)

1. History record of previous pregnancies
2. Plasma glucose concentration level
3. Blood pressure
4. Skin thickness
5. 2-hour serum insulin
6. Body mass index
7. Diabetespedigree function
8. Age

In an EHR of a patient, along with this information much, more information will be present. Feature Selection reduces the big data available into a lesser amount of data that can help in improving the prediction accuracy.

Dealing With Unstructured Data

Extracting information from unstructured data like a prescription of the doctors, clinical notes, etc is much more challenging. Normally, unstructured data will be transformed into a structured one manually for extracting information. The human resources required and the cost of this transformation is high. The Electronic Health Record consumes memory in kilobytes as it is structured, whereas clinical notes require a lot of memory. It is also difficult to process.

To automate the process of data extraction from clinical notes text, Natural Language Processing (NLP) can be adopted. NLP uses artificial intelligence techniques to extract meaningful information. Character Recognition, Pattern Recognition and Speech Recognition methods help in converting and mapping the data in EHR. Character Recognition helps in identifying letters from clinical notes, nursing notes, etc. Pattern recognition helps to identify patterns from Biomedical signals. Speech Recognition helps to convert the doctor's prescription directly to the text.

Pre-Processing the Images

X-rays, CT scan, mammography, radiology images, MRI scans play a vital role in the prediction of disease. Sometimes, the pregnancy-related video will also be present for detecting the movement of an embryo. The available images have to be enhanced during the pre-processing stage.

Image pre-processing involves image conversion, filtering of noises and image enhancement. The first stage involves the conversion of images to grayscale format as processing color information will take more time and unnecessary. The grayscale image is then resized and stored.

Noise removal techniques are applied to remove unwanted image variations. Salt and Pepper noise is used to remove the unwanted white and black pixels present in an image. Gaussian noise or Poisson noise is based on the probability density function. Speckle noise is a granular noise, which makes the interpretation to be difficult. Median Filter, Weiner Filter, Gaussian-filtering techniques are used to remove those noises.

Object detection and Image Segmentation techniques are used for template matching, identifying region growing in case of cancer tissues and other applications. Spatial Domain and Frequency domain enhancement techniques can be used to enhance the images for processing.

Sensor Data Processing

Sensors have a wide variety of applications in healthcare such as activity monitoring, intensive care monitoring, monitoring in operation rooms. Wearable sensors are used for activity monitoring. The data collection and processing from a sensor is a challenging task owing to various reasons as given below.

Sensors have a limited capacity of storage and it is important to transfer the data to the cloud using protocols. Bluetooth can be used to transfer the data from a sensor to a local device and then WiFi can be used to store the data to cloud in case of activity monitoring. Fall detection is an important research area in this field. The rapid change in the patient's behavior has to be monitored time to time. If a fall is detected, immediately it has to be informed to the caretakers, neighbors, and hospitals. The response time for this type of application must be very minimal owing to the severity of the situation.

Similarly, an intensive care unit has to be monitored using a temperature sensor. Any abrupt rise in temperature has to be detected and corrected.

With sensors, digital and analog output can be generated and the values can be easily collected.The main issue with the use of sensors is how to store the data. The local device has to be switched on all the time. If power failure occurs, the local device cannot transfer data. Energy efficiency is one of the most important things when sensors are considered.

Ingestible sensors are available for healthcare for monitoring the activities of various body parts. But harvesting energy for such applications is much challenging because of the proximity to the body. Real-time constraints are more in the case of such sensors.

Johannes Schobel, Rüdiger Pryss, Marc Schickler, Manfred Reichert (2016), discussed the usage of mobile devices for data collection in healthcare. They also discussed about the different scenarios of mobile data collection.

Integration of Data for Modelling

The pre-processing techniques available for various forms of data have been discussed earlier. The key challenge is how to integrate all the available data. Data integration has to be done both at the hospital level and at the global level. D. J. Berndt, J. W. Fisher, A. R. Hevner, J. Studnicki (2001) presented the unique challenges in maintaining a data warehouse for healthcare system.

At the hospital level, for each patient record, sensor data, image data, and EHR have to be integrated. At the global level, the records from various establishments are to be integrated. This helps to improve the research in the field of medical sciences. To achieve the real potential of the big data, all the data available in various healthcare centers and hospitals at the global level are to be integrated by creating data warehouses which form the education data. If an epidemic arises in a particular region, the causes for that can be easily analyzed if the data is available and accessible anywhere.

DATA FUSION AS PRE CLASSIFIER

Raw data may be in any form collected from various sources and may contain noise and many anomalies and outliers. The outliers may be the exact anomaly or it may not be the required information that can only be identified by training the network with more data sets. There is a possibility of missing some information in some places in the continuous data recording process that has to be replaced using average data.

Before moving to the classification method, information preprocessing and standardization are required. Due to the variability in the nature of the information sets, adding the data sets directly to the classifier model increases the false alarms and the complexity of the classifier. These artifacts, anomalies, and outliers should be used to solve these issues properly denoising and feature extraction methods. Choosing the right characteristics will enhance the precision of the classification and also reduce the complexity.

The following feature selection techniques will suit for the big and small data sets:

- Peak analysis
- Pulse and transition metrics
- Spectral measurements
- Bag of visual words
- Histogram of oriented gradients (HOG)
- Minimum eigenvalue algorithm
- Edge detection
- Timestamp decomposition
- Aggregate value calculation

Previous sections show different data collection and pre-processing techniques. Ramalatha Marimuthuct ct al. (2019) shows the purpose of going to Machine learning techniques is to handle the big datasets. When the size of the data set increases, it will also increase the complexity. To face these challenges, the feature reduction technique plays a vital role. Dimensionality reduction plays an important role to get the predominant features from the available data set.

Some of the feature reduction techniques are:

- Principal component analysis (PCA) — It is the method of dimension reduction and decreases the big dataset to a smaller size but retains most of the data.
- Linear Discriminant Analysis (LDA) — Maximizes the inter-class separation, which is a generalization of Fisher's Linear Discrimination Approach.
- Factor analysis—identifies correlations of variables in the dataset to provide representation in terms of a smaller number of unobserved latent, or common, factors.
- Independent Component Analysis (ICA) — If the subcomponents are non-Gussian in nature and also autonomous from each other, then this computing technique is more appropriate to separate a multivariate signal into additive subcomponents.
- Nonnegative matrix factorization — used for components of such as physical and nonnegative quantities.

The features which have a higher correlation of class information are extracted first followed by training on the features with the class label. Then the data without class labels are entered into the testing process. These data are considered as diagnosis data that are used for classification of diseases.

The data which are used for prediction of diseases are called intervention data, also named as Pervasive healthcare data. Providing improved services for the increasing population is a challenge that can be met with recent wireless technologies. Based on this we can say pervasive computing is the future of healthcare services with improved coverage and quality. Social media can also provide vast data with their variable symptoms concerning multiple illnesses if data can be properly collected. Information retrieval - supervised, semi-supervised and unsupervised is expected to be an important step in health care data analytics. Where signs, symptoms, laboratory records and other clinical data for a particular patient's situation are fed into the Dxplains and Quick Medical Reference (QMR). These web-based clinical support system or expert system offers ranked differential diagnoses for most illnesses, whether rare or common.

Jane B (1999) states that knowledge base enhancement is used to enhance the success rate of QMR. Peter L. Elkin (2010) demonstrates that expert systems like DXplain are helpful sources of understanding for clinicians. There is a growing need for clinicians to understand each day, so the need for instruments to provide high-quality, patient-specific data continues to develop just when it is most helpful. Bauer BA, (2002) shows DXplain, a web-based clinical diagnostic decision support system to provide more accurate, patient-specific information to assist clinicians in their best practice efforts.

Nowadays wearable sensors play an important role in health care. In the wearable sensor-based data collection the following features fetched in the time domain: Range, exact value, minimum and maximum value, zero crossing, Integrals, derivatives, sudden variation in signal. Statistical features are: Root Mean Square, Skew, Kurtosis, Mean, Median, Variance, Standard Deviation, Entropy.Similarity measures are, auto and cross-correlation. While processing an image, measures such as histogram, sharpening, filtering, averaging gives the valuable information about the image, which cannot be seen directly.

The following transformation methods such as Fourier Series, Fourier Coefficient, Discrete Fourier Transform, and Fast Fourier Transform are used to get signal and image frequency domain data. The Short-Term Fourier transforms are used to obtain both time and frequency domain data, the accessibility of which is mutually exclusive.

To get time, frequency and amplitude localization of signal or image the wavelet transform technique is used. Based on the dataset the appropriate transformation technique has been used. If the fetched signal follows the stationary pattern, then stationary wavelet transform can be used to derive the predominant information present in it. The real-time signal may follow different patterns based on that appropriate wavelet transform type is used.

F. Castanedo (2013) & Ashwin Belle et al. (2015) demonstrate the distinct information fusion models that play a significant part in mixing information at multiple levels such as signal level fusion, pixel level fusion, feature level fusion, and symbol level fusion. The Data is sampled from the sensors, smart watches, EMR and patient recorded information. This information is multi-modal in nature which is fused together with different techniques like:

Signal Level Algorithms

- Weighted averages
- Kalman Filter (KF)
- Particle Filtering (PF)
- Wiener Filtering
- Wavelet Filtering
- Non-Gaussianity through Kurtosis
- Non-Gaussianity through Negentropy

Feature Level Non-Parametric Algorithms

- *k-Nearest Neighbour (k-NN)*
- *Decision Trees (DT)*
- *Support Vector Machines (SVM)*
- Artificial Neural Network (ANN) and Deep Learning

Feature Level Parametric Algorithms

- Gaussian mixture model (GMM)
- *k-Means* – *k*-means is an unsupervised iterative

Decision Level Algorithms

- *Bayesian inference*
- *Fuzzy logic*
- *Topic models*

Based on the data pattern, the data's are merged in the classifier phase and then entered into the classification method with the listed data fusion methods.

MACHINE LEARNING TECHNIQUES FOR MEDICAL DATA ANALYTICS

Nowadays there is a huge number of healthcare data available in cloud, coupled with the different tools, these made machine Learning for Healthcare research subjects an interesting, accurate and more useful technology. Machine Learning techniques help to discover and understand hidden patterns in a given dataset which may not be possible by normal visualization of the medical data. Selecting suitable Machine learning techniques in healthcare data can be confusing and difficult most of the time owing to the volume and variety of data. Now, most Machine Learning algorithms are available for healthcare data analysis, but it is difficult for people with little knowledge of Machine learning to choose suitable Technique. This work aims to analyze Machine Learning techniques, used for the different healthcare datasets for identifying, predicting and analyzing.

Machine Learning evolved based on the human cognitive brain and neuron learning. There are distinct kinds of learning available: supervised, unsupervised and reinforced learning. After preprocessing the data are entered into the training phase, then validation and testing are performed. Limits are generalized, depending on the features. In Tom's M. Mitchell (2013) view will adjust the training model's bias, variance and based on estimate and generalization tradeoff.

Statistical Techniques

Linear model predicts the gradually differing disease's symptoms. These are the distinct linear regression models: linear feature models, decomposition of bias-variance, linear regression of Bayesian (D. Barber, 2012).

Classification of these models is listed as: Discriminating features use the least-squares for classification, Fisher's linear discriminating strategy utilizes either two classes or various classes.

In certain special situations where acute conditions are identified, a nonlinear model can be used. The symptoms and test reports will not provide accurate disease identification, so the nonlinear model is included.

Ex: Dengu, malaria, flu, seizure & sudden cardiac arrest. These are some of the illnesses and circumstances in which the symptoms are not always rapidly recognizable, so these can only be predicted with nonlinear models.

Recently, the Support Vector Machine classifier is gaining popularity for the processes of Linear, Nonlinear and also kernel-based classification. To determine whether or not an individual has a disease (where two-class SVM is appropriate), a hyperplane is drawn between the information points separating one class from the other. The best hyperplane separating the two classes is the biggest margin between the two classes. The advantage of going with SVM, which suits unknown, unstructured and semi-structured data, is that it won't be hit with local optima, thereby jeopardizing classification precision.

The model of regression is used to forecast the reaction based on the data set's ongoing data.

Eg: In order to predict the heart disease problem, from the hospital EHR data's (Heart Valve issue, Earlier Heart attack information) are collected then it is mapped with the risk score using the regression model.

Unsupervised Learning and Clustering

Clustering and unsupervised learning are used to categorize the following datasets:

- when the data set is not marked.
- or has no supervisor to group the information
- or without sophisticated or prior information about the grouping concept.

Clustering can be classified as hard and soft clustering methods based on the nature of the information:

1. **Hard Clustering Techniques:** (If the data points belong to only one cluster)
    a. K-means clustering: group the data into k number of mutually exclusive clusters.
    b. Clustering of K-Medoids: cluster centers coincide with information points.
    c. Hierarchical Clustering: Analysis of similarities between points pairs and grouping of objects into a binary, hierarchically nested tree.
    d. Self-organizing map: a clustering based on a neural network that converts a 2D map that preserves topology
2. **Soft Clustering:**(if the data point belongs to more than one cluster)
    a. Fuzzy c-Means: clustering based on partitions, where the information is split into many cluster numbers
    b. Gaussian Mixture Model: Clustering based on partitions where information points come with certain probabilities from various multivariate normal distributions.

If information grouping is not evident, use self-organizing technique or hierarchical clustering to search for feasible structures in the information. Otherwise use cluster assessment to search for a specified cluster algorithm for the "best" amount of groups.

Ex: Prediction of heart disease is done with clustering approach. Risk level is predicted by grouping the high blood pressure and cholesterol level of the patient.

Probabilistic and Graphical Approaches

This approach is preferred, when the Identification of illness is done with few of the disease symptoms. Some of the model are listed, such as:Graphic models such as Directed graphic models-Bayesian network, Markov Random field inference in graphic models-Markov model-Hidden Markov Models (HMMs).

Graphical model traces the increase in temperatures and gradual worsening of the patient's circumstances. To know the time taken to achieve a limit that is equivalent to the severity of the situation. With this, we can predict the known symptoms causes and impacts.

The primary objective is to assist the physician with the expert system to make informed choices rather than assumptions in critical instances. Classification and regression tree methods may be used for this Decision tree. For instance, when they happen, these methods can be used to classify the various fever kinds.

Fever is the first sign of the disease. Viral infection, bacterial infection, climate shift, prevalent cold, or even indigestion is indicated with rise in temperature. The causes and symptoms are used for framing the use of Rule-based Expert Systems to diagnose the correct type of fever.

Neural Approach

This operates based on the principle of brain computing theory. The neural strategy comprises of the layer of input, the hidden layer and the layer of output. The input layer is made up of characteristics like neurons. The hidden layer connects the layers of input and output. Neurons of the output layer act as the class labels. The amount of hidden layers and hidden neurons is fixed based on the implementation or complexity of the issue.

To optimize the output layer, the consecutive hidden layer neurons should always have fewer neurons. For distinct applications, the suitable activation function can be identified using either trial and error or iteration based methods. Some of the activation functions are sigmoidal, tangent, linear functions.

Neural Network is the classifier that is monitored. First, with feed-forward neural networks, the specialist system with the recognized class label should be taught. The classification mistakes are reduced with error reduction based the backpropagation algorithm and network pruning in single to multi-layer perceptron classification (Mohri, 2012). Hand-crafted characteristics and backpropagation learning convergence are some of the constraints that will reduce classification precision and increase false alarms. With Generalized Radial Base Function Networks, Neural Convolution Network, and Deep Neural Network, these can be overcome.

With the following machine learning techniques, an expert system (Mitchell, 2013) can be developed, which accepts the data and gives the disease information.

- Deep Belief Network (DBN)
- Convolutional Neural Network (CNN)
- Deep Recursive Neural Network (RNN)
- Deep Fusion
- Natural Language Processing (NLP)
- Symbolic Argumentation
- Restricted Boltzmann Machine (RBM)
- Stacked Auto-Encoders

Any machine learning method or a mix of machine learning methods can be selected based on the signs, symptoms and accessibility of clinical information of the information set.

E.g.: handwriting of physicians in EHR are identified by Language Processing method.

Health analytics reduces the doctor's diagnostic time to enable patients to receive immediate care that can save patients a lifetime. Large amounts of data can be addressed using either the mobile network or IoT integrated cloud computing techniques. The classifier model's effectiveness and classification enhanced with proper preprocessing, extraction of features and selection methods (Wen-TsaiSung Ming-HanTsai, 2012). Information accuracy improved with online (multi-sensor) and offline (accessible cloud) information integration on the IoT platform. The SWOT analysis indicated the strength, weakness, opportunities and threats in the healthcare system. The table below demonstrates the available methods for eliminating threats and weaknesses and enhancing strengths using a Machine-based strategy to teaching.

CONCLUSION

Data collection is essential for the identification, treatment and diagnosis of different illnesses. This work shows the accessible information gathering techniques and lists the various pre-processing approaches along with the various health care data associated issues. Statistical, clustering, probabilistic and graphical methods used for diagnosis based on the nature of the information. Combining data with techniques such as selection of features and algorithms in signal level, feature level and decision level can provide precise data about the disease. A SWOT analysis shows the strengths and weaknesses of the various online and offline information and their characteristics to assist technologists create an appropriate model of machine learning before testing.

Table 2. Appropriate machine learning techniques derived from SWOT analysis

S.No	Data Resources	Focus	Techniques	Outcome
1.	EMR data	Electronic patient information and information in real-time can be combined to define patterns of disease	Statistical Techniques, Probabilistic and Graphical modelling, Data fusion techniques	Interpretation of data leads to a good source of patient disease data, which is more helpful for disease assessment.
2.	Sensor data	Different sensors for continuous monitoring of patients are installed on the human body. Whenever an abnormality happens, an instant warning will be sent to caregivers and physicians or ambulance services nearby..	Feature Extraction and Selection Techniques, Sensor and IoT based Optimization Techniques	Multiple sensors provide extensive sources of data to monitor acute disease. For the choice of features and using optimization techniques, the sensor data must be gathered and processed. This improves the predictability and precision time
3.	Prescription, insurance, and billing data	To predict the insurance quantity, there are many medical insurance companies. They concentrate only on their business, which can be prevented with the professional healthcare system based on ML.	Prediction Algorithms, Neural Approach Statistical Techniques, Probabilistic and Graphical modelling,	It is possible to do the demands of doctors, caretakers and technicians, infrastructure and price prediction.
4.	Data collection through survey and feedback	Machine learning methods create surveys and feedback simpler to evaluate. The various methods of data fusion can be used to collect the information	Data Fusion Techniques, Statistical Techniques, Probabilistic and Graphical modelling,	It enhances disease diagnosis and hospital management.
5.	Research data collected through various means	Machine learning technique is suitable for big and complicated information. It also efficiently handles missing information.	Statistical Techniques, Probabilistic and Graphical modelling, Neural approach Optimization Techniques	Many pharmaceutical companies are seeking machine learning in healthcare for the latest drug development. To generate precise models, the scientist can use predictive analytics.

REFERENCES

Islam, M. S., Hasan, M. M., Wang, X., Germack, H. D., & Noor-E-Alam, M. (2018). A systematic review on healthcare analytics. *Application and Theoretical Perspective of Data Mining Healthcare (Basel, Switzerland)*, *6*(2), 54. doi:10.3390/healthcare6020054 PMID:29882866

Ashwin, B., Thiagarajan, R., Reza Soroushmehr, S. M., Navidi, F., Beard, D. A., & Najarian, K. (2015). Big Data Analytics in Healthcare, *Biomed Res Int.* 2015: 370194. Published online July 2, 2015. doi:10.1155/2015/370194

Barber, D. (2012). *Bayesian reasoning and machine learning*. Cambridge, UK: Cambridge University Press.

Bauer, B. A., Lee, M., Bergstrom, L., Wahner-Roedler, D., Bundrick, J., & Litin, S. (2002). Internal medicine resident satisfaction with a diagnostic decision support system (DXplain) introduced on a teaching hospital service. *Proc AMIA Symp.*, 31–35. PMID:12463781

Berndt, D. J., Fisher, J. W., Hevner, A. R., & Studnicki, J. (2001). Healthcare data warehousing and quality assurance. *Computer IEEE Journal, 34(12), Dec. 2001.*

Castanedo, F. (2013). A review of data fusion techniques. *The Scientific World Journal*, *2013*, 1–19. doi:10.1155/2013/704504 PMID:24288502

Dxplains. (n.d.). Retrieved from http://www.mghlcs.org/projects/dxplain

Elkin, P. L., Liebow, M., Bauer, B. A., Chaliki, S., Wahner-Roedler, D., Bundrick, J., ... Barnett, G. O. (2010, November). The introduction of a diagnostic decision support system (DXplain™) into the workflow of a teaching hospital service can decrease the cost of service for diagnostically challenging diagnostic related groups (DRG) s. *International Journal of Medical Informatics*, *79*(11), 772–777. doi:10.1016/j.ijmedinf.2010.09.004 PMID:20951080

Gajare, S., & Sonawani, S. (2018). Automatic feature selection from EHR & DNN modeling. Maharashtra Institute of Technology, Pune. International Journal of Advance Research, Ideas, and Innovations in Technology, 4(1).

Haughton, J., Wadsworth, J., Falk, L. H., & Horstmeier, P. (2014). *The changing role of healthcare data analysts—how our most successful clients are embracing healthcare transformation (Executive report).* HealthCatalyst.

Lee, C., Luo, Z., Ngiam, K. Y., Zhang, M., Zheng, K., Chen, G., ... Wei, L. J. Y. (2017). *Big healthcare data analytics: challenges and applications. Handbook of large-scale distributed computing in smart healthcare.* Scalable Computing and Communications. *Springer International Publishing.* doi:10.1007/978-3-319-58280-1_2

Lemaire, J. B., Schaefer, J. P., Martin, L. A., Faris, P., Ainslie, M. D., & Hull, R. D. (1999). Effectiveness of the quick medical reference as a diagnostic tool. *CMAJ, 161*(6), 725-728.

Lu, J., Hales, A., Rew, D., & Keech, M. (2016). Timeline and episode-structured clinical data: Pre-processing for Data Mining and analytics. *IEEE 32nd International Conference on Data Engineering Workshops (ICDEW)*. doi:10.1109/ICDEW.2016.7495618

Marimuthu, R., Shivappriya, S. N., & Malarvizhi, K. (2019). Machine learning-based cognitive support system for healthcare. *Body Area Network Challenges and Solutions.* pp. 87-103. doi:10.1007/978-3-030-00865-9_5

Marsland, S. (2014). Machine learning - an algorithmic perspective (2nd ed.), Chapman and Hall/CRC. Machine learning, and Pattern recognition series.

Mitchell, T. M. (2013) *Machine learning* (1st ed.), McGraw Hill Education.

Mohri, M., Rostamizadeh, A., & Talwalkar, A. (2012). *Foundations of machine learning*. Cambridge, MA: MIT Press.

National Institute of Diabetes and Digestive and Kidney Diseases database. Retrieved from https://www.kaggle.com/uciml/pima-indians-diabetes-database

Reddy, C. K., & Aggarwal, C. C. (2015). *Healthcare data analytics", Chapman &Hall/CRC, Data Mining and Knowledge Discovery Series*. Boca Raton, FL: CRC Press.

ReferenceQ. M. (QMR). Retrieved from http://www.openclinical.org/aisp qmr.html

Schobel, J., Pryss, R., Schickler, M., & Reichert, M. (2016). Towards flexible mobile data collection in healthcare. *IEEE 29th International Symposium on Computer-Based Medical Systems (CBMS),* doi:10.1109/CBMS.2016.43

Smith, J. W., Everhart, J. E., Dickson, W. C., Knowler, W. C., & Johannes, R. S. (1988). Using the ADAP learning algorithm to forecast the onset of diabetes mellitus. In *Proceedings of the Symposium on Computer Applications and Medical Care.* (pp. 261-265). IEEE Computer Society Press.

Soley, M. (2013). *Dealing with missing data: Key assumptions and methods for applied analysis, Bori, Report*. Boston University School of Public Health, Department of Health Policy and Management.

Staheli, R. (2014) How to avoid the 3 most common healthcare analytics pitfalls and related inefficiencies. Retrieved from https://www.healthcatalyst.com/avoid-common-healthcare-analytics-pitfalls-related-inefficiences

Staheli, R. (2016). *4 ways healthcare data analysts can provide their full value.* Retrieved from https://www.healthcatalyst.com/insights/healthcare-analytics-best-practices

Sung, W.-T., & Tsai, M.-H. (2012). Data fusion of multi-sensor for IOT precise measurement based on improved PSO algorithms. *Computers & Mathematics with Applications (Oxford, England)*, *64*(5), 1450–146. doi:10.1016/j.camwa.2012.03.092

Wadsworth, J. (2017). *The best organizational structure for healthcare analytics.* Retrieved from https://www.healthcatalyst.com/best-organizational-structure-healthcare-analytics

Chapter 6
Data to Analytics to Insight:
Role of rtDashboard at St. Joseph Mercy Health

Mohan Tanniru
https://orcid.org/0000-0002-9584-0090
College of Public Health, University of Arizona, USA

Matt Nawrocki
St. Joseph Health Systems, USA

David Bobryk
St. Joseph Health Systems, USA

Anupam A. Sule
https://orcid.org/0000-0002-5931-3381
St. Joseph Health Systems, USA

ABSTRACT

Continual feedback to adapt to external regulatory and competitive environment is essential in today's complex healthcare landscape, and hospital leadership needs to transform its strategic planning process to reflect the market dynamic. Digital artifacts such as performance dashboard track operational data and transform these into key performance indicators (KPIs) to set organizational goals and align unit level operations. However, the velocity of change occurring in the marketplace needs a dynamic approach: a real-time aggregation of operational data into KPIs for a daily or weekly review to gain insights and respond quickly to evolving market expectations. This chapter discusses how an rtDashboard (real time dashboard) has evolved to become a key artifact that transformed the way a hospital in SE Michigan engaged in its strategic planning process.

DOI: 10.4018/978-1-7998-2310-0.ch006

INTRODUCTION

Ever since organizations have started to use IT to streamline operations, they had two primary goals: *improve operational productivity and enhance decision making*. The first goal led to the automation of several operational activities which in turn led to inter-departmental-unit integration of transactions with customers, suppliers and other stakeholders. The *data collected from these transactions led to analysis* of gaps in responsiveness and/or inefficient use of resources so they can be addressed quickly and effectively. The second goal is to enhance decision making in a continually evolving market landscape, which is increasingly influenced by advances in technology and growing demand for consumer services using these technologies. Traditionally, organizations have used executive information systems or performance dashboards to aggregate data from transactions into key performance indicators (KPI) to assess performance gaps and develop strategic plans to address these gaps or revise targets for KPI.

Organizational KPIs representing management goals get cascaded down to the operational units to direct and influence their activities. However, the velocity of change occurring in the marketplace needs a dynamic approach: a real time aggregation of operational data into KPIs for a daily or weekly review to gain insights. These insights surface evolving changes in the market (external intelligence) or changes in customer expectations reflected by deviations in operational level targets (internal intelligence). Such continual *insight gained from analysis* of external and internal sources must be integrated with established KPIs, so that key decision makers can continue to align goals and actions.

Continual feedback to make organizations adapt to external environment is an essential characteristic of complex adaptive systems. Leadership of these organizations must support adaptation using any process methodology and/or an artifact that both tracks real time data in order to make KPIs both current and relevant, as well as integrate this data with key human insights. This chapter discusses how a rtDashboard (real time dashboard) has become a key artifact--along with multiple process changes--to help a hospital align their goals in both the operating units and in administration, and to adapt over time both the artifact and the planning process in order to reflect the changing environment. The chapter is organized into four sections:

1. Context and complexity of decision making in the hospital under discussion.
2. Stage 1: *Transitioning from current to exploratory platform* (Phases I and II) – Current process uses an adhoc technology and process environment that is highly dis-jointed and semi-automated. The exploratory platform integrates data from operational units to seek goal alignment at the corporate level, while creating a culture of accountability and responsibility.
3. Stage 2: Transitioning from *an exploratory platform* to a *mature platform* (Phases III and IV) – Once shown to be effective, the next two phases are used to integrate data from multiple systems and support the decision needs of both units and hospital administration, while seeking greater acceptance and use within the broader healthcare ecosystem.
4. Stage 3. Going forward –*Mature to Dynamic Platform*: Moving the artifact and supporting processes to become a *dynamic platform* that combines multitude of data and insights from internal and external sources.

The key takeaways from this chapter are the following:

- Learn about how designing technical artifacts to improve decision making must integrate the roles of multiple actors (both machine and human) synergistically.
- Building maturity in the use of machines and human actors is an evolving process, and each needs to adapt to changes in the other if artifacts must become an integral part of an organizational resource
- Complex environments organizations operate in today call for an organizational system, people, machines or both, to integrate resources (technology and data) to gain insights and adapt to stakeholder expectations

CONTEXT OF HOSPITAL AND COMPLEXITY IN DECISION MAKING

SJMO is a 443-bed multi-specialty community teaching hospital serving the Oakland County in Michigan. It is part of the Saint Joseph Mercy Health System, which serves five counties in Southeastern Michigan through its six hospitals, including SJMO. SJMO is recognized for excellence in the overall care it provides and especially for heart and lung treatment, joint replacement and orthopedics, and breast cancer. Equipped with the latest diagnostic and imaging technologies and state of the art outpatient surgical center, it specializes in cutting edge procedures across specialties. Its breast imaging center is one of the five in the state of Michigan that is nationally accredited as a center of excellence. For improved access, it also has four urgent care facilities located in Oakland County.

Over its 85 year existence, it has earned recognition for clinical excellence: consistently ranks among the nation's top hospitals in clinical quality; figures among the top 100 heart hospitals; nine-time award winner for excellence in cardiovascular care; a two-time Top 50 Cardiovascular Hospital; a 2012 Leapfrog Top Hospital for patient safety and quality; five-star rated for women's health services; verified as a Level II trauma center for emergency care by the American College of Surgeons; and rated Michigan's #1 primary certified stroke center (people needing immediate care are assured to be seen by a physician within 20 minutes of arrival at the emergency center).

Despite its record for clinical excellence, SJMO continues to look for opportunities to improve its operational efficiencies and patient outcomes. SJMO operates in a highly competitive environment with several hospital systems such as Beaumont, Ascension and Henry Ford, located in its vicinity. Faced with a healthy, but fierce competition in its vicinity, SJMO must continuously look for creative ways, not just to survive, but thrive. In early 2012, SJMO was staring at several challenges in its external and internal environment.

Complexity in Decision Making

Decision making in any organization is based on Simon's three phases: intelligence, design and choice (Simon 1947). The gathering of intelligence in any evolving competitive landscape comes from internal (data from operations and market forecasts) as well as external sources. Clinical units like radiology, pediatrics, cardiology, etc. have used advances in technologies and clinical procedures to improve both patient diagnosis and treatment recommendations as well as tracking changes in regulatory and reimbursement guidelines to address quality and appropriate coding of clinical procedures to generate revenues.

The design/choice phase is often based on choosing advances in medical devices or care practices to improve hospital along for competitive criteria such as reputation of the hospital on various clinical quality and specializations and attracting of top-notch physicians. Hospitals, unlike other businesses, have a dual organizational structure (Morrisey et al. 1990, Trybou et al. 2011, Tanniru et al. 2018). All clinical specialties have an administrative structure. The head of each clinical department leads the physician staff of that department. These heads report to the chief of staff, who reports directly to the board. The chief of staff is responsible for the quality of care provided in the hospital. The CEO is the head of the administrative structure of the hospital and reports directly to the board as well. The CEO works with the CFO, COO, CIO, Chief of Nursing, and the Quality and HR managers to run the hospital's operations. The staff they manage includes clinical staff (nurses, advance practice providers, pharmacists, lab technicians, etc.) and operations staff (those who manage emergency, operating and patient rooms, lab/ diagnostic test facilities, housekeeping etc.).

This was not a major concern for quite some time when hospitals were paid under "fee for service" model and physicians are often regarded as the primary customers of hospitals, as they bring patients to hospitals. Hospitals were reimbursed for clinical diagnosis and tests they order to create treatment plans based on the standard codes used for care delivery. It helped generate revenues and address various costs, even if the costs were managed by hospital administrators. These costs included both physician costs as well as costs incurred due to physician actions. These include other clinical staff payments (e.g. nurses and anesthesiologists) as well as costs of other resources such as labs, patient transports, quality assurance and facility costs.

With rising healthcare costs becoming a hot button issue in the public and political discourse, insurance providers and government agencies were exerting pressure to control costs, resulting in declining reimbursements for the hospitals. With the passing of the Affordable Care Act (ACA) in 2010, the pressure on hospitals and healthcare networks to reduce costs and increase efficiencies had started to grow. Unanticipated costs due to service gaps resulting in patient falls and hospital acquired infections as well as non-reimbursable costs attributed to ACA such as readmissions, penalties for low patient satisfaction scores and bundled payments for care provided inside and outside a hospital have created major operational challenges.

In early 2012, SJMO faced other operational challenges such as long turnaround times in several operational processes, all leading to inefficiencies and adversely affecting patient satisfaction. For instance, in the Radiology department, there was a 12 to 24-hour delay for the report to reach concerned physicians/nurses after a diagnostic procedure was performed on a patient, contributed by process-related bottlenecks and lack of an effective monitoring mechanism. The patient volume was increasing, but asset utilization was declining across asset categories, which was typical of the inefficiencies in the operational processes.

The unique organizational structure and the fast-changing regulatory and competitive environment has called for a significant alignment of goals of both clinical and administrative units. The strategic planning and budgeting process has become both dynamic and needed to adapt to reflect the goals of each. There was a heightened urgency at SJMO to research various outcome measures and develop new KPI metrics that could shed light on operational inefficiencies and process related bottlenecks. To address such goal alignment, the senior leadership team (SLT) consisting of the CEO, CMO, CIO, Nursing Administrators, and operational VPs discussed various ideas and came up with strategic long-term plans. These are further cascaded into annual strategic initiatives and action items with budgets and responsibilities assigned. The VPs of various functional units were assigned action items pertaining to the unit/function to directors/managers, who may in turn assign responsibilities to their associates. Next section discusses how SJMO developed a multi-stage approach to align the operational decisions with strategic goals.

Stage 1. Transitioning From Current System to rtDashbaord: Phases 1 and II

Given SJMO's commitment to excellence, the leadership team decided to seek innovative solutions in order to bridge these gaps in alignment between the SLT and the middle management (VPs/Divisional Managers). To support dynamic monitoring and develop actionable follow-up on the various strategic initiatives and action items in real time, technology implementation coupled with meaningful human process changes and education has become an important strategy. This led to the first stage – transitioning the organization to use rtDashboard to seek both alignments in goals/actions at various levels and develop a culture of shared responsibility and accountability.

Both the CEO and CIO viewed this as a radical transformation as it was designed to integrate data from disparate systems of various technological maturity (paper, excel spreadsheets, to data from Cerner EMR system) and influence key stakeholder actions more transparently. Using advanced digitization to align the activities of multiple units with organizational goals is a significant challenge, especially in hospitals where unique care related specialties often dictate both clinical and treatment operations and financial reimbursements. However, as the focus of hospitals shifts to care optimization to address a wide range of organizational metrics, there is a greater need for accountability across units to ensure that their action plans are aligned with these metrics. In support of this effort, SJMO has implemented rtDashboard using the following strategy, as discussed in Table 1 (Phases I and II).

Table 1 provides various steps taken by the CIO and CEO, with each focusing on their respective roles in making rtDashboard address the key alignment and strategic planning goals. The implementation is done in four phases to align IT and executive leadership goals with the project goals.

Phase I

Senior leadership, in collaboration with the medical staff, set the vision and high-level targets for the organization. At each tier of the management hierarchy, the high-level goals were translated into a set of coherent, consistent, understandable, and attainable actions that could be cascaded to each subsequent level of the hospital. At each grade, managers and employees personally participated in the translation

Table 1. A timeline of rtDashboard evolution

			Technology Leadership	**Business Leadership**
Phase I	Mar – Aug, 2011			
9-Mar-11	Purchase and acquisition of rtDashboard	Patient flow initiative to help improve capacity management issues, i.e., the capacity levels by units. Capacity management was the first dashboard created because it had a high impact on the organization.	Low Investment in technology and leverage existing software	Metrics chosen to show the value of dashboard to managers IS dynamism
11-May	Metric selection	The chosen team evaluated the metrics in terms of the information currently available and the value to the organization.		
May-July 2011	Automation of inputs	Teletracking software provided automation of input to the rtDashboard. The data presented by rtDashboard allowed unit comparisons with other units and supported industry-wide benchmarking.		
	Introduction of other metrics	Other metrics added: how long a patient was in observation, EVS turnaround time metrics, ER turnaround time metrics, and clinical quality metrics, including the federal government's Meaningful Use.	Focus on user training in the use of dashboard	Business users select applications and continue to sustain the culture
11-Jul	Operational innovations	After four months of training, the organization started multi-disciplinary rounds and daily huddles utilizing rtDashboards. The goal is to use past data to respond quickly to changes. Unit huddles allowed nurse managers to use real time metrics to change their operations.		
Phase II	Sept 11- Feb 13			
11-Sep	Technology challenges continue to persist	Only 10% of the rtDashboard (e.g. key volume indicators and capacity) was getting real time data.	Create a technology team and process to select projects	Standardizing application priorities
Fall 2012	BI Team formation	A business intelligence team was created to start prioritizing data requests for new dashboard development and maintenance.		

of the strategy into detailed action plans to attain their respective targets. These targets were reviewed and interpreted daily. Both through the planning and policy deployment, this integrated rtDashboard became the basis for tracking various performance metrics and providing opportunities for goal alignment, resource optimization across care processes, the elimination of siloed thinking, and priority setting. In other words, a technology product innovation helped support a process innovation (change in the planning process).

During the first few months (March to July 2011), the IT leadership used a relatively small financial investment and internal resources to purchase a rtDashboard platform. This platform supported the analysis of a few currently managed operational metrics (e.g. capacity management and patient satisfaction) and provided these to senior unit managers in order to get an early buy-in from them on both the value and need for aligning unit operations and hospital administration's organizational goals along a few key performance metrics.

At a department/process level, these real-time metrics were to be used for continuous improvement. On the huddle boards, the daily metrics were shown to front-line associates regarding their unit performance in a user-friendly and intuitive manner. For example, some key metrics monitored by staff included:

- Current emergency room/inpatient census – What is the current hospital census (by unit)? How many patients are in the emergency room? The emergency waiting room?
- Patient volume – How many admissions/emergency visits occurred yesterday? What about monthly and/or year-to-date? How many were brought by emergency medical service companies?
- "Door-to-doc" time in the emergency room – How long do patients wait to be seen by physicians or advanced practice providers in the emergency room? Operationally, how does this impact staffing levels, patient safety, and patient/employee satisfaction?
- "Decision to admit to departure" in the emergency room – How long does it take from the time the emergency physician decides to admit a patient to the time the patient leaves the emergency room to an inpatient bed?
- Number of patients who leave without being seen (LWBS) in the emergency room–Functionally, LWBS visits are an indication of emergency room crowding and associated with longer wait times.
- Department-specific quality metrics (falls, hand hygiene compliance, etc.).
- Department-specific patient satisfaction scores.

Figure 1.

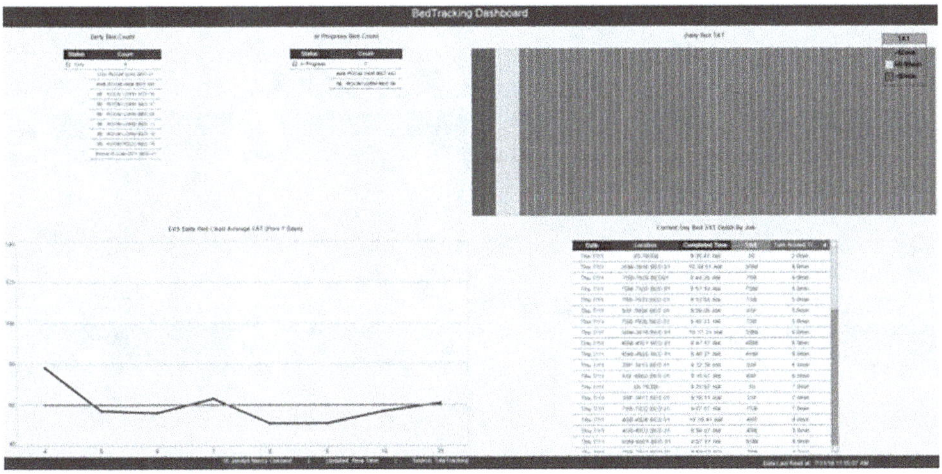

Phase II

As any great plan requires commitment and execution of all players involved, the leadership team developed internal organizational practices--such as daily and periodic rounds--to get managers to openly discuss their unit level performance. This would require an organizational culture of change and the willingness to find better solutions to existing problems. In order to facilitate this level of trust organizationally, leadership created a highly transparent and evidenced-based culture to supplement this powerful rtDashboard technology. Executive leadership was personally engaged in these periodic rounds to make clear their commitment to use real time data sharing and unit level activity tracking as a source for collaboration and continual improvement, and not a distraction or cause of blame games. The leadership also encouraged and assisted management at various tiers in developing new dashboard applications using several other metrics from available data.

IT leadership continued to support dashboard applications by becoming an active and lead member of a newly created committee tasked with assigning priorities among various requests based on their organization-wide impact and/or to address unit level efficiencies. The rtDashboard, with its ability to display trends (daily, weekly, monthly, etc.), has started to help monitor appropriate metrics and performance, as well as reinforce the culture of transparent and open learning with data. This dashboard technology allowed the organization to integrate data from multiple sources into a single chart in real-time (see Figures 1-4). Speedometer charts with easy-to-understand metrics were displayed on all units, and the metrics were made fully transparent throughout the organization and every unit had three

Figure 2.

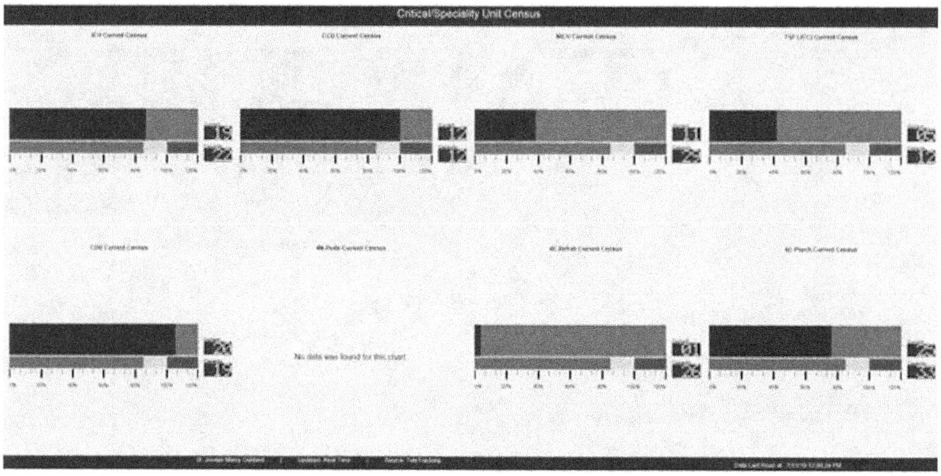

Figure 3.

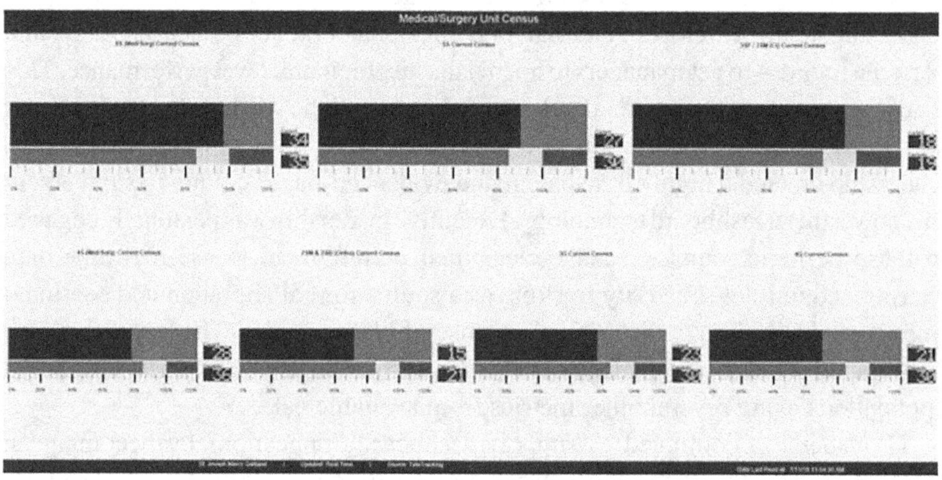

Figure 4.

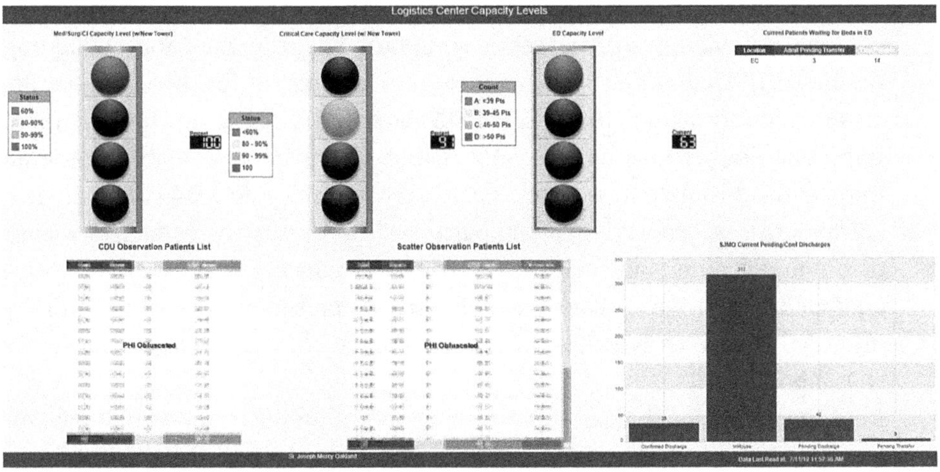

flat-screen monitors installed that displayed continuous real-time data for their unit's specific KPIs.

The dashboard product was also made available on every computer in the hospital so that everyone in the organization was aware of the long-term strategic goals and key performance metrics. The data transparency created a healthy competition between units as it created impetus to out-perform their peers. rtDashboard is a web-based user interface that supports all browser types and devices to display on, including mobile devices on Android and iOS. Each dashboard can be setup with role-based permissions, as well as allow for sensitive data to be seen only by those who need the access. In addition, it allows for real-time user filtering to drill down to the granular level, view historical data, select criteria to filter, synchronized and multiple pivots, input parameter controls and, dynamic picklists. The early benefits of using this system are discussed below.

- Enhanced ability to manage through metrics – For example, our organization's '*decision to admit to departure*' for the Lean-Track patient improved from 164 minutes (Jan'12) to 112 minutes (Feb'14), a 32% improvement (See Appendix). The '*decision to admit to departure*' for Acute-Track patients improved from 343 minutes (Jan'12) to 223 minutes (Feb'14), a 35% improvement.

- Empowering employees – The visibility of performance through rtDashboard allows everything to be out in the open, thereby allowing everyone to efficiently work toward the same end-goal. For example, after obtaining the Level II Trauma Service Certification Designation for the organization, closely monitoring daily/monthly EMS Ambulance run trends became more important and by making this KPI visible, the hospital was able to see an improvement of 29% in only two years (894 in Feb'13 to 1,244 in Jan'15).
- Dashboards vs. reports – rtDashboard is utilized as a very effective means of communicating information for which spreadsheets or reports are ill-equipped. Reports may have been effective at presenting raw data, but they often fail to deliver dynamic insight into the data in such an effective way as rtDashboard
- Real-time alerts/analytics – Real-time analytics on the dashboard allows for users to perform dynamic calculations on real-time data. Using conditional logic, real-time data analytics results are delivered with intuitive visual displays. Combining this analytical ability with real-time alerts, users can receive alerts based on desired thresholds for KPIs. The alerts monitor the data at specific points in time and send an email and/or an SMS text message when those thresholds are reached; more importantly, the user does not have to be logged into the dashboard to receive alerts. For example, our organization's number of patients who left without being seen (LWBS) in the emergency room improved from almost 4% (165 patients in Mar'12) to 1.25% (64 patients in Feb'14) (please refer to Appendix 2).
- Ease of use / scalability – rtDashboard is extremely intuitive and user-friendly for all levels of users. The plug-in-based flash engine in rtDashboard is designed to provide a fast response with an interactive user experience.

These benefits led to sustained interest in developing more applications as a part of maturity phase and this is discussed in Stage 2 of the platform evolution (Phases III and IV)

Stage 2. Exploratory Platform to Mature Platform (Phase III and IV)

Eighteen months after the dashboard's introduction, the focus of IT leadership shifted to technology platform standardization and data integration from multiple systems. These technology issues had taken a back seat up to this time, with the early focus being on the diffusion of technology to the user population. Since new technologies can often cause user backlash if implemented poorly, the leadership team ensured that the adoption could be as high as possible by focusing strongly on the user of the technology first, and secondarily focusing on technological improvement once adoption started to take hold. Once a certain maturity in usage was reached, the IT leadership started to look for greater system efficiencies through standardization and portability to support future dashboard applications. Refer to Phase III and Phase IV of Table 2.

Phase III

Prior to rtDashboard, the data shared among organizational units was in Excel file format sent through secured email. After its implementation, rtDashboard was able to integrate data, often through manual input, from multiple sources into a single chart in real-time using speedometer charts with easy to-understand metrics displayed in all units. However, over time these data files needed automation to gain operational efficiencies. The focus during this phase is to look for more mature and standardized technologies as well as process standards for application development. The goals here are:

- Make rtDashboard available on every computer in the hospital so everyone in the organization is aware of the long-term strategic goals and key performance metrics;
- Create a web-based user interface that supports all browser types and devices, including mobile devices on Android and iOS;
- Support role-based permissions, so sensitive data can be seen only by those who need the access;
- Using real-time user filtering to drill down to the granular level, support viewing historical data based on select criteria as well as support synchronized and multiple pivots, helps set up input parameter controls, etc.

With connectivity established through ODBC link to the source database (Oracle & Microsoft SQL Server databases), data can be queried, and results loaded on to staging databases via ETL packages. The rtDashboard product today provides real-time alerts when certain conditions are met and sends these alerts via email and/ or SMS text to individuals or groups of users based on the established escalation levels for potential action.

Table 2.

<table>
<tr><th></th><th></th><th></th><th>Technology Leadership</th><th>Business Leadership</th></tr>
<tr><td>Phase III</td><td>Mar 13-Jun 15</td><td></td><td></td><td></td></tr>
<tr><td>Spring 2013</td><td>Attempt to address technology challenge</td><td>An upgraded Teletracking software was explored to automate Excel files for direct input to the dashboard.</td><td rowspan="5">Start to streamline technologies used in supporting dashboard – diverse data integration to support KPI</td><td rowspan="5">Let standardized processes and data sharing become a part of organizational culture</td></tr>
<tr><td>Late 2013</td><td>Committee Creation</td><td>Data Validation team was created to review prioritized completed reports and receive approval to send to staff/ external entities.</td></tr>
<tr><td>Fall 2014</td><td>Recruitment of business intelligence (BI) staff</td><td>A BI staff member helped automation of Press Ganey data input to rtDashboard. This team was able to accept a Press Ganey data file and clean the file up prior to sending it out to SJMO for patient satisfaction metrics.</td></tr>
<tr><td>Spring 2014</td><td>Enhancing the automation effort</td><td>Three new reporting services were purchased from Teletracking, and the BI Team worked with the vendor to automate capacity management and enhance EVL/Transport tracking. Dashboard automation moved 10% to 80-85%.</td></tr>
<tr><td>Early 2015</td><td>Legacy system integration</td><td>SJMO was finally able to get Cerner (legacy system) to integrate the corporate system data with the dashboard for direct access to some of the data.</td></tr>
<tr><td>Phase IV</td><td>July 2015-</td><td></td><td></td><td></td></tr>
<tr><td>15-Jul</td><td>External recognition</td><td>SJMO received a national award for rtDashboard, Innovator Finalist award as a top-six healthcare IT project in the US.</td><td rowspan="2">Standardize the software platform</td><td rowspan="2">Leadership's focus is to expand the use to other regions</td></tr>
<tr><td>Fall 2015</td><td>Regional strategy for rtDashboard</td><td>rtDashboard has become a part of the regional strategy for St Joseph Mercy Health System South Eastern Michigan. Some systems were the same in the region, which became easy to replicate, and some new systems in the region were new dashboard developments.</td></tr>
</table>

Phase IV

When the approach used for introducing rtDashboard for performance monitoring was identified for expansion as a part of the regional strategy of the St. Joseph Mercy hospital system in Michigan, a business intelligence team was created without adding any additional full-time employees. The members included individuals from various departments such as Patient Placement Center, Clinical Informatics, Quality, Finance, Process Excellence, Outcomes Management, Nursing Education, Desktop Support, and Patient Satisfaction. The low-cost nature of the software makes it feasible for even small, independent hospitals that are looking to improve outcomes, increase performance, and harness the talent in house. A few challenges have arisen since the effort to scale the rtDashboard to other regions has begun:

- Operational - Ann Arbor/Chelsea/Livingston (West Region) had a huddle but was unable to view metrics in real time or in detail. Given that a health campus like Ann Arbor is spread out and difficult to operationalize a daily personal huddle, they may utilize Web Ex.
- Metrics and Standardization-The Livonia facility uses "mean score" to measure patient satisfaction, while SJMO uses top box scores. Also, metrics chosen initially were focused around people to emphasize people centered care, develop national leadership, encourage effective stewardship and operational excellence, and engage colleagues.

To address these regionalization challenges, three regional teams were formed: (1) A weekly process excellence team gets into the granular level of detail in rtDashboards; (2) A monthly operations team focuses on standardization of metrics and new dashboard creation; and (3) The steering team meets monthly with account executives to give them the status and seek needed guidance to move the regionalization project forward. The regional dashboard is to include a clinical quality scorecard for all Southeastern Michigan. Currently, the organization is moving to Stage 3, making the mature platform dynamic, i.e. learn to adapt to the changing nature of the market landscape.

Stage 3. Moving from Mature Platform to Dynamic Platform

Over the time rtDashboard has evolved from adhoc to exploratory to maturity phases, organization realized that the processes used to make decisions, technology enabling these decisions and people making these decisions have to learn to adapt to each other as well as the external market place demands if the performance dashboard is to continue to be relevant and create value. A few of these evolutions are identified below and these are being undertaken independent of the changing organizational leadership (i.e. changing of CEO, Chief of Staff and Director of medical informatics) and technology landscape (i.e. organization moving from Cerner system to Epic system).

Process Evolution

In the early stages of automation, access to "clean" data for reporting using dashboard tools (e.g. dashboards, tableau, etc.) was still allowing front line users to make operational and strategic decisions but with significant difficulty. As automation and optimization of how units and organization aligned their decisions continue to occur in the exploration phase, the organization has learnt to minimize the need to clean data and sanitize processes, so connections among units and units and administration have become visible. With this maturity, units have started to explore disparate pieces of data to run new applications and this called for meta models on the data to ensure data integrity and validation. It is anticipated that, as this process matures, rtDashboard will be able to use machine learning and predictive capabilities to develop best practices using real time data and push these to help decision makers. Making organization, using its real time data, adapt to marketplace changes and "build practices" is more contextually relevant than simply looking for generalized models developed elsewhere, or ideas generated from theory.

Technology Evolution

Technology in the early stages is merely one that allowed data to be processed and displayed using Excel spreadsheets and PowerPoint presentations and transfer across processes became cumbersome and versioning an issue. As we moved to shared systems (intranet file share) with version controls and dashboard and reporting tools allowing users to access a single version in a centralized location (i.e. on a server and in some database-like structure), organization is able to use charts, graphs and trend lines of historical as well as real time performances for retrospective analysis. It is hoped that, in the future, the same dashboard will use machine learning (ML) and business intelligence (BI) tools to provide descriptive, predictive, and prescriptive versions of information to support decision making, i.e. providing meaningful information to improve decision quality.

People or User Evolution

User interpretability and ease of understanding has been key in the early phases to allow managers to access and use data to improve their operations. As they started to adopt the technology and move to exploratory phase, they have started to use operational charts supporting their individual units while also sharing the data and utilizing dashboards and reports to align their operations with the overall goals daily. As they move from exploratory to maturity phase, the data driven decision making has become a part of the organizational culture. The goal here is to reinforce the direction where units will continue to optimize their operations, while keeping in mind the larger picture of what the healthcare organizations need to do to stay competitive. In the future, as organizations move from mature phase to dynamic phase, units need to scan the environment and discover specific situations that call for assessment, learning and potential adaptation. This may make units use drill-down capabilities of the dashboard to a granular level to assess changes that need to be made and help units adapt to these new situations quickly.

In summary, any tool used to support organizational decision making must evolve with the needs of the organization – people and decision processes they use to compete in a competitive marketplace. It is not the vendor that dictates when a new version of the artifact will become available for an organization to adapt, but let the organization define the versions the artefact must undergo. After all, the best practices are those that organizations learn from within, as they explore new innovations, become mature in their use to help make better decisions, and dynamically adapt to address marketplace changes. In other words, technology, along with people, together are the “organizational actors” that are networked to evolve and adapt to changes in the organizational ecosystem.

REFERENCES

Morrisey, M. A., Alexander, J. A., & Ohsfeldt, R. L. (1990). Physician integration strategies and hospital output. *Medical Care, 28*(7), 586–603. doi:10.1097/00005650-199007000-00005 PMID:2366600

Simon, H. A. (1947). *Administrative behavior*. New York, NY: Macmillan.

Tanniru, M., Khuntia, J., & Weiner, J. (2018). Hospital leadership in support of digital transformation, *Pacific Asia Journal of Association of Information Systems, (PAJAIS), 10*(3), Article 1.

Trybou, J., Gemmel, P., & Annemans, L. (2011). The ties that bind: An integrative framework of physician-hospital. *BMC Health Services Research, 11*(1), 36. doi:10.1186/1472-6963-11-36 PMID:21324128

Chapter 7
Deep Learning of Data Analytics in Healthcare

Yang Lu
https://orcid.org/0000-0002-3027-3064
College of Charleston, USA

ABSTRACT

The importance of data as the fuel of artificial intelligence is self-evident. As the degree of informatization in various industries deepens, the amount of accumulated data continues to increase; however, data processing capability lags far behind the exponential growth of data volume. To gather accurate results, more and more data should be collected. However, the more data collected, the slower the processing and analyzing of that data. The emergence of deep learning solves the problem of how to process large amounts of data quickly and precisely. With the advancement of technology, the healthcare industry has achieved a promising level of needed data. Moreover, if deep learning can be used to aid disease diagnosis, patient data can be processed efficiently, useful information can be screened, valuable diagnostic rules can be mined, and disease diagnosis results can be better formulated and treated. It is foreseeable that deep learning has the potential to improve the effectiveness and the efficiency of healthcare and relevant industries.

DOI: 10.4018/978-1-7998-2310-0.ch007

DEVELOPMENT OF DEEP LEARNING

In 1986, while serving as a professor of the University of Toronto, the father of machine learning and the father of neural networks Geoffrey Hinton invented the BP (backpropagation) algorithm for the multilayer perceptron (MLP) and used Sigmoid for nonlinear mapping to effectively solve his linear classification and learning problems. However, in 1991, the BP algorithm was found to have an issue; there was a problem of gradient disappearance, which directly hindered the further development of deep learning. In addition, in the mid-1990s, the support vector machine (SVM) algorithm was created, and various shallow machine learning models were proposed. SVM is a supervised learning model for pattern recognition, classification, and regression analysis. Support vector machines are based on statistical data and are very different from neural networks. The implementation of algorithms such as support vector machines hinders the development of deep learning.

To this end, Hinton and his students published an article in Science that proposed a solution to the gradient disappearance problem in deep network training: unsupervised pre-training to initialize weights and supervised training to fine-tune. In terms of their in-depth research, Stanford University, New York University, and the University of Montreal in Canada attach great importance to this study for academic and industrial use.

In 2011, the ReLU activation function was proposed, to effectively suppress the gradient disappearance problem. Since then, Microsoft has used deep learning for speech recognition for the first time and has made a major breakthrough. The world's top speech recognition researchers use DNN (deep neural network) to reduce speech recognition error rates by 20% to 30%, which is the biggest advancement in speech recognition for more than a decade. In 2012, DNN technology achieved remarkable results in the field of image recognition, reducing the error rate of ImageNet evaluation from 26% to 15%. In that same year, DNN was also applied to a pharmaceutical company's drug activity forecast and achieved the best results in the world.

At the same time, in order to prove the potential of deep learning, in 2012, the Hinton team participated in the ImageNet Image Recognition Competition for the first time. The CNN (Conventional Neural Network) established by AlexNet won the championship and attracted a lot of attention. With the development of the deep learning, GPU hardware training methods and continuous improvement are also expanding in other fields. The detailed development of artificial intelligence and deep learning is described in the following table (Table 1).

Table 1. Evolution of artificial intelligence (Excerpted from Lu, 2019)

Time	Events	Country
The Initial Phase (1956-1980)		
1950	Alan Turing published a landmark paper indicating that machines were, possibly, intelligent. The Turing Test was the first proposal in the philosophy of artificial intelligence.	UK
1956	The Dartmouth Conference in the United States gathered the first researchers to determine the name of and mission for artificial intelligence. This event was the starting point for artificial intelligence.	USA
1957	Frank Rosenblatt, a psychologist at Cornell University, implemented a neural network "perceptron."	USA
1957	GPS (General Problem Solving) extended Wiener's feedback principle and solved many problems.	
1958	McCarthy developed LISP (List Processing) language.	USA
1967	Waseda University launched the WABOT project in 1967 and assembled the first full-size smart humanoid robot WABOT-1 in 1972.	Japan
1969	The International Federation of Artificial Intelligence was established in Seattle, USA, and held its first meeting.	USA
1974-1980, because of the limitation of computing and related techniques, AI was under a low level of development.		
The Industrialization Phase (1980-2000)		
1980	Carnegie Mellon University designed an expert system called XCON for DEC (the Digital Equipment Corporation) and achieved great success.	USA
1982	Japan invested 850 million US dollars to develop artificial intelligence computers. The goal is to enable machines to think in the same way as humans, achieving human-computer interaction, language translation, and image recognition.	Japan
1982	Physicist John Hopfield invented a neural network that could learn and process information in new ways.	USA
1986	The appearance of multi-layer neural networks and BP response propagation algorithms improved the accuracy of automatic recognition.	
1980-1987, companies around the world have adopted artificial intelligence programs called "expert systems", and knowledge expression systems have become the focus of mainstream artificial intelligence research.		
1988	The German Artificial Intelligence Research and Center, the world's largest non-profit artificial intelligence research organization, was established.	Germany
1997	The "Deep Blue" machine defeated the chess champion. After being influenced by Moore's Law, computing power began to increase dramatically.	USA
1987-1993, AI was under a low level of development for the second time.		
The Explosion Phase (2000-)		
2003	Garry Kasparov ties Deep Junior	USA
2003	Garry Kasparov tied X3D-FRITZ	Germany
2005	Stanford's robots automatically drove 131 miles on desert roads.	USA
2006	Hinton proposed an unsupervised learning training method based on a deep belief network. His doctrine prompted the academic community to begin in-depth research into deep learning.	Canada
2011	IBM Waston defeated human.	USA
2012	Deep learning has begun to be widely used in different fields	
2014	The a chatbot named Eugene Goostman passed the Turing Test, organized by the Royal Society of England, for the first time.	UK
2016	AlphaGo defeated former World Go Champion.	USA

Figure 1.

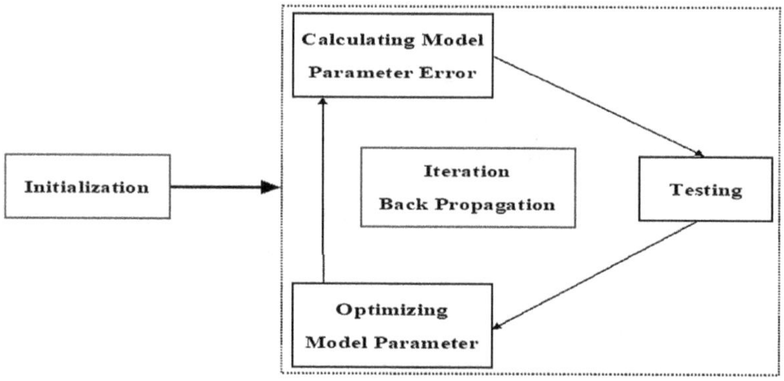

So, what is deep learning technology and what is its specific application in the medical field? How will future medical activities change? This chapter will introduce the related concepts, theories, and specific applications in the field of deep learning and it will explore the potential issues that deep learning will needs to deal with in the field of healthcare.

Deep Learning Algorithms

Deep learning, also known as the deep neural network, was developed from an artificial neural network model. Deep learning is divided into multiple deep neural network models based on problem solving and application fields. The concept of deep learning was first proposed by Hinton et al. in 2006. Deep learning is an important research area for artificial neural networks. In deep learning, the core concept is to simulate multi-level information processing of the brain, to interpret the input information hierarchically, and to obtain a series of features for the input information. Deep learning increases the number of hidden layer nodes, with excellent representation and generalization capabilities. In general, deep learning consists of three processes: initiation, iteration, and acceleration (Figure 1).

"The initialization process first introduces the model parameters with random numbers and then needs to pre-train some models. This process can help the model avoid falling into local optimization in subsequent iteration training. The iterative training process first reads and processes the training data and compares the actual output to the expected output to obtain training errors. The training error and parameter error are then propagated layer by layer through the Error Back Propagation. Based on the comparison and calculation, the model parameters are upgraded by the optimization algorithm. Finally, testing whether the conditions of the iterative training are met to terminate or continue the iterative process" (Lu, 2019).

Based on structural and technical applications, deep learning is divided into unsupervised (generated), supervised (differential), and hybrid deep learning networks (Table 2). Common unsupervised learning models are the RBM (Restricted Boltzmann Machine), the DBN (Deep Belief Network), the DBM (Deep Boltzmann Machine), the AE (Auto-Encoder), the SAE (Sparse Auto-Encoder), and the DAE (Denoising Auto-Encoder). The first three models are based on energy, and the latter three models are based on AE. Typical supervised learning models include the CNN (Convolutional Neural Network), the RNN (Recurrent Neural Network), and the DSN (Deep Stacked Network). To compensate for the deficiencies of the generated model, the hybrid model is often supplemented by the results of an unsupervised or supervised model. Representative models are mixed depth neural networks, such as DNN-HMM and DNN-CRF, and mixed deep belief networks, such as DBN-HMM (Dahl, Yu, Deng, & Acero, 2011; Dahl, Yu, Deng, & Acero, 2011 May).

APPLICATIONS OF DEEP LEARNING IN HEALTHCARE

In the medical field, in order to achieve accurate diagnosis and treatment, it is usually necessary to obtain an image via an imaging device (for example, ultrasound imaging, X-ray, CT, MRI, etc.). Following this, accurate image interpretation is required. Currently, the interpretation of medical images mainly depends on the completion of the doctor and on the influence of the doctor's subjectivity and the doctor's experience upon the interpretation results. Doctors are prone to fatigue after repeated work for a long time, and this can increase the risk of misreading a medical image. Many technology companies are using deep learning techniques for medical image recognition and disease diagnosis to help doctors make more effective decisions. The following table (Table 3) lists several popular deep learning applications in healthcare system.

Medical Image Analysis

Medical image analysis is an integral part of modern medical activities. In traditional image recognition, doctors' work efficiency can be reduced due to fatigue, and some novice doctors may even have recognition errors, due to lack of experience. Through deep learning algorithms, the above problems can be effectively solved and the accuracy of image interpretation can be improved. Deep learning has many successful applications in medical image analysis, such as lung cancer and lung nodule detection, pathological section detection, skin cancer detection, and retinopathy detection, etc. For example, the primary method used by pathologists to diagnose cancer cells is biopsy. This method is complicated and time consuming. Some small

Table 2. Summary of typical unsupervised and supervised models (Excerpted from Lu, 2019)

Model	Structure	Evaluations	Article
Unsupervised Learning			
RBM (Restricted Boltzmann Machine)	No connection within a layer, full connection between layers	Provide pre-training for supervised learning models; Unable to calculate the representation effectively	(Nair & Hinton, 2010) (Larochelle & Bengio, 2008)
DBN (Deep Belief Network)	Full connection between the two top layers, directional connection between the other layers	Prevent overfitting; Unable to train effectively	(Hinton, Osindero, & Teh, 2006) (Mohamed, Dahl, & Hinton, 2012)
DBM (Deep Boltzmann Machine)	Full connection with the layers, multiple hidden layers	Provide pre-training for supervised learning models; solving Bayesian variational inference problem; low efficiency	(Salakhutdinov & Larochelle, 2010) (Srivastava & Salakhutdinov, 2012)
AE (Auto-Encoder)	Consisting of encoder and decoder	Used for feature extraction and dimensionality reduction; slow learning	(Bengio, Lamblin, Popovici, & Larochelle, 2007) (Deng, et al., 2010) (Sainath, Kingsbury, & Ramabhadran, 2012)
SAE (Sparse Auto-Encoder)	Consisting of encoder and decoder, sparse restriction	For dimensionality reduction and coding; poorer performance than supervised	(Bengio, Courville, & Vincent, 2013) (Hinton, et al., 2012)
DAE (Denoising Auto-Encoder)	Consisting of encoder and decoder, random noise	Used to predict missing values; robustness	(Vincent, Larochelle, Bengio, & Manzagol, 2008) (Bengio, Yao, Alain, & Vincent, 2013)
Supervised Learning			
CNN (Convolutional Neural Network)	Alternate connection between the convolutional layer the down sampling layer	Used to process image data, to solve overfitting	(Krizhevsky, Sutskever, & Hinton, 2012) (Abdel-Hamid, Deng, & Yu, 2013)
RNN (Recurrent Neural Network)	Directional acyclic structure, directional recurrent in the hidden layer	Focusing on processing sequence data; Strong computational and modeling capabilities	(Martens, & Sutskever, 2011) (Sutskever, Martens, & Hinton, 2011) (Graves & Jaitly, 2014)
DSN (Deep Stacked Network)	Block stacking	Convex optimization problem; Solving overfitting	(Deng, Yu, & Platt, 2012) (He, Zhang, Ren, & Sun, 2016)

tissue samples are difficult to observe and to explain with the naked eye. Hence, it is necessary to develop a machine learning mechanism to improve the accuracy of interpretation. IBM researchers use deep learning to identify features of tissue samples and to assess tumor spread, in order to produce a recognition accuracy that is comparable to that of human experts.

Table 3. Applications of deep learning in healthcare system

Case	Explanation	Algorithm
Medical Image Analysis		
Clinical of Colorectal Cancer	By extracting high-dimensional features, the deep information in medical images is fully explored, and the heterogeneity of tumors is comprehensively characterized to diagnose the specific conditions of the disease.	CNN (convolutional neural network), GAN (generative adversarial networks), SAE (sparse auto-encoder)
Pulmonary Nodule and Lung Cancer	Deep learning plays a reliable role in detecting abnormalities, quantitative measurements, tracking and differential diagnosis.	Imaging processing and detection mechanisms
Disease Diagnosis		
DR Diagnosis	Deep learning techniques are used to establish sensitivity (87% to 90%) and specificity (98% to 98.5%) for DR (diabetic retinopathy) and DME (diabetic macular edema) automated detection algorithms.	AE (Auto-Encoder)
Diagnosis of Liver Diseases	The application of deep learning in liver imaging has gradually increased, such as the screening of chronic liver diseases, assessment of the severity of illness, differentiation and classification of focal liver lesions, assisted physician diagnosis, image segmentation algorithm for liver diseases, automatic assessment of image quality, etc.	SVM (support vector machine) and k-NN (k-nearest neighbors)
Data Analytics in Healthcare		
ICU Disease History	By appropriate deep learning mechanisms, multivariate time series data and information is analyzed.	CNN (Convolutional Neural Network) and CRF (Conditional Random Field),
Other Applications in Healthcare		
Healthcare Intelligent Management System	Deep learning has the potential to improve the healthcare management system and to provide decision-making advice for medical quality monitoring, operation management and medical assistance diagnosis.	LSTM (long-short memory network)

Disease Diagnosis

Deep learning can not only play a role in medical image recognition, but can also intelligently diagnose diseases. In 2011, Watson was introduced. More recently, Watson has been studying textbooks on cancer, medical journals, and other medical literature. Watson is now clinically used for the diagnosis and treatment of cancer and to introduce cancer to patients for potential treatment. In the field of cancer treatment, NVIDIA researchers and the National Cancer Institute have developed artificial intelligence systems to assist in cancer research. The system uses deep learning techniques to explore the rules and patterns of cancer treatment and the causes of tumor spread, using a large amount of medical data, and then it recommends the most appropriate treatments for cancer patients. There are hundreds of different types of cancer in the world, each with a different etiology. Therefore, choosing the right treatment plan can be a difficult problem in the field of cancer treatment. In 2017, Stanford University professor Andrew Ng and his research teams demonstrated a deep learning model that recognizes arrhythmias from electrocardiograms (ECGs); this can diagnose potentially fatal arrhythmias more reliably than cardiologists. In some geographic areas with low levels of care, this intelligent approach can improve heart disease diagnosis.

Data Analytics in Healthcare

The EPR (Electronic Patient Record) contains a huge amount of digital and textual information, which is the medical record of the patient's treatment, including the patient's symptoms, medication records, treatments, etc. Deep learning can extract information, obtain useful medical data, provide decision support for medical treatment, and provide patients with personalized treatment solutions to assure accurate medical treatment.

Other Applications in Healthcare

In addition to applications in the above areas, deep learning can improve the collection and the processing efficiency of medical data and predictive genes and can predict gene expression. In traditional drug research and development, there are problems such long development cycles, high costs, and complicated processes. Through the deep learning system, the drug development cycle can be shortened, research and development costs can be reduced, the process flow can be simplified, and drug development efficiency can be improved. At the same time, deep learning technology has been applied to remote medicine; it can monitor the health of patients in real time through sensors and can provide patients with viable treatment options.

ISSUES OF DEEP LEARNING IN HEALTHCARE

Although deep learning technology has made great progress, its sustainable development still faces more problems. Especially in the medical field, there are still many practical problems that need to be solved.

The premise of deep learning is the accumulation of big data, and data is the key to its effectiveness. The deep learning system must swallow data until it finds a pattern or feature in the data to output meaningful results. The data source can be (1) a specialized design project that can recruit a large number of subjects and generate new data, (2) published research data, and (3) the data generated by daily actual medical activities written by doctors. Medical records are an important foundation. Data accumulation in the medical field has always been a problem, and data regarding patient compliance often presents great challenges; especially after treatment, the data is often inaccurate or incomplete. How to quickly and efficiently ensure accurate, fast, and comprehensive access to data is a continuing crucial problem.

The positioning of artificial intelligence in the medical field is still a sensitive issue. The patient's right to life and health is of paramount importance. As technology advances, it may be entirely prudent to consider a diagnosis or to rely on it for treatment. Clinical treatment is a complex holistic thinking process. The diagnosis and treatment of the disease is an important part of the overall diagnosis and treatment process, but it is not all. The general condition of the patient, his or her compliance, and the ability of the family to afford and to accept the treatment are important factors in determining the disease's treatment. In the past, this part of the judgment was completed by a doctor as a rational person. Whether artificial intelligence can do this is still an issue.

The more prominent question in deep learning in healthcare is how to verify its new findings, compared to the "best" doctors or to design experiments. If people can't understand the mechanism by which it produces the results, how can it be discovered? There are also ethical and legal issues that have not been explicitly discussed, namely who is responsible for the error, how to develop an effective quality control plan, and so on. If incomplete, inappropriate, biased, or unstable data is used during the deep learning procedure, the best outcome of erroneous data may be that the analysis is meaningless; in fact, the worst outcomes may lead to misleading or even harmful analysis. What kind of data is "correct" data? How much is enough? What is the cost of getting the data? How can one detect and understand possible deviations or errors in the data? How can those important but non-quantifiable data be utilized? All of these issues will be dealt with by deep learning in healthcare industry.

A CASE STUDY OF DEEP LEARNING IN HEALTHCARE

Deep learning has been used to solve many big data problems, such as computer visualization, speech recognition, and natural language processing. In healthcare, artificial intelligence based on deep learning is also being gradually integrated into the clinic. At present, its application range is the automatic analysis and auxiliary diagnosis of medical images such as the benign or malignant classification of pulmonary nodules and the benign or malignant identification of breast lesions. In the musculoskeletal system, there are also attempts to analyze the structure of bones and cartilage. Many AI-based tools have been developed to support decision-making in healthcare. Through the joint analysis of various inspection methods, the accuracy of diagnosis can be improved. Through the analysis of electrocardiogram and MRI (Magnetic Resonance Imaging), diagnosis of medical functional diseases such as arrhythmia and cognitive disorders can be achieved.

As an algorithm for learning and characterizing data in machine learning, deep learning can be expressed in various ways. It is easier to implement from a specific expression using a specific representation. For example, for an image – for example, recognizing a facial or facial expression – a vector of each pixel intensity value is employed or, more abstractly, is represented as a series of edges, regions of a particular shape, and the like. The advantage of deep learning is that it replaces traditional manual feature acquisition with unsupervised or semi-supervised learning and a hierarchical feature extraction.

Feature extraction is critical and is more important than algorithms. For example, in orthopedic clinics, data for some patients is classified. If the expected result is to obtain the structure of the bone, if the extracted feature is muscle, then no matter what classification algorithm is used, the effect will not be good; if the extracted feature is the length of the bone, although there will still be errors, it will be better than the merely including information about the muscle. If the extraction is a strong feature, such as a bone cell chromosome, the classification is, basically, not wrong. That is to say that, if the features that can be extracted most accurately match the classification algorithm, the classification will be more correct. This requires doctors and artificial intelligence experts with rich clinical experience to design the system.

Take an orthopedic spine scaffold as an example. Physical plastic surgery for scoliosis is a very complex system. The 3D (three-dimensional) correction of the laterally curved spine requires attention to the improvement of multiple parameters. It is difficult to obtain an ideal 3D orthopedic effect by orthopedic surgery having a single parameter or several parameters. The traditional approach is to compare normal X-ray or CT fluoroscopy with the patient's, so that the patient can clearly understand the symptoms and so that an orthotic with a manual plaster model can be made.

Figure 2.

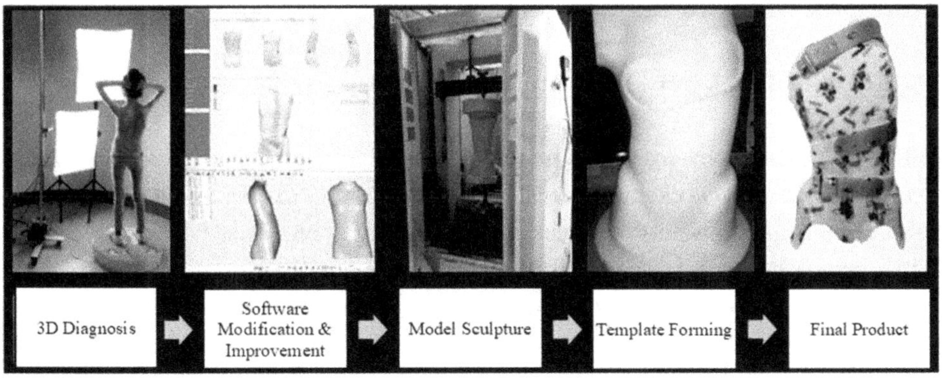

The mechanical principle of scoliosis correction is that it can be corrected in three aspects by the three-point correction principle; that is, the main correction force is applied to the highest vertebrae of the frontal surface, and the reaction force is applied to the upper and lower ends, in order to correct the lateral curvature. As the accuracy of the calibration requirements increases, the amount of data required increases, and it becomes increasingly difficult to obtain such data by conventional manual methods. At this stage, in addition to the traditional imaging assessment, comprehensive assessment of various instruments to improve the physical condition of patients with scoliosis, to obtain comprehensive and objective scoliosis data, is needed.

Orthopedic 3D effects have been validated in clinical trials. These upgrade the two core technical parts of the traditional production process (**Figure 2**), such as 3D diagnosis (mold sampling and mold repair, replacing the manual with 3D technology), software modification and improvement (and upgrading the roughing process to precision molding), model sculpture (continuing to pay attention to details), template formation (improving and enhancing the orthopedic effect), and the final product (enhancing the product's quality).

HOW TO DEVELOP DEEP LEARNING EXPERTISE

Artificial Intelligence (AI) has grown exponentially over the past decade, and the concept of AI that previously existed only in science fiction have now become a reality. Automatic software has been introduced to the workplace and personal life, taking on major tasks and making our lives easier and more convenience. In this section, both the individual and organizational levels of developing deep learning expertise are addressed and discussed.

Organizational Level

In the process of development, human history has experienced four industrial revolutions, namely workshop management, production management, information resource management and green intelligent management. It is now in the fourth industrial revolution Industry 4.0 (Lu, 2017), which is artificial intelligence AI-based on massive data, covering green products, green manufacturing and green living. For example, sharing automatic cars can increase full load and resource utilization, and effectively control carbon emissions.

The challenge that Industry 4.0 brings to organizations is deep learning based on smart manufacturing and services. The intelligent management of an organization can be explained by the "pyramid" structure. The pyramid is divided into four layers, the bottom layer is data, the second layer is information, the third layer is intelligence, and the highest level is deep learning. The data layer is from shallow to deep and from theory to application. The information layer is based on accurate and reliable data. The intelligent layer is based on massive data, and simultaneously performs secondary processing and matrix analysis on different information systems to form results and decisions. The deep learning layer is based on massive data, multiple information subsystems, and computational analysis.

In order to comply with the trend of enterprise management change, what enterprises need to do is to strengthen the data collection process of the manufacturing process. The second is to strengthen the data collection of customers in the process of product use. The third is to reconstruct the computer software and hardware platform after the formation of massive data. The fourth is to build a smart and in-depth learning team. With the development of smart manufacturing, one reality that companies cannot avoid is that employees at different levels may face cuts. Workers, such as planners, dispatchers, quotas, purchasers, quality inspectors, etc., will be greatly reduced. Some skill-based workers will also be replaced by intelligent machines. In order to meet the needs of Industry 4.0, the strategic management, developing strategies, and corporate culture of enterprise are inseparable from the assistance and development of smart manufacturing and deep learning.

Individual Level

With the rapid development of deep learning, companies need deep learning relevant professionals to adapt to the new trend of market development and increasingly fierce commercial competition. Therefore, as an individual, grasping one type of skills associated with deep learning will be an advantage that help the personnel achieve relatively high career development. The question is how to improve the deep learning skill for an individual. It is different to various groups of people.

For instance, as a college student, the school may offer degree or certificate related to deep learning. Student have the opportunity to systematically learn the knowledge about artificial intelligence and deep learning, and to consistently exercise and practice neural networks in the real world. As an employee, employees are best trained in the basics and applications of deep learning. Using algorithms to analyze the collected data is not easy, but you should know in advance the purpose of data mining and the process of deep learning mechanisms. As a manager, it is important to understand management decisions such as trends, competitive advantage and potential profits. Deep learning is a very powerful decision-making tool that helps managers judge expectations and assessments based on actual data and information. A project-oriented plan is a good way for managers to implement deep learning algorithms and put their insights into practice.

CONCLUSION

This chapter combs the concept and the development of deep learning in healthcare, with the aim of studying its development, applications, and problems in healthcare industries. There are still many problems to be solved in deep learning associated with healthcare, both in theory and in practice. With the advent of the "big data" era and the massive increase in computing resources and artificial intelligence technology, the verification cycle of new models and new theories will be greatly shortened. All of this will inevitably change the world – not just healthcare industry.

Artificial intelligence based on deep learning has gradually been integrated into healthcare, but many of its challenges still await resolution. For example, despite its prospects, deep learning still can't answer what causes a disease or how a disease develops. Properly addressing these issues will greatly improve the medical level of the entire society and will benefit patients.

REFERENCES

Abdel-Hamid, O., Deng, L., & Yu, D. (2013, August). Exploring convolutional neural network structures and optimization techniques for speech recognition. In Interspeech (Vol. 2013, pp. 1173-5).

Bengio, Y., Courville, A., & Vincent, P. (2013). Representation learning: A review and new perspectives. *IEEE Transactions on Pattern Analysis and Machine Intelligence*, *35*(8), 1798–1828. doi:10.1109/TPAMI.2013.50 PMID:23787338

Bengio, Y., Lamblin, P., Popovici, D., & Larochelle, H. (2007). Greedy layer-wise training of deep networks. In Proceedings Advances in Neural Information Processing Systems (pp. 153-160).

Bengio, Y., Yao, L., Alain, G., & Vincent, P. (2013). Generalized denoising auto-encoders as generative models. In Proceedings Advances in Neural Information Processing Systems (pp. 899-907).

Deng, L., Seltzer, M. L., Yu, D., Acero, A., Mohamed, A. R., & Hinton, G. (2010). Binary coding of speech spectrograms using a deep auto-encoder. In *Eleventh Annual Conference of the International Speech Communication Association.*

Deng, L., Yu, D., & Platt, J. (2012, March). Scalable stacking and learning for building deep architectures. In *Proceedings 2012 IEEE International Conference on Acoustics, Speech, and Signal Processing (ICASSP),* (pp. 2133-2136). IEEE. 10.1109/ICASSP.2012.6288333

Graves, A., & Jaitly, N. (2014, January). Towards end-to-end speech recognition with recurrent neural networks. In *Proceedings International Conference on Machine Learning* (pp. 1764-1772).

He, K., Zhang, X., Ren, S., & Sun, J. (2016). Deep residual learning for image recognition. In *Proceedings of the IEEE conference on computer vision and pattern recognition* (pp. 770-778).

Hinton, G., Deng, L., Yu, D., Dahl, G. E., Mohamed, A. R., Jaitly, N., ... Kingsbury, B. (2012). Deep neural networks for acoustic modeling in speech recognition: The shared views of four research groups. *IEEE Signal Processing Magazine*, *29*(6), 82–97. doi:10.1109/MSP.2012.2205597

Hinton, G. E., Osindero, S., & Teh, Y. W. (2006). A fast learning algorithm for deep belief nets. *Neural Computation*, *18*(7), 1527–1554. doi:10.1162/neco.2006.18.7.1527 PMID:16764513

Krizhevsky, A., Sutskever, I., & Hinton, G. E. (2012). Imagenet classification with deep convolutional neural networks. In Advances in Neural Information Processing Systems (pp. 1097-1105).

Larochelle, H., & Bengio, Y. (2008, July). Classification using discriminative restricted Boltzmann machines. In *Proceedings of the 25th International Conference on Machine Learning* (pp. 536-543). ACM.

Lu, Y. (2017). Industry 4.0: A survey on technologies, applications and open research issues. *Journal of Industrial Information Integration*, *6*, 1–10. doi:10.1016/j.jii.2017.04.005

Lu, Y. (2019). Artificial intelligence: A survey on evolution, models, applications and future trends. *Journal of Management Analytics*, *6*(1), 1–29. doi:10.1080/23270012.2019.1570365

Martens, J., & Sutskever, I. (2011). Learning recurrent neural networks with hessian-free optimization. In *Proceedings of the 28th International Conference on Machine Learning (ICML-11)* (pp. 1033-1040).

Mohamed, A. R., Dahl, G. E., & Hinton, G. (2012). Acoustic modeling using deep belief networks. *IEEE Transactions on Audio, Speech, and Language Processing*, *20*(1), 14–22. doi:10.1109/TASL.2011.2109382

Nair, V., & Hinton, G. E. (2010). Rectified linear units improve restricted Boltzmann machines. In *Proceedings of the 27th international conference on machine learning (ICML-10)* (pp. 807-814).

Sainath, T. N., Kingsbury, B., & Ramabhadran, B. (2012, March). Auto-encoder bottleneck features using deep belief networks. In *Proceedings 2012 IEEE International Conference on Acoustics, Speech, and Signal Processing (ICASSP),* (pp. 4153-4156). IEEE. 10.1109/ICASSP.2012.6288833

Salakhutdinov, R., & Larochelle, H. (2010, March). Efficient learning of deep Boltzmann machines. In *Proceedings of the Thirteenth International Conference on Artificial Intelligence and Statistics* (pp. 693-700).

Srivastava, N., & Salakhutdinov, R. R. (2012). Multimodal learning with deep Boltzmann machines. In Advances in Neural Information Processing Systems (pp. 2222-2230).

Sutskever, I., Martens, J., & Hinton, G. E. (2011). Generating text with recurrent neural networks. In *Proceedings of the 28th International Conference on Machine Learning (ICML-11)* (pp. 1017-1024).

Vincent, P., Larochelle, H., Bengio, Y., & Manzagol, P. A. (2008, July). Extracting and composing robust features with denoising autoencoders. In *Proceedings of the 25th International Conference on Machine Learning* (pp. 1096-1103). ACM. 10.1145/1390156.1390294

Chapter 8
Integration of BI in Healthcare:
From Data and Information to Decisions

Xue Ning
University of Colorado, Denver, USA

ABSTRACT

In the digital age, the healthcare industry is generating a huge amount of data and information. Although there are structured data such as EHRs, the major data type is unstructured data such as clinical text. The sources of health data are also diversified, including medical data, clinical data, patient-generated data, and social media data. Different methods are applied to analyze the variety of data and obtain health information. When the various types of information are generated, information retrieval and extraction techniques can be used for further decision-making. Data and information-enabled decision-making is a complex process. Many tools and methods are developed to support decision-making in healthcare. Along with the benefits of integrating business intelligence in healthcare, issues and challenges exist. This chapter discusses the health data and information and how they support decision-making in healthcare.

DOI: 10.4018/978-1-7998-2310-0.ch008

DATA AND INFORMATION IN HEALTHCARE

Big Data and Text Data Analysis

In the big data era, healthcare industry also generates huge amount of data in different formats, including sensor data, biomedical signal and image data, and various text data (Wang, Kung, & Byrd, 2018). Text data in healthcare can be structured format such as part of the EHR text, but most clinical text data is unstructured, for example, free-style doctor notes (Dong et al., 2016). The clinical text refers to reports written by the clinicians for describing patients, their pathologies, personal, social, and medical histories, findings made during interviews or procedures, etc.

It is critical to converting the unstructured clinical text into a structured format for user convenience. The traditional manual coding method is costly and time-consuming. Currently, one of the most popular and powerful methods is natural language processing (NLP). NLP is an interdisciplinary effort between linguistics and computer science domain, which is considered as a subfield of artificial intelligence (AI). The first step of NLP approach in healthcare is generating and understanding the natural language, then creating syntactic and semantic language knowledge on top of domain knowledge. Data mining from unstructured text with NLP approaches can process large volume of clinical text to automatically encode clinical information in a timely manner (Kreimeyer et al., 2017).

NLP methodologies are useful for the clinical text preprocessing such as text segmentation, text irregularities handling, identification of domain specific abbreviation and missing punctuations. More advanced processing includes the application of syntactic and semantic interpreter, algorithms, database handler to convert the clinical text into a format that is compatible for database storage (Friedman & Johnson, 2006).

The NLP methodology consists of some text analysis methods as the core components. For example, morphological analysis, lexical analysis, syntactic analysis, and semantic analysis (Chopra, Prashar, & Sain, 2013). Morphological analysis refers to the process of converting a sentence into a sequence of tokens that are mapped to their canonical base form. For instance, go is the canonical base form of goes and went. Lexical analysis is based on lexicon (i.e., a special dictionary), which provides the necessary rules and data for carrying out linguistic mapping. Syntactic analysis requires grammatical knowledge and parsing techniques. This method can identify the formal relationship between words in the text. The semantic analysis determines the words or phrases in the text that are clinically relevant and extracts their semantic relations. By applying these text analysis techniques, the analyzed data is classified and standardized for database storage.

For better clinical text analysis and mining, the training and testing of clinical text corpora is the key to the performance of any NLP system. There are different evaluation metrics for the measure of performance quality, for example, linguistic realism, accuracy, and consistency (Resnik et al., 2006). Linguistic realism is the set of well-designed tags that can bring together the words of the same category. Accuracy refers to the percentage of correctly tagged words in the text corpus. It is reflected through precision, recall, F-measure, overgeneration, undergeneration, error, and fallout calculation. Consistency calculates the percentage of allows and disallows agreed by the annotators.

Clinical text analysis is complex because of the diverse formants, and there are many challenges (Raghupathi & Raghupathi, 2014). For example, the analysis needs domain knowledge to understand the abbreviations, it should concern the confidentiality and intra/interoperability issue of clinical text, and it needs experts to interpret the outcome information. Nevertheless, the clinical text analysis has wide application in healthcare. For instance, it can be used to summarize patient information in clinical reports, identify vaccine reactions, and extract tumor-related clusters from records (Raja, Mitchell, Day, & Hardin, 2008). It can also be used for the decision-making support based on EHR and other decision support systems, and for the surveillance purpose.

Other Data Sources

Chemical and biological data can be used to predict interactions between chemical compounds and biological targets, which is very helpful for pharmaceutical discovery. There are several methods to model the interaction between drugs and proteins as well as predict the outcome (Meng, Zhang, Mezei, & Cui, 2011). For example, network-based approaches are used to construct a prediction network structure for the interactions. It first constructs the network, then predicts new interaction based on relevant factors.

Some other types of data include patient-generated data such as social media posts, web search logs, and healthcare related online forums, from which medical information can be extracted. Reports reveal that 72% of American adults are using social media and 61% of American adult seek health information online (Lenhart, Purcell, Smith, & Zickuhr, 2010). Social media data provides both fine granularity and pervasiveness and can be used to extract patterns and knowledge with descriptive and predictive models. Various methods are used for social media analytics, including methods for aggregate health trends spotting, methods for processing and fine-grained analysis, and the pyramid model of public health impact.

Healthcare organizations need timely and accurate disease surveillance techniques. The traditional way of disease outbreaks tracking is based on survey and primary data aggregation (Chew & Eysenbach, 2010). One example of such an effort of syndromic surveillance systems is influenza-like illness (ILINet). However, this kind of method is high cost and has time delay. Social media analysis is an alternative to address such issues for tracking and detecting infectious disease outbreaks. Social media data can be obtained in near real-time and the volume of social media data is almost unlimited with the publicly available data (Chew & Eysenbach, 2010). Statistically, the social media data has the huge population sample size and contains geographical metadata.

With information technology, one emerging domain for disease detection is the infodemiology or information epidemiology (Eysenbach, 2009). It is the intersection of computer science and public health. It develops methodologies and measures to understand patterns and trends for general public health research. These trends are used to identify disease outbreaks. Infodemiology is also for exploring and quantifying knowledge interpretation gaps, as well as for early detection of a disease outbreak by understanding and predicting the online search and content generation behavior. For example, report found that there are about 8 million people searching for online health information daily. It is suggested that by tracking such health-related information searching behavior, public health can be monitored and used for syndromic surveillance. Based on IP address, users' geographical information and search engine logs can be collected and mined systematically to obtain additional and valuable health information.

Google Flu Trends is one of the disease tracking system examples. This tool tracks influenza rates daily based on the search queries volumes to estimate the current flu activity. It can provide flu trend estimation 7 to 10 days faster compared to the FluView operated by the Centers for Disease Control and Prevention (CDC) (Paul & Dredze, 2011). However, the limitation of using search queries and website access logs is there is no contextual information about the search.

Twitter and Blogs data is another source to obtain health information. Compared to other website search logs, Twitter data has more contextual information for the disease outbreak detection. Twitter users' profiles can be used as metadata for more detailed and sophisticated analysis. Another advantage of Twitter data is the frequent updates and the huge amount of public data. Researchers have used Twitter data analytics for infectious disease such as H1N1 pandemic surveillance (Signorini, Segre, & Polgreen, 2011). Twitter data provide different granularity for the research by setting up the time period as daily or every five days. By combining with other data sources, Twitter data analytics can generate better disease surveillance outcome. For blogs data, the impacts of influential blogs depend on several factors such as PageRank, betweenness centrality, and closeness.

Research methods used for Twitter data analytics include simple methods such as *n*-gram based models for tweet classification, methods for improved classification based on syntactic or lexical features, and more advanced methods that consider spatial proximity such as Bayesian approach based on the Spatio-temporal Markov Network (Ghiassi, Skinner, & Zimbra, 2013). The simple methods are easy to apply but many subtle differences are ignored by the simple methods. This limitation can be addressed by the methods that allow fine-grained classification of tweets. For example, such methods can distinguish flu infection-related tweet and flu awareness tweets, as well as the differences between self-reported sick cases and others-reported sick cases.

When comparing the performance of twitter-based methods and the abovementioned Google Flu Trends regarding disease tracking, there are subtle differences (Paul & Dredze, 2011). For instance, the Twitter method is better than Google Flu Trends if there is no excessive news coverage or if the time is before the influenza season peak. In other words, when media attention declines, the accuracy of most social media surveillance systems also decreases; also there is time series effect. Social media data provides rich datasets such as textual, geographical, and network data thus can generate better information than traditional sentinel-based system. This does not mean traditional surveillance systems are not necessary, considering the limitation of social media data. For example, it cannot describe the global impact of an emerging disease outbreak or the epidemiology completely. New techniques are suggested as solution. In the first phase of the new methods, a classifier is used to detect sick individuals, then the methods estimate the physical interactions between sick and healthy people based on their online activities.

Information Retrieval

Beyond clinical and health data, the information in healthcare is also useful for decision making. Information retrieval refers to the process of searching, acquisition, and organization of information (Pluye, Grad, Dawes, & Bartlett, 2007). Knowledge-based information is information based on scientific research rather than patient-specific information. It can be primary information, such as the information from original research in journals and books or secondary information that synthesizes or reviews the primary information. For example, the most common secondary literature source is traditional textbooks.

In the healthcare industry, there are different types of information needs, including unrecognized need, recognized need, pursed need, and satisfying need based on clinician awareness and information seeking outcome (Gorman, Yao, & Seshadri, 2004). Information seeking topics are diversified, including certain medical treatment or procedure, hospitals or other medical facilities, specific disease or medical problem, health insurance, doctors or other health professionals, food safety, etc.

There are different knowledge-based information resources to seek bibliographic content, full-text content, annotated content, aggregated content, and web catalog (Hersh, 2008). Bibliographic content refers to the bibliographic or literature reference database that contains citations to the medical literature. For example, MEDLINE and other specialized databases by National Library of Medicine (NLM). Some other non-NLM bibliographic databases are CINAHL which has a focus on the nursing field and EMBASE which is the European version of MEDLINE. Full-text content includes online versions of book and journals. Beyond electronic books such as e-textbooks, many websites also provide full-text contents. Examples are Wikipedia, web blogs, and commercial health and biomedical websites. Annotated content is stored in database management systems instead of web pages in discrete information types, including biomedical image, citation, evidence-based medicine, and genomic information. There are many genomics databases and citation databases are available on the Internet.

Aggregated content is the combination of the bibliographic contents, full-text contents, and annotated contents. As a result, it has various types of information for different usage purposes. Currently, the largest aggregate consumer information resource is MedlinePlus that is run by the NLM (Silbajoris, McDuffee, & Olney, 2007), from where clinicians can find the aggregations of a wide variety of content. For genomics researchers, model organism databases provide the widely used aggregated contents.

Biomedical literature is another source for hypothesis generation and knowledge representation. It provides a wide range of resources for healthcare information, not only for drug-adverse events predictions. In biomedical literature for pharmacogenomics, genotypes, phenotypes, and pharmacological entities are the three main entities for resolutions and recognition. Furthermore, HealthFinder, HON select, open directory are the most popular examples of the web catalog (Trivedi, 2009).

Information retrieval and extraction can be complicated. Exact-match retrieval and partial-match retrieval are the two main types of information retrieval. The former one is based on Boolean operator such as AND, OR, and NOT, while the latter method is more popular in Web search engines. The most common approach for partial-match retrieval is to calculate the sum of term weights derived from the queries of a document and give each document a score based on the calculation (Alshari, Azman, Mustapha, Doraisamy, & Alksher, 2016). For example, query expansion is one long-lasting useful retrieval technique that used without relevance information but based on the number of top-ranking documents.

One typical example of information retrieval is the PubMed system (Herskovic, Tanaka, Hersh, & Bernstam, 2007). It allows basic search and advanced features based on the basic search results. Instead of using the traditional reverse-chronological order, PubMed system sorts the search results by relevance ranking. For example, when a user finds a journal paper, the user is able to assess additional features around the found paper. With the increased information retrieval needs, the number and functions of search engines are also growing.

Information Extraction

Information extraction methodologies are also used to mine information from the clinical text in order to extract and uncover knowledge from the unstructured text (Savova et al., 2010). These techniques also need preprocessing such as spell checking, distinguish word sense ambiguation, and different level of parsing. Parsing is the process of determining the complete syntactic structure of a sentence or a string of symbols in a language. While there are shallow and deep parsing, the shallow parsing has better speed and robustness compared to deep parsing.

The information extraction can from either context or code. For the context-based extraction, concept extraction, association extraction, coreference resolution, explicit negation detection systems, and temporality analysis are the relevant techniques (Yanshan Wang et al., 2018). Concept extraction is based on concepts such as symptoms, drug, and diagnoses. It has contextual features such as negation, historicity, and experiencer. The baseline approach of concept extraction is lexical analysis based on a dictionary or lexicon. Other methods such as conditional random fields also can be used for concept extraction. The rationale for association extraction is the connection between clinical concepts in the clinical text. This method is used to identify and extract meaningful relationships or association between the clinical concepts. Because coreferential expressions are common in clinical narratives, coreference resolution is another way for concept extraction. Coreference resolution methodologies consist of heuristics-based approaches, supervised and unsupervised machine learning, applying in multi-pass system (Zheng, Chapman, Crowley, & Savova, 2011). Temporality analysis of time expression and events in clinical notes is important for better medical treatment, more accurate summary of patient history, and further clinical study. For the code-based extraction, it is based on code systems such as the International classification of diseases (ICD) 9, ICD 10, and Systematized Nomenclature of Medicine Clinical Terms (SNOMED–CT). This method uses NLP techniques to extract the codes mapped to controlled sources from clinical text.

To sum up, the rule-based and pattern-based methods are the current two major methodologies for information extraction (Zhou et al., 2011). Rule-based approaches use a set of rules to identify possible textual relationship and encode similar structures in expressing relationship. Patter-based methods rely on a set of word patterns that are coded based on the biomedical entities and their relation keywords to extract information. The emerging machine learning algorithms aim to develop machines that can lcarn and adapt from their experiences like human beings. This method is considered as the future direction for information extraction.

MAKING DECISION BASED ON DATA AND INFORMATION

Decision Making Support Systems

Decision-making is based on data and information, and there are different tools and ways for decision-making in healthcare. Clinical decision support systems (CDSS) refers to computer systems that assist clinicians' decision-making for the diagnosis and treatment of the patient (Johnston, Langton, Haynes, & Mathieu, 1994). The use of CDSS brings various benefits, including care quality improvement, patient cost decrease, accuracy increase, errors reducing, etc. CDSS can also be applied in pharmacy and billing fields. From the earliest Caduceus/Internist to the latest Isabel, CDSS has evolved a lot in the last four decades (Moore & Loper, 2011). Caduceus was developed in the 1970s as an artificial intelligence model for the use in CDSS based on a probabilistic method to rank the diagnoses. However, the diagnostic accuracy of Caduceus was not good. Compared to Caduceus, quick medical reference (QMR) is more flexible and it combines the inputs from clinicians. But it required frequent updates and its accuracy is not good either. MYCIN was developed in the 1970s also to identify infectious diseases and recommend antibiotics for treatment. It is rule-based system and is similar to the expert system. This system worked very slow and as one type of expert system, there was accountability issue to fully trust the computerized results. Iliad is one of the later CDSS. It uses the Bayes model for analysis such as recognizing multiple diseases in a single patient. The three modes of using Iliad are consultation, simulation, and simulation test. VisualDx is dcvclopcd to aid visualization in the diagnosis by healthcare providers. Rather than a specific diagnosis, VisualDx is organized by symptoms and other clues. But it only provides very brief summary for each image. In the late 1980s, the American Medical Association developed DXplain. It is a web-based diagnosis system with increased liability, cost efficiency, and accuracy. It is also user-friendly for physicians who have little computer experience. Isabel is one of the latest and most comprehensive CDSS. It is also a web-based system that highly improves the ease of use and accuracy for physician.

Generally, CDSS can be categorized as knowledge-based and nonknowledge-based (Berner & La Lande, 2007). The knowledge-based CDSS aim to replicate the logic and reasoning of a human decision-maker and try to make decisions based on existing knowledge. For example, medicine is a good domain for decision-making based on existing knowledge. The four main parts of a knowledge-based CDSS are input, inference engine, knowledge base, and output (Berner & La Lande, 2007). The input of CDSS determines the quality of its output. The key is the match between the vocabulary of CDSS and the clinician's keywords. An implicit time model that contains part of the specified user input as temporal information is used to improve the match. Still, there can be temporal ambiguity. For example, the word recent can means last year or last week. The inference engine combines user input with other data source to avoid confusion and applies Bayes' rule to computes the conditional probabilities for probabilistic estimation. It adds a system of logic to the knowledge base and makes the knowledge base smarter. The knowledgebase is a compiled information set and contains all relevant medical information and necessary rules and conditions for analysis. The medical information can be either declarative or procedural knowledge. There are four forms of knowledge representation in a knowledge base, including logic, procedural, network, and structured systems (Kong, Xu, & Yang, 2008). One of the crucial challenges for implementing the knowledge bases is the missing of probabilities in many real-life clinical environments. The output can be in either textual or graphical format. In most cases, it is in the form of probabilistically ranked list of solutions. It can also be other factors instead of probability. User communication method which allows clinician to input the relevant data of patient is also used in the knowledge-based CDSS. With this method, clinician is able to get corresponding results based on the relevant inputs.

The most popular nonknowledge-based CDSS is based on machine learning techniques such as an artificial neural network (ANN) (Berner & La Lande, 2007). ANN build neurodes and weighted connections based on evaluation and learning from existing occurrences, in order to simulate human thinking. Input, hidden data processor, and output are the three main components of ANN. This method finds patterns in the patient data and identifies correlations between the symptoms and possible diagnosis for patients. The advantages of ANN are no need for expert input, no need of manually writing rules, and ability to analyze incomplete data. But the data should be trained first, which is time-consuming, and the results of this method are hard to interpret.

Some other nonknowledge-based systems are based on the genetic algorithm, which is aligned with Darwin's theories of natural selection and survival of the fittest (Berner & La Lande, 2007). By using this algorithm, the output solutions are ranked by their fitness scores, and the assumption is the higher fitness of a solution, the greater the likelihood that solution has to create new solutions. The application of this method is a cumbersome process.

Other Support Systems and Issues of CDSS

There are more types of decision support systems for specific applications and contexts. CPOE systems refer to the systems that provide decision support during care provider order entry by allowing clinicians to input digital medical orders of their patients (Miller, Waitman, Chen, & Rosenbloom, 2005). Besides the ability to create complete, legible, correct, and actionable orders, CPOE systems also can optimize clinical care, provide just-in-time focused education on patient care, and provide specific clinical decision support for patients. Therefore, CPOE systems are very useful for clinical productivity, education support, and patient care quality improvement. However, the effectiveness of CPOE varies based on the orders created by the clinicians, which is influenced by clinicians' expertise level and specific condition. Moreover, physicians and nurses have different viewpoints regarding the orders from the pharmacists and radiologists who carry out the orders. As a result, some unidentified errors may impose risks to patients.

Another example is diagnostic decision support systems (DDSS), which is designed to diagnose conditions and diseases based on the input parameters (Safdar, Zafar, Zafar, & Khan, 2018). DDSS is the most user-centered systems that provide questionnaires about patients' family history, current health conditions, and other specific patients relevant questions such as depression test, family medical guide, etc. The application of DDSS aims to replicate clinicians' diagnosis process in a computerized format, however, to what extent can human users accept the computer-generated medical advice remains considerable disagreement. Therefore, human-intensive techniques are applied in DDSS to increase the inputs from real-life clinical experts, including knowledge sharing, knowledge preservation. The knowledge acquisition of a CDSS improves its ability to learn and function in the same manner as a human expert, forming a solid basis for decision support. To reveal experts' underlying skills, human knowledge engineer and knowledge authoring system enable the process of identifying and utilizing knowledge from external sources.

Nevertheless, the use of CDSS faces multiple challenges (Berner & La Lande, 2007). For example how to improve the effectiveness of CDSS, how to create new CDSS interventions, how to disseminate existing CDSS knowledge and interventions, and how to address some technical design issues. To improve the effectiveness of

CDSS, the system should have an improved human-computer interface, improve the ability to filter and prioritize recommendations to the user, allow the use of unstructured data for clinical decision support, and enable the combination of recommendations for patients with comorbidities as well as patient-level information summary. Users can create new CDSS interventions and even new CDSS system by prioritizing CDSS content development and implementation based on large clinical databases mining. It becomes possible to disseminate existing CDSS knowledge and interventions by disseminating best practices in CDSS design, development, and deployment, by creating online clinical decision support repositories, and by creating a platform to share executable CDSS modules and services. Some technical issues along with the CDSS design include how to add structure to medical knowledge, the consideration of data and knowledge representation formats. The data representation formats can be the framing, relational databases, and object-oriented database management systems for structural data and other formats for special data types. The knowledge representation formats involve logic-based knowledge representation, procedural knowledge representation, network, and other structured representation.

Engle Jr (1992) summarized the three decades of experience of using computer to support diagnostic decision making and categorized the CDSS challenges as non-critical issues and critical issues. The non-critical issues include the dubious reliability of computers, the overall complexity of computer systems, fear of competition among clinicians regarding the effectiveness of their CDSS, and the generally limited nature of these programs. The critical issues of CDSS mentioned in his article are shallow domain knowledge, a lack of robustness and flexibility, a marked inability to give detailed explanations of conditions and decisions, difficulties in verifying the validity of a decision, an inability for such systems to learn from their own experience, and an inability to properly work with specialized data. Furthermore, as the nature of human-computer interaction nature of CDSS, there are legal and ethical issues of using the CDSS.

Data Visualization for Decision Making

Visual analytics is another powerful technique to aid decision making in healthcare by combining analytical techniques and interactive visual interfaces (Raghupathi & Raghupathi, 2018). It is especially helpful for interpretation of complex data. Human cognition has its limitation and can only handle certain amount of information. Information overload will cause misunderstanding, overlooking, and confusion. As a solution, visual analytics can present information in interactive manner and facilitate the exploration of large-scale datasets. Data visualization is an interdisciplinary domain that involves visualization, data mining, data processing, graphics, data fusion, statistics, and cognition. There are many software applications are available for data visualization, for example MicroStrategy and Tableau.

The basic techniques to visualize clinical data include histograms, line plots, pie charts, scatter plots, etc. These standard techniques can be combined into a single chart to display multiple variables. Such high-dimensional data visualization enables interactive exploration of complex clinical datasets and helps users identify previously unknown patterns. Most EHRs provide heatmaps, maximum intensity projection (MIP), and other mechanisms to illustrate tabular and imaging data, while line chart is the most common visualization technique available within EHRs. In addition, infographics enable easy understanding with the increased visually appealing; parallel coordinates is a powerful method for visualizing multidimensional data; hierarchical trees and treemaps are the two main techniques for hierarchical data analysis. There are also many techniques and systems for the visualization of imaging data. For example, picture archiving and communication system (PACS) is the primary system used to store, manipulate, and visualize clinical scans such as MR, CT, or PET scans (Im et al., 2010).

Various methods of visual analytics are widely used in public health and population research (Raghupathi & Raghupathi, 2018). Geospatial analysis is one of the most widely used techniques in support of public health applications. The most famous example of geospatial analysis is the broad street map during a cholera outbreak in 1854 London developed by John Snow, who is a founding father of modern epidemiology. The method of choropleth maps represents a map as a collection of non-overlapping spatial regions, each of which is rendered with a color or texture that represents the value to be visualized. This method can be used to represent a wide range of data including scalar, ordinal, and categorical variables. One example of choropleth maps is the US Health Map, which shows United States counties shaded in a specific color that represents the prevalence of smoking among females according to a dataset from 2012. However, the limitation of choropleth maps is uniformly distributed population density cannot be reflected properly. Some researchers combine the geospatial representations, the statistical analyses or automated data mining and machine learning algorithms, and even the data collected from social media to overcome the mismatch between geographic area and population distributions (Gittelman et al., 2015).

To reveal the critical nature of time in many investigations, temporal analysis is applied to chart temporal data for cohorts of patients. For example, Florence Nightingale's Rose Diagram is used to demonstrate the seasonal impact on soldier mortality at a field hospital. However, because temporal trends are not always correlated with a cyclical time structure, many temporal patterns play out over time marked by a "starting event." For such cases, a linear timeline-based visualization technique that covers common time zero, aggregation process, interactive visualization can be more effective. It captures population proportions by grouping similar patient timelines into event pathways which no longer graphically represent each patient individually. Recently, a network visualization technique is used to view social network structures, disease propagation models, or medication use within online communities (Shneiderman, Plaisant, & Hesse, 2013). With multiple coordinated views, domain experts can contribute to the exploratory data analysis and decision-making. With the user-centered design, users needs are considered in the design process.

As a further application of visual analytics, business intelligence dashboards are used for clinical workflow (Nagy et al., 2009). The dashboards provide summary displays of visual analytics outcome and better understanding of the overall clinical workflow. The dashboards can cover almost all aspects of a healthcare organization, from billings, coding patterns, waiting times, patient outcomes details to differences/similarities between providers, frequencies of specific diagnoses, and effectiveness of particular treatments. The outcomes are improved management efficiency of patient flow and patient monitoring, reduced cost, advanced care quality, and increased medication safety. In other words, visual analytics can be beneficial for both clinicians and patients. For example, the above-mentioned temporal analysis provides temporal presentation of patient data with focus on individual patient records rather than broad populations. Therefore, clinicians could access more detailed information across multiple modalities and integrate data from multiple sources for individual patient. On the other hand, visual analytics aids patients' comprehension of their health information in an easier way. It also allows patients get involved and manage different aspects of their daily lives with the empowerment through visualization. The visual interfaces encourage patients to understand their health treatments and procedures.

Social Media Analytics for Decision Making

Social media analytics can also support decision-making in healthcare (Priyanka & Kulennavar, 2014). A variety of syndromic surveillance systems based on social media can be used for public health research. For example, the online system FluNearYou which can visualize the current and retrospective flu activity in the United States and Canada. There are different methods can be used to analyze content generated by social media users and the structure of their online social networks. For instance, topic models such as latent Dirichlet allocation (LDA) and ailment topic aspect model (ATAM) are applied to analyze health-related content (Paul & Dredze, 2014). The LDA models are probabilistic hidden variable generative models that can generate disease-related topics from health-related tweets. The ATAM assumes that each health-related tweet corresponds to a latent ailment such as flu and allergy.

Traditional detection methods of adverse medical events and drug reactions are based on clinical trial data, chemical or pharmacological databases, EMRs, and spontaneous reporting systems. With the growing social media usage, one new source for detection is the posts generated by social media users. Social media data such as tweets data can also be used to characterize lifestyle and well-being, which is an important public health topic (Schwartz et al., 2013). To sum up, social media is changing the way doctors and patients interact. It becomes possible and easy for severely ill patients to find a doctor globally and communication with doctors via social media, thus narrow the information gap between providers and patients. Social media also improves patients engagement and empowerment by spreading health information. However, the sample bias, trustworthiness, and other issues and limitations should be noted while using social media data (Olteanu, Castillo, Diaz, & Kiciman, 2019).

CONCLUSION

This chapter explore the integration of business intelligence in healthcare, with a focus on the process from data and information to decisions. This chapter first examined the data and information in healthcare from four perspectives: big data and text data analysis, other data sources such as social media data, the processes of information retrieval, and the methods of information extraction. Next, this chapter discusses how different types of decision-making support systems such as CDSS, CPOE, and DDSS, and techniques such as data visualization and social media analytics support the decision-making process in healthcare, which is enabled by the obtained data and information. Challenges and issues in the processes are also discussed.

With the comprehensive discussion, this chapter indicates methods and issues, provides fundamental knowledge and summary, and informs the applications and practice of business intelligence in healthcare. This chapter also offers several implications. For example, with the increasing amount of unstructured data (e.g., text data), healthcare organizations should improve the capability of text data analysis, information retrieval and extraction. Also, the significance of social media data should be identified and explored well in the future. Moreover, although different types of systems and techniques are helpful for healthcare practitioners' decision making based on data and information, they should be able to select the appropriate methods and address the potential challenges in the decision-making process.

REFERENCES

Alshari, E. M., Azman, A., Mustapha, N., Doraisamy, S. C., & Alksher, M. (2016). Prediction of rating from comments based on information retrieval and sentiment analysis. In *Proceedings 2016 Third International Conference on Information Retrieval and Knowledge Management (CAMP)*. 10.1109/INFRKM.2016.7806330

Berner, E. S., & La Lande, T. J. (2007). Overview of clinical decision support systems. In *Clinical decision support systems* (pp. 3–22). Springer. doi:10.1007/978-0-387-38319-4_1

Chew, C., & Eysenbach, G. (2010). Pandemics in the age of Twitter: Content analysis of tweets during the 2009 H1N1 outbreak. *PLoS One*, *5*(11). doi:10.1371/journal.pone.0014118 PMID:21124761

Chopra, A., Prashar, A., & Sain, C. (2013). Natural language processing. *International Journal of Technology Enhancements and Emerging Engineering Research, 1*(4), 131-134.

Dong, X., Qian, L., Guan, Y., Huang, L., Yu, Q., & Yang, J. (2016). A multiclass classification method based on deep learning for named entity recognition in electronic medical records. In *Proceedings 2016 New York Scientific Data Summit (NYSDS)*. 10.1109/NYSDS.2016.7747810

Engle, R. L. Jr. (1992). Attempts to use computers as diagnostic aids in medical decision making: A thirty-year experience. *Perspectives in Biology and Medicine*, *35*(2), 207–219. doi:10.1353/pbm.1992.0011 PMID:1557299

Eysenbach, G. (2009). Infodemiology and infoveillance: Framework for an emerging set of public health informatics methods to analyze search, communication and publication behavior on the Internet. *Journal of Medical Internet Research*, *11*(1). doi:10.2196/jmir.1157 PMID:19329408

Friedman, C., & Johnson, S. B. (2006). Natural language and text processing in biomedicine. In *Biomedical Informatics* (pp. 312–343). Springer. doi:10.1007/0-387-36278-9_8

Ghiassi, M., Skinner, J., & Zimbra, D. (2013). Twitter brand sentiment analysis: A hybrid system using n-gram analysis and dynamic artificial neural network. *Expert Systems with Applications*, *40*(16), 6266–6282. doi:10.1016/j.eswa.2013.05.057

Gittelman, S., Lange, V., Crawford, C. A. G., Okoro, C. A., Lieb, E., Dhingra, S. S., & Trimarchi, E. (2015). A new source of data for public health surveillance: Facebook likes. *Journal of Medical Internet Research*, *17*(4). doi:10.2196/jmir.3970 PMID:25895907

Gorman, P. N., Yao, P., & Seshadri, V. (2004). *Finding the answers in primary care: information seeking by rural and nonrural clinicians.* Paper presented at the Medinfo.

Hersh, W. (2008). Information retrieval in literature-based discovery. In *Literature-Based Discovery* (pp. 153–172). Springer. doi:10.1007/978-3-540-68690-3_10

Herskovic, J. R., Tanaka, L. Y., Hersh, W., & Bernstam, E. V. (2007). A day in the life of PubMed: Analysis of a typical day's query log. *Journal of the American Medical Informatics Association*, *14*(2), 212–220. doi:10.1197/jamia.M2191 PMID:17213501

Im, K. C., Choi, I. S., Ryu, J.-S., Eo, G. S., Kim, J. S., & Moon, D. H. (2010). PET/CT fusion viewing software for use with picture archiving and communication systems. *Journal of Digital Imaging*, *23*(6), 732–743. doi:10.100710278-009-9227-3 PMID:19657696

Johnston, M. E., Langton, K. B., Haynes, R. B., & Mathieu, A. (1994). Effects of computer-based clinical decision support systems on clinician performance and patient outcome: A critical appraisal of research. *Annals of Internal Medicine*, *120*(2), 135–142. doi:10.7326/0003-4819-120-2-199401150-00007 PMID:8256973

Kong, G., Xu, D.-L., & Yang, J.-B. (2008). Clinical decision support systems: A review on knowledge representation and inference under uncertainties. *International Journal of Computational Intelligence Systems*, *1*(2), 159–167.

Kreimeyer, K., Foster, M., Pandey, A., Arya, N., Halford, G., Jones, S. F., ... Botsis, T. (2017). Natural language processing systems for capturing and standardizing unstructured clinical information: A systematic review. *Journal of Biomedical Informatics*, *73*, 14–29. doi:10.1016/j.jbi.2017.07.012 PMID:28729030

Lenhart, A., Purcell, K., Smith, A., & Zickuhr, K. (2010). Social media & mobile internet use among teens and young adults. Millennials. *Pew internet & American life project.*

Meng, X.-Y., Zhang, H.-X., Mezei, M., & Cui, M. (2011). Molecular docking: A powerful approach for structure-based drug discovery. *Current Computer-aided Drug Design*, *7*(2), 146–157. doi:10.2174/157340911795677602 PMID:21534921

Miller, R. A., Waitman, L. R., Chen, S., & Rosenbloom, S. T. (2005). The anatomy of decision support during inpatient care provider order entry (CPOE): Empirical observations from a decade of CPOE experience at Vanderbilt. *Journal of Biomedical Informatics*, *38*(6), 469–485. doi:10.1016/j.jbi.2005.08.009 PMID:16290243

Moore, M., & Loper, K. A. (2011). An introduction to clinical decision support systems. *Journal of Electronic Resources in Medical Libraries*, *8*(4), 348–366. doi:10.1080/15424065.2011.626345

Nagy, P. G., Warnock, M. J., Daly, M., Toland, C., Meenan, C. D., & Mezrich, R. S. (2009). Informatics in radiology: Automated Web-based graphical dashboard for radiology operational business intelligence. *Radiographics*, *29*(7), 1897–1906. doi:10.1148/rg.297095701 PMID:19734469

Olteanu, A., Castillo, C., Diaz, F., & Kiciman, E. (2019). Social data: Biases, methodological pitfalls, and ethical boundaries. *Frontiers in Big Data*, *2*, 13. doi:10.3389/fdata.2019.00013

Paul, M. J., & Dredze, M. (2011). *You are what you tweet: Analyzing twitter for public health.* Paper presented at the Fifth International AAAI Conference on Weblogs and Social Media.

Paul, M. J., & Dredze, M. (2014). Discovering health topics in social media using topic models. *PLoS One*, *9*(8). doi:10.1371/journal.pone.0103408 PMID:25084530

Pluye, P., Grad, R. M., Dawes, M., & Bartlett, J. C. (2007). Seven reasons why health professionals search clinical information-retrieval technology (CIRT): Toward an organizational model. *Journal of Evaluation in Clinical Practice*, *13*(1), 39–49. doi:10.1111/j.1365-2753.2006.00646.x PMID:17286722

Priyanka, K., & Kulennavar, N. (2014). A survey on big data analytics in health care. *International Journal of Computer Science and Information Technologies*, *5*(4), 5865–5868.

Raghupathi, W., & Raghupathi, V. (2014). Big data analytics in healthcare: promise and potential. *Health information science and systems, 2*(1), 3.

Raghupathi, W., & Raghupathi, V. (2018). An empirical study of chronic diseases in the United States: A visual analytics approach to public health. *International Journal of Environmental Research and Public Health*, *15*(3), 431. doi:10.3390/ijerph15030431 PMID:29494555

Raja, U., Mitchell, T., Day, T., & Hardin, J. M. (2008). Text mining in healthcare. Applications and opportunities. *Journal of Healthcare Information Management, 22*(3), 52–56. PMID:19267032

Resnik, P., Niv, M., Nossal, M., Schnitzer, G., Stoner, J., Kapit, A., & Toren, R. (2006). Using intrinsic and extrinsic metrics to evaluate accuracy and facilitation in computer-assisted coding. In *Proceedings Perspectives in Health Information Management Computer Assisted Coding Conference*.

Safdar, S., Zafar, S., Zafar, N., & Khan, N. F. (2018). Machine learning based decision support systems (DSS) for heart disease diagnosis: A review. *Artificial Intelligence Review, 50*(4), 597–623. doi:10.100710462-017-9552-8

Savova, G. K., Masanz, J. J., Ogren, P. V., Zheng, J., Sohn, S., Kipper-Schuler, K. C., & Chute, C. G. (2010). Mayo clinical text analysis and knowledge extraction system (cTAKES): Architecture, component evaluation and applications. *Journal of the American Medical Informatics Association, 17*(5), 507–513. doi:10.1136/jamia.2009.001560 PMID:20819853

Schwartz, H. A., Eichstaedt, J. C., Kern, M. L., Dziurzynski, L., Lucas, R. E., Agrawal, M., . . . Seligman, M. E. (2013). *Characterizing geographic variation in well-being using tweets*. Paper presented at the Seventh International AAAI Conference on Weblogs and Social Media.

Shneiderman, B., Plaisant, C., & Hesse, B. W. (2013). Improving healthcare with interactive visualization. *Computer, 46*(5), 58–66. doi:10.1109/MC.2013.38

Signorini, A., Segre, A. M., & Polgreen, P. M. (2011). The use of Twitter to track levels of disease activity and public concern in the US during the influenza A H1N1 pandemic. *PLoS One, 6*(5). doi:10.1371/journal.pone.0019467 PMID:21573238

Silbajoris, C., McDuffee, D., & Olney, C. (2007). Creating the first MedlinePlus "Go Local" service: Lessons and recommendations from the evaluation of NC Health Info. *Medical Reference Services Quarterly, 26*(2), 75–86. doi:10.1300/J115v26n02_07 PMID:17522010

Trivedi, M. (2009). A study of search engines for health sciences. *International Journal of Library and Information Science, 62*(68), 062-073.

Wang, Y., Kung, L., & Byrd, T. A. (2018). Big data analytics: Understanding its capabilities and potential benefits for healthcare organizations. *Technological Forecasting and Social Change, 126*, 3–13. doi:10.1016/j.techfore.2015.12.019

Wang, Y., Wang, L., Rastegar-Mojarad, M., Moon, S., Shen, F., Afzal, N., ... Sohn, S. (2018). Clinical information extraction applications: A literature review. *Journal of Biomedical Informatics*, *77*, 34–49. doi:10.1016/j.jbi.2017.11.011 PMID:29162496

Zheng, J., Chapman, W. W., Crowley, R. S., & Savova, G. K. (2011). Coreference resolution: A review of general methodologies and applications in the clinical domain. *Journal of Biomedical Informatics*, *44*(6), 1113–1122. doi:10.1016/j.jbi.2011.08.006 PMID:21856441

Zhou, L., Plasek, J. M., Mahoney, L. M., Karipineni, N., Chang, F., Yan, X., ... Rocha, R. A. (2011). Using medical text extraction, reasoning and mapping system (MTERMS) to process medication information in outpatient clinical notes. In *Proceedings AMIA Annual Symposium*.

Chapter 9
A Proposed Architecture to Sustain Public-Private Partnership:
The Case of the Arizona ASHLine

Mohan Tanniru
https://orcid.org/0000-0002-9584-0090
College of Public Health, University of Arizona, USA

Mark Martz
College of Public Health, University of Arizona, USA

ABSTRACT

Information technology has enabled tertiary health care providers to improve patient access to preventive and post-discharge care transition services. When such services are supported by facilities that are under the control of the hospital, hospitals can still influence the delivery and overall quality of patient care services. However, for a variety of reasons, many hospitals rely on external care providers who operate relatively independently from the hospital to deliver these services. As such, service delivery intended to create efficiency and value to patients can become complex, challenging to deliver, and resource intensive—especially if the service delivery spans a prolonged time horizon. This chapter discusses one case of an intermediary who helps hospitals address the smoking cessation needs of patients. Using service dominant logic research, the service exchanges among three different ecosystems (healthcare providers, intermediary, and patients) are modeled and intelligence needed to align their goals using blockchain architecture is highlighted.

DOI: 10.4018/978-1-7998-2310-0.ch009

INTRODUCTION

With the rapid evolution of the Worldwide Web, social media, wearables and telehealth technologies, potential for patient engagement in preventive and post-discharge care transition has increased, bringing with it the resources providers, patients and other actors found within patient ecosystem can employ to improve access to care. This has motivated healthcare organizations to evolve their care delivery models to reduce costs and address both regulatory (e.g. reimbursement penalties and patient satisfaction, etc.) and administrative challenges (e.g. congestion in hospitals, distributed nature of clinical competencies such as counseling and rehabilitation, etc.). These emerging care models promote patient engagement of care extenders outside a hospital setting where a patient can receive the continued care hospitals plan for them to receive after they discharge from an acute care setting. Examples of services care extenders can provide include physical and speech therapy, dialysis, and chronic disease and pain management interventions. Each of these service exchanges can influence the overall care provided to patients initially within a hospital that is then extended outside the hospital over time (i.e. value created or cocreated).

One of the resources healthcare systems have been utilizing over the past decade to connect services provided within an acute care setting to those provided within community is the electronic health record, or EHR (Shiver & Cantiello, 2016). Using electronic health records to extend care is a relevant and meaningful exercise as doing so improves access to care, reduces duplication of effort, and as a result improves patient outcomes and saves costs, i.e., Triple Aim (Weber, Bloom, Pierdon, & Wood, 2008). Harnessing the power of the electronic medical record to achieve a lofty goal such as the Triple Aim comes at a cost. Developing, implementing, and maintaining electronic records can present a significant financial barrier for those wishing to incorporate EHRs into their workflow (Soumeri & Koppel, 2012), particularly among providers who do not have necessary economies of scale that large hospital and insurance providers may have, and have limited trust in the resources they share among each other.

As a result, the use of alternative technologies must be sought and used to gain intelligence on collective performance of stakeholders across multiple ecosystems. This chapter highlights the need to address gaps in alignment among stakeholders when patient care is managed by a mix of public and private enterprises and discusses the role intelligence in performance tracking to bridge the gaps using blockchain technology. Transparency in resource sharing and trust in the architecture used to support communication and coordination is essential if patient care is the shared goal of all involved. The next section discusses the organizational context and the third section discussed the model used to analyze the service exchanges among multiple stakeholders. Section four develops strategies to address some of these challenges using blockchain technologies and section five provides concluding remarks and future research directions.

ORGANIZATIONAL CONTEXT

Tobacco use remains the leading cause of preventable death in the United States (CDC, 2014). The negative health and economic impact of tobacco use has been well established with billions of dollars being expended annually to treat the deleterious health and societal effects caused by smoking in addition to the billions of dollars in societal productivity that are forgone as a result of smoking. In an effort to address and provide solutions to reduce smoking prevalence and improve individual and population health comprehensive tobacco control measures have been developed and deployed systematically at the national, state, and local level for decades. One example of a tobacco control measure that has been in existence the longest is the provision of tobacco cessation services via state tobacco quitlines (NAQC, 2018). Every state in the United States supports a tobacco quitline. In Arizona, the Arizona Smokers' Helpline (ASHLine), supported by the state tax on tobacco products and operated by the University of Arizona's Mel and Enid Zuckerman College of Public Health, serves a the tobacco cessation service intermediary. Primary objectives of the ASHLine are to:

- Provide education and training to providers to inform patients on the harms and dangers of using tobacco products, the benefits of quitting, and how to refer patients to cessation services offered via the ASHLine.
- Provide opportunities for individuals to make a successful quit attempt by providing access to online resources and applications, behavioral counseling, and over the counter nicotine replacement therapy.
- Tailor cessation interventions and services to meet the specific needs of special populations who express higher prevalence of nicotine use as compared to the general population. Special populations include individuals with a co-occurring mental illness, ethnic minorities, LGBTQ members of community, Native Americans, and those who live at or below the poverty line.

In many ways, the providers of this intermediary are the state public health agency whose mission is to improve population health by investing tobacco tax dollars to prevent tobacco use initiation and provide a variety of cessation approaches for individuals wanting to make a successful quit attempt. The operations of the ASHLine are to promote its services to healthcare system providers[1] and the public at large, refer individuals to the quitline, and enroll patients who have an interest in quitting smoking and engaging patients in a series of service exchanges that may include counselling and pharmacotherapy, with an overall goal of reducing tobacco use prevalence over time. To ensure the ASHLine is accomplishing its operational objectives and utilizing the tobacco tax dollars that support its operations to their highest and best use, the ASHLine has developed a performance dashboard that tracks client participation in the program and generates reports to the state public health agency, referring health care providers, and stakeholders.

Service Demand

Stakeholders who interact within the tobacco cessation service delivery marketplace have grown over the years, including healthcare providers who want their patients to quit smoking. These providers include physicians, dentists, pharmacists, physician assistants, nurses, nurse practitioners, community health workers, promoters, and substance use disorder treatment therapists, as well as trusted members of community. Resources dedicated to cessation efforts come from a variety of sources. These may include taxes collected from the sale of tobacco products, federal funds provided to states in the form of grants, and incentives employers provide to employees when an employee becomes tobacco free. As with any resource, particularly those connected to a government source (tobacco tax, federal grants) there is a limitation on the amount of resources that may be available. In addition, there are no guarantees of an ongoing steady stream of incoming resources to maintain current service delivery levels to meet future demand. And finally, other competing interests and priorities can generate a gravitational pull that can result in resources being shifted to meet the needs of other competing interests or emerging issues, i.e., the opioid crisis.

Service Utilization

Currently, all Arizonans referred to the quitline by a provider, regardless of insurance status, can receive behavioral counseling and over the counter nicotine replacement therapy from the ASHLine. While this policy supports a desire to provide cessation services to all those who request it, this policy may not be sustainable. For example, a large percentage of individuals who utilize the quitline are privately insured, approximately 30% of all clients (ASHLine, 2019) and have access to a robust set of cessation services through their employer or insurer. As a result, the quitline is not able to dedicate as much of its scarce resources to service the needs of its priority populations (opportunity cost), especially the uninsured and individuals who fall within a special population category. In other words, due to a lack of effective cost sharing for services provided to patients who have access to cessation services through private insurance, one may argue the ASHLine is unable to provide comprehensive support to the most vulnerable, high-prevalence populations who are in most need of services and who, without access to comprehensive services, express poorer health outcomes as compared to individuals who have access to comprehensive services while also exacting a significant (avoidable) cost burden upon the health care system over time.

Balancing Service Demand and Resource Utilization

It becomes paramount for all stakeholders to be mindful of the resources they have and plan strategically the ways in which scarce resources are being utilized. This leads to a financial challenge – how to create a sustainable funding model for the services ASHLine provides by charging for these services appropriately, i.e. have providers of insured patients co-produce the value they receive while dedicating limited tax dollars to support access to comprehensive cessation services for those who need them the most.

Today, ASHLine tracks its patient enrollment and counselling services and provides this information to state agencies (one set of providers) by summarizing patient participation in counselling services. While it provides some reports to other providers who refer insured patients to the quitline, they are often either not sought actively or do not track detailed information on patient focused services. If ASHLine wants to seek payment from providers of insured patients, it may need to match the benefits providers receive currently for free against the costs it incurs to provide cessation services such as contacting the patient, scheduling a trained cessation specialist to help the patient quit smoking and processes that support all other provider-intermediary-patient communication and coordination.

The next section models the service exchanges that take place among the three ecosystems as they are configured today and explores re-structuring services to not only support effective tracking of costs/value generated to providers but to also help re-configure the system to achieve effective communication, coordination, and service delivery.

Modeling of the Service Exchanges

Figure 1 illustrates the value created and value in use dynamic that occurs between provider and patient. Service Dominant (S-D) logic argues that value created by a service provider (hospital) and customer (patient or healthcare customer) must be judged by value in use (i.e. how the value is perceived and judged by patients and their adherence to care plans) (Vargo and Lusch, 2008). Intelligence gathered from value-in-use should lead to changes in the treatment care plans (i.e. next instance of value creation cycle), and many such value creation-and value in use analysis

Figure 1.

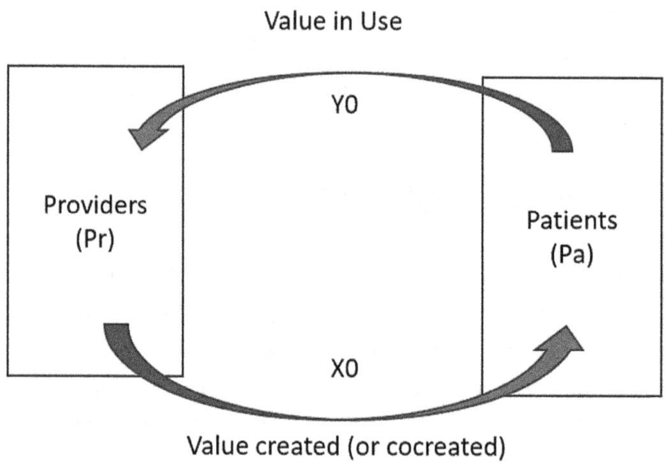

Figure 2.

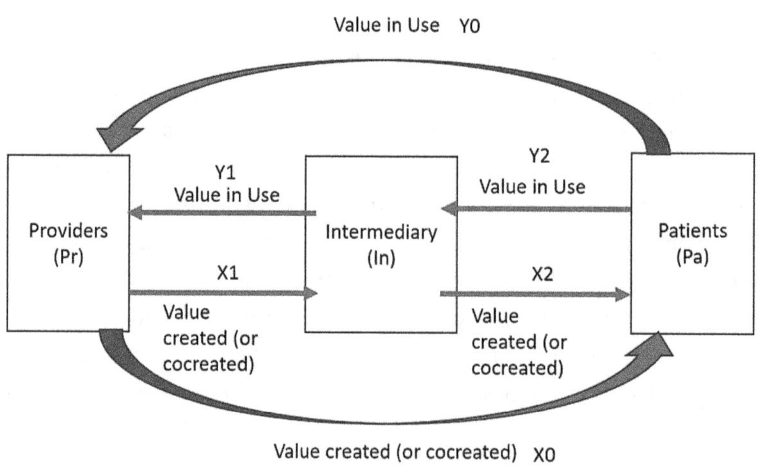

cycles are needed to sustain patient care. While such intelligence of value-in-use can be gathered and used to create new value when a provider is in direct contact with the patient using surveys, follow-up phone calls, frequent consultations, etc., this becomes complex when an intermediary such as ASHLine is involved in engaging the patient as seen in Figure 1 and 2.

If X and Y represent value created and value in use, Figure 1 shows how differences in X0 and Y0 (gathered through intelligence from patients) can lead to multiple {X0, Y0} value instances to ensure care plans are adhered to. However, in Figure 1b, while intelligence on Y0, even if tracked by regular patient surveys, is influenced by other {X, Y} value cycles such as how provider creates value with intermediary (sharing resources and seeking alignment with) and how intermediary creates value cycles with patients. In other words {X1,Y1} are focused on how effectively provider communicates with the intermediary on care related goals and ensures that the value-in-use (i.e. intermediary's ability to fulfill this value) is aligning provider/ intermediary goals. Similarly, {X2, Y2} are focused on how intermediary transfers the provider goals into action plans to create value to patients and how intelligence gathered from them changes intermediary's strategy in creating or transferring provider value effectively to patients.

In summary, there are three ecosystems (provider, intermediary and patient) with associated actors and resources, who dictate how effectively the combination of {X1, Y1} and {X2, Y2} are addressing the goals of provider-patient engagement {X0, Y0}. The goal of this chapter is to discuss how these three ecosystems are interacting in a smoking session program in Arizona and what can be explored to address the challenges in aligning the shared goals of the actors within each of these ecosystems. Aligning goals needs the partnership of multiple stakeholders, which is key to any agile service organizations (Lusch and Nambisan, 2015).

In Figure 2, the intermediary is replaced by ASHLine. Providers co-create value with ASHLine between each other: provider sending patient referrals to ASHLine with provider being reimbursed for services rendered (i.e., delivering intervention, submitting referral). This is X1. To ensure that this value in fulfilled, ASHLine tracks all referrals by provider and generate invoices (Y1) to providers ASHLine contract with but do not currently generate financial reports for providers it does not contract with, which is most provider/referral locations today.

ASHLine in-turn creates value to the patients by providing tailored services in a timely manner to ensure their adherence (X2) and value-in-use here corresponds to tracking patient adherence to the services provided (incomplete, decrease smoking, quit at 7month follow-up) and their overall satisfaction of the services (Y2).

Provider creates value to patients by referring those who need services to ASHLine or select services of ASHLine to help them quit smoking (X0). While ASHLine may be currently providing a single service (X0 and X2 may be similar), it may in the future co-create distinct value-based services such as tele-services and knowledge-based services for self-motivated patients with providers, so patients with varying capabilities and interests can be offered choices.

Figure 3. Service objects connecting providers and patients to ASHLine

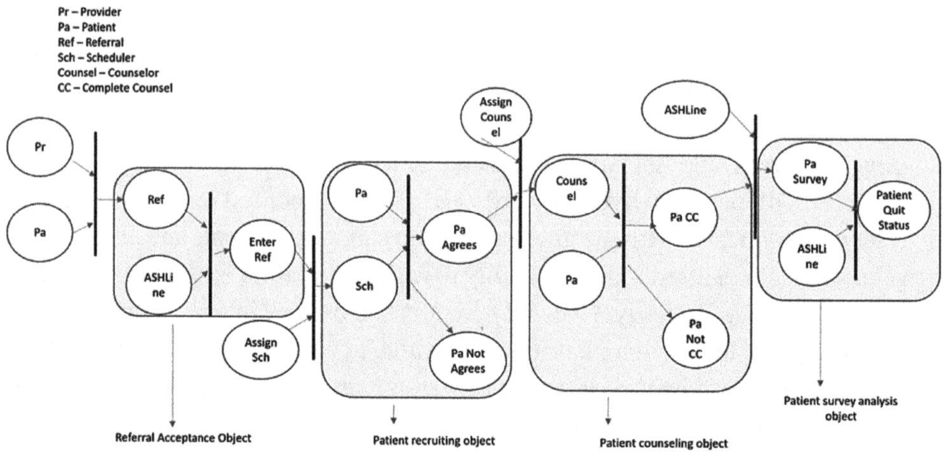

Similarly, the value-in-use Y0 today is like Y2, but it may vary if providers wish to directly contact patients for evaluation of the services, especially if patients are provided multiple services for smoking cessation besides ASHLine. Also, providers and ASHLine may co-create the value-in-use tracking of patient data to ensure it meets provider goals. The service model of the basic interaction among these three ecosystems is shown in Figure 3.

While the first service object describes the basic referral process, the next three service objects describe the detailed service exchanges between ASHLine and the patient – first to enroll the patient, second to counsel the patient, and the third to seek feedback from the patient. The value-in-use from the services provided to patients is captured by tracking the number of patients engaged in each service exchange and the proportion who have completed the recommended counseling sessions. This is shown in Figure 4.

Challenges in Current System Operation

Besides the anticipated financial challenges, as discussed in the previous section, there are some other operational challenges that impact the timely processing of referrals (referral acceptance object) and effective capture and transmission of the various value-in-use reports to the providers, if ASHLine has to engage in shared value co-creation with the provider, i.e. provide value to provider for seeking reimbursement for the service. These operational challenges include:

Figure 4. Value-in-use tracking of patient services

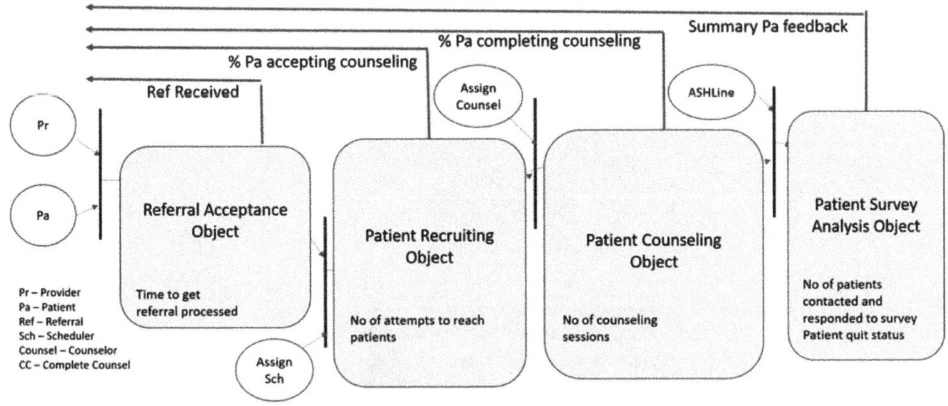

- 90% of the referrals from providers come in Fax and these are printed and re-input into an internal dashboard – this takes away a small window provider must convince a patient, through ASHLine, to enroll in the smoking cessation program
- Many of the value-in-use reports are generated at various points in time, not generated in real time for monitoring and follow up on patient engagement
- Many of the providers are not easily connected to the ASHLine dashboard system for effective and faster transmission of the value-in-use reports to providers, for their follow-up with patients if needed
- No micro or macro-level analysis is feasible today because of a single consolidated data source with needed provider, patient and other related demographic information

This calls for reconfiguration of the current system architecture – automation of some of the referral inputs for faster processing and re-architecting the current ASHLine dashboard to generate reports in a timely manner. Ultimately, ASHLine needs a communication and coordination architecture that can help it track value-in-use data in order to alter its value creation potential. Blockchain technology has been shown most appropriate when there is no central coordinating entity that has the interest or resources to manage the activities of many actors as they share resources in a secure manner. It has been applied within the financial service industry for sharing financial transactions (Gomber et al. 2018). Managing distributed records in blockchain (Lemieux, 2017), sharing data in a decentralized marketplace (Subramanian, 2018), and building applications in a decentralized digital architecture (Glacer, 2017) all illustrate how multiple actors in distributed and different enterprises can share resources to address a common goal by leveraging the distributed resource

Figure 5. A pilot blockchain implementation

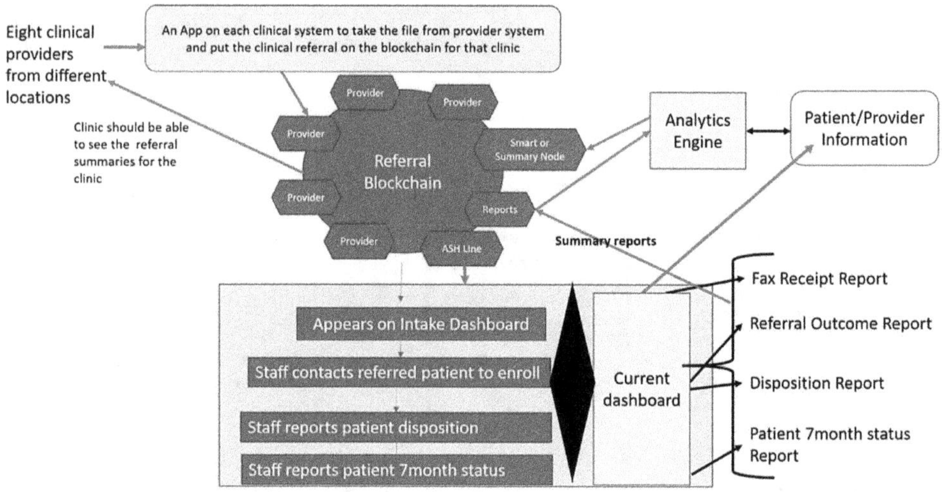

sharing characteristic of blockchain technology. This is similar to the case of care delivery outside a hospital when they have to rely on intermediaries, clinical and non-clinical, to support patient care with no centralized trusted institution. This is discussed in the next section.

RECONFIGURATION OF ASHLINE SYSTEM USING BLOCKCHAIN ARCHITECTURE

While ASHLine can create and coordinate a centralized data base and software system that can interact with multiple providers to generate the needed intelligence on referral process and patient adherence, it is viewed as cost prohibitive with the current financial funding model, especially given that all its resources to the extent possible be devoted to serving patients. For this reason, a pilot application using blockchain architecture is being explored. This is presented in the figure below and discussed briefly.

Features of the Prototype

- A provider with several clinics will be selected
- An app is developed to be placed on the provider system to upload the current referral request (which is sent as a fax) to appropriate clinic nodes on the blockchain add appendix showing referral information collected from existing fax form
- ASHLine uses an app on their dashboard to download the referral request and send a quick SMS message to the patient acknowledging their interest in the program
- The appropriate applications of the dashboard are revised to immediately contact the patient and solicit their participation – using a mechanism they prefer to contact them (phone, email, text, etc.)
- Assign the counseling staff to initiate the patient engagement sessions
- Reports generated are automatically uploaded to the report node of the blockchain, so providers can have real time access to the patient and/or referral status

Another node on the blockchain is used to perform macro or micro level analysis of patients by providers to inform providers on their patient status/adherence. Such analysis may include:

- What patient ecosystem characteristics are related to their adherence?
- How quickly are patients responding to scheduling calls? (for possible change in use of text or other options)
- How quickly is counseling done and what other metrics can help determine counseling effectiveness?
- What insight can patient adherence inform both ASHLine and Provider response – difference in patient insurance and eco system characteristics?
- How much effort is spent to cost justify referable process for patients who are insured vis-à-vis uninsured?

Figure 6. A database schema of the referral system

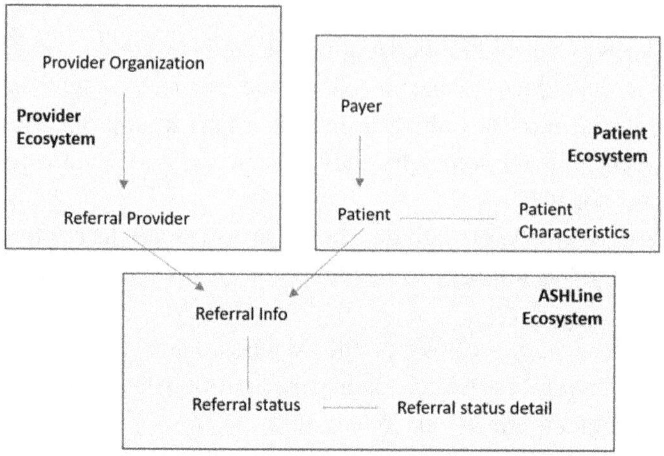

Benefits of Utilizing a Blockchain Model

- Safe, secure permissioned network to share patient health information in a HIPAA-compliant network
- Transmits mirrored provider-intermediary-patient information in real time
- Engages patients while motivation to quit is high
- Network can exist outside of traditional EHR providing cost savings to providers who may not have tens of thousands of dollars to invest in an EHR or want to modify their current EHR to accommodate the referral process
- Process can be applied in other contexts, e.g., managing ambulatory care service delivery, supporting other health interventions (behavioral health, diabetes)
- Creates high value for all stakeholders utilizing a low-cost solution
- Achieves the Triple Aim

Potential Issues and Challenges

The high level view of the database architecture that supports the referral system is shown in Figure 6 below. The data is a part of three different ecosystems that interact and collaborate in support of smoking cessation program. Some of the data needed for the referral ecosystem is generated from existing electronic health record (EHR) at some of the provider sites, and needs to be shared with ASHLine referral system, referred to here as performance dashboard, along with some of the patient data, some on the provider ecosystem and some is not a part of any system at present but is needed for effective analysis and support. One of the first challenge is determining which part of the data needs to be distributed via the blockchain that supports communication and coordination of care providers, ASHLine staff and patients, and which can remain outside the blockchain and referred to consultation and analysis.

A second challenge is determining how much of the data stored in the blockchain needs to remain on the network after certain time period, as blockchains typically timestamps the data blocks and stores with no ability to change unless it is a part of consensus protocol. However, many of the referrals lose their relevance over time, especially if the patient completes and moves out of the program or dies because of smoking related complications. Keeping the referrals to perpetuity appear to serve no purpose.

A third challenge is one scalability. As more providers are added to the system with different patient populations, the scalability of the network can become an issue and an alternative here is to form different blockchain networks by clustering these providers based on some criteria such as size of patient population, geographical region, etc. However, patients do move from one provider to another over time and this becomes an issue if providers are on different networks and patients complete or stop the program they are enrolled in under one provider and return to with a referral from another provider to continue counseling sessions. In such cases, there needs to be some level of synchronization of patient data across networks, if broader analysis of ASHLine effectiveness on patient adherence is needed over time. Similar issue arises if providers merge or some providers leave the care delivery system.

CONCLUSION

In a time of resource scarcity, heightened competition among stakeholders, and an ever-increasing demand for quality health care services, it is imperative for decision makers to continuously look for new ways to develop, implement, and analyze novel solutions that are capable of efficiently and effectively addressing the complexities of health care service delivery. Using a state tobacco quitline as a contextual example, principles of business intelligence coupled with its analysis towards the development of a novel information technology architecture (i.e. blockchain) is proposed as a potential solution to create value across multiple ecosystems.

The architecture proposed is to designed to be a secure platform for communication and coordination of those involved in addressing the needs of smoking population who want to quit. Future research is needed to see how such a shared platform can be used to gain insight on value provided (i.e. patient adherence to cessation counseling) and look for alternative resources that be can be obtained through public private partnership to improve patient adherence.

Another area of future research includes using the conceptual model and blockchain architecture to assess both the degree to which tailored models of smoking cessation can be developed to address select population segments, as well as apply similar framework to other types of counseling to populations distributed across regions and among several providers.

REFERENCES

Arizona Smokers' Helpline. (2019). *Arizona Smokers' Helpline Annual Report, 2019. University of Arizona*. Tucson, AZ: Author.

Centers for Disease Control and Prevention. (2014). Best practices for comprehensive tobacco control programs, 2014. U.S. Department of Health and Human Services, Centers for Disease Control and Prevention, National Center for Chronic Disease Prevention and Health Promotion, Office on Smoking and Health. Atlanta.

Glaser, F. (2017). *Pervasive decentralization of digital infrastructure: a framework for blockchain enabled system and use case analysis*. Hawaii: HICSS.

Gomber, P., Kauffman, R. J., Parker, C., & Weber, B. W. (2018). On the Fintech revolution: interpreting the forces of innovation, disruption, and transformation in financial services. *Journal of Management Information Systems* (35:1), pp. 220-265.

Limieux, V. (2017). Blockchain and distributed leaders as trusted record keeping systems: an archival theoretic evaluation framework. *Future Technology Conference*, Vancouver, Canada.

Lusch, R. F., & Nambisan, S. (2015). Service innovation: a service-dominant logic perspective. *Management Information Systems Quarterly*, *39*(1), 155–175. doi:10.25300/MISQ/2015/39.1.07

NAQC. (2018). *Adoption of best practices among state quitlines. North American Quitline Consortium*. Phoenix, AZ: Author.

Shiver, J., & Cantiello. (2016). *Managing integrated health systems*. Jones & Bartlett, Burlington, MA.

Soumerai, D., & Koppel, R. (2012, Sept. 18). A major glitch for digital health records. *The Wall Street Journal*, A17.

Subramanian, H. (2018, January). Decentralized blockchain-based electronic market places. *Communications of the ACM*, *61*(1), 78–84. doi:10.1145/3158333

Vargo, S. L., & Lusch, R. F. (2008). Service-dominant logic: continuing the evolution. *Journal of the Academy of Marketing Science*, *36*(1), 1–10. doi:10.100711747-007-0069-6

Weber, V., Bloom, F., Pierdon, S., & Wood, C. (2008). Employing the electronic health record to improve diabetes care: a multifacted intervention in an integrated delivery system. *Journal of General Internal Medicine*, *23*(4), 379–382. doi:10.100711606-007-0439-2 PMID:18373133

ENDNOTE

1 Examples of providers include physicians, pharmacists, mid-level practitioners, ancillary care providers, health extenders, and community health workers.

Chapter 10
Patient Empowerment and Analytics

Sumate Permwonguswa
Assumption University, Thailand

Dobin Yim
Loyola University Maryland, USA

ABSTRACT

The healthcare system is focusing more on patient empowerment leading to patients with active health management. In this process, although some mechanisms exist, there is a need for patient empowerment to move to a new realm where the empowerment process is activated remotely from the patient's side. With the increasing importance of Internet and e-health, it is believed that patient empowerment can be facilitated in the online setting and can be more effective than traditional face-to-face setting. Facilitating patient empowerment online also paves way to data analytics as various online activities can be tracked and the emerging analytic techniques can be utilized to gain insight into the data. This chapter provides knowledge on patient empowerment, data analytics, and their relationship including the role of patient empowerment in data analytics.

DOI: 10.4018/978-1-7998-2310-0.ch010

INTRODUCTION

Patient empowerment has long been proven to be useful in the healthcare industry (Anderson, 2007). Physicians suggest that patient empowerment is effective in helping patients who suffer from chronic symptoms and various severe diseases. Patient empowerment has been incorporated into the treatment regimen in many areas such as breast cancer, diabetes, and several types of psychological disorders.

In this era, when Internet has played an important role in connecting people around the world and even connecting various kinds of devices (i.e. wearable devices), the realm of patient empowerment has been moving towards the online world. More and more research has focused on how online technologies can not only inform but also intervene in managing personal health. Extant research studies examined factors such as demographics associated with online patient empowerment, generating and sharing medical knowledge and experience to complement existing system of knowledge (Permwonguswa, Khuntia, Yim, Gregg, & Kathuria, 2018). More recent studies explore how patient empowerment and participation contribute to their well-being and improve their health outcome, and the role of online technologies in augmenting or mediating end outcome.

Pervasive use of smart devices and increased bandwidth on communication technologies reduce inefficiencies in delivering medical knowledge to patients, as well as geographical distance between patients and medical experts, thereby enhancing patient accessibility to services. Self-help mobile monitoring apps such as diet, exercise, and sleep, as well as reminders to take medicine or keep appointments greatly improve patients to manage their own health effectively. In addition, medical conditions related to mental health are mentioned as areas for new opportunities as technologies provide privacy and anonymity.

For example, a 12-week internet-based cognitive behavioral therapy program improved patients with body dysmorphic disorder through reading self-help texts, completing interactive worksheets, and communicating with therapists via a messaging app within the platform (Enander et al., 2019). Mobile apps such as Woebot and Happify provide self-help to those with mild depression or mental health related issues to cope with daily stress (Carpenter et al., 2017).

Proliferation of websites, social networking technologies, and mobile apps enabled not only users from diverse background adopting these technologies to consume but also generate tremendous amount of data for new applications, especially in healthcare. The infrastructure, platform, and service availability on the cloud to store and process huge amounts of data necessitated a shift in data analytics paradigm. Moreover, the Internet of Things revolution is rapidly transforming disconnected systems of sensors, medical equipment, and hospitals and service facilities into a truly connected healthcare ecosystem.

The emerging trend of data analytics has also shed light on the healthcare industry hoping to gain some benefits from the emerging technologies. Some scholars have investigated the applications, the factors deterring the adoption, costs and benefits, managerial issues, and other relevant topics in the context of data analytics in healthcare industry.

The purpose of this chapter is to introduce the concept of online patient empowerment and suggest some practical implications of data analytics on patient empowerment. The chapter will start by discussing patient empowerment in general and how online technologies facilitate patient empowerment. The chapter follows by some factors influencing online patient empowerment and how data analytics can be leveraged to help magnify the effect of patient empowerment.

PATIENT EMPOWERMENT

Patient empowerment is the process of enabling and encouraging patients to actively take appropriate health actions to stabilize their health conditions or even to heal better and faster (Anderson, 2007; Samoocha, Bruinvels, Elbers, Anema, & van der Beek, 2010). Patient empowerment is a long-term process usually for patients with chronic diseases (Bravo et al., 2015). Patients who encounter chronic diseases (i.e. diabetes, blood pressure conditions, chronic back pain) usually suffer from mild discomfort to severe pain. The frequency of these conditions may vary from patient to patient. Regardless of the severity and frequency, many patients find it difficult to live their normal lives. Even worse, some lose jobs due to their chronic health conditions (Hannah, 2017). These personal problems collectively can be aggravated to a wider scope in the long run (i.e. public health issues, economic issues). Some studies associate unemployment with health and healthcare spending (Pellegrini, Rodriguez-Monguio, & Qian, 2014). It is still controversial whether health issues cause unemployment or vice versa. However, it is clear that health issues cause major issues to the world's economy as the healthcare spending is increasing every year (OECD Data, 2019) while the US healthcare spending alone has skyrocketed to $3.65 trillion in 2018 (Sherman, 2019). Therefore, this problem needs immediate attention, and patient empowerment has been proved to alleviate the symptoms resulting in a better health outcome.

There is no consensus of the definition of patient empowerment as there are different definitions and scopes of patient empowerment used in different research studies (Bravo et al., 2015; McAllister, Dunn, Payne, Davies, & Todd, 2012). Some definitions focus on the process of patients gaining control over their own health (Martha M Funnell & Anderson, 2004; Martha M. Funnell, Nwankwo, Gillard, Anderson, & Tang, 2005). Some focus on the change in personal attitudes and psychological states that encourages patient to take active actions toward a better health (Aujoulat, d'Hoore, & Deccache, 2007; Lau, 2002). Some focus on the social support and intention to help other patients gain control over their health (Gibson, 1991). Although the definitions of patient empowerment are a bit different, they all evolve around the concept of encouraging patients to actively manage their own health.

Previous research conceptualizes psychological empowerment, an individual level of patient empowerment, as a multi-dimensional construct comprises four dimensions: meaningfulness, autonomy, self-efficacy, and impact (Deng, Khuntia, & Ghosh, 2013). Meaningfulness refers to how important the treatment option is for the patient. Autonomy is the patient's freedom to make his or her own decision on the treatment options. Self-efficacy is the patient's confidence or perception of the ability to manage his or her own health. Finally, impact refers to the perception of how and how much the treatment options will affect the patient's health conditions and the long-term consequence of their life. These dimensions are sometimes referred to as cognitive and emotional empowerment (Christens, Collura, & Tahir, 2013; Zimmerman, 2000).

In a bigger picture, the patient will go through the 'situation interpretation' phase, which will happen before the treatment. The psychological empowerment will happen in the treatment phase. Along the treatment process, psychological empowerment will lead to the patient's behaviors such as the change in his or her lifestyle, medication adherence, and treatment intervention. As the consequence, the patient's behaviors will influence the effectiveness of the treatment and the final health outcomes (Bravo et al., 2015).

A recent research expands the concept of patient empowerment to cover patient level, provider level, and health system level (Bravo et al., 2015). The study proposes a conceptual model, which covers a broader perspective of patient empowerment as it covers all stakeholders in the patient empowerment process. The model consists of five key components: underpinning ethos, moderators, interventions, indicators, and outcomes. According to Merriam-Webster Dictionary, *ethos* is defined as "the distinguishing character, sentiment, moral nature, or guiding beliefs of a person, group, or institution" (Merriam-Webster, 2019). Hence, the underpinning ethos refer to the internal characteristics manifested in a person's or community's beliefs, ideas, or culture. The underpinning ethos vary across the three levels of stakeholders. For example, autonomy, which is a dimension of psychological empowerment, is conceptualized as a part of ethos at the patient level whereas respect to patient's autonomy is the ethos at the healthcare provider level. Interestingly, self-efficacy, which is another dimension of psychological empowerment, is still an indicator of patient empowerment in Bravo's model. This conceptual model is derived from structured analysis of previous literature; hence its coverage is more comprehensive.

HEALTH INFOMEDIARY

Health infomediary is an emerging tool that leverages the power of Internet to facilitate patient empowerment (Permwonguswa, Khuntia, Yim, & Gregg, 2017; Permwonguswa et al., 2018). Hagel III combined the word "information" with "intermediary" and coined it as "infomediary", which means a person who provides information relevant to a specific topic in one place (Hagel III & Rayport, 1997; Zahedi & Song, 2008). Online infomediaries include all types of online information providers i.e. online discussion forums and web portals (Zahedi & Song, 2008). A *health infomediary* is defined as an online health platform that facilitates interactions between patients and providers with the purpose of sharing experience and knowledge for health management (Koch-Weser, Bardshaw, Gualtieri, & Gallagher, 2010; Schwartz et al., 2006).

There exist two broad types of infomediaries: general-purposed and specific-purposed infomediaries. Examples of general-purposed infomediaries are answers.com and ask.com. They provide general information covering a wide range of purposes. On the other hand, some infomediaries serve more specific purposes such as mechanics, travel, food. Health infomediaries are among the specific-purposed infomediaries connecting patients and providers together. However, there are some properties of health infomediaries that are different from those of other infomediaries: (1) The nature of information shared, (2) the importance of information quality, (3) factors driving the information sharing (Permwonguswa et al., 2018).

The knowledge being shared on health infomediaries is uniquely different in that people are often sharing their *personal information* – including their *private* and *sensitive* information. In general-purposed infomediaries, people may be sharing information on miscellaneous topics (Adamic, Zhang, Bakshy, & Ackerman, 2008). For instance, people share rating and reviews about their favorite restaurants on Yelp. People share mechanical knowledge and review different types of vehicles on car forums. On the other hand, people share their experience of breast surgery or erectile dysfunction on health infomediaries. Sometimes, they even show their private pictures. These knowledge and information shared on health infomediaries are much more personal and sensitive than the information shared on other infomediaries, and this is one of main properties that distinguishes health infomediaries from others (Yim, Khuntia, & Argyris, 2015).

The information shared on health infomediaries can lead to life or death situation as it involves patient's health and treatments (Sharma, Xu, Wickramasinghe, & Ahmed, 2006). If a patient receives the wrong information related to health conditions or treatments, his or her conditions could be worse. In the worst case, he or she could end up dead. For instance, an early-stage cancer patient seeks out more information from a low-quality health infomediary and believes in the false information that the cancer can be cured using a non-FDA approved elixir instead of undergoing an appropriate treatment regimen. The consequence could be a tragedy. In contrast, a well-informed decision based on the right information may help prolong a patient's life, or at least, minimize the affliction. Hence, the quality of the shared information is extremely important on health infomediaries (Permwonguswa et al., 2018).

On health infomediaries, the factors driving information sharing are likely to be different from those on other infomediaries; the magnitude of the effects are also likely to be different (Permwonguswa et al., 2018). Trust is a well-known factor influencing information sharing on online infomediaries (Zahedi & Song, 2008). However, as the information shared on health infomediaries involves life and death situations, much higher trust is required to drive a person to share private information and to seek for health information on health infomediaries (Permwonguswa et al., 2018). When people seek advice for specific issues, the advice from experts and persons who have direct experience is more valuable than the advice from people who do not have direct experience or expertise in relevant areas. For example, an advice from a mechanic is perceived as more valuable and trustworthy than an advice from a car owner when it is about the engine problems. Similarly, the experience and expertise of the information sharers on health infomediaries contribute to the value of the information being shared. Among the patients with chronic conditions, the information from patients with the same diseases or conditions can be more valuable than the information from doctors or nurses (Khuntia, Yim, Tanniru, & Lim, 2017). This is probably because patients have direct experience on the sufferings caused by the diseases while doctors may not have direct experience on the sufferings. Hence, it can be inferred that direct experience is more valuable than knowledge in some cases.

BIG DATA TECHNOLOGY

The term big data has been a trendy word recently. People usually think of big data as a large amount of data. The question that follows the idea of big data is 'how large should it be to be considered as big data?'. A previous literature suggests that big data refers to a large amount of data that exceeds the capability of regular software to handle it within a reasonable amount of time (Snijders, Matzat, & Reips, 2012). However, this definition suffers from inability of provide a clear cut-off point as the capability of the software increases rapidly over time (Brock & Moore, 2006). Hence, another approach to define big data has been proposed. Some scholars suggest that the nature of the big data does not involve only the volume of the data, but also involves some other properties of the data. Extant literature has defined big data as having a different number of properties. Some literature defines big data as having three properties (3 V's): volume, variety, and velocity (Garlasu et al., 2013). Volume is self-explanatory. Variety refers to the nature of online data, which can be in various forms. Velocity refers to the speed at which the data is generated. The data generated from the online interactions on the Internet are always flowing at an extremely fast rate, and hence it requires a well-designed infrastructure to handle a rapid flow of data stream. This definition of big data is commonly adopted by academicians i.e. in the textbooks (Coronel & Morris, 2018; Hoffer, Venkataraman, & Topi, 2018) and by practitioners i.e. CISCO (Gerhardt, Griffin, & Klemann, 2012).

Regarding the variety of data, it is worth a little further clarification. The data can be grouped into three broad categories: structured, semi-structured, and unstructured (Monica & Kumar, 2013). Structured data refers to a well-defined data stored in a non-proprietary system i.e. data in a relational database or data warehouse where a clear structure must be defined prior to the collection and the storage of the data into the system. Unstructured data refers to the data that do not have a clear systematic structure. Videos and images are usually considered unstructured data. At the time of writing, the technology that allows extraction and analysis of videos and images is still a state-of-an-art, and therefore, it is still extremely difficult to extract some insight from these data. On the other hand, unstructured text data (i.e. comments and discussions) can be extracted and analyzed using some advanced text mining techniques to gain insight from these data. Lastly, semi-structured data refers to anything between structured and unstructured data. For example, vast amount of data on the Internet has some pre-defined structure. Although the structures vary depending on the owner of the data, some structures can be found. For example, online data in the form of JSON and XML are considered semi-structured. Semi-structured data can be extracted and analyzed using some programming skills and advanced analytical techniques (Arasu & Garcia-Molina, 2003).

Nonetheless, additional big data properties were proposed by Inderpal Bhandar, Chief Data Officer at Express Scripts, in the presentation at the Big Data Innovation Summit in Boston (Normandeau, 2013). Veracity was most emphasized while validity and volatility were also brought to attention of data scientists. Veracity, mentioned as the greatest challenge, refers to the biases and noises in the data, which may cause wrong results or misinterpretation in data analytics. Validity refers to the correctness and accuracy of the data. Lastly, volatility refers to the time period when the data is valid and length of time the data should be stored. This property emphasizes the need to determine the expiry date of the data. An additional property of big data, value, is found in some literature (Kaisler, Armour, Espinosa, & Money, 2013; Khan et al., 2014; Money, Kaisler, Armour, & Espinosa, 2017). Value refers to the usefulness of the data in decision making (Gantz & Reinsel, 2011; Kaisler et al., 2013).

To sum up, the existing literature has mentioned seven properties (7 V's) of big data, which are volume, variety, velocity, veracity, validity, volatility, and value. However, only the first three have been widely referred to both in academia and practical world.

DATA ANALYTICS IN HEALTHCARE

Proliferation of big data produced by consumers using connected devices and social networking technologies such as Facebook, Twitter, Instagram, to name a few has renewed interest in the data analytics. Data analytics has played a pivotal role in winning a presidential election(Stieglitz & Dang-Xuan, 2013). The same benefits can be expected in the healthcare industry. For instance, crowdsourced detection and tracking infectious diseases such as Google Flu Trends and Twitter has reduced the costs while raising public awareness of outbreaks and epidemics. Popularity of Apple Watch, Fitbits, and other health devices and apps have enhanced our understanding of personal lifestyle and well-being.

The data generated from consumers can complement and enrich health data sources in the healthcare ecosystem such as sensors, medical equipment, patient and provider records. Health providers can leverage data analytics to make existing healthcare processes efficient, as well as enabling new use cases, ranging from reducing diagnostic errors to accelerating drug and treatment discoveries.

The advances in big data technologies have enabled data analytics to leverage both primary and secondary data sources for healthcare applications in two ways. First, parallel processing and machine learning algorithms have improved data processing speed and volume and quickly generating insights. Second, reduced startup cost and ease of accessing the cloud infrastructure as a software service have democratized the use of big data technologies to both large and small healthcare service providers. Thus, integrating data across *primary* sources – patient health records, physicians' clinical notes, hospital or other providers' admission records, physical data such as sensors, X-rays, Computed Tomography (CT) scans, and so forth – with *secondary sources* – social media, personal health app, wearable devices, etc. – are now possible to derive richer insights. However, challenges in training existing healthcare workforce to process data from diverse sources, as well as educating managers how to interpret the analysis outcomes have slowed the adoption of big data technologies in the healthcare industry. Despite these challenges, progress is being made across healthcare industries, with developments in standardization efforts such as HL7 for data interoperability to connect disjointed healthcare information systems, such as electronic health records (EHR), clinical document architecture (CDA), and fast healthcare information resource (FHIR).

Data analysis techniques commonly known as descriptive analysis start with simple summarization of transactions and service records, and aligning highest or lowest ranking of entities such as patient or disease categories, service quality of physicians or facilities, and so forth, at or over various time periods to performance metrics, thus improving decision making process. Extracting information from various data sources in timely manner involves the use of tools such as data warehouse, data marts, data visualization, and other business intelligence toolsets with vendors such as IBM, Teradata, SAS, and offering a suite of products customized for healthcare.

The next level of data analytics broadly categorized under predictive analytics extend extracted and structured data from a large dataset to predict or learn important outcomes for individual patients. The key distinction between descriptive and predictive analytics is the emphasis on summarizing a sampled population (i.e. descriptive) vs. making inferences or recommendation for an individual (i.e. predictive). Algorithms developed from computer science and statistics can be developed to *teach* machines to identify important patterns in underlying data, so that the learned patterns in turn can be used to predict individual outcome with optimal accuracy.

Prediction techniques such as decision tree, k-nearest neighbor, support vector machines, logistic regression, have been getting widespread use. Neural networks and especially deep neural network-based techniques are gaining more prominence as computing costs are getting more affordable. These techniques typically require a large dataset with known outcomes so that the machines can recognize patterns and derive rules from the dataset to make accurate predictions. This limitation of having *labeled* (i.e. known health outcome) potentially limits its immediate application. Related and more practical class of machine learning techniques known as unsupervised algorithms, which includes k-means and hierarchical clustering, and dimensionality reduction techniques such as PCA or matrix factorization, may be used identify useful patterns to reduce complexity within a dataset for application such as identifying patient risk groups.

Some of the use cases in healthcare include, but not limited to, increasing diagnostic accuracy and assisting clinical practice, quicker enumeration of treatment options, enhanced monitoring and alerting potential risk associated with prescriptions. More innovative applications have been discovered recently such as predicting disease discovery through analysis of retinal images (Odaibo et al., 2019). Other innovation leveraging advanced machine learning techniques also include predicting health outcome through genomic sequencing (Leung, Delong, Alipanahi, & Frey, 2015), and genetic modification for intervention, which also raises ethical concerns with the use of such technology.

PATIENT EMPOWERMENT AS A DATA SOURCE

A number of clinical studies have found online patient empowerment to be effective contributing to better health outcomes (Glasgow et al., 2012; Nguyen et al., 2013; Warmerdam, van Straten, Twisk, Riper, & Cuijpers, 2008). Furthermore, a more recent study suggests that online patient empowerment can be fostered by manipulating the environment or interactions on the health infomediaries to nurture the self-efficacy and social identity of the participants and to avoid intimating those who suffer from internalized self-stigma (Permwonguswa et al., 2018). These activities also influence knowledge sharing on health infomediaries – a source of data that can be the input for data analytics in healthcare.

Patient empowerment in health infomediaries is an ongoing process including blog posts, comments, discussions, conversations, connections, likes, and ratings. For example, PatientsLikeMe and RealSelf allow patients to connect to each other, talk, and create sub-communities on the platforms (Khuntia et al., 2017; Yim et al., 2015). These online activities constantly generate a huge amount of data on the platform. Furthermore, some other data exist and can be captured using Clickstream technology. For instance, how long each user spends on each page, the sequence of page viewed by each user, the browser and the device each user uses to view or interact on the platform. All these activities and interactions are not explicit data but can be converted into data if the platform is well aware of the opportunity and has prepared appropriate infrastructure to capture the data.

As suggested by previous literature, patient empowerment and engagement, and knowledge sharing on the health infomediaries can be fostered if the platforms understand the dynamics of the patients or users on their platforms and tailor the user experience to facilitate and encourage the interactions on the platforms (Permwonguswa et al., 2018). As a consequence, higher volume of data can be captured, and higher opportunity will be available for health data analytics.

In addition, health infomediaries may take another step to boost the volume of data by providing a feature for users to sync the data from their wearable devices on to the platforms (Google Play, 2019). Popular brands of activity trackers like Garmin and FitBit allow their customers to upload the data on to their platforms through web sites and apps, and to connect with friends to create online communities to promote health. Similar concept can be added as a new feature on health infomediaries to boost up the user engagement as well as the volume of the data.

Table 1 maps the online data sources with the characteristics of data based on the criteria broadly discussed in the Big Data Technology section. Data from health infomediaries are classified as secondary data, similar to data from social media. Various types of data exist on health infomediaries. They can be categorized into structured, semi-structured, and unstructured data. Descriptive and prescriptive

Table 1. Mapping of Online Health Data Sources and Characteristics of Data

<table>
<tr><th colspan="3" rowspan="2"></th><th colspan="3">Examples and Characteristics of Data</th></tr>
<tr><th>Structured</th><th>Semi-structured</th><th>Unstructured</th></tr>
<tr><td rowspan="3">Data Source</td><td>Primary</td><td>EHR</td><td>Patient Records
Encounters
Treatment Regimens
Vital Data</td><td></td><td>MRI
CT Scan
X-ray</td></tr>
<tr><td rowspan="2">Secondary</td><td>Health Infomediary</td><td>Diseases
Symptoms
Duration of Infliction</td><td>Likes
Ratings
Connections
Usage Time
Frequency of Usage
Log files
User behaviors</td><td>Blog posts
Comments
Discussions
Conversations</td></tr>
<tr><td>Social Media</td><td>Social Media Platforms
Followed Accounts</td><td>Likes
Shares
Connections</td><td>Posts
Comments</td></tr>
</table>

analytical techniques can be applied to structured and semi-structured data. However, for unstructured data, more advanced techniques i.e. text mining and analytics are required in order to extract meaningful insights from large amount of text data. The results from text mining and text analytics can then be further analyzed using predictive analytical techniques to learn the patterns useful for decision making or crafting future empowerment strategies.

FINAL THOUGHT ON PATIENT EMPOWERMENT AND DATA ANALYTICS

To recapitulate, the relationship between patient empowerment and data analytics is a two-way relationship. In short, patient empowerment provides input for data analytics as a secondary data source. On the other hand, the patterns possibly discovered by data analytics will provide insight on how to empower the patients more effectively. This, in turn, will create more data, which will be the input for the refinement of future empowerment strategies.

There is no single analytical technique that is appropriate for patient empowerment data. The appropriate technique depends on the researcher's objective. Descriptive techniques may be used if the main objective is to provide the summary data to help in decision making. More advanced predictive techniques may be used if the objective is unclear (i.e. when the researcher wants to explore and learn more insight from the data). High-level machine learning techniques may be applied to identify some patterns useful in crafting more efficient and effective strategies.

REFERENCES

Adamic, L. A., Zhang, J., Bakshy, E., & Ackerman, M. S. (2008, April 21). Knowledge sharing and yahoo answers: everyone knows something. In *Proceedings 17th International Conference on World Wide Web*. 10.1145/1367497.1367587

Anderson, B. (2007). Collaborative care and motivational interviewing: improving depression outcomes through patient empowerment interventions. *The American Journal of Managed Care, 13*(Sup4), S103-S106.

Arasu, A., & Garcia-Molina, H. (2003). Extracting structured data from web pages. In *Proceedings of the 2003 ACM SIGMOD International Conference on Management of Data*. 10.1145/872757.872799

Aujoulat, I., d'Hoore, W., & Deccache, A. (2007). Patient empowerment in theory and practice: polysemy or cacophony? *Patient Education and Counseling*, *66*(1), 13–20. doi:10.1016/j.pec.2006.09.008 PMID:17084059

Bravo, P., Edwards, A., Barr, P. J., Scholl, I., Elwyn, G., & McAllister, M. (2015). Conceptualising patient empowerment: A mixed methods study. *BMC Health Services Research*, *15*(1), 252. doi:10.118612913-015-0907-z PMID:26126998

Brock, D. C., & Moore, G. E. (2006). *Understanding Moore's law: four decades of innovation*. Chemical Heritage Foundation.

Carpenter, J., Crutchley, P., Zilca, R. D., Schwartz, H. A., Smith, L. K., Cobb, A. M., & Parks, A. C. (2017). Correction: Seeing the "big" picture: Big data methods for exploring relationships between usage, language, and outcome in internet intervention data. *Journal of Medical Internet Research*, *19*(12). doi:10.2196/jmir.8099 PMID:29258059

Christens, B. D., Collura, J. J., & Tahir, F. (2013). Critical hopefulness: a person-centered analysis of the intersection of cognitive and emotional empowerment. *American Journal of Community Psychology*, *52*(1-2), 170–184. doi:10.100710464-013-9586-2 PMID:23793530

Coronel, C., & Morris, S. (2018). *Database systems: Design, Implementation, & Management* (13th ed.). US: Cengage.

Deng, X., Khuntia, J., & Ghosh, K. (2013, Dec. 15-18). Psychological empowerment of patients with chronic diseases: the role of digital integration. In *Proceedings 34th International Conference on Information Systems*, Milan, Italy. dblp computer science bibliography.

Enander, J., Ljótsson, B., Anderhell, L., Runeborg, M., Flygare, O., Cottman, O., ... Ivanov, V. Z. (2019). Long-term outcome of therapist-guided internet-based cognitive behavioural therapy for body dysmorphic disorder (BDD-NET): A naturalistic 2-year follow-up after a randomised controlled trial. *BMJ Open*, *9*(1). doi:10.1136/bmjopen-2018-024307 PMID:30647044

Funnell, M. M., & Anderson, R. M. (2004). Empowerment and self-management of diabetes. *Clinical Diabetes*, *22*(3), 123–127. doi:10.2337/diaclin.22.3.123

Funnell, M. M., Nwankwo, R., Gillard, M. L., Anderson, R. M., & Tang, T. S. (2005). Implementing an empowerment-based diabetes self-management education program. *The Diabetes Educator*, *31*(1), 53–61. doi:10.1177/0145721704273166 PMID:15779247

Gantz, J., & Reinsel, D. (2011). Extracting value from chaos. *IDC iview*, *1142*(2011), 1-12.

Garlasu, D., Sandulescu, V., Halcu, I., Neculoiu, G., Grigoriu, O., Marinescu, M., & Marinescu, V. (2013). A big data implementation based on Grid computing. In *Proceedings the 2013 11th RoEduNet International Conference.* 10.1109/RoEduNet.2013.6511732

Gerhardt, B., Griffin, K., & Klemann, R. (2012). Unlocking value in the fragmented world of big data analytics. *Cisco Internet Business Solutions Group, 7.*

Gibson, C. H. (1991). A concept analysis of empowerment. *Journal of Advanced Nursing*, *16*(3), 354–361. doi:10.1111/j.1365-2648.1991.tb01660.x PMID:2037742

Glasgow, R. E., Kurz, D., King, D., Dickman, J. M., Faber, A. J., Halterman, E., ... Ritzwoller, D. (2012). Twelve-month outcomes of an internet-based diabetes self-management support program. *Patient Education and Counseling*, *87*(1), 81–92. doi:10.1016/j.pec.2011.07.024 PMID:21924576

Google Play. (2019). Android apps on Google Play: Health and fitness. Retrieved from https://play.google.com/store/apps/category/HEALTH_AND_FITNESS

Hagel, J. III, & Rayport, J. F. (1997). The coming battle for customer information. *Harvard Business Review*, *75*(1), 53. PMID:10174454

Hannah, L. (2017). What it was like losing my job because of my illness. Retrieved from https://themighty.com/2017/04/losing-job-for-being-sick/

Hoffer, J., Venkataraman, R., & Topi, H. (2018). *Modern database management* (13th ed.). US: Pearson.

Kaisler, S., Armour, F., Espinosa, J. A., & Money, W. (2013). Big data: Issues and challenges moving forward. In *Proceedings the 2013 46th Hawaii International Conference on System Sciences.* 10.1109/HICSS.2013.645

Khan, N., Yaqoob, I., Hashem, I. A. T., Inayat, Z., Ali, M., Kamaleldin, W., ... Gani, A. (2014). Big data: Survey, technologies, opportunities, and challenges. *The Scientific World Journal*, 2014. PMID:25136682

Khuntia, J., Yim, D., Tanniru, M., & Lim, S. (2017). Patient empowerment and engagement with a health infomediary. *Health Policy and Technology*, *6*(1), 40–50. doi:10.1016/j.hlpt.2016.11.003

Koch-Weser, S., Bardshaw, Y. S., Gualtieri, L., & Gallagher, S. S. (2010). The Internet as a health information source: Findings from the 2007 Health Information National Trends Survey and Implications for Health Communication. *Journal of Health Communication, 15*(Sup3), 279-293.

Lau, D. H. (2002). Patient empowerment: A Patient-centred approach to improve care. *Hong Kong Medical Journal*, *8*(5), 372–374. PMID:12376717

Leung, M. K., Delong, A., Alipanahi, B., & Frey, B. J. (2015). Machine learning in genomic medicine: A review of computational problems and data sets. *Proceedings of the IEEE*, *104*(1), 176–197. doi:10.1109/JPROC.2015.2494198

McAllister, M., Dunn, G., Payne, K., Davies, L., & Todd, C. (2012). Patient empowerment: The need to consider it as a measurable patient-reported outcome for chronic conditions. *BMC Health Services Research*, *12*(1), 157. doi:10.1186/1472-6963-12-157 PMID:22694747

Merriam-Webster. (2019). Dictionary by Merriam-Webster. Retrieved from https://www.merriam-webster.com

Money, W. H., Kaisler, S. H., Armour, F., & Espinosa, J. A. (2017). Big data: The path to maturity. *International Journal of Systems and Service-Oriented Engineering*, *7*(2), 1–23. doi:10.4018/IJSSOE.2017040101

Monica, N., & Kumar, K. R. (2013). Survey on Big Data by coordinating mapreduce to integrate variety of data. *International Journal of Science and Research (IJSR) (Online)*, 2319-7064.

Nguyen, H. Q., Donesky, D., Reinke, L. F., Wolpin, S., Chyall, L., Benditt, J. O., ... Carrieri-Kohlman, V. (2013). Internet-based dyspnea self-management support for patients with chronic obstructive pulmonary disease. *Journal of Pain and Symptom Management, 46*(1), 43–55. doi:10.1016/j.jpainsymman.2012.06.015 PMID:23073395

Normandeau, K. (2013). Beyond volume, variety and velocity is the issue of big data veracity. *Inside big data.* Retrieved from https://insidebigdata.com/2013/09/12/beyond-volume-variety-velocity-issue-big-data-veracity/

Odaibo, S. G. MomPremier, M., Hwang, R. Y., Yousuf, S., Williams, S., & Grant, J. (2019). Mobile artificial intelligence technology for detecting macula edema and subretinal fluid on OCT scans: Initial results from the DATUM alpha Study. *arXiv preprint arXiv:1902.02905.*

OECD Data. (2019). Health resources: Health spending. Retrieved from https://data.oecd.org/healthres/health-spending.htm

Pellegrini, L. C., Rodriguez-Monguio, R., & Qian, J. (2014). The US healthcare workforce and the labor market effect on healthcare spending and health outcomes. *International Journal of Health Care Finance and Economics, 14*(2), 127–141. doi:10.100710754-014-9142-0 PMID:24652416

Permwonguswa, S., Khuntia, J., Yim, D., & Gregg, D. (2017). *Empowerment and knowledge sharing in health infomediary: empirical evidence from reconstructive surgery patients.* Paper presented at the Americas Conference on Information Systems 2017, Boston, MA.

Permwonguswa, S., Khuntia, J., Yim, D., Gregg, D., & Kathuria, A. (2018). Knowledge sharing in a health infomediary: Role of self-concept, emotional empowerment, and self-esteem. *Health Systems (Basingstoke, England), 7*(3), 181–194. doi:10.1080/20476965.2017.1405875 PMID:31214347

Samoocha, D., Bruinvels, D. J., Elbers, N. A., Anema, J. R., & van der Beek, A. J. (2010). Effectiveness of web-based interventions on patient empowerment: a systematic review and meta-analysis. *Journal of Medical Internet Research, 12*(2). doi:10.2196/jmir.1286 PMID:20581001

Schwartz, K. L., Roe, T., Northrup, J., Meza, J., Seifeldin, R., & Neale, A. V. (2006). Family medicine patients' use of the internet for health information: a metronet study. *Journal of the American Board of Family Medicine, 19*(1), 39–45. doi:10.3122/jabfm.19.1.39 PMID:16492004

Sharma, S. K., Xu, H., Wickramasinghe, N., & Ahmed, N. (2006). Electronic healthcare: issues and challenges. *International Journal of Electronic Healthcare*, *2*(1), 50–65. doi:10.1504/IJEH.2006.008693 PMID:18048234

Sherman, E. (2019). *U.S. health care costs skyrocketed to $3.65 trillion in 2018.* Retrieved from https://fortune.com/2019/02/21/us-health-care-costs-2/

Snijders, C., Matzat, U., & Reips, U.-D. (2012). Big data: Big gaps of knowledge in the field of internet science. *International Journal of Internet Science*, *7*(1), 1–5.

Stieglitz, S., & Dang-Xuan, L. (2013). Social media and political communication: A social media analytics framework. *Social Network Analysis and Mining*, *3*(4), 1277–1291. doi:10.100713278-012-0079-3

Warmerdam, L., van Straten, A., Twisk, J., Riper, H., & Cuijpers, P. (2008). Internet-based treatment for adults with depressive symptoms: randomized controlled trial. *Journal of Medical Internet Research*, *10*(4), e44. doi:10.2196/jmir.1094 PMID:19033149

Yim, D., Khuntia, J., & Argyris, Y. (2015). Identifying bands in the knowledge exchange spectrum in an online health infomediary. [IJHISI]. *International Journal of Healthcare Information Systems and Informatics*, *10*(3), 63–84. doi:10.4018/IJHISI.2015070104

Zahedi, F. M., & Song, J. (2008). Dynamics of trust revision: using health infomediaries. *Journal of Management Information Systems*, *24*(4), 225–248. doi:10.2753/MIS0742-1222240409

Zimmerman, M. A. (2000). Empowerment theory. In J. Rappaport, & E. Seidman (Eds.), *Handbook of community psychology* (pp. 43–63). New York: Springer. doi:10.1007/978-1-4615-4193-6_2

Chapter 11
Guiding Assistive-Technology Adaptations Through Intelligent Stream Mining of Patient Data

William Robinson
Georgia State University, USA

Tianjie Deng
University of Denver, USA

Andrea Aria
Georgia State University, USA

ABSTRACT

Users with cognitive impairments use assistive technology as part of a treatment plan. As the AT interface is manipulated, data stream mining techniques are used to monitor user goals. In this context, data mining aids caregivers in tracking user behaviors as they attempt to achieve their goals. Divergences over consecutive stream-mined models identify potential changes in user goal attainment, as the user learns his or her personalized emailing system. When a data-mined model diverges significantly from recent models, the user's behavior is flagged as a significant behavioral change. The specific changes in behavior are then characterized by analyzing model divergence as well as the underlying data. This chapter describes how divergence analysis of decision-tree and hidden Markov models can aid recognition and diagnoses of behavioral changes in support of AT adaptation, in a case study of cognitive AT for emailing. The technique may be more widely applicable to other behavior monitoring contexts.

DOI: 10.4018/978-1-7998-2310-0.ch011

INTRODUCTION

One in 4 U.S. adults (61 million Americans) have a disability that impacts major life activities (Okoro et al., 2017). More than one million adults in the U.S. are diagnosed each year with cognitive impairments (CI) due to neurological disease or trauma. Currently, there are between 13.3 to 16.1 million Americans living with chronic brain disorders and associated CI (Alliance, 2001). In addition, approximately 4 million Americans have developmental disabilities that impact cognitive functioning (Services, 2002). Cognitive impairments prevent this large and growing segment of our society from fully integrating into society (McColl et al., 1998).

Assistive technology (AT) should help. However, studies have found that AT systems are abandoned by CI users at shockingly high rates (de Joode et al., 2010a; LoPresti et al., 2004; Wilson et al., 2001a; Wright et al., 2001). One major cause of abandonment is an eventual misalignment between: (1) user goals and abilities, and (2) the functionality delivered by the system. Research described in this chapter supports the monitoring of this relationship between user goals and their satisfaction by the system. In a case study, users are given an email system to aid in their activities of daily living (ADLs). At appropriate times, the system is adapted to meet the changing needs of the user. By monitoring a user's event stream, post-clinic care teams and researchers can notice changes in user behavior that indicate that the system should be adapted. This work has mitigated this misalignment for dozens of clients engaged in cognitive rehabilitation. This technology is applicable to personalized user monitoring and generalizes to monitoring voluminous streams of event data.

AT-Supported Integrated Intelligent Health Systems

As noted by Acampora et al. (2015), the exploitation of information technology for implementing autonomous and pro-active healthcare servers are becoming extremely beneficial to the society. As a result, computer assistive technologies are becoming a common component of integrated health systems. Assistive technologies provide post-clinical support to clients such as assisted rehabilitation for individuals with disabilities (Robinson et al., 2012a), self-management of chronic diseases, medication management, and remote health monitoring (Acampora et al., 2015; Broek et al., 2010). Such low cost, post-clinical health systems embedded within home and other living environments enable the healthcare industry to utilize the limited resources more efficiently and effectively (Acampora et al., 2015; Nakashima et al., 2009).

Figure 1. Components of an AT-based integrated health monitoring system

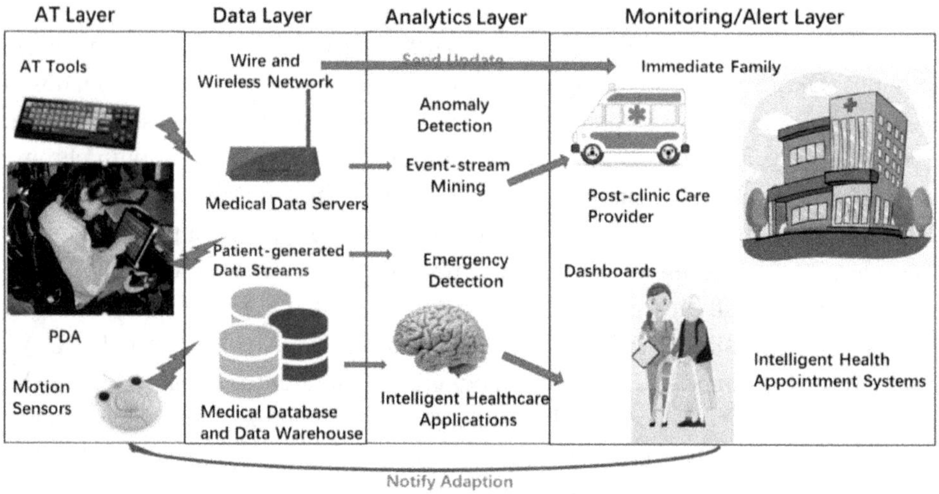

Figure 1 summarizes major components of an AT-based integrated health monitoring system. In the first layer, the client uses assistive technology to engage in healthcare-related activities such as self-management of chronic diseases and post-clinical rehabilitation (Broek et al., 2010). Where the AT is embed in an environment that includes a variety of devices, such as mobile phones, computers, PDAs, embedded devices, and wired or wireless sensors the environment is called Ambient Assisted Living (AAL) (Li et al., 2015). Clients in an AAL generate large amounts of event-stream data as they engage in activities of daily living (ADLs) and interact with AT devices, and those data are transmitted to and subsequently saved in medical data servers (as noted in the Data Layer). Often such data are monitored by care providers as noted in the Monitor Layer in Figure 1, so that the client's progress can be constantly evaluated. Based on such evaluation, care providers can notify the AT system to adapt to the client's changing needs.

Research into assistive technology for those with cognitive impairments overlaps but is distinct from AAL (Siegel et al., 2017). Marshall (2000) defines AT as "[...] any item, piece of equipment, product or system, whether acquired commercially, off-the-shelf, modified or customized, that is used to increase, maintain or improve functional capabilities of individuals with cognitive, physical or communication disabilities." An AT is used by the client primarily to aid cognition, rather than part of a diffuse, ambient, infrastructure primarily for client monitoring as is common to AAL systems (Bharucha et al., 2009). AT for CI provides support for symptoms of dementia, social contact, health monitoring and perceived safety (Siegel et al., 2017).

In particular, social isolation has been identified as a critical problem (McHugh et al., 2012) for which AT may have the greatest impact (Sixsmith et al., 2007).

Clients use AT, whereas AAL is ambient infrastructure. Thus, clients abandon AT, whereas they may not notice AAL infrastructure enough to even consider abandoning it. Consequently, AT developers monitor AT usage to inform AT adaptations that involve the client and maintain compatibility with client goals (Brodwin et al., 2004; Sohlberg et al., 2011; Sutcliffe et al., 2006; Todis et al., 2005). Thus, monitoring client AT usage with respect to client goal achievement is critical to maintaining AT compatibility, and more generally the perception that the AT is necessary (Peek et al., 2014). Thus, models of client goal achievement with the AT is important research that contributes to the success of AT systems.

Analytic Support to AT Health Systems

With the coming increase in the elderly population, there is increasing research into assisting the daily activities for those with physical and mental impairments, including cognitive decline. The multidisciplinary field of Ambient Assisted Living (AAL) investigates innovative technologies to provide assistance as well as healthcare and rehabilitation to senior people with impairment, especially for people with some cognitive impairment living on their own (Li et al., 2015). The scenarios addressed by this field include daily task facilitation, mobility assistance, healthcare and rehabilitation, and social inclusion and communication. The envisioned assistance mostly assumes an internet of things (IoT) that enable smart software services in support of a client. As Li et al. (2015) note, AAL faces a number of challenges, including the gap between the AAL services and user acceptance.

As an illustration of an AAL system, consider the work of Monekosso et al. (2010). They embedded sensors in a single occupant home and recorded various environmental parameters. To detect trends and deviations from the normal behavior of the inhabitant, where a behavior is identifiable pattern in a sequence of observations, they use hidden Markov models (HMM). They compare the predicted model with actual sequences and recognize significant differences as behavioral anomalies. Coronato et al. (2014) take a similar approach to AAL. Features are extracted from sensor data, which are then classified (using neural or Bayes networks), and then false positives are pruned using knowledge encoded in situational calculus. This approach is used to monitor physical manifestations of cognitive disorders (Coronato et al., 2013; Coronato et al., 2017).

In similar fashion, a variety of models have been applied to the problem of characterizing streams of sensor data common in the support of AAL systems. These include HMMs (Duong et al., 2005), Bayesian networks (Cardinaux et al., 2008), artificial neural networks (Li et al., 2008), multi-layer perceptron neural networks

(Tseng et al., 2006), recurrent neural networks (Mahmoud et al., 2013), and fuzzy data analysis (Lee et al., 2004). Such statistic-based models are often selected because of wide variations in the sensor data as well as the physical behaviors of the modeled client as they engage in ADLs within their home or similar context.

As noted above, research into assistive technology for those with cognitive impairments overlaps but is distinct from AAL (Siegel et al., 2017). The client uses the cognitive AT primarily to aid cognition. Thus, the models are not of the client and environment, but rather of the client and the AT. Both approaches have becoming increasingly dependent on machine learning. Such machine learning methods help researchers obtain insights from the wealth of user-generated data (Acampora et al., 2015), including rehabilitation software usage data (Robinson et al., 2012a) and sensor data. The research into cognitive AT, as presented herein, attempts to data-mine the AT user's progress and generate timely alerts back to caregivers (Acampora et al., 2015), as illustrated by the Analytics and Monitoring Layers on Figure 1.

This chapter presents some machine learning techniques that support the development of cognitive AT. Such techniques help to close the gap between user needs and system functionality, thereby facilitating AT-supported health systems maximize their capabilities.

The case study herein illustrates the automatic monitoring of the relationship between user goals and their satisfaction by the AT. Next, concepts and challenges in AT monitoring are presented (the AT layer and Monitoring layer of Figure 1). Then, a brief review of current AT monitoring techniques is presented (facilitated by the Analytics layer of Figure 1). An illustrative case study shows how to improve the efficiency of the monitoring, by the analytics layer. In the case study, clients are given an email system to aid in their ADLs. At appropriate times, the system is adapted to meet the client's changing needs. By monitoring an AT user's event stream, researchers notice changes in user behavior that indicate that the system should be adapted. This chapter concludes by discussing how this technique can be applied to other behavioral monitoring problems in health IT.

SUPPORTING INFRASTRUCTURE AND TECHNOLOGY

The case introduced in this chapter is an AT-based program initially called Think and Link (TAL) project, later commercialized as CogLink[1]. TAL, supported by Department of Education, sought to evaluate the effects of email interfaces that are usable by people with impairments in memory and learning as a result of brain injuries (Fickas et al., 2005; Sohlberg et al., 2005; Todis et al., 2005). Two components of this system are: (1) an assessment process called Comprehensive Overview of Requisite

Email Skills (CORE) and (2) the Think and Link (TAL) email interface. A TAL installation is continually monitored to determine how well it supports clinical and personal goals (Fickas et al., 2005). When satisfaction wanes, the system is updated to provide higher-quality software.

The TAL project derived new personalized design principles, including the following *methodology principles*, which are critical to success.

- An individual assessment process, e.g., CORE, is needed to glean the specialized goals, skills, and obstacles of each user with CI (hereafter, simply user). This is not to say that each user has a *unique* context. Instead, each user has a personal context, i.e., there is no one-size-fits-all design for the population(Sutcliffe et al., 2006).
- User goals can be divided into those that can be achieved from the outset, and those that must be deferred until more favorable conditions exist. Deferred goals provide guidance for both follow-on training and adaptation.
- Training must be integrated into the (holistic) system design. Training provides new skills to a user. As training progresses, the user may become more capable. As the system is adapted to reflect the new user skills, new training issues arise with the added system complexity. There is a cycle of learning, system adaptation, and training.

From previous TAL experience, the authors acquired the following *project principles*:

- A multi-disciplinary team, including cognitive rehabilitation specialists, assess a client's needs and specifies a rehabilitation plan that includes use of assistive technology (AT). Clinical goals such as *increased brain function* and *support user ADLs* are refined into subgoals that are desired by the user (i.e., user goals) and supported by the AT, such as *use email to communicate with friends*.
- The client becomes a user of the AT software system. The use of the AT is monitored, and results are continually analyzed by the team. If the user attains a user goal (e.g., *email a friend*), then the user is encouraged to attain new goals. A user may also fail to achieve previously attained goals (i.e., forget) in which case they are encouraged to re-attain them.
- The AT system is adapted under the direction of the team, as a means to assist the user in attaining goals supported within the AT.

While a client is a user of the AT, he or she seeks to satisfy his or her own personal goals (e.g., *use email to communicate with friends*), which in turn satisfy clinical rehabilitation goals (e.g., *increased brain function*). Monitoring AT usage is critical to ensure that the client will not reject the AT (i.e., quit emailing) and will continue to attain new personal goals, and thus achieve the clinical rehabilitation goals.

A Cognitive Rehabilitation Scenario

Assume that Jill is interested in learning to use email. Jill acquired a brain injury in an auto accident and has impairments in both memory and executive functions rendering it difficult to learn new skills. Jill has no memory of using a computer in the past, although her closet contains several computers, which were given by friends and family. Jill is unable to use her computers. She decides to work with one of our TAL staff members, Andrew, to explore the use of email. Andrew uses the CORE methodology to obtain two important items (Sohlberg et al., 2002): (1) Jill's personal goals for using email, and (2) Jill's existing skills for using email independently. (Other information is obtained but omitted here for brevity.) Using this information, Andrew produces a user profile containing (1) a specification of an initial system to deliver to Jill, and (2) a training plan broken into a set of lessons. Notice that Jill's personal goals play an important role here (and will continue to play a role in the future): they filter from all possible skills the subset that is necessary to meet Jill's needs. In essence, this is goal-directed training. Similarly, the system that is delivered is one that fits with both Jill's current skills and her personal goals—some of which are deferred. It's important to note that Jill has high aspirations for her use of email. She would eventually like to contribute articles to the online newsletter, published by a local group that advocates for the disabled. This goal, however, is not realizable given her current skills. Thus, it becomes a deferred goal that will be monitored.

Next, the email system is delivered to Jill. A family care provider, Jill's daughter-in-law Ann, assists in the training task. Soon, Jill is busy using the email system to reconnect with family and friends that have dropped out of touch. Both Jill's daily usage, and her training sessions with Ann, produces raw data. This data includes that which is generated from the email system itself, along with Ann's input on training progress. Data is also collected periodically from Jill and her email buddies through online questionnaires.

Figure 2 is a snapshot of a TAL email interface. This configuration is minimal in terms of functions and prompts, as required by users. As can be seen, Jill currently has eight email buddies. The email system is closed—only accessible to the user's buddies. The interface must adapt with the user. For example, when the user becomes successful—even bored—with emailing, then a new buddy may be added to the list. To avoid device abandonment, TAL automatically and continuously adapts

Figure 2. One configuration of the TAL email interface

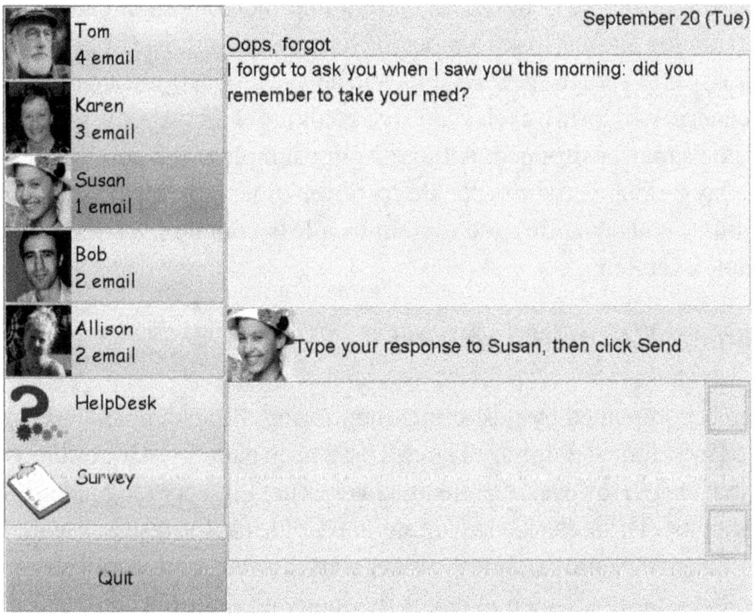

the TAL email system to individual users—each user has their own continuously personalized email interface. To inform the adaptation process, an automated method for analyzing CI behavior with respect to their goals is a prerequisite.

As a user operates TAL, events are logged and then analyzed in support of decision-making about deferred goals. Working backwards, Jill has goals that are not satisfied currently. Each of these goals has preconditions, in terms of skills, that enable them. Each skill, in turn, has measured activities that signal the learning and retention of the skill. These measures can be evaluated from the collected data. Raw data is monitored. This data is evaluated for evidence of existing, and eventually, new skills, shown as an arrow back to Jill's skill set. Eventually, a match is made between a goal deferred and the skills necessary to achieve it. At this point, email system adaptation becomes the means to enabling the goal. With Jill's deferred goal of contributing to the online advocacy newsletter, the following skills are among those required: {be able to initiate email, avoid inappropriate language, keep email within a given length, use proper spelling and grammar}. Evidence for these skills can be measured. Suppose that all but the last skill has been demonstrated. At this point, two options are possible: (1) continue to train Jill in spelling and grammar, or (2) provide automated support through her email system. A spelling checker and a grammar checker are two of the functions that can be added to Jill's system. A decision is made to adapt Jill's system to include a spell checker, deferring the decision on the grammar checker until a later point. Two explicit products come from the adaptation: (1) a newly designed system that includes spell checking, and (2) additional training lessons to accommodate the new design. The implicit outcome is forward progress toward the needed skill, and hence, progress toward a deferred goal.

This scenario will form a cycle: deferred goals are achieved, new goals may arise, and other goals may be dropped. Although our examples are optimistically forward driven, it may be that certain skills are lost over time, making system *retraction* a real possibility, thus adapting the system to a less complex version rather than a more complex version.

Post-Clinical Health Monitoring

AT is often accompanied by post-clinic monitoring. For example, TAL clients are not enrolled in a clinical program. They all have been patients of the clinic associated with research team. However, that treatment does not last very long given the limited financial support. Through research grants and CogLink, the research team monitors the clients. Given the ratio of clients to caregivers, however, this entails less oversight than a clinical program, which in fact is the motivation for the automation. We use the term *post-clinical* care for this context.

The research team monitors client progress toward their emailing goals. It does so by using a *warning and review* process. First, the team relies on the monitor to raise a warning when some behavioral change occurs. Second, the team reviews the emailing behavior, technical context, and social context to derive a consensus on TAL adaptations. When the team reaches consensus, the adaptation is discussed with the client and then it is applied (e.g., adding a new buddy or including a reply button).

Next section presents related research that supports automated monitoring.

MONITORING USER-GENERATED STREAM DATA: APPLICATIONS AND TECHNIQUES

Many integrated health systems rely on machine learning to analyze the user-generated data supported by AT systems. This section introduces three major monitoring tasks and supporting analytical methods (from the Analytic Layer in Figure 1) that are commonly used for analyzing user-generated data to assist client activity monitoring. These techniques make it possible to obtain insights from the wealth of user-generated data from AT systems, and provide timely recommendations and alerts for system adaptation.

Activity Recognition

One common use of AT in healthcare is the embeddedness of pervasive healthcare applications in homes or other non-clinical living environment, to monitor people with conditions and healthcare requirements (Sow et al., 2015). Such smart environments (often called smart homes or smart offices) need to the support of researcher or post-clinic providers to monitor users' daily activities. Those activities are normally divided into two categories: (1) Activities of Daily Living: fundamental daily self-care activities such as eating, dressing, taking medication, etc.; and (2) Instrumental Activities of Daily Living (IADL) (Bookman et al., 2007): daily social-related activities an individual perform to live independently in his or her community, such as shopping, housekeeping, and managing money. To evaluate if the user can function independently at his or her own home, caregivers need to know if the users can complete certain ADLs and IADLs. Thus, one key monitoring task is the automation recognition of such activities.

The classification models applied for activity recognition research falls under two major categories: generative models, and discriminative models (van Kasteren et al., 2008). Hidden Markov models (HMM), as a type of generative probabilistic model, are commonly used to recognize activities from a stream of user-event data, with the hidden state representing possible activities (Sow et al., 2015). For example, Borazio et al. (2012) use an HMM classifier to study sleep: they show that the HMM classifier could identify and differentiate sleep state and awake state. Other work that uses HMM models includes (Brand et al., 2002; Cao et al., 2010; Tapia et al., 2004; Van Kasteren et al., 2010). Examples of generative models are decision trees (Maurer et al., 2006), dynamic Bayesian networks(Liao et al., 2007; Wilson et al., 2010), and Naive Bayes (Maurer et al., 2006; Tapia et al., 2004; van Kasteren et al., 2008). Stikic et al. (2008) use a combination of RFID data and accelerometer data, and apply three classification models: HMM, Naïve Bayes, and Joint Boosting, to recognize 10 housekeeping activities. They found that Naive Bayes and HMM classifiers perform well when classifying low-level activities such as sitting, standing and walking. The Joint Boosting method overcomes limitation of the sensing and feature extraction and achieves the best performance with the combined data. One disadvantage of such generative models, however, is that they depend on the explicit specification of the dependencies between the observed data and the activities. However, long term dependencies in activity recognition are often difficult to model (Van Kasteren et al., 2010). As a result, discriminative models are introduced into this field. Examples of discriminative models include conditional random fields (Lafferty et al., 2001; Vail et al., 2008) and support vector machines (Cortes et al., 1995). Van Kasteren et al. (2010) compare the potential and performance between generative models and discriminative models in an activity monitoring scenario and discuss consideration of selecting the models.

Behavioral Pattern Discovery

While it is a common task for health systems to recognize a set of pre-defined activities in a supervised manner, it is also valuable for such systems to be able to discover unlabeled behaviors such as recurring sequence of activities (Acampora et al., 2015). For example, in the elderly population, frequent awakening episodes can indicate prostatism, gastro-esophageal reflux, or degenerative joint disease (Lo et al., 2007). Frequent pattern mining has been commonly used in this field of research, including methods such as mining frequent patterns using regular expression (Barger et al., 2005), motif analysis (Robinson et al., 2012a), and frequent-periodic pattern mining (Rashidi et al., 2010). FP-Stream is a frequent pattern mining algorithm which incorporates temporal information by mining a data stream at different granularities (Giannella et al., 2003). Another example of a frequent pattern mining algorithm is Closet+ (Wang et al., 2003), which finds closed frequent patterns using optimized search methods. It also offers computational advantages over existing mining techniques in terms of runtime, memory usage and scalability.

Research extends those early methods to look for more complex patterns (Acampora et al., 2015) with more advanced techniques. Ali et al. (2008) extend the FP and Closet+ methods described above, and propose a Routine-Tree data structure, which maps time to frequent behavioral patterns, and thus reduced time and cost of mining. They apply this framework to the output data of the e-AR (ear-worn activity recognition) sensor developed at Imperial College London (Lo et al., 2007), to identify and update a variable-resolution representation of frequent behavioral patterns. The authors show that they can analyze both routine behavior as well as deviations. Coronato et al. (2014) presented a technique and an infrastructure for detecting repetitive and stereotyped behaviors in patients with Autism Spectrum Disorders, from sequences of data generated by patients' accelerometers. They apply Artificial Neural Network algorithm to the feature set extracted from the data. Three classifiers were evaluated based on Artificial Intelligence algorithms: Neural Networks, Naive Bayes and Bayesian Networks. Ruotsalainen et al. (2007) design and develop the GAIS method, seeking to detect interleaved sequential patterns from data. This method allows for pattern detection from erroneous data, which contains multiple interleaved.

The preceding techniques derive behavioral models from data mining user data. Another approach includes a priori model specification, which is used to check for user compliance against the model. Finally, behavioral changes can be detected by differencing behavioral models derived from user data. Research on these two approaches are summarized below.

Model-Based Monitoring

Runtime monitoring of software for specified behaviors is increasingly of importance to software engineering (Robinson, 2010). Here is a partial list demonstrating a variety of concerns and techniques that influence the interpretation and directed adaptation of a running AT system.

- Functional models describe the states and transitions allowed by system (Robinson, 2002; Robinson, 2006).
- Goal models typically augment a functional model to describe user behaviors that can be refined to operational specifications of system behaviors(van Lamsweerde et al., 1995).
- User models describe user goals and capabilities, including cognitive impairments or software skills (Fickas et al., 2005).
- Anti-models describe undesirable behaviors, such as attackers, to support analysis of anticipated problems (van Lamsweerde, 2004).
- QoS models describe qualitative measures of systems, which may be included in a goal model (Ludwig et al., 2004).
- Diagnostic models infer causes of property violations (Wang et al., 2007).
- Architectural and related models describe software architecture, design, and code models, often in support of QoS analysis (van Lamsweerde, 2003).
- Evolution models describe potential changes to the system, typically focusing on software changes; however, user changes, such as skill learning, are possible. Evolution models can be associated with QoS and or cost models (Zhang et al., 2007).
- Discovery models, such as data mining or learning, enable dynamic discovery of behaviors, such as hacking attacks, as well as predictions of eventual property violations and successes (Kargupta et al., 2004).
- Decision models, such as utilities, use the other models to select an appropriate evolution path (Chung et al., 2004).

Change Detection

Detecting changes in data-streams is important for monitoring AT systems. Often researchers and health providers need to recognize deviations from the client's routine behavior to identify possible health issues (Acampora et al., 2015), relapse, or even progress (Robinson et al., 2012a). Two types of algorithms are common: (1) distribution detection, which watches for changes in the data distributions, and (2) burst detection, which watches for sudden large and unusual changes in a data-stream. Distribution detection algorithms have two common forms: (1) data from two windows (current and reference) are compared using some distance measure, (2) a predictive model is created from a prior window and then its prediction is compared with the current window—high prediction error indicates a significant change.

Many data stream techniques address change detection of item sets (e.g., (Aggarwal et al., 2003; Agrawal et al., 1995; Chakrabarti et al., 1998; Ganti et al., 2002; Kifer et al., 2004; Silberschatz et al., 1996)) . For example, Agrawal et al. (1995) and (Chakrabarti et al., 1998) monitor the change on the support of an item set over temporally ordered transactions. Ganti et al. (2002) propose a framework, FOCUS, in which changes are detected by quantifying the difference between the two models induced by the datasets. Two trees are first extended so that they become identical, and then they are compared to derive a numeric difference value.

Anomaly Detection

Although it is very important to recognize common, normal behaviors, it is necessary for certain health systems to identify abnormal, irregular events (Acampora et al., 2015), which often imply health issues that require medical assistance. Tong et al. (2013) use an HMM-based method to detect and predict fall from tri-axial acceleration data. The authors show that their algorithm can predict falls 200~400 ms before the collision and can successfully distinguish fall events from ADLs with high sensitively and specificity. There are two major challenges in anomaly detection. First, it is hard to define anomaly in specific scenarios, making anomaly detection a challenging task (Acampora et al., 2015). Second, there is a dearth of training data due to the fact that collected data are often biased towards normal data (abnormal events are rare), resulting in models with high false positive rate (Yin et al., 2008). Different approaches have been suggested to tackle such challenges. One stream is the model-based approach, which employs similarity or distance measures on models to detect outliers (Bay et al., 2004). Plan recognition methods, have also been applied (Jarvis et al., 2005). Yin et al. (2008) suggest a two-phase approach in which they first train a well-estimated SVM model for *normal* activities, and then derive *abnormal* activity models from the normal activity model using kernel nonlinear regression.

Deep Learning Models

Deep learning-based approaches are becoming increasingly popular in the area of user behavior recognition from sensor data, because of their ability to model complex relationships by utilizing multi-layered neural networks (LeCun et al., 2015).

A Recurrent Neutral Network (RNN) has been proved to perform well when modeling sequential data (Zhu et al., 2017). In particular, a Long Short Term Memory (LSTM) is one type of RNN architecture which is designed to model temporal sequences and their long-term dependencies, and often has higher accuracy compared to conventional RNNs (Sak et al., 2014). Inspired by the successful applications of RNN in other domains, Bashivan et al. (2015) propose to use an RNN to model cognitive events from Electroencephalography (EEG) data. Their LSTM model reaches an accuracy of 85.05% when classifying mental load conditions from thirteen subjects in a working memory experiment. Their model outperforms a series of models such as SVM, random forest, and logistic regression. In the context of smart living, Zhang et al. (2017) propose a 7-layer LSTM model to classify EEG signals for smart living user intent recognition, to help patients with motor impairments. The model reaches a mean accuracy of 95.53%, in tests of five intents recognition on ten subjects.

Deep learning models require vast amounts of training data or, in the case of transfer learning, a moderate amount of data for an existing model built from similar data. Consequently, deep learning may be more successful for AAL systems, with their voluminous user data. Conversely, deep learning models are a challenge for cognitive AT systems, where each system is customized to an individual client and the client's AT usage may be limited. Moreover, change or anomaly detection is commonly applied techniques for AT monitoring, but may be a challenge for the deep learning classifiers. Nevertheless, as AT usage grows, aggregating AT usage data will facilitate the use of deep learning.

Next, TAL's model-based monitoring techniques are presented, followed by an illustrative case study.

Table 1. Design rationale for the monitor design

		Approach	Other Considerations
Strategic	How to recognize transitions?	Compare mined predictions to actual events—predictive error indicates transition.	Data, rather than model, comparisons may require more effort with no better results.
	How to diagnosis transitions?	Analyze divergence between two models to find model changes.	Decision trees and Markov models have efficient divergence algorithms.
Tactical	Which mining algorithms to apply?	Decision tree and Markov model	Markov models consider event sequencing, while decision trees provide attribute ordering.
	How to select data window size?	Sufficient data for good accuracy while not being so long that differences as less and results are delayed.	Larger windows can increase accuracy but delay results and miss small transitions.
	Which data attributes to mine?	Predicting event type is the focus. Attributes that improved that prediction were included.	Some logged data was dropped because had no predictive value.

MONITOR DESIGN

The TAL monitor is designed to provide feedback to caregivers about AT usage by clients. Two data analytic goals are central:

- Identify transitions in a user's behavior, where a user's behavior is represented by the stream of events that they initiate with the AT
- Diagnose transitions of a user's behavioral change, as characterized by the most influential behavioral differences around a moment of change

In support of these goals, Table 1 presents design rationale for the monitor. Two strategic decisions are: how to recognize transitions, and how to diagnose transitions. The authors chose to use model predictive error to identify transitions and model divergence for diagnoses. The tactical, case-specific, decisions of Table 1 led us to decision trees and Markov models, because of their modeling accuracy and divergence algorithms.

TAL Data Stream

An example facilitates an explanation of mining methods. The TAL project provides an automated custom logger, which appends to a text file. To obtain real-time data access, the client's log file is monitored with changes sent to a server. Here is a simplified entry from the log file.

```
09:48:41 NewMailEvent [id=765406159;in-reply-to=311149530;
chars=770; words=179; sentences=16]
```

This logged event specifies the time, the TAL event, and its associated arguments. The example logs the arrival of a new email that is in reply to previous e-mail; the identity of the sender and receiver and characteristics of the e-mail message, such as its length, are also included. This data is transformed, cleaned, and stored in a relational database on the server. The result is a continuously updated SQL view of the data stream.

Much of the data analysis addresses the following classification problem, which uses a subset of the available data:

- **Input**: event type, (email) word count, day segment, day of week, week of year, month of year
- **Predict**: event type, day segment, day of week

The DaySegment attribute represents a range of hours in the day, for example, from 2 A.M. to 4 A.M., with 12 segments. The relevant event types are: read email, compose email, delete email, and new (arriving) email. The dataset for one client included 3,695,086 records.

Identifying Transitions

The approach to identifying transitions relies on data mined models of user behavior, based on the TAL events, to recognize significant changes in those events. Changes in mined-model qualities are considered to indicate changes in user behavior. This approach depends on a few assumptions:

- User behavior is characterized by the stream of events that user initiates with the user interface (e.g., the TAL emailing client).
- User behavior can be characterized as planned event sequences for goal fulfillment.
- User behavior is less consistent when involved in less familiar tasks, and more consistent when involved in more familiar, routinized tasks.

Based on these assumptions, the monitor analyzes patterns in event sequences to find inconsistent behaviors, which are interpreted as *goal transitions*, i.e., moving from a state of low goal achievement to a state of higher goal achievement (or vice versa). Consider a user goal set, $\mathbf{G}_i$, which specifies the currently attained goals. The researchers want to know when a user transitions to new goal set, $\mathbf{G}_j$, where the difference between the user goal attainment is one goal, i.e., $\mathbf{G}_j - \mathbf{G}_i = g$. The monitor applies a data-stream mining approach to identify unusual behavioral patterns that are most likely to be associated with goal transitions.

Model Changes are Behavioral Changes

TAL has applied two approaches to identifying model changes, which imply user behavioral changes. Both assume that event mining produces a sequence of models, m_1 .. m_n, that predict the behavior observed in the subsequent windows w_2 .. w_{n+1}. Significant changes in the event stream can be identified with (1) changes between consecutive models or (2) changes in the predictive accuracy of the models. In the latter case, a predicted window is observed, w_i, and the prediction quality of the last model is computed, $q(m_{i-1}, w_i) = [0,1]$. There are a number of ways in which quality can be defined. For example, the classic metrics of *accuracy* and *precision* can be used individually or in combination. Accuracy measures how error-free the model's predictions are, according to this equation.

accuracy = (true negative cases + true positive cases) / all cases

where all cases = true negative + true positive + false negative + false positive cases;
Precision measures fidelity, according to this equation.

precision = true positive cases / (true positive + false positive cases)

Predictive quality can be automatically evaluated with each new window during stream mining. Given that model m_i is trained over window w_i, one can evaluate the predicted values of m_i against the data in w_{i+1}.

Consider the case where the predictive quality is nearly a constant 0.9. This suggests that the models are good and that the behavior from one window to the next is nearly constant. Now, consider a sequence of some *n* predictions, with q_1 .. q_n, where each $q_i \approx 0.9$ with the exception of q_k $(1 < k < n)$ which is 0.1. Again, this suggests that the models are good with the exception of m_{k-1}, which was trained on window w_{k-1} to predict window w_k. From this, we infer that something interesting happened during window w_k. That is, the events in window w_k are so different from the events of window w_{k-1} that the model trained on w_{k-1} cannot reasonably classify the new window w_k behavior. This technique can be used to recognize the window in which significant behavioral changes occurred. This window is the transition window.

The predictive quality change over time is *dq/dt*. Thus, when this change over time is significant, $|q'| > \varepsilon$, it implies behavioral changes from window w_{k-1} to window w_k. One can also consider how quickly the predictive quality changes, which is q''. An analysis of typical domain values for q' and q'' can provide guidelines that distinguish normal behavioral variations from significant behavioral changes (Robinson et al., 2010).

The other transition identifying technique is that of directly comparing consecutive models. For every consecutive model pair, the divergence of the newer model from the older is calculated. High divergence indicates significant behavioral changes.

Divergence is well defined for hidden Markov models (HMM). To find the divergence between two HMMs, one can apply the Kullback-Leibler algorithm (Kullback, 1997), also known as *KL divergence,* which compares two probability distributions. The KL divergence compares both HMM's in their entirety. It measures the information divergence, in bits, between the two probably distributions representing the sequential data. Thus, KL divergence provides an accurate measure of information change (Sahraeian et al., 2011). Moreover, KL divergence is not a symmetric, in that $D^{kl}(m_2, m_1) \neq D^{kl}(m_1, m_2)$. Thus, the divergence from a window absent evidence of goal attainment *g*, to a window demonstrating goal *g*, differs from when the goal *g* is no longer attained.

Model accuracy and model divergence both identify behavioral transitions. As a client uses the AT, their actions are logged and modeled, consecutive models are compared, and consequently model differences reveal real differences in client actions with the AT. Because HMMs model sequential probabilities, whereas decision trees only model event distributions, HMMs more precisely model the sequential user behavior, and their differences more accurately characterize differences in client behavior. Some differences are minor, while others reflect a client's transition from one level of AT usage to the next, as characterized by their goal achievement through skill attainment. Through analysis of these differences, and consultation with the caregivers, a difference threshold is established that corresponds to events that caregivers identify as real client transitions. For KL divergence of HMMs, that difference is three standard deviations over a running mean of model divergences (Robinson et al., 2017).

Good Model Quality is Sufficient

A good model is sufficient for finding significant differences in a model sequence. Great or nearly perfect predictive models are wonderful, but unnecessary for identifying transitions. The model differences are more important. Of course, low quality models will have substantial variance from model to model in stream mining. Good quality models have less variance and thus their differences will be striking. The key is that the differences are more prominent than the random variance in the models. In the TAL domain, our goal has been better than 70% for both accuracy and precision.

There are many ways to improve model quality, including selecting the best mining technique, apply multiple techniques simultaneously, and apply multiple window sizes simultaneously.

Selecting the appropriate window size, *ws*, is important. If *ws* is small, then insufficient data will be available when the mining model is derived. Conversely, if *ws* is large, then the analysis must wait for sufficient data to arrive before the model is derived. Finally, large data windows have a *regression to the mean problem*—short variations in behavior will be discounted in favor of more common behavior, and thus short variations may not be represented in the mined model. Thus, widow size affects model quality and analysis of their divergence.

In the case studies, the authors have applied: (1) multiple concurrent windows, (2) two kinds of models (decision tree and HMM), and (3) two kinds of model divergence (quality difference and KL divergence). Once a transition is identified, the authors use decision tree models to diagnose the cause of the transition, which is describe next.

Diagnosing Transitions

A discovered transition change begs the question, “what exactly has changed?” Diagnosing a transition provides an answer, which is used by caregivers to decide if a goal transition has occurred. If it has, then a system adaptation or training may follow, as directed by the caregivers. In the TAL diagnosis context, a transition can reveal that the user “now sends more emails on Wednesday than in the past”. (Failing to take medications on Wednesday was an underlying cause for this real example.)

Model divergence reveals the most significant changes between two models. A data mined model, m_i, provides a model of the data observed in window w_i. When models diverge from w_{k-1} to window w_k, it means that the data varies substantially

Figure 3. A decision tree classifying compose events

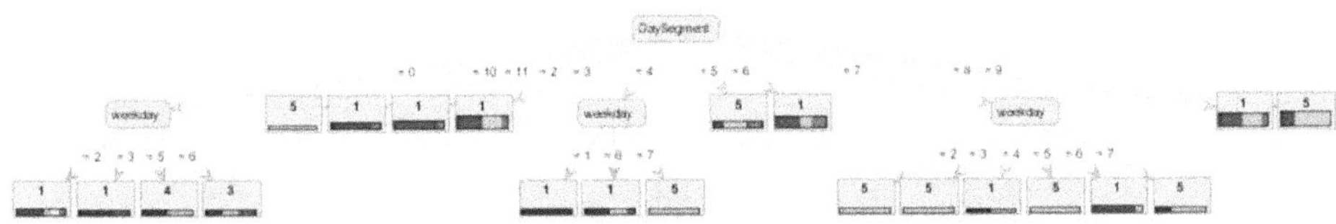

from w_{k-1} to window w_k. Thus, given model divergence, three data windows are of interest: w_{k-1} (before change data), w_k (change data), and w_{k+1} (after change data). To determine if the new behavior persists, we compare the models associated with windows w_{k-1} with w_{k+1}. We consider w_k (change data) of lesser importance because it represents the transition from between two models of more consistent behavior. Next section illustrates decision-tree model comparisons.

Decision Tree Divergence

Figure 3 illustrates a portion of a decision tree that models user email events. For a data window, the model summarizes the kind of email event (Event: read, receive, delete, compose), the day of the week (weekday: 1-7), and a 2-hour period in which the event occurred (DaySegment: 0 - 11). The leaves of the tree represent the email events. A path from the root to a leaf can be considered a proposition that characterizes the leaf data. For example, the path DaySegment = 4, weekday = 1 leads to the events satisfying those two attribute values.

In Figure 3, the data distribution is represented by the colored bar chart on the leaves. Thus, the bottom left leaf shows that the path DaySegment = 4, weekday = 1 has only read email events. On the other hand, other leaves have a mix of colors, indicating a mixed distribution of email events. (The node is labeled with the dominant event number—read = 1, compose = 5.)

To illustrate decision tree divergence, consider two hypothetical decision trees. The first has only read events for day segment 1, while the second has only read events for day segment 2. The divergence of the two models (m_2 - m_1) reveals that read has shifted from DaySegment 1 to DaySegment 2 (i.e. DaySegment 1 is dropped and DaySegment 2 is added). This observation is the basis for our diagnosis. By comparing two decision trees, one can characterize the change. Our algorithm is sufficiently efficient because it stops on each branch comparison when it finds the first difference (Robinson et al., 2011). There are, however, some issues with comparing decision trees.

Figure 4. A decision tree that classifies DaySegment =2

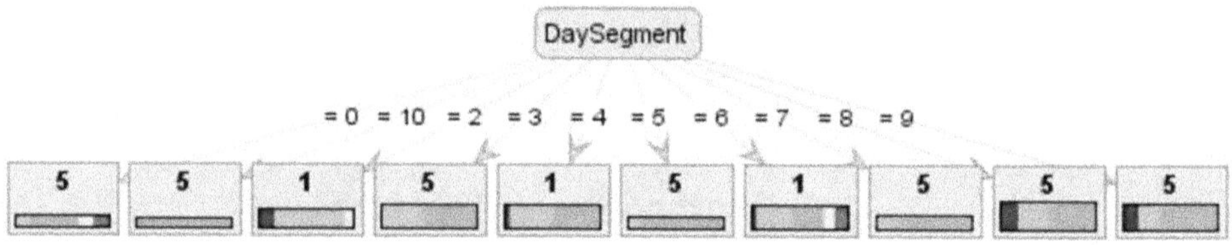

Significant Attributes in Decision Trees

In general, completely comparing unordered trees is computationally expensive (NP-complete) (Bille, 2005). Even if we assume ordered trees, which is common for decision trees, the algorithmic complexity of complete comparison is high. The complexity arises because a node in tree A may move to anywhere within the next tree B (however unlikely in practice). In practice, we have found that the comparing sequential decision trees reveal small changes in the tree, such as the attribute or attribute value changes. Even complete comparison is practical for small decision trees. Yet, we do not need a complete comparison for our diagnostic problem. Instead, an algorithm that returns the most influential changes is sufficient.

Decision trees use an attribute selection measure as a criterion for splitting at a node. Popular choices include information gain, Gini impurity measure, and gain ratio. The attribute with the highest metric determines the splitting rule. The improvement at each node is calculated using the selection measure and fraction of data split. For each attribute, the importance measure is derived using a weighted sum of the improvements due to that attribute. Such importance values are used to rank the decision tree attributes.

More influential attributes are found at the top of the tree, while less influential attributes are found closer to the leaves (Wu et al., 2008). Thus, when comparing two trees, the most significant differences are found by first comparing the roots

Figure 5. A decision tree that lacks DaySegment =2

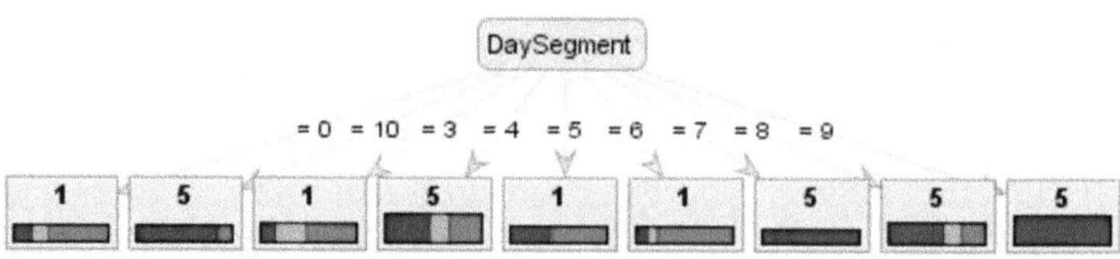

and working towards the leaves. We apply this method, stopping along each branch when either a difference or a leaf-node is found (Robinson et al., 2011).

By comparing structures of two trees based on the order in which attributes appear near the top, we can determine the divergence in attribute influence between two models. This ordering of attributes by significance simplifies comparison and is one reason why we use decision trees to diagnose behavior.

Given two decision trees, there are two kinds of differences to consider: (1) value differences at the nodes, and (2) attribute difference. Additionally, it is possible that the two models have nothing in common.

Model Divergence in Attribute Values

Given two decision tree models, it is possible that they have an attribute value divergence. As an illustration, consider the models in Figure 4 and Figure 5. The two trees branch on day segment. The absence of a branch for DaySegment =2 in Figure 5 is the only structural difference.

Dropping a tree branch, from m_1 to m_2, occurs when the latter model is constructed from a dataset lacking data for the branch. In the case of Figure 5 compared to the prior model of Figure 4, the user quit reading email during DaySegment =2.

Model Divergence in Attributes

Given two decision tree models, it is possible that they have an attribute divergence. As an illustration, compare Figure 4 with the previous Figure 3. The attribute difference occurs in the path DaySegment =4. In Figure 4, there is no subsequent branching, whereas in Figure 3 DaySegment =4 is segmented into three weekday branches (1, 6, and 7).

Adding an attribute, from m_1 to m_2, occurs when the latter model is constructed from a dataset that includes data for the branches (e.g., weekdays 1, 6, and 7), and that data is non-uniformly distributed over the attribute (weekday). Thus, we can infer from Figure 3 that the user, during DaySegment =4, mostly had email events on weekdays 1, 6, and 7.

We cannot infer specific quantity changes from attribute differences alone—the addition of weekday in Figure 3 does not suggest that more events occurred during weekdays 1, 6, and 7. Instead, it shows that the distribution of events changed from Figure 4 to Figure 3. It is likely, however, that fewer events occurred for the weekdays other than 1, 6, and 7, thereby creating a non-uniform distribution.

It is worth noting here the pathological case of two identical models, m_1 to m_2, for which the events occur with the same distribution, but different quantities. For example, consider Figure 4. There is no indication of the quantity of DaySegment =10; the figure simply indicates that at least one event occurred at DaySegment =10. It is possible, but not likely, that another model, identical to that of Figure 4 would have twice as many total events with the same distribution. Therefore, the decision-tree model differencing is a diagnostic aid, which can be improved by comparing the classified quantities in each leaf. Once a tree divergence is identified, the algorithm does compute the difference in data counts. However, analysis is not applied to identical trees, because the pathological case is exceedingly unlikely in practice.

Models with No Common Attributes

Given two decision tree models, it is possible that they have no attributes in common. For example, model m_1 branches only on DaySegment 1 and model m_2 branches only on weekday 1. From this example, we can deduce that the concentration of email events was first on DaySegment 1, uniformly distributed for all weekdays, while the second model concentration shifted to weekday 1 uniformly distributed on all hours. Such a dramatic change has not occurred in our data but may occur in other domains. In such cases, the algorithm reports the entire two trees as the differences.

ANALYSIS OF THE DATA-MODEL STREAM MINING APPROACH

This chapter applies a design science approach to the analysis of the analytic techniques (Hevner et al., 2004). This section summarizes a case study, as applied to a randomly selected client from the TAL project. The data includes 26,185 email events collected over two years. The approach identifies four important goal transitions.

Data Mining Models

Transition detection requires a good quality model. In pre-testing, we considered a variety of classification models, including decision trees, Bayesian networks, neural networks, and association rules. The authors settled on Hidden Markov models (HMM) and three decision tree algorithms, which were the best in quality.

Figure 6. Predictive quality for the read models

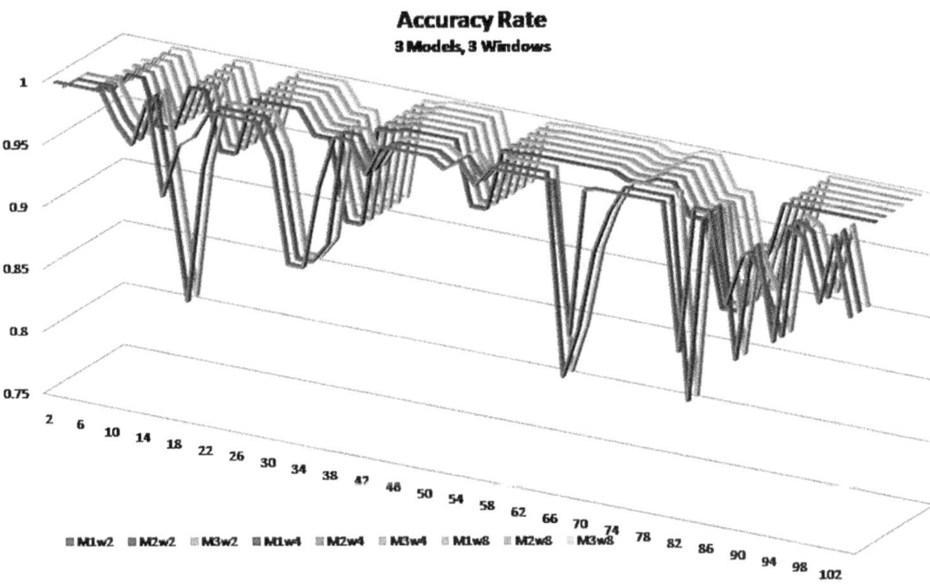

- M1: Gain Ratio (C4.5) is a successor of ID3.
- M2: Information Gain (ID3) minimizes the information needed to classify the data represented as tuples and the resulting partitions reflect the least randomness or impurity in these partitions.
- M3: Gini Index (CART) uses a formula based on probability to branch on nodes.

The authors also considered a variety of data window sizes. We settled on running three window sizes simultaneously: two-, four-, and eight-week windows. These allowed us to consider short-term and long-term behavioral patterns. Shorter than two weeks produced poor quality models because of insufficient data, while longer than eight weeks was not valued for diagnoses.

Identifying Transitions With Decision Trees

The decision-tree models predict the event type for a time-segment within a day-of-week. Table 2 summarizes accuracy and precision for the read and compose event types. The values for the different window sizes are very similar. Notice that the read models are very good—meaning that the models predict well the number of emails that will be read during a time-segment on a day-of-week. The composing model is not as good. It weakly predicts the number of emails that will be composed during

Table 2. Qualities of model M1 for read and compose email

		Read		Compose	
		Accuracy	Precision	Accuracy	Precision
2-week window	Average	0.967	0.970	0.631	0.484
	StdD.	0.049	0.018	0.241	0.144
4-week window	Average	0.984	0.971	0.657	0.478
	StdD.	0.027	0.011	0.202	0.119
8-week window	Average	0.983	0.971	0.657	0.478
	StdD.	0.027	0.011	0.202	0.119

a time-segment on a day-of-week. Because read models have the best quality and least variability, we rely on them to predict behavioral changes. The compose graph mostly supports the same transition points, but with less accuracy.

Consider the read model. The predictive qualities of the three data mined models (M1, M2, M3) for three windows are graphed in Figure 6. The graph shows that the models roughly track the same events. Windows of four and eight weeks are nearly the same. They both diminish events considered interesting by the two-week window (e.g., weeks 66 – 68). In general, the two-week window analysis has greater variability and foreshadows the larger window analysis, as expected. Notice that week 34 has poor predictive quality (q) as identified in both the two- and four-week window analysis. Moreover, the quality in the immediately surrounding weeks is good; thus, the rate in change of the quality (q') around week 34 is also high.

Table 3. First derivative of accuracy, q'

Week	2-Week Window			4-Week Window		
	M1	M2	M3	M1	M2	M3
10	-0.012	-0.012	-0.012	0.000	0.000	0.000
12	-0.007	-0.007	-0.007	-0.018	-0.018	-0.018
16	-0.037	-0.037	-0.037	0.018	0.018	0.018
18	0.021	-0.043	-0.043	0.000	0.000	0.000
20	0.005	0.054	0.054	-0.023	-0.023	-0.023
Ö						
30	-0.014	-0.014	-0.014	0.000	0.000	0.000
32	-0.040	-0.040	-0.040	-0.010	-0.010	-0.010
36	0.033	0.009	0.009	-0.032	-0.032	-0.032

Figure 7. Selecting potential learning inflection points from model divergences

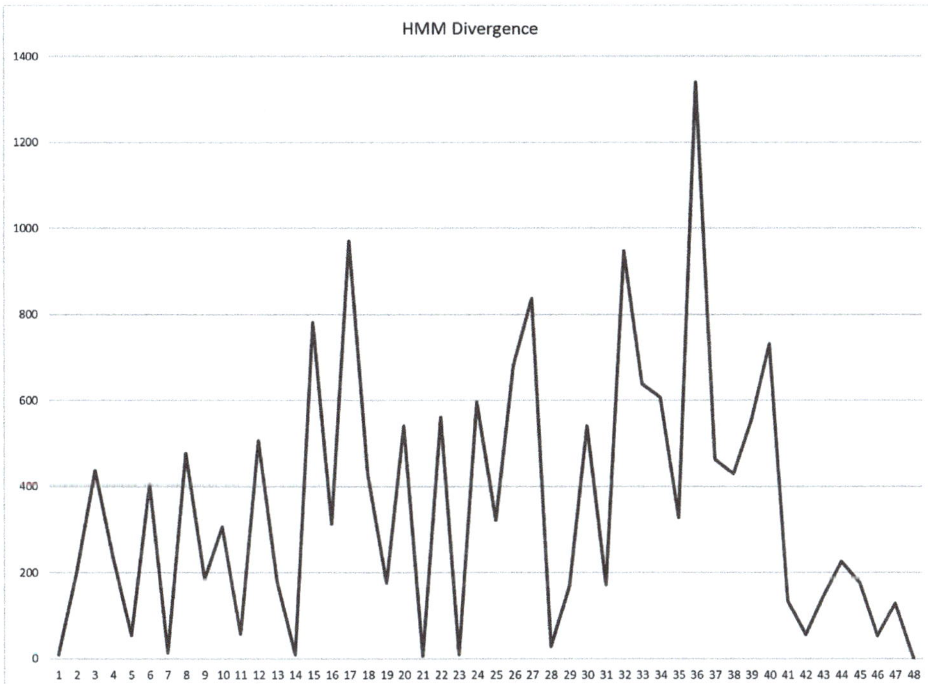

Together the dramatic decrease in *q* and zeroing of *q*' suggest that week 34 may be a behavioral inflection point worthy of further analysis.

Table 3 presents *q*' for two- and four-week windows for the three models; it illustrates the significance of our transition identification technique. The table shows where *q*' turns negative between 0 and 36 weeks. The analyst can combine these values—for example, using average, logical And or logical Or—to automate the recognition of interesting events. The rule for our case study is that two consecutive *q*' windows mean that the transition began on the first window. Table 3 shows that week 12 and 32 are transitions.

Identifying Transitions With HMMs

Transitions can be identified with changes in the predictive accuracy of the models, as illustrated above with the decision-trees, or with changes between consecutive models, which we illustrate here using hidden Markov models.

Table 4. Significant changes in composing email

Weeks	Compose in Selected Hours	Total Compose for Model	% Activity	Δ Activity
10 PM				
10 - 12	7	111	6%	
14 - 16	0	115	0%	-6%
Tuesday (6-12 AM and 2-8 PM)				
32-34	3	46	6%	
36-38	14	67	21%	15%
Saturday				
50-52	0	55	0%	
54-56	39	81	48%	48%
Saturday, Sunday, Monday and Friday (6-12 AM)				
80-82	5	31	16%	
84-86	23	91	25%	9%

For use with the HMMs, the TAL events are divided into two-week data windows. Every two weeks of events are segmented into 6 segments (4 hours each). An HMM is generated from a day segment of two combined 4-hour segments, each from the same weekday for two weeks. This results in time-based data windows within each two-week period. (For example, one Sunday segment between 12 PM – 4 PM for each two-week window.) Thus, for two weeks, there will be a total of 6 X 7 = 42 HMMs.

Next, we analyzed the HMMs using an inflection point algorithm. Corresponding HMM pairs over two-week data windows are compared, for 52 weeks of data. Thus, for example, every two consecutive Sunday noon segments are compared.

Figure 7 graphs the maximum divergence for 52 weeks of data, where each point represents the comparison of two models. Thus, point 16 on Figure 7 corresponds to week 32 in Figure 6. According to the HMM inflection point algorithm, there are four most significant inflection points 16, 26, 31 and 35, which correspond to points 32, 52, 62, and 70 in Figure 6. (The significance threshold is set at three standard deviations among a running mean of model divergences, cf. Robinson et al. (2019).) Thus, both transition identification approaches consider find common transitions. Modeling sequences is the key difference between the HMM and decision-tree models, which results in the slightly varying transitions points between the two approaches.

Figure 8. Stack graph showing the read counts, by buddy, for weeks 50 – 56

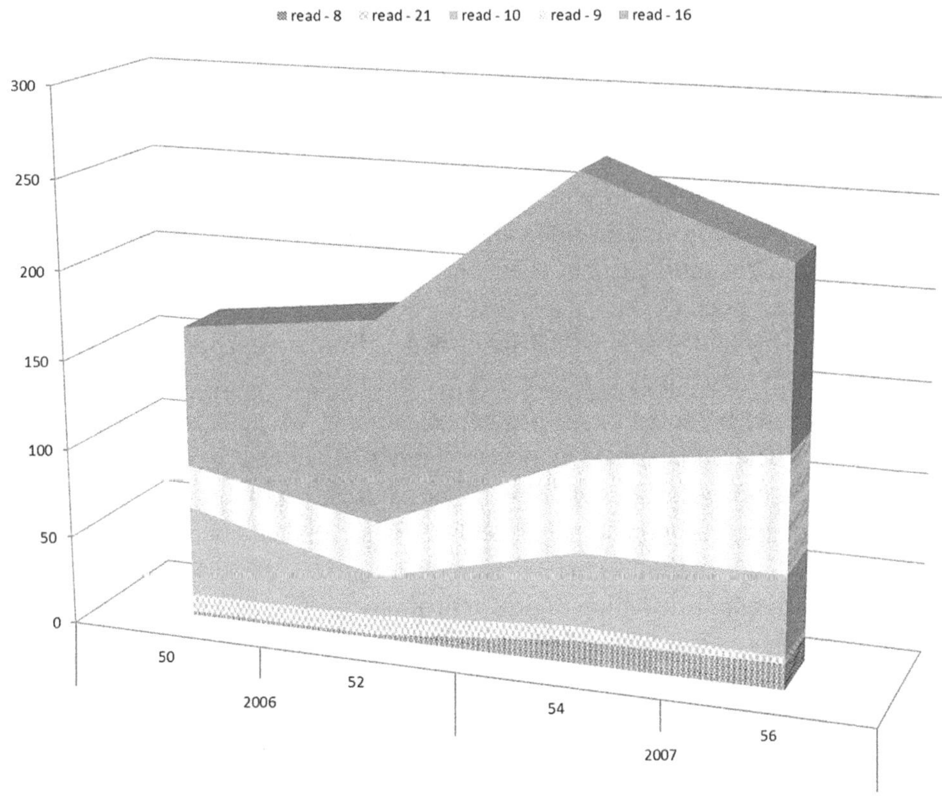

Diagnosing Transitions

As transitions are identified, diagnosis is automatically applied. Table 4 and Figure 6 and Figure 7 summarize the diagnostic analysis for the goal transitions identified in the *read email* and *compose and send email* data streams underlying Figure 6. We present the results of comparing pairs of M3 (CART) decision trees over 2-week windows. However, the results are similar for the other models and windows.

Table 4 presents the results of decision-tree model divergence found in the *compose and send email* data stream. One potential goal transition occurs during the two weeks of 32 and 33 of the datasets. The three data windows for this inflection point begin at 32, 34, and 36 weeks. The model differencing technique compares the models beginning at 32 and 36—it does not consider the intervening transitional model. For the transition at week 32, there was a 15% increase in email composition during the periods from 6 to 12 A.M. and 2 to 8 P.M. There were 48% and 9% increases for the inflection points of beginning at weeks 50 and 80, respectively. These changes indicate an increased attainment for the compose email goal.

Figure 8 presents a stack graph showing the differences in read count, with the top-5 buddies, for weeks 50 – 56. The graph shows that some buddy increases and decreases occurred in the transition week 52, followed by general increases in week 54. The graph reveals the increase in the number of reads, which was identified in the metrics of Table 4. This illustrates the value of the metrics—rather than generating and reviewing numerous graphs, the metrics point to windows where the data and their graphs have the most change. These changes indicate an increased attainment for the read email goal.

The preceding tables summarize how model divergence applies. The tables demonstrate how transitions can be characterized by their underlying behavioral changes. It should be noted that, for this presentation, we collapsed consecutive time segments. The actual mined model considered 2-hour day segments. Thus, for example, the Saturday statistics of Table 4 is an aggregation of the 12 time-periods. The other statistics are automatically calculated (e.g., total and percent). Finally, it should be noted, that the results are calculated in real-time, as each window closes, immediately after the calculation of goal transitions.

The TAL caregivers used the diagnostic results to evaluate client behavior. The *read* and *compose email* models guide goal evaluation of a TAL client, Don. Logical property-based analysis is used to evaluate the satisfaction of achievement goals, like *After receiving an email, a user shall read and reply to the sender, within k days* (Fickas et al., 2005; Lamsweerde, 2008; Robinson et al., 2009). In the case study, as transitions were discovered, new buddies were introduced to increase the interest, and the emailing, of Don. Review of the transition diagnosis quickly directs clinicians to the most important behavioral changes. These changes may not include the anticipated increase or decrease of a goal, like *email composition*. Instead, the changes can include other attributes, such as time, day of week, *etc*. Table 4 shows an increase in weekend behavior and some decrease in late evening (10 P.M.) behavior. Such unanticipated diagnoses have been helpful in understanding the total changes a client is undergoing. In Don's case, he had less AT usage during traditional sleep times—a sign of improvement. Don's emailing behavior, technical context, and social context direct the research to consensus. Consequently, the team encouraged Don to explore new functions, including *reply*—an adaptation that was included in the TAL user interface.

In practice, a data analyst assists a clinician in reviewing the event stream data. With each mouse click on the TAL email interface, the recorded events are stored in a database. As each data window is filled, mining automatically applies and results are stored in a database. Periodically, the team conducts a review session. A data analyst displays the diagnostic results using pivot tables and graphs, such as shown in the prior figures. Along with the event data, the team considers any significant events unrepresented in the data stream, such as a client's medication change or family visit, or changes to the TAL interface or power outages, *etc*. When the team reaches consensus, an adaptation is applied (e.g., a new buddy or including a reply button). Prior to the adaptation, the client is informed of the recommendation.

Validation

The researchers have discussed the monitored analysis with the other TAL researchers and caregivers. The goal transitions do reflect persistent changes in behavior. One example may be revealing. Week 34 of the data corresponds to 8/20/2006 - 8/26/2006, while week 82 of the data corresponds to 7/29/2007 - 8/4/2007 (week 31 of 2007). We hypothesize that something interesting happens to the client in the August summer holiday, such as a family member visit. Client anonymity prevented us from directly correlating such real-world events, but it was confirmed that real-world events of significance occurred at the identified transition. Consequently, the caregiver team found the TAL monitoring to be useful.

Don's event data shows a general trend of increasing email usage. He consistently composes email and replies to emails, which is in support of his *know and use basic email skills*. Don also has periodic behavior of increasing emails after the introduction of a new buddy (Fickas et al., 2005). An analysis of Don's sequences (e.g., read followed by compose), revealed that Don was becoming (1) more consistent over time because of the increasing length of non-variable sequences, and (2) becoming more conversational with email because of the increased usage of reply (Robinson et al., 2012b). This latter point is significant, because it suggests that Don may be transitioning from using email for simple notifications (e.g., "I'm low on meds") or requests (e.g., "I need a ride to the library.") to dialogs (e.g., "I do remember that about our father. That reminds me of ..."). Prior analysis of simple metrics (e.g., message length, composition speed, *etc*.) supports this common trend of TAL users becoming increasingly skilled emailers (Sohlberg et al., 2005).

Generalizing the Approach

Model quality and model divergence are appropriate for user behavioral monitoring, as demonstrated here for the CI domain. That alone is a significant contribution. However, can model quality and model divergence be applied effectively to other domains, such as business activity monitoring or network analysis? This open question has provided us a new research opportunity in the area of financial business activity monitoring.

Consider the problem of monitoring personal credit card transactions (Robinson et al., 2017), which is similar to the problem we are undertaking. Although simpler than rehabilitation goals, users do have goals for using credit cards, such as short-term payment, long-term payment, and insured (rental car) transaction. Financial models can be stream mined from transactional data. Behavioral changes can be inferred from model quality changes and characterize via model differences. Consequently, as a user transitions from short-term financing to long-term financing, the techniques described herein can automatically flag and characterize the change—at least our initial efforts suggest that his may be appropriate. It's fair to say that analyses of stream-mined models, such as quality metrics and differencing, provides future research opportunities for real-time data analytics.

CONCLUSION

This chapter presents techniques for monitoring and diagnosing behavioral changes from an event stream of user actions.

To analyze user behavior, we analyze the divergence of models generated, in sequence, by mining the stream of user events. Large divergence suggests significant changes in user behavior. These transitions can suggest the need for AT adaptation, moving forward with plan achievement and revisiting prior treatments with user regression. The entire process is automated—from event acquisition in the AT software to recognizing and diagnosing changes in model quality.

Like the work on which we build, this research is important to the field of AT-based therapy. Dynamically interpreting and adapting therapy plans for individuals currently requires substantial effort of caregivers. With the CI user population increasing, the need for some automation in therapy analysis is critical. Methods, such the one we describe herein, will be a critical factor in addressing the needs of the millions of people with cognitive disabilities.

ACKNOWLEDGMENT

This research was supported by the National Science Foundation, grant number 0613698.

REFERENCES

Acampora, G., Cook, D. J., Rashidi, P., & Vasilakos, A. V. (2015). Data analytics for pervasive health. *Healthcare Data Analytics*, 533-576. doi:10.1201/b18588

Activity recognition in the home using simple and ubiquitous sensors 158-175. (2004).

Aggarwal, C. C., Han, J., Wang, J., & Yu, P. S. (2003). A framework for clustering evolving data streams. *Proceedings of the 29th International Conference on Very Large Data Bases-Volume 29*. Berlin, Germany. 10.1016/B978-012722442-8/50016-1

Agrawal, R., & Psaila, G. (1995). Active data mining. *In Proceedings of the First International Conference on Knowledge Discovery in Databases and Data Mining*. Montreal, Canada.

Ali, R., ElHelw, M., Atallah, L., Lo, B., & Yang, G. Z. (2008). Pattern mining for routine behaviour discovery in pervasive healthcare environments. In *Proceedings 5th Int. Conference on Information Technology and Applications in Biomedicine, ITAB 2008 in conjunction with 2nd Int. Symposium and Summer School on Biomedical and Health Engineering, IS3BHE 2008*. 10.1109/ITAB.2008.4570576

Alliance, F. C. (2001). Incidence and prevalence of the major causes of brain impairment. Retrieved from http://www.caregiver.org/caregiver/jsp/content_node.jsp?nodeid=438

Barger, T. S., Brown, D. E., & Alwan, M. (2005). Health-status monitoring through analysis of behavioral patterns. *IEEE transactions on systems, man, and cybernetics. Part A, systems and humans*, *35*(1), 22–27. doi:10.1109/TSMCA.2004.838474

Bashivan, P., Rish, I., Yeasin, M., & Codella, N. (2015). Learning representations from eeg with deep recurrent-convolutional neural networks. *arXiv preprint arXiv:1511.06448*.

Bay, S. D., & Schwabacher, M. (2004). *Mining distance-based outliers in near linear time with randomization and a simple pruning rule*. Association for Computing Machinery.

Bharucha, A. J., Anand, V., Forlizzi, J., Dew, M. A., Reynolds, C. F. III, Stevens, S., & Wactlar, H. (2009). Intelligent assistive technology applications to dementia care: Current capabilities, limitations, and future challenges. *The American Journal of Geriatric Psychiatry*, *17*(2), 88–104. doi:10.1097/JGP.0b013e318187dde5 PMID:18849532

Bille, P. (2005). A survey on tree edit distance and related problems. *Theoretical Computer Science*, *337*(1-3), 217–239. doi:10.1016/j.tcs.2004.12.030

Bookman, A., Harrington, M., Pass, L., & Reisner, E. (2007). *Family caregiver handbook*. Cambridge, MA: Massachusetts Institute of Technology.

Borazio, M., & Van Laerhoven, K. (2012). *Combining wearable and environmental sensing into an unobtrusive tool for long-term sleep studies: Association for Computing Machinery*. doi:10.1145/2110363.2110375

Brand, M., Oliver, N., & Pentland, A. (2002). *Coupled hidden Markov models for complex action recognition. Institute of Electrical and Electronics Engineers*. IEEE.

Brodwin, M. G., Star, T., & Cardoso, E. (2004). Computer assistive technology for people who have disabilities: Computer adaptations and modifications. *Journal of Rehabilitation, 70*(3), 28.

Broek, G. V. D., Cavallo, F., Odetti, L., & Wehrmann, C. (2010). AALIANCE ambient assisted living roadmap 2010. *Ambient Intelligence and Smart Environments, 6*, 110.

Cao, X. Q., & Liu, Z. Q. (2010). Human motion detection using Markov random fields. *Journal of Ambient Intelligence and Humanized Computing, 1*(3), 211–220. doi:10.100712652-010-0015-1

Cardinaux, F., Brownsell, S., Hawley, M., & Bradley, D. (2008). *Modelling of behavioural patterns for abnormality detection in the context of lifestyle reassurance*. Paper presented at the Iberoamerican Congress on Pattern Recognition. 10.1007/978-3-540-85920-8_30

Chakrabarti, S., Sarawagi, S., & Dom, B. (1998). Mining surprising patterns using temporal description length. In *Proceedings of the 24th International Conference on Very Large Data Bases*. San Francisco, CA.

Chung, L., & Subramanian, N. (2004). Adaptable architecture generation for embedded systems. *Journal of Systems and Software, 71*(3), 271–295. doi:10.1016/S0164-1212(03)00009-8

Coronato, A., & De Pietro, G. (2013). Situation awareness in applications of ambient assisted living for cognitive impaired people. *Mobile Networks and Applications, 18*(3), 444–453. doi:10.100711036-012-0409-8

Coronato, A., De Pietro, G., & Paragliola, G. (2014). A situation-aware system for the detection of motion disorders of patients with autism spectrum disorders. *Expert Systems with Applications, 41*(17), 7868–7877. doi:10.1016/j.eswa.2014.05.011

Coronato, A., & Paragliola, G. (2017). A structured approach for the designing of safe AAL applications. *Expert Systems with Applications, 85*, 1–13. doi:10.1016/j.eswa.2017.04.058

Cortes, C., & Vapnik, V. (1995). Support-vector networks. *Machine Learning*, *20*(3), 273–297. doi:10.1007/BF00994018

de Joode, E., van Heugten, C., Verhey, F., & van Boxtel, M. (2010a). Efficacy and usability of assistive technology for patients with cognitive deficits: A systematic review. *Clinical rehabilitation*, *24*(8), 701–714. doi:10.1177/0269215510367551 PMID:20543021

de Joode, E., Van Heugten, C., Verhey, F., & Van Boxtel, M. (2010b). Efficacy and usability of assistive technology for patients with cognitive deficits: A systematic review. *Clinical rehabilitation*, *24*(8), 701–714. doi:10.1177/0269215510367551 PMID:20543021

Duong, T. V., Bui, H. H., Phung, D. Q., & Venkatesh, S. (2005). Activity recognition and abnormality detection with the switching hidden semi-Markov model. In *Proceedings 2005 IEEE Computer Society Conference on Computer Vision and Pattern Recognition (CVPR'05)*. 10.1109/CVPR.2005.61

Fickas, S., Robinson, W., & Sohlberg, M. (2005, September). The role of deferred requirements: A case study. In *Proceedings International Conference on Requirements Engineering (RE'05)*, Paris, France. 10.1109/RE.2005.70

Ganti, V., Gehrke, J., Ramakrishnan, R., & Loh, W. Y. (2002). A framework for measuring differences in data characteristics. *Journal of Computer and System Sciences*, *64*(3), 542–578. doi:10.1006/jcss.2001.1808

Giannella, C., Han, J., Pei, J., Yan, X., & Yu, P. S. (2003). Mining frequent patterns in data streams at multiple time granularities. In H. Kargupta, A. Joshi, K. Sivakumar, & Y. Yesha (eds.), Next generation data mining, 191-212. doi:10.1.1.14.2327

Hevner, A. R., March, S. T., Park, J., & Ram, S. (2004). Design science in information systems research. *Management Information Systems Quarterly*, *28*(1), 75. doi:10.2307/25148625

Jarvis, P. A., Lunt, T. F., & Myers, K. L. (2005). Terrorist activity with AI plan-recognition technology. *AI Magazine*, *26*, 73–81. doi:10.1609/AIMAG.V26I3.1827

Kargupta, H., Bhargava, R., Liu, K., Powers, M., Blair, P., Bushra, S., ... Vasa, M. (2004). Vedas: A mobile and distributed data stream mining system for real-time vehicle monitoring. *Proceedings of the SIAM International Data Mining Conference, Orlando, FL*. 10.1137/1.9781611972740.28

Kifer, D., Bendavid, S., & Gehrke, J. (2004). Detecting change in data streams. In *Proceedings of the International Conference on Very Large Data Bases*.

Kullback, S. (1997). *Information theory and statistics*. Dover Pubns.

Lafferty, J. D., McCallum, A., & Pereira, F. C. N. (2001). Conditional random fields: Probabilistic models for segmenting and labeling sequence data. *Proceedings of the Eighteenth International Conference on Machine Learning*.

Lamsweerde, A. V. (2008). *Requirements engineering: From system goals to UML models to software specifications*. Wiley.

LeCun, Y., Bengio, Y., & Hinton, G. (2015). Deep learning. *nature, 521*(7553), 436.

Lee, B.-S., Martin, T. P., Clarke, N. P., Majeed, B., & Nauck, D. (2004). Dynamic daily-living patterns and association analyses in tele-care systems. In *Proceedings Fourth IEEE International Conference on Data Mining (ICDM'04)*. 10.1109/ICDM.2004.10023

Li, H., Zhang, Q., & Duan, P. (2008). *A novel one-pass neural network approach for activities recognition in intelligent environments*. Paper presented at the 2008 7th World Congress on Intelligent Control and Automation.

Li, R., Lu, B., & McDonald-Maier, K. D. (2015). Cognitive assisted living ambient system: A survey. *Digital Communications and Networks*, *1*(4), 229–252. doi:10.1016/j.dcan.2015.10.003

Liao, L., Patterson, D. J., Fox, D., & Kautz, H. (2007). Learning and inferring transportation routines. *Artificial Intelligence*, *171*(5-6), 311–331. doi:10.1016/j.artint.2007.01.006

LoPresti, E., Mihailidis, A., & Kirsch, N. (2004). Assistive technology for cognitive rehabilitation: State of the art. *Neuropsychological Rehabilitation*, *14*(1-2), 5–39. doi:10.1080/09602010343000101

Ludwig, H., Dan, A., & Kearney, R. (2004). Crona: An architecture and library for creation and monitoring of ws-agreents. *Proceedings of the 2nd international conference on service oriented computing* (pp. 65-74). New York, NY: ACM Press. 10.1145/1035167.1035178

Mahmoud, S., Lotfi, A., & Langensiepen, C. (2013). Behavioural pattern identification and prediction in intelligent environments. *Applied Soft Computing*, *13*(4), 1813–1822. doi:10.1016/j.asoc.2012.12.012

Marshall, M. (2000). *Astrid: A social and technological response to meeting the needs of individuals with dementia and their carers; a guide to using technology within dementia care*. London, UK: Hawker.

Maurer, U., Smailagic, A., Siewiorek, D. P., & Deisher, M. (2006). Activity recognition and monitoring using multiple sensors on different body positions. *Proceedings - BSN 2006: International Workshop on Wearable and Implantable Body Sensor Networks*. 10.21236/ADA534437

McColl, M., Carlson, P., Johnston, J., Minnes, P., Shue, K., Davies, D., & Karlovitz, T. (1998). The definition of community intergration: Perspectives of people with brain injuries. *Brain Injury: [BI]*, *12*(1), 15–30. doi:10.1080/026990598122827 PMID:9483334

McHugh, J., Wherton, J., Prendergast, D., & Lawlor, B. (2012). Identifying opportunities for supporting caregivers of persons with dementia through information and communication technology. *Gerontechnology (Valkenswaard)*, *10*(4), 220–230.

Mining of sensor data in healthcare: A survey 91-125. (2015). CRC Press.

Monekosso, D. N., & Remagnino, P. (2010). Behavior analysis for assisted living. *IEEE Transactions on Automation Science and Engineering*, *7*(4), 879–886. doi:10.1109/TASE.2010.2049840

Nakashima, H., Aghajan, H., & Augusto, H. (2009). Handbook of ambient intelligence and smart environments. Handbook of Ambient Intelligence and Smart Environments. doi:10.1007/978-0-387-93808-0

Okoro, C. A., Hollis, N. D., Cyrus, A. C., & Griffin-Blake, S. (2017). *Prevalence of disabilities and health care access by disability status and type among adults — United States, 2016*. In S. T. Peek, E. J. Wouters, J. Van Hoof, K. G. Luijkx, H. R. Boeije, & H. J. Vrijhoef. (2014). Factors influencing acceptance of technology for aging in place: A systematic review. *International Journal of Medical Informatics*, *83*(4), 235–248.

Phillips, B., & Zhao, H. (1993). Predictors of assistive technology abandonment. *Assistive Technology*, *5*(1), 36–45. doi:10.1080/10400435.1993.10132205 PMID:10171664

Rashidi, P., & Cook, D. J. (2010). Mining sensor streams for discovering human activity patterns over time. *Proceedings - IEEE International Conference on Data Mining, ICDM*. 10.1109/ICDM.2010.40

Real-time pervasive monitoring for postoperative care, 122-127 (2007).

Robinson, W. N. (2006). A requirements monitoring framework for enterprise systems. *Requirements Engineering Journal*, *11*(1), 17–41. doi:10.100700766-005-0016-3

Robinson, W. N. (2002, Jan. 7-10). Monitoring software requirements using instrumented code. In *IEEE Proceedings of The 35th Annual Hawaii International Conference on Systems Sciences*, Hawaii.

Robinson, W. N., & Akhlaghi, A. (2017). Sequential fraud detection for prepaid cards using hidden Markov model divergence. *Expert Systems with Applications.*

Robinson, W. N., & Akhlaghi, A. (2010, Jan. 5-8). Monitoring behavioral transitions in cognitive rehabilitation with multi-model, multi-window stream mining. In *Proceedings Hawaii International Conference on Software Systems*, Kauai, HI. 10.1109/HICSS.2010.279

Robinson, W. N., Akhlaghi, A., Deng, T., & Syed, A. R. (2012a). Discovery and diagnosis of behavioral transitions in patient event streams. *ACM Transactions on Management Information Systems*, *3*(1), 1–28. doi:10.1145/2151163.2151167

Robinson, W. N., Akhlaghi, A., & Syed, A. (2011, January). *A framework for mining behaviors in clinical data streams.* Paper presented at the IEEE Draft, HI.

Robinson, W. N., & Aria, A. (2019). Fraud detection using hidden Markov model divergence. *IEEE Security and Privacy.*

Robinson, W. N., & Fickas, S. (2009). Talking designs: A case of feedback for design evolution in assistive technology. In K. Lyytinen, P. Loucopoulos, J. Mylopoulos, & W. Robinson (Eds.), Design requirements engineering: A ten-year perspective (pp. 215-237): Springer-Verlag.

Robinson, W. N., Syed, A. R., Akhlaghi, A., & Deng, T. (2012b, Jan. 4 - 12). Pattern discovery of user interface sequencing by rehabilitation clients with cognitive impairments. In *Proceedings Hawaii International Conference on Software Systems*, Hawaii. 10.1109/HICSS.2012.467

Ruotsalainen, M., Ala-Kleemola, T., & Visa, A. (2007). Gais: A method for detecting interleaved sequential patterns from imperfect data. *Proceedings of the 2007 IEEE Symposium on Computational Intelligence and Data Mining, CIDM 2007.* 10.1109/CIDM.2007.368920

Sahraeian, S. M. E., & Yoon, B.-J. (2011). A novel low-complexity hmm similarity measure. *IEEE Signal Processing Letters*, *18*(2), 87–90. doi:10.1109/LSP.2010.2096417

Sak, H., Senior, A., & Beaufays, F. (2014). *Long short-term memory recurrent neural network architectures for large scale acoustic modeling*. Paper presented at the Fifteenth Annual Conference of the International Speech Communication Association.

Services, U. S. D. O. H. A. H. (2002). *Add fact sheet*. Retrieved from http://www.acf.dhhs.gov/programs/add/Factsheet.htm

Siegel, C., & Dorner, T. E. (2017). Information technologies for active and assisted living—Influences to the quality of life of an ageing society. *International Journal of Medical Informatics*, *100*, 32–45. doi:10.1016/j.ijmedinf.2017.01.012 PMID:28241936

Silberschatz, A., & Tuzhilin, A. (1996). What makes patterns interesting in knowledge discovery systems. *IEEE Transactions on Knowledge and Data Engineering*, *8*(6), 970–974. doi:10.1109/69.553165

Simultaneous tracking and activity recognition (star) using many anonymous, binary sensors. 62-79. (2010).

Sixsmith, A. J., Gibson, G., Orpwood, R. D., & Torrington, J. M. (2007). Developing a technology 'wish-list'to enhance the quality of life of people with dementia. *Gerontechnology (Valkenswaard)*, *6*(1), 2–19. doi:10.4017/gt.2007.06.01.002.00

Sohlberg, M. K. M., Turkstra, L. S., & Wilson, B. A. (2011). *Optimizing cognitive rehabilitation: Effective instructional methods*. The Guilford Press.

Sohlberg, M. M., Ehlhardt, L., Fickas, S., & Todis, B. (2002). Core: comprehensive overview of requisite e-mail skills. In M. M. Sohlberg, S. Fickas, L. Ehlhardt, & B. Todis, (Eds.), *The longitudinal effects of accessible email for individuals with severe cognitive impairments. Aphasiology*, *19*(7), 651–681.

Stikic, M., Huỳnh, T., Laerhoven, K. V., & Schiele, B. (2008). Adl recognition based on the combination of RFID and aeeelerometer sensing. *Proceedings of the 2nd International Conference on Pervasive Computing Technologies for Healthcare 2008, PervasiveHealth*. 10.1109/PCTHEALTH.2008.4571084

Sutcliffe, A., Fickas, S., & Sohlberg, M. K. M. (2006). Pc-re: A method for personal and contextual requirements engineering with some experience. *Requirements Engineering*, *11*(3), 157–173. doi:10.100700766-006-0030-0

Todis, B., Sohlberg, M. M., Hood, D., & Fickas, S. (2005). Making electronic mail accessible: Perspectives of people with acquired cognitive impairments, caregivers and professionals. *Brain Injury: [BI]*, *19*(6), 389–401. doi:10.1080/02699050400003957 PMID:16101262

Tong, L., Song, Q., Ge, Y., & Liu, M. (2013). Hmm-based human fall detection and prediction method using tri-axial accelerometer. *IEEE Sensors Journal*, *13*(5), 1849–1856. doi:10.1109/JSEN.2013.2245231

Tseng, C.-C., & Cook, D. (2006). Mining from time series human movement data. In *Proceedings 2006 IEEE International Conference on Systems, Man and Cybernetics*. 10.1109/ICSMC.2006.384617

Vail, D. L., Veloso, M. M., & Lafferty, J. D. (2008). *Conditional random fields for activity recognition. Association for Computing Machinery.*

van Kasteren, T., & Krose, B. (2008). *Bayesian activity recognition in residence for elders. Institution of Engineering and Technology.*

Van Kasteren, T. L. M., Englebienne, G., & Kröse, B. J. A. (2010). An activity monitoring system for elderly care using generative and discriminative models. *Personal and Ubiquitous Computing*, *14*(6), 489–498. doi:10.100700779-009-0277-9

van Lamsweerde, A. (2003). From system goals to software architecture. *Formal Methods for Software Architectures*, 25–43.

van Lamsweerde, A. (2004). Elaborating security requirements by construction of intentional anti-models. In *Proceedings 26th International Conference on Software Engineering, 2004. ICSE 2004.* 148-157.

van Lamsweerde, A., Darimont, R., & Massonet, P. (1995, March 27-29). Goal-directed elaboration of requirements for a meeting scheduler: Problems and lessons learnt. In *Proceedings IEEE Second International Symposium on Requirements Engineering*. 10.1109/ISRE.1995.512561

Wang, J., Han, J., & Pei, J. (2003). Closet+: Searching for the best strategies for mining frequent closed itemsets¤. *Proceedings of the ninth ACM SIGKDD international conference on Knowledge discovery and data mining - KDD '03*, 236. doi:10.1145/956750.956779

Wang, Y., Yu, Y., & Mylopoulos, J. (2007). An automated approach for monitoring and diagnosing requirements. In *Proceedings the 22nd IEEE/ACM International Conference on Automated Software Engineering*, Atlanta, GA. 10.1145/1321631.1321675

Wilson, B. A., Emslie, H. C., Quirk, K., & Evans, J. J. (2001a). Reducing everyday memory and planning problems by means of a paging system: A randomised control crossover study. *Journal of Neurology, Neurosurgery, and Psychiatry*, *70*(4), 477–482. doi:10.1136/jnnp.70.4.477 PMID:11254770

Wilson, B. A., Emslie, H. C., Quirk, K., & Evans, J. J. (2001b). Reducing everyday memory and planning problems by means of a paging system: A randomised control crossover study. *Journal of Neurology, Neurosurgery, and Psychiatry*, *70*(4), 477–482. doi:10.1136/jnnp.70.4.477 PMID:11254770

Wright, P., Rogers, N., Hall, C., Wilson, B., Evans, J., Emslie, H., & Bartram, C. (2001). Comparison of pocket-computer memory aids for people with brain injury. *Brain Injury: [BI]*, *15*(9), 787–800. doi:10.1080/02699050110045161 PMID:11516347

Wu, X., Kumar, V., Ross Quinlan, J., Ghosh, J., Yang, Q., Motoda, H., ... Yu, P. (2008). Top 10 algorithms in data mining. *Knowledge and Information Systems*, *14*(1), 1–37. doi:10.100710115-007-0114-2

Yin, J., Yang, Q., & Pan, J. J. (2008). Sensor-based abnormal human-activity detection. *IEEE Transactions on Knowledge and Data Engineering*.

Zhang, J., Cheng, B., & Goldsby, H. (2007, Sept. 30 – Oct. 5). *Amoeba-rt: Run-time verification of adaptive software.* Paper presented at the Models@Run.Time'07 Workshop, ACM/IEEE 10th International MoDELS 2007, Nashville, TN.

Zhang, X., Yao, L., Huang, C., Sheng, Q. Z., & Wang, X. (2017). Intent recognition in smart living through deep recurrent neural networks. In *Proceedings International Conference on Neural Information Processing*. 10.1007/978-3-319-70096-0_76

Zhu, Y., Li, H., Liao, Y., Wang, B., Guan, Z., Liu, H., & Cai, D. (2017). What to do next: Modeling user behaviors by time-LSTM. In *Proceedings IJCAI*. 10.24963/ijcai.2017/504

ENDNOTE

1 www.think-and-link.org, www.coglink.com.

Chapter 12
Ethically Building Business Intelligence in Healthcare:
A Value-Sensitive Perspective

Majid Dadgar
University of San Francisco, USA

K. D. Joshi
University of Nevada, Reno, USA

ABSTRACT

This chapter advocates the use of a value-sensitive design (VSD) approach toward deriving patient intelligence by illustrating that the insights provided by the healthcare data that captures patients' concerns, needs, and desires—known as values—provide more sustainable care. Authors examine three cases extracted from top information systems (IS) peer-reviewed journals in which medical data is collected and analyzed and in which intelligence is derived through a VSD framework. VSD is a three-part methodology that comprises conceptual, empirical, and technical investigations. This chapter investigates the value sensitivity of the following key activities and tasks that result in intelligence from data: data collection, data analysis, and data reporting.

INTRODUCTION

Advanced information and communication technologies (ICTs) designed and employed in the healthcare sector support and automate the activities that are required during the care process (Cortez, Cohen, & Kesselheim, 2014). Patients are more and more frequently participating in the care process enabled by these

DOI: 10.4018/978-1-7998-2310-0.ch012

ICTs (Bardhan & Thouin, 2013). As such, we argue that disruptive ICTs must be adaptive to each patient's needs, desires, and concerns in order to become effective tools. Data generated and employed by these technologies and systems is processed and analyzed to provide insight into and intelligence about the patient care process. Healthcare providers recommend clinical treatments based on the system's generated and obtained patient data. We believe such data must capture patients' needs, desires, and concerns (i.e., human values), otherwise the medical recommendations become incomplete and the ICTs used during the care process become ineffective. In order to ensure patients' human values are captured, data collection, analysis, and reporting should be sensitive to these values.

There is a gap between the knowledge and practice of ethical responsibilities in the complicated care process that provides health care, treatment, and service for the patients (Concannon, Gillibrand, & Jones, 2019). Healthcare providers and healthcare data workers collect and analyze healthcare data during the care process to gain insight into the patient's care and treatment. We believe it is the ethical responsibility of the healthcare providers and scholars to ensure the intelligence gained from healthcare data is ethically derived. This chapter's objective is to introduce a value-sensitive perspective to derive insight from healthcare data that captures patient's concerns, needs, and desires (Friedman, 1997). We examine three cases extracted from top information systems (IS) peer-reviewed journals in which medical data is collected and analyzed and in which intelligence is derived through a value-sensitive design (VSD) framework (Friedman, Kahn, & Borning, 2008). VSD is a three-part methodology that comprises conceptual, empirical, and technical investigations. In this chapter, we investigate the value sensitivity of the following key activities and tasks that result in intelligence from data: data collection, data analysis, and data reporting.

BACKGROUND: HEALTHCARE DATA & ETHICS

Healthcare ethics primarily involves policies, regulations, guidelines, and activities to ensure ethical and professional conduct and providing medical and social benefits (Concannon et al., 2019). Healthcare data is collected from multiple sources to be used by different stakeholders for different purposes. The healthcare data collected to improve patients' care should take into account patients' values in forms of feelings, needs, and desires. It is the ethical responsibility of those collecting, analyzing, and reporting patients' healthcare data to ensure that the patients have a say in the process. The intelligence derived from patients' data for their care and treatment, should be sensitive to their values and not just focus on clinical outcomes. The patients' intelligence will be more congruent with ethical considerations if the important steps of the data lifecycle, data collection, analysis, and reporting, are sensitive to the values of the patients as humans.

The ethical view on the use of healthcare data is well reflected in the protocols and policies to minimize harm, ensure patients are aware that how and why their data is collected and used to obtain their informed consent (Mouton Dorey, Baumann, & Biller-Andorno, 2018) with full control and autonomy (Rumbold & Pierscionek, 2017), protect their privacy (Bassan & Harel, 2018), and design healthcare systems that are stress-free and user-friendly (Mueller, Heger, & Niehaves, 2018). This ethical perspective centers around patients' rights to know how their healthcare data is being used (e.g., for research, for social or individual benefits). This view aims to maximize the social and medical benefits of the healthcare data by protecting the patients' privacy. This ethical view on healthcare data is limited to the medical considerations to achieve high quality of care and technical specifications to protect data security and privacy, and does not satisfy all the ethical responsibilities towards patients' healthcare data. Ethics is a means to achieve the end of higher data quality (Wade, 2007). Patients' engagement in the data collection and analysis provides an opportunity for a joint effort between patients and healthcare providers to improve care (Manafo, Petermann, Mason-Lai, & Vandall-Walker, 2018) but should capture what patients need and desire as human beings. An ethical empathy with the patients-humans during data collection and analysis allows patients engage in the care process and share their needs and desire with the healthcare providers and data worker (Concannon et al., 2019).

It is ethical to protect the privacy of the patients' data. The content of the healthcare data that is fully protected from the privacy threats, may contain data that does not reflect the human needs and desires of a patient as a human. The intelligence derived from data that is collected, analyzed, and reported by keeping patients values in mind is not limited to privacy concerns and provides better insights about how patients want to be take care of. Technical specifications and policies, and political limitations can eliminate patients' privacy concerns such as protection of healthcare big data that is collected from multiple sources (Bassan & Harel, 2018). Patients want their values reflected in the care they receive, and therefore, their values should be reflected in their healthcare data and the intelligence that is derived from it. Data governance may satisfy privacy and informed consent values of the patients (Mouton Dorey et al., 2018) but does not fully support all their values. Privacy in addition to the other ethical values that are important for the patients should be protected and supported in the healthcare data.

In the following sections we propose and use a framework that is sensitive to the patients' values. The value that is central to the framework principles has ethical import. The values defined and conceptualized based on the human ethics and they are sensitive to the ethical values of the humans. We use the framework to investigate healthcare data that is generated and analyzed from healthcare systems to obtain insight and provide better care, is sensitive to the patients' values. The patients' values investigated and discussed for the healthcare systems reflect to what extent the data collected, analyzed, and reported through those systems has been done through an ethical process. Our investigation shows to what extent the intelligence gained from healthcare data and analyzed to improve patients' care has been and can be sensitive to the patients' ethics as humans.

Value Sensitive Data and Business Intelligence Ethics

The use of ICTs in the healthcare context is increasing (Bardhan, Chen, & Karahanna, 2017), and ICT-enabled healthcare solutions have become clinical tools that can potentially improve the quality of patients' care (Bailey, Belter, Pandit, & Carpenter, 2013). This proliferation of ICT use in the healthcare context is generating a large volume of data that is being transformed into intelligent insights that recommend healthcare treatments and improve health altogether (Yang, Guo, & Wu, 2015). Although patients are involved in the decision-making process regarding their treatment options, they are primarily peripheral to the collection, analysis, and reporting of the data that drives those options. Data concerning patients' conditions, illnesses, and treatments are critical for generating intelligence to provide more efficient patient care at reasonable costs, but we argue that the data is inadequate because it is primarily gathered and used from a clinical perspective without much input or involvement from the patients themselves. The key premise of this book chapter is that patients' deep involvement in the collection, analysis, and reporting of their healthcare data—wherein they are the co-creators of the intelligence that is converted from data to insights—leads to more favorable health outcomes than those that result when patients are not involved.

In this chapter, we offer a solution to the issue of inadequate data by advocating for a patient's ***value-sensitive*** perspective in collecting, analyzing, and reporting his/her data. Despite the economic and medical values implicated in the healthcare systems, patients' values that are of moral and ethical import are not similarly incorporated into both the system and the data generated by those systems that aim to improve patients' health conditions. The health systems and solutions that are insensitive to patients' values can become ineffective over time (Dadgar & Joshi, 2018). In order for the intelligence derived from patients' healthcare data to be considered valuable, we recommend that patients' data be sensitive to their values during all stages of data collection, analysis, and reporting. We believe in the modern care models wherein patients are active in the care process and partner with their healthcare providers to improve their health conditions (Bodenheimer, Lorig, Holman, & Grumbach, 2002); it is further essential that they are involved in the production and delivery of the data that concerns them and their treatments. Such engagement in transforming data into insights will produce value-sensitive intelligence that is more closely aligned with patients' needs and desires.

We use the VSD framework to illustrate how sensitizing healthcare data by aligning it with patients' values leads to outcomes that patients desire. The VSD framework is a tripartite methodology that examines the sensitivity of the technological products and processes to the aforementioned human values (Friedman et al., 2008). An initial set of proposed values are believed to be universal, although several studies have redefined and adapted the universal values within new contexts (Yetim, 2011); thus, we have redefined the VSD's universal values in the healthcare context (Dadgar & Joshi, 2018). Value is of ethical import in the VSD framework, which differs from the restricted economic view of the value-based systems proposed by Porter (Porter, 2012).

The VSD framework is employed in the literature for various technological, political, medical, and social applications and research projects, such as the incorporation of patients' values into ICT-enabled self-management systems (Dadgar & Joshi, 2017, 2018), the designing of Internet browsers that are sensitive to users' privacy (Xu, Crossler, & Belanger, 2012), the empowerment of microtask workers in crowdsourced workspaces (Deng, Joshi, & Galliers, 2016), and the provision of a voice to the constituents in technology-related policies (Young, Magassa, & Friedman, 2019). There are seventeen methods to use VSD including stakeholder analysis, value source analysis, value scenario, scalable assessments of information dimensions, and value-oriented coding manual (Friedman & Hendry, 2019, pp. 61–64). These methods are adaptive to the differences between concepts, contexts, and technologies. Our goal in this book chapter is to investigate and illustrate the importance of patients-humans' values in the three main stages of data lifecycle, data collection, analysis, and reporting, that result in the intelligence. We choose value-source analysis and value-oriented coding manual methods. These methods serve the purposes that we aim to achieve in the next section. The purpose of value source analysis is to identify and distinguish among the project values, users', providers' and system developers' values.

We discussed in the background that the ethical considerations in the collection and analysis of the data are primarily concerned with data protection, control, and governance is inadequate. A broader perspective which accounts for patients' values in a more comprehensive manner is needed. In order to distinguish and discuss the different values and highlight the importance of patients' values the value source analysis method will be utilized. The method of value-oriented coding manual serves the purpose of value analysis. This method is used for the coding of the data to illustrate values based on a coding scheme. The coding scheme that we use in this book chapter to investigate three intelligence-based healthcare systems and their data is the set of values proposed by Dadgar and Joshi (2018) which is the most comprehensive list of human values that capture the needs, desires, and concerns of the patients.

MAIN FOCUS OF THE CHAPTER

Investigative Approach

We selected three cases (papers) from top IS journals to illustrate how the collection, analysis, and reporting of healthcare data can be conducted sensitively to patients' values. Three papers were selected that extensively discuss the data collection, analysis, and reporting stages of deriving intelligence from healthcare data. We chose articles-cases based on the criteria that each article has to be peer-reviewed, published in a top IS journal, provide information about the business intelligence processes and activities of the data collection, analysis, and reporting processes and activities, and discuss the details of the patient-centric care delivery with the central role of the intelligence and insight gained from the healthcare data. Our literature search resulted in 15 articles and the authors suggested and reviewed their top choices to select the final three articles that best satisfy their selection criteria. In these cases, ICTs are an integral element involved in streamlining and improving the care process as well as facilitating decision making for the healthcare providers. The designs of the ICT-enabled healthcare systems selected for this study from the related literature have the integral role of collecting and analyzing data generated by those systems to report insight and intelligence for patients.

Inventories of the universal human values have been suggested by Friedman et al. (2008), and the contextualized values proposed by Dadgar and Joshi (2018) are identified and explained based on the VSD framework as well as used to investigate healthcare systems and their sensitivity to patients' values. In this book chapter, we employ the VSD framework to illustrate the importance of patients' values in the intelligence derived from their data. Table 1 lists the human values in the healthcare context proposed by Dadgar and Joshi (2018). The proposed values are specific to patients with diabetes but can be generalized to any severe healthcare condition. The descriptions of the values have been minimally changed to match the data related, value-sensitive investigation of this study. We hope this small change makes the values' descriptions relevant to the context of healthcare business intelligence.

A patient depends upon a portfolio of interplaying values, and values may impact other values—a phenomenon known as swing values (Dadgar & Joshi, 2018). For example, a patient may feel her privacy is being violated if her medical data is or is expected to be continuously measured. Privacy is a human value; in response to

Table 1. Value repository used in healthcare

Human Value	Description
Accessibility	Properties of being available when needed
Accountability	Properties that ensure an entity's actions may be traced uniquely to that entity
Autonomy	Patients' ability to independently decide, plan, and act in ways they believe will help them achieve their goals
Compliance	Adherence to activities such as taking drugs, using medical devices and ICTs for self-care and self-directed exercises
Dignity	A sense of pride and self-respect in oneself, which captures both the positive and negative consequences of preserving dignity; on one hand, solid control over one's health conditions provides a sense of pride although on the other hand impedes the care process as patients try to withhold information or fail to seek help in an attempt to preserve their pride.
Empathy	The ability to understand and share patients' feelings
Feedback	Information concerning patients used as a basis for reminders, improvement, or positive reinforcement
Hope	A patient's motivation to achieve future-oriented expectations and personally valued goals that instill meaning and are dependent upon personal activity or characteristics
Sense making	The ability to ascribe meaning to data that captures patients' activities and behaviors
Joy	The feeling of pleasure
Privacy	An individual's claim, entitlement, or right to determine what one's information about oneself (e.g., medical data, medication taking, diabetes diagnosis) can be communicated to others.
Trust	Expectations (of reliability, truth, and/or the ability to do the right thing) that exist between people and/or technology

the violation of privacy, patients may not fully cooperate with the data collection process. Patients who are harshly addressed by their healthcare providers during the care process may not report their medical signs or numbers in an attempt to maintain their human value of dignity, which consequently makes continuous technology-enabled data collection ineffective. Patients who decide to maintain their dignity may not remain compliant with treatment instructions; the values of privacy, dignity, and compliance interact and change one another in this example.

Patient Intelligence: A Value-Sensitive Perspective

We define patient intelligence as data-driven insights into patients' care that are derived by transforming data into actionable knowledge. Patient intelligence involves three key activities: data collection, data analysis, and data reporting. Patients' data collection is a critical step in the data lifecycle—from the origin or source to the destination or use. The analysis and reporting steps depend upon the data collection step, and intelligence derived from data depends upon the quality of the data collected. We discuss below that patients should be engaged in the data collection process and that their involvement should be designed and defined in conjunction with what they value. Patients' voices and perspectives regarding the care process and its activities should be captured in the data, otherwise we may ascertain that the data lacks completeness. Healthcare data that is indifferent to patients' needs and desires results in ineffective and slow care processes, ranging from doctor's visits to treatment to recovery and, further, to post-recovery. The care processes become slow and ineffective when they are not congruent with patients' expectations (e.g., what is important to them is not discussed or incorporated in their care process). Patients' apathy manifests as their reluctance to participate and engage in the care process which in turn impedes the quality of care (Concannon et al., 2019). Healthcare data regarding patient care should be collected both with and by patients themselves.

The analysis of healthcare data should also be sensitive to patients' values. Patients' health data should be interpreted through the lens that considers patients' needs and desires and should not solely focus on clinical outcomes. Patients should be involved in the interpretation of the results data, and they should be allowed and encouraged to explore and understand their health data. New care models in healthcare promote the development of partnership between patients and healthcare providers, wherein patients are actively engaged in the care process. We believe this partnership should be reserved for the critical steps of the care process that affect healthcare providers' final recommendations. The collection, analysis, and reporting of healthcare data throughout the care process are critical points that may create the opportunity for providers to collaborate with their patients and subsequently improve their care. We believe this collaboration is effective when it is decided based on the needs and desires of patients who must follow their healthcare recommendations. A value-sensitive interpretation and analysis of patient data can more thoroughly explain its details as well as facilitate the development of a more collaborative care process alongside the patients themselves.

The reporting of a patient's data analysis should be sensitive to her values. The available reporting tools and features should allow that patients present the data analysis results in a customizable way; these tools include customized visuals, numbers, and table-graphing options. Analysis results should be presented with positive feedback such that patients maintain their positive outlook on both their health conditions and the care process. Data that is sensitive to patients' values involves their needs and concerns, which are gathered during the data analysis and reporting steps, as well as their clinical data and vital signs.

Next, we discuss and examine the value sensitivity of ICT-based healthcare solutions during the three main stages that result in data-derived intelligence. The selected stages of the data lifecycle are discussed for three cases, each of which is a peer-reviewed research article published in a top-tier IS journal. First, we explain the ICT-enabled healthcare solution discussed in each case. Next, we exemplify and illustrate each case's importance with regard to value sensitivity at each of the three data lifecycle stages.

Case #1: The Patient Self-Reporting System

Kallinikos and Tempini (2014) propose a web-based social network platform that automates medical data collection and allows that patients with severe conditions enter and report their medical data. Patients subscribe to the network for free and socialize with other patients who possess similar health conditions. Symptoms, treatments, body measures, and other health-related factors can be tracked and reported on the platform. The platform collects data from each patient's living environment to provide realistic and timely data. The system encourages patients to enter data at their convenience, and data is collected and analyzed on a continuous basis.

Data Collection

The system collects data through online electronic questionnaires and forms that are available to network members. Collected data is consistently and continuously analyzed, and patients are encouraged to report their health status:

data collection in the network is predicated on an inclusive, holistic understanding of health that goes far beyond the medically recognizable conditions of particular diseases. Data collection is, to a degree, use-agnostic, open to the recording of rather broad aspects of patient life. In the hope that all data might turn out relevant, the network seeks to capture a wide range of circumstances, beyond those that medical researchers would traditionally earmark for data collection in the context of specific research undertakings. As we show in the context of symptoms data collection, patients can choose to track a range of symptoms that is much more granular and extensive than expert terminologies often allow for (Kallinikos & Tempini, (2014)p. 827).

This approach allows patients to identify and take inventory of their symptoms and thus account for their views and experiences in derivation of medical facts. Patients' inclusion in the data collection activity broadens the participation that can help in "reducing biases, errors, and conflicting interests" (Kallinikos & Tempini, 2014, p. 827). We concur with the argument Kallinikos and Tempini (2014) make in that healthcare providers might be biased in their analysis and interpretation of patients' data, which therefore indicates they should involve patients in the measurement, analysis, and understanding of their health data:

By controlling data entry, clinicians have the ultimate word on what a symptom really is. The patient plays a dependent role in data collection, and only so far as perceptions and feelings are part of the phenomena under investigation, such as when reporting symptoms. The patient is otherwise excluded from the assessment of all other reportable and observable medical entities (clinical signs) and has no relevant role to play in measurement, nor in inference (p. 824).

A patient's understanding of her health conditions is partially shaped by what she shares with others, specifically those who have similar health conditions. The interactions of a patient with an external entity—that is, another patient, friend, or relative—are part of the patient's efforts in following her medical treatments. Seeking information from any external entity is an important element in understanding a treatment's efficiency. Why must a patient seek more information? What kind of information is sought? Interactions with external entities can be held through social networking applications to connect with others who share the same health conditions, share experiences, and verify what is already known. The healthcare solution discussed in this case possesses the social networking features that allow a patient to interact and communicate about their health conditions with other patients. A patient's collected health data may be partially shaped by the data she collects from her social networks.

The prescriptive medical recommendations derived from clinical data lack the presence of the patient as a living human with feelings and whose input is important. Data collected from patients at medical institutions separate them from their living environment, and such data does not fully capture a patient's context or setting; patients may follow medical treatments while merely living their daily lives outside the clinical settings wherein data is collected. Medical recommendations should speak to each patient's perspective concerning a treatment's circumstances, conditions, and requirements. Collecting data from patients and by patients throughout their daily lives reduces the chance of reaching incompatibilities between medical recommendations and patients' daily routines:

Thus, the attribution of a local clinical situation to an illness profile, medical category, or classification system is established by the clinician, and their expert knowledge. Against this backdrop, the routine generation of medical data by patients themselves represents an entirely new development that breaks with the history of medical records being used for research purposes and the institutional settings within which these records have commonly been generated (Kallinikos & Tempini, 2014, p. 824).

In addition, such an approach to data collection captures granular data that encourages a more nuanced view of patients' conditions. The following excerpt from the above paper further explains the importance of capturing data at the granular level in patients' life contexts:

Data collection is longitudinal, encouraging reporting at all stages of patient life. It is also continuous, seeking to obtain patient inputs as frequently and regularly as possible. The longitudinal and continuous data collection is based on the assumption or belief that it is worth capturing the patient experience in significant detail, transcending the standard focus of most institutional care and research. Patients are free to enter data as often as they believe necessary, as the technology automates many of the transactions involved (Kallinikos & Tempini, 2014, p. 827).

Data collection's breakthrough outside institutional settings and within a patient's living environment is rather effective although potentially intrusive. In response to excessive exposure to data collection technologies and routines, patients might choose to be more private and share less data during the data collection process. Patients will take responsibility for their medical conditions and take actions to comply with medical treatments if their privacy is not violated and if they do not feel stressed or pressed to provide data regarding their treatments. Failure to comply with medical treatments may be rooted in data collection activities, as patients who receive negative feedback from their healthcare providers when they do not comply with or remain accountable for their treatments often attempt to protect their pride and remain private (Dadgar & Joshi, 2018). If patients' pride is violated, they may not fully involve themselves in reporting their medical statistics because they dread the negative feeling of lost pride that is influenced by their failure to comply with their medical treatments. Data collection should be sensitive to what a patient considers important about her treatments such that the data analysis accounts for compatibility between her daily life and her treatment regimen. The data analysis should be sensitive to the possibility that compliance to medical treatment is not in place in the event that a patient feels her pride and privacy are being violated.

Data Analysis

The objectives of the data analysis for the purposes of patient care are inadequate if they are not value sensitive or based primarily on clinical criteria. Most data analyses in the medical field are not free from knowledge experts' and healthcare providers' assumptions; expectedly, bias towards data is not conducive to an accurate analysis of a patient's health status or her accountability to and compliance with her medical treatments. A patient's treatment compliance is largely affected by how those treatments fulfill her needs and desires. Therefore, failure to comply should not be exclusively interpreted as the fact that a patient has not followed her prescribed treatment. Patients' values as well as their difficulties with and barriers to complying with their treatments should be included in the medical narrative that helps them understand their health conditions and provides medical recommendations, as is supported by Kallinikos and Tempini (2014):

Our data analysis and interpretation continued after the fieldwork period, mainly through the crosschecking of the empirical material with a view to identifying a consistent narrative about the phenomena under investigation. In this process, we compared our empirical findings on the processes of data collection and analysis used at the field site to data collection processes depicted in the literature on medical research and medical knowledge creation. Much of that comparison took place against a wider understanding of the role of social media, data, and computation. After several iterative readings and analyses, we selected the most relevant pieces of evidence and assembled them into a case study narrative, following retroductive logic to produce our explanations (p. 830).

We believe patient intelligence is co-created by healthcare providers and patients themselves. The co-creation of patient intelligence is indirectly affected by patients' co-created healthcare data and is directly affected by the analysis of healthcare data alongside a patient. Healthcare providers should discuss patients' health data with the patients themselves before forming their understanding of that data, which may be accomplished either electronically or in person, when patients and healthcare providers meet for discussion. When providers share their interpretations, patients become engaged in the analysis of their own health data, both parties are assuredly on the same page regarding the data's progress over time, and patients are informed about the patterns and fluctuations in the tables and visuals that will be reported during the next data lifecycle stage.

Data Reporting

Patient intelligence is affected by how the intelligence derived from data is provided and presented to patients. An ineffective representation of the data conveys only part of that intelligence or otherwise incomplete and inaccurate intelligence. This derived intelligence is represented in data reports and should be easy to understand and follow. Patients should be educated on understanding their health data and the reports generated from their health data by their healthcare providers, healthcare systems, and themselves. Patients' health data should be presented to them in a way that allows that they customize and manipulate it to create a report that is most meaningful to them. Patients should be supported while and after they interpret their health data through access to additional resources, such as healthcare providers who are available to answers questions and concerns, opportunities to share feelings and thoughts with other patients with similar health conditions, and access to medical facts stored and represented in digital documents, articles, visuals, or videos. Following this interpretation, patients should be supported with positive feedback such that they may continue complying with their treatments and adhering to their prescribed medications.

Providing positive reinforcement in the form of positive comments and encouragement motivates patients to take action in response to their results data. Patients who have immediate access to additional informative resources can more thoroughly understand the data presented to them. Kallinikos and Tempini (2014) further explain the importance of easily interpreting data and quickly accessing the necessary information:

Patients can explore information about their own health through various forms of data output. Through data aggregation techniques, the system dynamically constructs and displays profile pages on specific kinds of medical entities (conditions, symptoms, treatments, labs, and others), represented in the form of scores, descriptive statistics, and visualizations. Patients can thus browse a range of reports that put their profile data in perspective and offer a complex picture of the individual. Patients can also browse data representing the health aspects of entire patient populations. Patients access a wealth of information that the system generates by aggregating the data contributed by patient members across the network (p. 832).

Case #2: Patient Flow Models

Adeyemi, Demir, and Chaussalet (2013) discuss patient flow modelling, which is used to optimize the steps a patient follows from admission to discharge. The case focuses more closely on the re-admission step of the patient flow, while the information resulting from the flow models is employed in the decision support tools to monitor and optimize patients' flows in healthcare settings. The patient flow model enables healthcare providers to understand how to reduce inefficiencies, obtain more favorable clinical and operational outcomes, and improve the comprehensive patient experience (Adeyemi et al., 2013).

Data Collection

Part of the data collected for this study originates from the data provided by the Department of Health in England, which contains personal and medical information of the patients admitted to the hospitals. The study of Adeyemi et al. (2013) intends to understand and improve the patient experience. We believe patients' values—that is, their concerns, needs, and desires—bridge the empirical data with the patient experience (Friedman et al., 2008). Clinical, personal, and administrative data used in the study may be useful for statistically analyzing data based on demographic and administrative variables, which do not capture the patient's experience beyond traditional medical and clinical data. The experience measured in this case centers around the improvement of the patient's "clinical (disease progression) and operational (movement) experience during the process of care" (Adeyemi et al., 2013, p. 118). This is an incomplete picture of the patient experience because it lacks the human and ethical aspects of the patient experience. For example, data collected during the care process may contain time of care, medication, and the chemical levels in the body but may not capture how patients feel about taking medications or their high/low chemical levels.

Patients may not even be aware of the human values that are infused in their care experience, and some data should be collected from patients with regard to their human experiences through the care process. Healthcare providers should learn from patients how they experienced the care process and its flow, and they should thus include the insights gained while striving to meet their data analysis objectives. In the present case, the patient experience is reduced to her number of readmissions. The chronic disease that is studied in this case is a lifelong experience that should be investigated as a bigger picture that is not limited to the narrow scope of clinical and operational data. Furthermore, data concerning a patient's experience should capture the human aspect of that experience.

Data Analysis

Data is grouped and analyzed by age and gender based on patients' demographic information, while further analysis is conducted to determine whether or not the patient experience improves in terms of one's number of readmissions:

We want to determine the probability of a patient belonging to any of the lower group[s] advancing to a higher group as a function of patient characteristics, such as gender, age, readmission history, total length of stay in hospital prior to discharge, number of previous readmissions, Charlson co-morbidity index, index of multiple deprivation (IMD), ethnicity, reasons for discharge and discharge destinations (Adeyemi et al., 2013, p. 121).

According to the objectives of the data analysis, the human aspect of the patient experience should be included to capture the complete picture of that experience. The value-sensitive data collection in the prior stage of the data lifecycle makes analyzing, identifying, and understanding the human aspect of the patient experience an easier task. The patient experience is created not only by medical and clinical facts, but also by patients' concerns, needs, and desires. From a patient's admission to a healthcare clinic to her discharge to the post-recovery phase, her feelings and experiences relative to the care process should be analyzed and included in the data analysis objectives.

Data Reporting

Patients can be informed or guided by relevant data, such as "patient readmission progression" (Adeyemi et al., 2013, p. 124). Patients can use the information presented to them regarding their care flow and progress to adapt and learn about the ways by which the care flow can become more effective and efficient as well as subsequently support their comprehensive experience (including the human aspect). Trend lines, for example, can be an effective visualization technique to demonstrate the longitudinal progress of the care flow. This flow cannot be improved without the patient's direct contribution to the flow's improvement and without her clear understanding of a flow, which can and should be both efficient and effective. Patients make daily decisions while living with their chronic diseases, and these decisions are informed by data that these patients must continuously access, such as descriptions of the flow's steps, the individuals involved in the care process and their responsibilities, and quick contact information. The health systems designed with the most effective decision-making features become ineffective when their procedures are not properly followed or understood.

Case #3: Online Physician Service Delivery

Yang, Guo, and Wu (2015) examine the impact of care delivery through an online health community focused on patient satisfaction. The online health community under study was developed based on web 2.0 networking technologies to facilitate interaction and communication between patients and physicians. Patients seek information and emotional support through their membership and engagement in these online communities, and this system benefits high-risk patients more so than low-risk patients.

Data Collection

In this case, data was collected from one of the largest online health communities in China by a Java program that scrapes Internet data related to that community. This automated data collection program downloads webpages that contain any information about a physician's response to a patient, the goal being to determine the response speed and frequency from the scraped and collected webpages. Data was additionally collected from the online forum, which includes responses from physicians who are grouped into disease categories. Physicians' responses to patients' questions have metadata for future analysis, descriptions of patients' conditions, and the exact time each physician gave a response. Data on patient satisfaction was collected from the patients' ratings upon completion of their consultation with a physician, where more positive ratings indicate higher levels of patient satisfaction. Other data used in the statistical model to measure satisfaction include "the physician's ranking (director physician, associate director physician, chief physician, and physician), academic titles (professor, associate professor, and lecturer), patients' digital gifts and thank you letters, and contribution value" (Yang et al., 2015, p. 117).

The variables used to measure patient satisfaction result in patient intelligence that merely reflects one's satisfaction with the medical and clinical services provided through the online system. The satisfaction data collected in this study is limited to statistical ratios of positive ratings, which represents a beneficial step in data collection that is however insufficient for capturing every aspect of a patient's satisfaction. The data scraped from the web is easily collectible yet may nevertheless lack important elements that affect patient satisfaction, including patients' needs and concerns. This online health community is a technology patients use to seek alternative information and emotional support regarding their health conditions (Yang et al., 2015). Seeking information and support is an organic and continuous activity many patients perform in different contexts and situations for various needs and concerns. Thus, due to patients' continuous and critical use, the data collected for patient satisfaction regarding online care delivery should capture aspects beyond satisfactory clinical and medical uses and outcomes.

Data Analysis

The study of Yang et al. (2015) aims to examine whether or not response speed and interaction frequency between patients and physicians in online care delivery affect patients' satisfaction and the role of disease risk in this relationship. The objectives of the data analysis include targeting the improvement of the system's functionality and clinical outcomes: "The dependent variable of this research is patient satisfaction. We used the ratio of the number of positive ratings to the number of patients as a proxy for patient average satisfaction rate" (Yang et al., p. 116). The data analysis objectives should reach beyond statistical comparisons and include the needs and concerns of patients who, as humans, utilize online health communities to seek more information or emotional support while containing the psychological effects of their health conditions, such as stress, anxiety, and depression (Schulman-Green et al., 2012). Patient satisfaction is shaped within the life context and requires contextual intelligence beyond the independent variables of "the mean response speed and mean interaction frequency" (Yang et al., p. 116).

Data Reporting

This case was conducted in China, and data was collected from Chinese patients and physicians. As such, cultural differences should be considered when reporting and interpreting medical and clinical measures. A Chinese patient with diabetes may have different needs and concerns than an American patient with the same condition, as patients' values vary by culture. A representation of the data should be compatible with a patient's understanding of the data relationships and associations represented in the data reports, as the relationships and interactions between patients and physicians will vary across cultures and countries. The types of health data presented and reported to patients should support and address their needs and desires as humans living with their health conditions. Chinese patients may require data access and interpretation for their health management that differs from that of other countries, and healthcare management activities may additionally be followed and conducted differently in China. Thus, Chinese patients' need for positive feedback and support from their healthcare providers will more or less differ from what is required by patients in other parts of the world. Patients from different cultures may require different types of data, tools, or techniques in order to understand the health data that is reported and presented to them.

SOLUTIONS AND RECOMMENDATIONS

Data analysts and data scientists involved in designing, building, and operating business intelligence activities for the medical field should try mitigating their biases by being sensitive to patients' values while collecting, analyzing, and reporting their information. The process of acquiring data-driven insight should be transparent and patient centric (Friedman & Nissenbaum, 1996), and values that are important to patients should be incorporated into the data collection, analysis, and reporting steps that are conducted to drive insights into patient care. Patients should be involved in the data collection process while the interplay of their privacy and dignity values against their accountability and compliance values are captured and investigated during data collection and analysis. Technology-enabled data collection in patients' living environment, although effective, should be implemented with care such that it does not interfere in patients' lives or violate their privacy. Furthermore, data presented to each patient as insight for interpretation should be easy to understand and supported by positive feedback.

FUTURE RESEARCH DIRECTIONS

In regard to big data, healthcare providers are more and more frequently exploring new data analytics approaches that allow them to derive intelligence regarding healthcare and treatments, as new technologies enable the easier and quicker analysis of big data. As data grows in volume, velocity, veracity, and variety and as technologies become more advanced, the risk of compromising patients' needs and desires in the care process become evident as healthcare providers rely more heavily on clinical and medical data to recommend treatments for their patients. In order to derive patient intelligence that is significantly valuable and supports healthcare-related decision making and management, healthcare providers must capture and reveal what patients need and consider important in their care process. Healthcare big data analytics and intelligence should be sensitive to patients' human values along the three data lifecycle steps of data collection, analysis, and reporting.

The factors affecting the derivation of patient intelligence that are sensitive to patients' values reach beyond the data lifecycle, as healthcare systems and technologies continuously generate, collect, analyze, and report insights from patients' health data throughout the care process. The health systems and technologies used during the care process should possess features that allow patients to record and report the aspects that are important to them as well as enable healthcare providers to proactively collect comprehensive healthcare data that contains patients' values. The health systems that fail to view patients as members of healthcare provider teams are designed to exclusively collect clinical and medical data. This approach becomes ineffective over time because data management and governance approaches are disengaged with the realities of patients' lives. In order to avoid such a destiny, we strongly advocate that data management and intelligence delivery approaches take into account patients' values of ethical and moral import.

VSD in healthcare is an effective method and framework for investigating data's sensitivity to patients' values. The growth of consumerization concerning advanced technologies necessitates greater value sensitivity due to the danger that these new technologies may develop into functional tools that are effective in improving medical symptoms but simultaneously fail to fulfill patients' healthcare expectations and needs. Virtual, augmented, and artificial intelligence and realities should be developed and employed in healthcare to more thoroughly understand patients' human values by, for example, introducing augmented reality wearable technology that allows patients to know and learn about the medical tools and terms used through the care process as well as the knowledge employed when care management activities are performed, such as the monitoring of symptoms, the measurement of patients' health status, and communication with other patients, healthcare providers, and relatives.

CONCLUSION

This book chapter introduces the VSD framework and methodology to examine and investigate the sensitivity of patients' health data that is collected, analyzed, and reported to them. The patient intelligence derived from health data includes important and necessary clinical and medical data concerning patients and their health status but does not include their needs, desires, and concerns throughout the care process. We believe the VSD framework allows scholars in healthcare to be attentive and sensitive to what patients as living humans consider important, necessary, and desirable during the care process. Medical treatments and advice are based on the data collected, analyzed, and reported throughout the care process that highlights the importance of these steps in creating an effective and value-sensitive care process.

The three cases investigated in this book chapter are provided to illustrate the ethical importance of patients' values in the data that is generated and used by the systems and healthcare providers to improve patients' health and their quality of life. In the three cases-articles three systems are used that rely on the data intelligence to improve patients' health. We investigate these examples using two VSD methods of value source analysis and value-oriented coding manual. The investigation of the cases provides examples and instances of data collection, analysis, and reporting activities that underscore the importance of sensitivity to patients' values for better patient care. Our investigation of the cases and review of the healthcare data ethics literature suggest that the ethical considerations of the healthcare data is limited to privacy, protection, and governance. A broad and inclusive ethical perspective is needed to ensure that patient as a human is engaged in the data collection, analysis, and reporting and the intelligence is ethically derived. We use VSD, a value-sensitive critical framework, to illustrate examples of data collection, analysis, and reporting activities and processes that should be sensitive to the patients' values in order to provide an ethically derived patient's intelligence.

REFERENCES

Adeyemi, S., Demir, E., & Chaussalet, T. (2013). Towards an evidence-based decision making healthcare system management: Modelling patient pathways to improve clinical outcomes. [Retrieved from edselp.]. *Decision Support Systems*, *55*(1), 117–125. doi:10.1016/j.dss.2012.12.039

Bailey, S. C., Belter, L. T., Pandit, A. U., & Carpenter, D. M. (2013). *The availability, functionality, and quality of mobile applications supporting medication self management.*

Bardhan, I., Chen, H., & Karahanna, E. (2017). The role of information systems and analytics in chronic disease prevention and management. *MIS Quarterly*, (Call for Papers MISQ Special Issue).

Bardhan, I. R., & Thouin, M. F. (2013). Health information technology and its impact on the quality and cost of healthcare delivery. [Retrieved from edselp.]. *Decision Support Systems*, *55*(2), 438–449. doi:10.1016/j.dss.2012.10.003

Bassan, S., & Harel, O. (2018). The ethics in synthetics: Statistics in the service of ethics and law in health related research in big data from multiple sources. *Journal of Law and Health*, *31*(1), 87–117. PMID:30889335

Bodenheimer, T., Lorig, K., Holman, H., & Grumbach, K. (2002). Patient self-management of chronic disease in primary care. *Journal of the American Medical Association*, *288*(19), 2469–2475. doi:10.1001/jama.288.19.2469 PMID:12435261

Concannon, M., Gillibrand, W., & Jones, P. (2019). An exploration of how ethics informs healthcare practice. *Ethics and Medicine, 35:1*(Spring 201). Retrieved from https://pure.hud.ac.uk/en/publications/an-exploration-of-how-ethics-informs-healthcare-practice

Cortez, N. G., Cohen, G., & Kesselheim, A. S. (2014). FDA regulation of mobile health technologies. *The New England Journal of Medicine, 371*(4), 372–379. doi:10.1056/NEJMhle1403384 PMID:25054722

Dadgar, M., & Joshi, K. D. (2017). Value-sensitive review and analysis of technology-enabled self-management systems: A conceptual investigation. *International Journal of Electronic Healthcare, 9*(2/3), 157. doi:10.1504/IJEH.2017.083166

Dadgar, M., & Joshi, K. D. (2018). The role of information and communication technology in self-management of chronic diseases: an empirical investigation through value sensitive design. [JAIS]. *Journal of the Association for Information Systems, 19*(2), 86–112. doi:10.17705/jais1.00485

Deng, X., Joshi, K. D., & Galliers, R. D. (2016). The duality of empowerment and marginalization in microtask crowdsourcing: giving voice to the less powerful through value sensitive design. *Management Information Systems Quarterly, 40*(2), 279–A19. doi:10.25300/MISQ/2016/40.2.01

Friedman, B. (Ed.). (1997). *Human values and the design of computer technology.* CA: CSLI Publications.

Friedman, B., & Hendry, D. G. (2019). *Value sensitive design: shaping technology with moral imagination.* Retrieved from https://mitpress.mit.edu/books/value-sensitive-design

Friedman, B., Kahn, P. H., & Borning, A. (2008). *Value sensitive design and information systems* John Wiley & Sons. doi:10.1002/9780470281819.ch4

Friedman, B., & Nissenbaum, H. (1996). Bias in computer systems. *ACM Transactions on Information Systems, 14*(3), 330–347. doi:10.1145/230538.230561

Kallinikos, J., & Tempini, N. (2014). Patient data as medical facts: social media practices as a foundation for medical knowledge creation. *Information Systems Research, 25*(4), 817–833. doi:10.1287/isre.2014.0544

Manafo, E., Petermann, L., Mason-Lai, P., & Vandall-Walker, V. (2018). Patient engagement in Canada: A scoping review of the 'how' and 'what' of patient engagement in health research. *Health Research Policy and Systems, 16*(5).

Mouton Dorey, C., Baumann, H., & Biller-Andorno, N. (2018). Patient data and patient rights: Swiss healthcare stakeholders' ethical awareness regarding large patient data sets – a qualitative study. *BMC Medical Ethics*, 19. PMID:29514635

Mueller, M., Heger, O., & Niehaves, B. (2018, Jan. 3). Investigating ethical design requirements for digitalized healthcare support: the case of ambulatory physiotherapeutic assistance systems. In *Proceedings of the Hawaii International Conference on System Sciences (HICSS)*, Waikoloa Village, HI. 10.24251/HICSS.2018.372

Porter, M. E. (2012). Redefining German health care: Moving to a value-based system. Heidelberg, Germany: Springer. doi:10.1007/978-3-642-10826-6

Rumbold, J. M. M., & Pierscionek, B. K. (2017). A critique of the regulation of data science in healthcare research in the European Union. *BMC Medical Ethics*, *18*(1), 27. doi:10.118612910-017-0184-y PMID:28388916

Schulman-Green, D., Jaser, S., Martin, F., Alonzo, A., Grey, M., McCorkle, R., ... Whittemore, R. (2012). Processes of self-management in chronic illness. *Journal of Nursing Scholarship*, *44*(2), 136–144. doi:10.1111/j.1547-5069.2012.01444.x PMID:22551013

Wade, D. (2007). Ethics of collecting and using healthcare data. *BMJ (Clinical Research Ed.)*, *334*(7608), 1330–1331. doi:10.1136/bmj.39247.679329.80 PMID:17599978

Xu, H., Crossler, R. E., & Belanger, F. (2012). A value sensitive design investigation of privacy enhancing tools in web browsers. *Decision Support Systems*, *54*(1), 424–433. doi:10.1016/j.dss.2012.06.003

Yang, H., Guo, X., & Wu, T. (2015). Exploring the influence of the online physician service delivery process on patient satisfaction. [Retrieved from edselp.]. *Decision Support Systems*, *78*, 113–121. doi:10.1016/j.dss.2015.05.006

Yetim, F. (2011). Bringing discourse ethics to value sensitive design: pathways toward a deliberative future. *AIS Transactions on Human-Computer Interaction*, *3*(2), 133–155. doi:10.17705/1thci.00030

Young, M., Magassa, L., & Friedman, B. (2019). Toward inclusive tech policy design: A method for underrepresented voices to strengthen tech policy documents. *Ethics and Information Technology*, *21*(2), 89–103. doi:10.100710676-019-09497-z

ADDITIONAL READING

Friedman, B. (Ed.). (1997). *Human Values and the Design of Computer Technology*. CA: CSLI Publications.

Friedman, B., & Hendry, D. G. (2019). Value Sensitive Design: Shaping Technology with Moral Imagination. Retrieved from https://mitpress.mit.edu/books/value-sensitive-design

Yetim, F. (2011). Bringing Discourse Ethics to Value Sensitive Design: Pathways toward a Deliberative Future. *AIS Transactions on Human-Computer Interaction*, *3*(2), 133–155. doi:10.17705/1thci.00030

Compilation of References

Abdel-Hamid, O., Deng, L., & Yu, D. (2013, August). Exploring convolutional neural network structures and optimization techniques for speech recognition. In Interspeech (Vol. 2013, pp. 1173-5).

Abdel-Khalek, S., Ishak, A. B., Omer, O. A., & Obada, A.-S. (2017). A two-dimensional image segmentation method based on genetic algorithm and entropy. *Optik (Stuttgart)*, *131*, 414–422. doi:10.1016/j.ijleo.2016.11.039

Acampora, G., Cook, D. J., Rashidi, P., & Vasilakos, A. V. (2015). Data analytics for pervasive health. *Healthcare Data Analytics*, 533-576. doi:10.1201/b18588

Activity recognition in the home using simple and ubiquitous sensors 158-175. (2004).

Adamic, L. A., Zhang, J., Bakshy, E., & Ackerman, M. S. (2008, April 21). Knowledge sharing and yahoo answers: everyone knows something. In *Proceedings 17th International Conference on World Wide Web*. 10.1145/1367497.1367587

Adeyemi, S., Demir, E., & Chaussalet, T. (2013). Towards an evidence-based decision making healthcare system management: Modelling patient pathways to improve clinical outcomes. [Retrieved from edselp.]. *Decision Support Systems*, *55*(1), 117–125. doi:10.1016/j.dss.2012.12.039

Aggarwal, C. C., Han, J., Wang, J., & Yu, P. S. (2003). A framework for clustering evolving data streams. *Proceedings of the 29th International Conference on Very Large Data Bases-Volume 29*. Berlin, Germany. 10.1016/B978-012722442-8/50016-1

Agrawal, R., & Psaila, G. (1995). Active data mining. *In Proceedings of the First International Conference on Knowledge Discovery in Databases and Data Mining*. Montreal, Canada.

Al Sayed, C., Vinches, L., & Hallé, S. (2017). Validation of a wearable biometric system's ability to monitor heart rate in two different climate conditions under variable physical activities. *E-Health Telecommunication Systems and Networks*, *6*(02), 19–30. doi:10.4236/etsn.2017.62002

Ali, R., ElHelw, M., Atallah, L., Lo, B., & Yang, G. Z. (2008). Pattern mining for routine behaviour discovery in pervasive healthcare environments. In *Proceedings 5th Int. Conference on Information Technology and Applications in Biomedicine, ITAB 2008 in conjunction with 2nd Int. Symposium and Summer School on Biomedical and Health Engineering, IS3BHE 2008*. 10.1109/ITAB.2008.4570576

Alliance, F. C. (2001). Incidence and prevalence of the major causes of brain impairment. Retrieved from http://www.caregiver.org/caregiver/jsp/content_node.jsp?nodeid=438

Alshari, E. M., Azman, A., Mustapha, N., Doraisamy, S. C., & Alksher, M. (2016). Prediction of rating from comments based on information retrieval and sentiment analysis. In *Proceedings 2016 Third International Conference on Information Retrieval and Knowledge Management (CAMP)*. 10.1109/INFRKM.2016.7806330

Anderson, B. (2007). Collaborative care and motivational interviewing: improving depression outcomes through patient empowerment interventions. *The American Journal of Managed Care, 13*(Sup4), S103-S106.

Angst, C. M., & Agarwal, R. (2009). Adoption of electronic health records in the presence of privacy concerns: The elaboration likelihood model and individual persuasion. *Management Information Systems Quarterly, 33*(2), 339–370. doi:10.2307/20650295

Arasu, A., & Garcia-Molina, H. (2003). Extracting structured data from web pages. In *Proceedings of the 2003 ACM SIGMOD International Conference on Management of Data*. 10.1145/872757.872799

Arizona Smokers' Helpline. (2019). *Arizona Smokers' Helpline Annual Report, 2019. University of Arizona*. Tucson, AZ: Author.

ASHLine. (n.d.). Retrieved from https://uahs.arizona.edu/arizona-smokers-helpline-ashline

Ashrafi, N., Kelleher, L., & Kuilboer, J. P. (2014). The impact of business intelligence on healthcare delivery in the USA. *Interdisciplinary Journal of Information, Knowledge, and Management*, (9), 117-130.

Ashwin, B., Thiagarajan, R., Reza Soroushmehr, S. M., Navidi, F., Beard, D. A., & Najarian, K. (2015). Big Data Analytics in Healthcare, *Biomed Res Int*. 2015: 370194. Published online July 2, 2015. doi:10.1155/2015/370194

Atomwise. (2015). *Atomwise finds first evidence towards new ebola treatment*. Retrieved from http://www.atomwise.com/2015/03/24/atomwise-finds-first-evidence-towards-new-ebola-treatments/

Aujoulat, I., d'Hoore, W., & Deccache, A. (2007). Patient empowerment in theory and practice: polysemy or cacophony? *Patient Education and Counseling, 66*(1), 13–20. doi:10.1016/j.pec.2006.09.008 PMID:17084059

Avants, B. B., Tustison, N. J., Song, G., Cook, P. A., Klein, A., & Gee, J. C. (2011). A reproducible evaluation of ANTs similarity metric performance in brain image registration. *NeuroImage, 54*(3), 2033–2044. doi:10.1016/j.neuroimage.2010.09.025 PMID:20851191

Bailey, S. C., Belter, L. T., Pandit, A. U., & Carpenter, D. M. (2013). *The availability, functionality, and quality of mobile applications supporting medication self management.*

Baltzan, P. (2012). *Business driven technology*. McGraw-Hill/Irwin.

Barber, D. (2012). *Bayesian reasoning and machine learning*. Cambridge, UK: Cambridge University Press.

Bardhan, I., Chen, H., & Karahanna, E. (2017). The role of information systems and analytics in chronic disease prevention and management. *MIS Quarterly*, (Call for Papers MISQ Special Issue).

Bardhan, I. R., & Thouin, M. F. (2013). Health information technology and its impact on the quality and cost of healthcare delivery. [Retrieved from edselp.]. *Decision Support Systems*, *55*(2), 438–449. doi:10.1016/j.dss.2012.10.003

Barger, T. S., Brown, D. E., & Alwan, M. (2005). Health-status monitoring through analysis of behavioral patterns. *IEEE transactions on systems, man, and cybernetics. Part A, systems and humans*, *35*(1), 22–27. doi:10.1109/TSMCA.2004.838474

Barney, J. (1991). Firms resources and sustained competitive advantage. *Journal of Management*, *17*(1), 99–120. doi:10.1177/014920639101700108

Bashivan, P., Rish, I., Yeasin, M., & Codella, N. (2015). Learning representations from eeg with deep recurrent-convolutional neural networks. *arXiv preprint arXiv:1511.06448.*

Bassan, S., & Harel, O. (2018). The ethics in synthetics: Statistics in the service of ethics and law in health related research in big data from multiple sources. *Journal of Law and Health*, *31*(1), 87–117. PMID:30889335

Bauer, B. A., Lee, M., Bergstrom, L., Wahner-Roedler, D., Bundrick, J., & Litin, S. (2002). Internal medicine resident satisfaction with a diagnostic decision support system (DXplain) introduced on a teaching hospital service. *Proc AMIA Symp.*, 31–35. PMID:12463781

Bay, S. D., & Schwabacher, M. (2004). *Mining distance-based outliers in near linear time with randomization and a simple pruning rule*. Association for Computing Machinery.

Benatar, A. (2017). The pediatric electrocardiogram. *Ann Cardiol Cardiovasc Dis*, *2*(1), 1009.

Bengio, Y., Lamblin, P., Popovici, D., & Larochelle, H. (2007). Greedy layer-wise training of deep networks. In Proceedings Advances in Neural Information Processing Systems (pp. 153-160).

Bengio, Y., Yao, L., Alain, G., & Vincent, P. (2013). Generalized denoising auto-encoders as generative models. In Proceedings Advances in Neural Information Processing Systems (pp. 899-907).

Bengio, Y., Courville, A., & Vincent, P. (2013). Representation learning: A review and new perspectives. *IEEE Transactions on Pattern Analysis and Machine Intelligence*, *35*(8), 1798–1828. doi:10.1109/TPAMI.2013.50 PMID:23787338

Berndt, D. J., Fisher, J. W., Hevner, A. R., & Studnicki, J. (2001). Healthcare data warehousing and quality assurance. *Computer IEEE Journal, 34(12), Dec. 2001.*

Berner, E. S., & La Lande, T. J. (2007). Overview of clinical decision support systems. In *Clinical decision support systems* (pp. 3–22). Springer. doi:10.1007/978-0-387-38319-4_1

Bevan, N. (2001). International standards for HCI and usability. *International Journal of Human-Computer Studies*, *55*(4), 533–552. doi:10.1006/ijhc.2001.0483

Bharadwaj, A. S. (2000). A resource-based perspective on information technology capability and firm performance: an empirical investigation. *Management Information Systems Quarterly*, *24*(1), 169–196. doi:10.2307/3250983

Bharucha, A. J., Anand, V., Forlizzi, J., Dew, M. A., Reynolds, C. F. III, Stevens, S., & Wactlar, H. (2009). Intelligent assistive technology applications to dementia care: Current capabilities, limitations, and future challenges. *The American Journal of Geriatric Psychiatry*, *17*(2), 88–104. doi:10.1097/JGP.0b013e318187dde5 PMID:18849532

Bhatt, G. D., & Grover, V. (2005). Types of information technology capabilities and their role in competitive advantage: an empirical study. *Journal of Management Information Systems*, *22*(2), 253–277. doi:10.1080/07421222.2005.11045844

Bille, P. (2005). A survey on tree edit distance and related problems. *Theoretical Computer Science*, *337*(1-3), 217–239. doi:10.1016/j.tcs.2004.12.030

Birman-Deych, E., Waterman, A. D., Yan, Y., Nilasena, D. S., Radford, M. J., & Gage, B. F. (2005). Accuracy of ICD-9-CM codes for identifying cardiovascular and stroke risk factors. *Medical Care*, *43*(5), 480–485. doi:10.1097/01.mlr.0000160417.39497.a9 PMID:15838413

Blumenthal, D. (2010). Launching hitech. *The New England Journal of Medicine*, *362*(5), 382–385. doi:10.1056/NEJMp0912825 PMID:20042745

Bodenheimer, T., Lorig, K., Holman, H., & Grumbach, K. (2002). Patient self-management of chronic disease in primary care. *Journal of the American Medical Association*, *288*(19), 2469–2475. doi:10.1001/jama.288.19.2469 PMID:12435261

Bonney, W. (2013). Applicability of business intelligence in electronic health record. In *Proceedings of the 2nd International Conference on Integrated Information*. 10.1016/j.sbspro.2013.02.050

Bookman, A., Harrington, M., Pass, L., & Reisner, E. (2007). *Family caregiver handbook*. Cambridge, MA: Massachusetts Institute of Technology.

Boonstra, A., & Broekhuis, M. (2010). Barriers to the acceptance of electronic medical records by physicians from systematic review to taxonomy and interventions. *BMC Health Services Research*, *10*(1), 231. doi:10.1186/1472-6963-10-231 PMID:20691097

Boonstra, T. W., Nicholas, J., Wong, Q. J., Shaw, F., Townsend, S., & Christensen, H. (2018). Using mobile phone sensor technology for mental health research: Integrated analysis to identify hidden challenges and potential solutions. *Journal of Medical Internet Research, 20*(7). doi:10.2196/10131 PMID:30061092

Borazio, M., & Van Laerhoven, K. (2012). *Combining wearable and environmental sensing into an unobtrusive tool for long-term sleep studies: Association for Computing Machinery*. doi:10.1145/2110363.2110375

Botsis, T., Hartvigsen, G., Chen, F., & Weng, C. (2010). Secondary use of EHR: Data quality issues and informatics opportunities. *Summit on Translational Bioinformatics, 2010*, 1. PMID:21347133

Brand, M., Oliver, N., & Pentland, A. (2002). *Coupled hidden Markov models for complex action recognition. Institute of Electrical and Electronics Engineers*. IEEE.

Bravo, P., Edwards, A., Barr, P. J., Scholl, I., Elwyn, G., & McAllister, M. (2015). Conceptualising patient empowerment: A mixed methods study. *BMC Health Services Research, 15*(1), 252. doi:10.118612913-015-0907-z PMID:26126998

Brock, D. C., & Moore, G. E. (2006). *Understanding Moore's law: four decades of innovation*. Chemical Heritage Foundation.

Brodwin, M. G., Star, T., & Cardoso, E. (2004). Computer assistive technology for people who have disabilities: Computer adaptations and modifications. *Journal of Rehabilitation, 70*(3), 28.

Broek, G. V. D., Cavallo, F., Odetti, L., & Wehrmann, C. (2010). AALIANCE ambient assisted living roadmap 2010. *Ambient Intelligence and Smart Environments, 6*, 110.

Bron, E. E., Smits, M., Niessen, W. J., & Klein, S. (2015). Feature selection based on the SVM weight vector for classification of dementia. *IEEE Journal of Biomedical and Health Informatics, 19*(5), 1617–1626. doi:10.1109/JBHI.2015.2432832 PMID:25974958

Brown, J., Kahn, M., & Toh, S. (2013). Data quality assessment for comparative effectiveness research in distributed data networks. Medical care, 51(8 0 3), S22.

Burt, C. W., & Sisk, J. E. (2005). Which physicians and practices are using electronic medical records? *Health Affairs, 24*(5), 1334–1343. doi:10.1377/hlthaff.24.5.1334 PMID:16162581

Campbell, H., Hotchkiss, R., Bradshaw, N., & Porteous, M. (1998). Integrated care pathways. *BMJ: British Medical Journal, 316*(7125), 133–137. doi:10.1136/bmj.316.7125.133 PMID:9462322

Cao, X. Q., & Liu, Z. Q. (2010). Human motion detection using Markov random fields. *Journal of Ambient Intelligence and Humanized Computing, 1*(3), 211–220. doi:10.100712652-010-0015-1

Cardinaux, F., Brownsell, S., Hawley, M., & Bradley, D. (2008). *Modelling of behavioural patterns for abnormality detection in the context of lifestyle reassurance*. Paper presented at the Iberoamerican Congress on Pattern Recognition. 10.1007/978-3-540-85920-8_30

Carpenter, J., Crutchley, P., Zilca, R. D., Schwartz, H. A., Smith, L. K., Cobb, A. M., & Parks, A. C. (2017). Correction: Seeing the "big" picture: Big data methods for exploring relationships between usage, language, and outcome in internet intervention data. *Journal of Medical Internet Research, 19*(12). doi:10.2196/jmir.8099 PMID:29258059

Castanedo, F. (2013). A review of data fusion techniques. *The Scientific World Journal, 2013*, 1–19. doi:10.1155/2013/704504 PMID:24288502

cdc.gov. 2014. Meaningful use. Retrieved from http://www.cdc.gov/ehrmeaningfuluse/

Centers for Disease Control and Prevention. (2014). Best practices for comprehensive tobacco control programs, 2014. U.S. Department of Health and Human Services, Centers for Disease Control and Prevention, National Center for Chronic Disease Prevention and Health Promotion, Office on Smoking and Health. Atlanta.

Chakrabarti, S., Sarawagi, S., & Dom, B. (1998). Mining surprising patterns using temporal description length. In *Proceedings of the 24th International Conference on Very Large Data Bases*. San Francisco, CA.

Chen, H., Chiang, R. H., & Storey, V. C. (2012). Business intelligence and analytics: From big data to big impact. *Management Information Systems Quarterly, 36*(4), 1165. doi:10.2307/41703503

Chew, C., & Eysenbach, G. (2010). Pandemics in the age of Twitter: Content analysis of tweets during the 2009 H1N1 outbreak. *PLoS One, 5*(11). doi:10.1371/journal.pone.0014118 PMID:21124761

Chismar, W. G., & Wiley-Patton, S. (2003, January). Does the extended technology acceptance model apply to physicians. In *Proceedings of the 36th Annual Hawaii International Conference on System Sciences*, 2003. (pp. 8-pp). IEEE. 10.1109/HICSS.2003.1174354

Chopra, A., Prashar, A., & Sain, C. (2013). Natural language processing. *International Journal of Technology Enhancements and Emerging Engineering Research, 1*(4), 131-134.

Christens, B. D., Collura, J. J., & Tahir, F. (2013). Critical hopefulness: a person-centered analysis of the intersection of cognitive and emotional empowerment. *American Journal of Community Psychology, 52*(1-2), 170–184. doi:10.100710464-013-9586-2 PMID:23793530

Chung, L., & Subramanian, N. (2004). Adaptable architecture generation for embedded systems. *Journal of Systems and Software, 71*(3), 271–295. doi:10.1016/S0164-1212(03)00009-8

Cimino, J. J. (2006). "Coding systems in healthcare." Methods of information in medicine 35 (1996): 273-284.

Clark, D. E., & Ahmad, S. (n.d.). Estimating injury severity using the Barell matrix. Injury Prevention, 12(2), 111–116. *PubMed.*

cms.gov. (2014). EHR incentive programs. Retrieved from http://www.cms.gov/Regulations-and-Guidance/Legislation/EHRIncentivePrograms/index.html?redirect=/EHRIncentivePrograms/

Cohen, M. X. (2014). *Analyzing neural time series data: theory and practice*. Cambridge, MA: MIT Press. doi:10.7551/mitpress/9609.001.0001

Coiera, E., & Tombs, V. (1998). Communication behaviours in a hospital setting: An observational study. *BMJ (Clinical Research Ed.)*, *316*(7132), 673–676. doi:10.1136/bmj.316.7132.673 PMID:9522794

Concannon, M., Gillibrand, W., & Jones, P. (2019). An exploration of how ethics informs healthcare practice. *Ethics and Medicine, 35:1*(Spring 201). Retrieved from https://pure.hud.ac.uk/en/publications/an-exploration-of-how-ethics-informs-healthcare-practice

Coronato, A., & De Pietro, G. (2013). Situation awareness in applications of ambient assisted living for cognitive impaired people. *Mobile Networks and Applications*, *18*(3), 444–453. doi:10.100711036-012-0409-8

Coronato, A., De Pietro, G., & Paragliola, G. (2014). A situation-aware system for the detection of motion disorders of patients with autism spectrum disorders. *Expert Systems with Applications*, *41*(17), 7868–7877. doi:10.1016/j.eswa.2014.05.011

Coronato, A., & Paragliola, G. (2017). A structured approach for the designing of safe AAL applications. *Expert Systems with Applications*, *85*, 1–13. doi:10.1016/j.eswa.2017.04.058

Coronel, C., & Morris, S. (2018). *Database systems: Design, Implementation, & Management* (13th ed.). US: Cengage.

Cortes, C., & Vapnik, V. (1995). Support-vector networks. *Machine Learning*, *20*(3), 273–297. doi:10.1007/BF00994018

Cortez, N. G., Cohen, G., & Kesselheim, A. S. (2014). FDA regulation of mobile health technologies. *The New England Journal of Medicine*, *371*(4), 372–379. doi:10.1056/NEJMhle1403384 PMID:25054722

Coyte, P. C., & Holmes, D. (2007). Healthcare technology adoption and diffusion in a social context. *Policy, Politics, & Nursing Practice*, *8*(1), 47–54. doi:10.1177/1527154407299646 PMID:17470771

Craft, S. (2017). A collaborative blueprint for reducing SNF readmissions: Driving results with quality reporting and performance metrics. *Health Intelligence Network*, July. Retrieved from www.hin.com

Dadgar, M., & Joshi, K. D. (2017). Value-sensitive review and analysis of technology-enabled self-management systems: A conceptual investigation. *International Journal of Electronic Healthcare*, *9*(2/3), 157. doi:10.1504/IJEH.2017.083166

Dadgar, M., & Joshi, K. D. (2018). The role of information and communication technology in self-management of chronic diseases: an empirical investigation through value sensitive design. [JAIS]. *Journal of the Association for Information Systems*, *19*(2), 86–112. doi:10.17705/jais1.00485

Dargie, W., & Poellabauer, C. (2010). *Fundamentals of wireless sensor networks: theory and practice*. John Wiley & Sons. doi:10.1002/9780470666388

Darwish, A., & Hassanien, A. E. (2011). Wearable and implantable wireless sensor network solutions for healthcare monitoring. *Sensors (Basel)*, *11*(6), 5561–5595. doi:10.3390110605561 PMID:22163914

Davis, F. D. (1989). Perceived usefulness, perceived ease of use, and user acceptance of information technology. *Management Information Systems Quarterly*, *13*(3), 319–340. doi:10.2307/249008

De Bleser, L., Depreitere, R., Waele, K. D., Vanhaecht, K., Vlayen, J., & Sermeus, W. (2006). Defining pathways. *Journal of Nursing Management*, *14*(7), 553–563. doi:10.1111/j.1365-2934.2006.00702.x PMID:17004966

De Coster, C., Quan, H., Finlayson, A., Gao, M., Halfon, P., Humphries, K. H., ... Romano, P. S. (2006). Identifying priorities in methodological research using ICD-9-CM and ICD-10 administrative data: Report from an international consortium. *BMC Health Services Research*, *6*(1), 77. doi:10.1186/1472-6963-6-77 PMID:16776836

de Joode, E., van Heugten, C., Verhey, F., & van Boxtel, M. (2010a). Efficacy and usability of assistive technology for patients with cognitive deficits: A systematic review. *Clinical rehabilitation*, *24*(8), 701–714. doi:10.1177/0269215510367551 PMID:20543021

Degaspari, J. (2013). NorthShore University Health System. *Healthcare Informatics*, *29*(1), 12–16. PMID:23505944

Deng, L., Yu, D., & Platt, J. (2012, March). Scalable stacking and learning for building deep architectures. In *Proceedings 2012 IEEE International Conference on Acoustics, Speech, and Signal Processing (ICASSP),* (pp. 2133-2136). IEEE. 10.1109/ICASSP.2012.6288333

Deng, X., Khuntia, J., & Ghosh, K. (2013, Dec. 15-18). Psychological empowerment of patients with chronic diseases: the role of digital integration. In *Proceedings 34th International Conference on Information Systems*, Milan, Italy. dblp computer science bibliography.

Deng, L., Seltzer, M. L., Yu, D., Acero, A., Mohamed, A. R., & Hinton, G. (2010). Binary coding of speech spectrograms using a deep auto-encoder. In *Eleventh Annual Conference of the International Speech Communication Association.*

Deng, X., Joshi, K. D., & Galliers, R. D. (2016). The duality of empowerment and marginalization in microtask crowdsourcing: giving voice to the less powerful through value sensitive design. *Management Information Systems Quarterly*, *40*(2), 279–A19. doi:10.25300/MISQ/2016/40.2.01

Devaraj, S., Sharma, S. K., Fausto, D. J., Viernes, S., & Kharrazi, H. (2014). Barriers and facilitators to clinical decision support systems adoption: A systematic review. *Journal of Business Administration Research*, *3*(2), 36. doi:10.5430/jbar.v3n2p36

Dong, X., Qian, L., Guan, Y., Huang, L., Yu, Q., & Yang, J. (2016). A multiclass classification method based on deep learning for named entity recognition in electronic medical records. In *Proceedings 2016 New York Scientific Data Summit (NYSDS).* 10.1109/NYSDS.2016.7747810

Dreyer, T. (2014). Care transitions: Best practices and evidence-based programs. *Home Healthcare Nurse*, *32*(5), 309–316. doi:10.1097/NHH.0000000000000069 PMID:24802602

Duong, T. V., Bui, H. H., Phung, D. Q., & Venkatesh, S. (2005). Activity recognition and abnormality detection with the switching hidden semi-Markov model. In *Proceedings 2005 IEEE Computer Society Conference on Computer Vision and Pattern Recognition (CVPR'05)*. 10.1109/CVPR.2005.61

Dxplains. (n.d.). Retrieved from http://www.mghlcs.org/projects/dxplain

Elkin, P. L., Liebow, M., Bauer, B. A., Chaliki, S., Wahner-Roedler, D., Bundrick, J., ... Barnett, G. O. (2010, November). The introduction of a diagnostic decision support system (DXplain™) into the workflow of a teaching hospital service can decrease the cost of service for diagnostically challenging diagnostic related groups (DRG)s. *International Journal of Medical Informatics*, *79*(11), 772–777. doi:10.1016/j.ijmedinf.2010.09.004 PMID:20951080

Enander, J., Ljótsson, B., Anderhell, L., Runeborg, M., Flygare, O., Cottman, O., ... Ivanov, V. Z. (2019). Long-term outcome of therapist-guided internet-based cognitive behavioural therapy for body dysmorphic disorder (BDD-NET): A naturalistic 2-year follow-up after a randomised controlled trial. *BMJ Open*, *9*(1). doi:10.1136/bmjopen-2018-024307 PMID:30647044

Engle, R. L. Jr. (1992). Attempts to use computers as diagnostic aids in medical decision making: A thirty-year experience. *Perspectives in Biology and Medicine*, *35*(2), 207–219. doi:10.1353/pbm.1992.0011 PMID:1557299

Eysenbach, G. (2009). Infodemiology and infoveillance: Framework for an emerging set of public health informatics methods to analyze search, communication and publication behavior on the Internet. *Journal of Medical Internet Research*, *11*(1). doi:10.2196/jmir.1157 PMID:19329408

Farmer, K. C. (1999). Methods for measuring and monitoring medication regimen adherence in clinical trials and clinical practice. *Clinical Therapeutics*, *21*(6), 1074–1090. doi:10.1016/S0149-2918(99)80026-5 PMID:10440628

Ferranti, J. M., Langman, M. K., Tanaka, D., McCall, J., & Ahmad, A. (2010). Bridging the gap: leveraging business intelligence tools in support of patient safety and financial effectiveness. *Journal of the American Medical Informatics Association*, *17*(2), 136–143. doi:10.1136/jamia.2009.002220 PMID:20190055

Fickas, S., Robinson, W., & Sohlberg, M. (2005, September). The role of deferred requirements: A case study. In *Proceedings International Conference on Requirements Engineering (RE'05)*, Paris, France. 10.1109/RE.2005.70

Fonkych, K., & Taylor, R. (2005). *The state and pattern of health information technology adoption*. Santa Monica, CA: RAND Corporation.

Ford, E. W., Menachemi, N., & Phillips, M. T. (2006). Predicting the adoption of electronic health records by physicians: When will healthcare be paperless? *Journal of the American Medical Informatics Association*, *13*(1), 106–112. doi:10.1197/jamia.M1913 PMID:16221936

Foshay, N., & Kuziemsky, C. (2014). Towards an implementation framework for business intelligence in healthcare. *International Journal of Information Management, 34*(1), 20–27. doi:10.1016/j.ijinfomgt.2013.09.003

Fowler, B. L. J., Johns, J., Tanniru, M. R., Ballijepally, V., Roumani, Y. F., Bobryk, D., & Mitchell, K. (2018). Engaging patients through multi-disciplinary rounding – The case study at a Michigan hospital. *Journal of Hospital Administration, 7*(5), 17–26. doi:10.5430/jha.v7n5p17

Friedman, B., & Hendry, D. G. (2019). *Value sensitive design: shaping technology with moral imagination.* Retrieved from https://mitpress.mit.edu/books/value-sensitive-design

Friedman, B. (Ed.). (1997). *Human values and the design of computer technology.* CA: CSLI Publications.

Friedman, B., Kahn, P. H., & Borning, A. (2008). *Value sensitive design and information systems* John Wiley & Sons. doi:10.1002/9780470281819.ch4

Friedman, B., & Nissenbaum, H. (1996). Bias in computer systems. *ACM Transactions on Information Systems, 14*(3), 330–347. doi:10.1145/230538.230561

Friedman, C., & Johnson, S. B. (2006). Natural language and text processing in biomedicine. In *Biomedical Informatics* (pp. 312–343). Springer. doi:10.1007/0-387-36278-9_8

Funnell, M. M., & Anderson, R. M. (2004). Empowerment and self-management of diabetes. *Clinical Diabetes, 22*(3), 123–127. doi:10.2337/diaclin.22.3.123

Funnell, M. M., Nwankwo, R., Gillard, M. L., Anderson, R. M., & Tang, T. S. (2005). Implementing an empowerment-based diabetes self-management education program. *The Diabetes Educator, 31*(1), 53–61. doi:10.1177/0145721704273166 PMID:15779247

Gajare, S., & Sonawani, S. (2018). Automatic feature selection from EHR & DNN modeling. Maharashtra Institute of Technology, Pune. International Journal of Advance Research, Ideas, and Innovations in Technology, 4(1).

Ganova-Iolovska, M., & Geraedts, M. (2009). Clinical pathways–the Bulgarian approach. *Journal of Public Health, 17*(3), 225–230. doi:10.100710389-008-0239-0

Gans, D., Kralewski, J., Hammons, T., & Dowd, B. (2005). Medical groups' adoption of electronic health records and information systems. *Health Affairs, 24*(5), 1323–1333. doi:10.1377/hlthaff.24.5.1323 PMID:16162580

Ganti, V., Gehrke, J., Ramakrishnan, R., & Loh, W. Y. (2002). A framework for measuring differences in data characteristics. *Journal of Computer and System Sciences, 64*(3), 542–578. doi:10.1006/jcss.2001.1808

Gantz, J., & Reinsel, D. (2011). Extracting value from chaos. *IDC iview, 1142*(2011), 1-12.

García, E., Oliver, A., Diez, Y., Diaz, O., Lladó, X., Martí, R., & Martí, J. (2017). Similarity metrics for intensity-based registration using breast density maps. In *Proceedings Iberian Conference on Pattern Recognition and Image Analysis*. 10.1007/978-3-319-58838-4_24

Garg, A. X., Adhikari, N. K., McDonald, H., Rosas-Arellano, M. P., Devereaux, P. J., Beyene, J., ... Haynes, R. B. (2005). Effects of computerized clinical decision support systems on practitioner performance and patient outcomes: A systematic review. *Journal of the American Medical Association, 293*(10), 1223–1238. doi:10.1001/jama.293.10.1223 PMID:15755945

Garlasu, D., Sandulescu, V., Halcu, I., Neculoiu, G., Grigoriu, O., Marinescu, M., & Marinescu, V. (2013). A big data implementation based on Grid computing. In *Proceedings the 2013 11th RoEduNet International Conference.* 10.1109/RoEduNet.2013.6511732

GDAHC. (n.d.). Retrieved from http://www.gdahc.org/

Gerhardt, B., Griffin, K., & Klemann, R. (2012). Unlocking value in the fragmented world of big data analytics. *Cisco Internet Business Solutions Group, 7.*

Ghiassi, M., Skinner, J., & Zimbra, D. (2013). Twitter brand sentiment analysis: A hybrid system using n-gram analysis and dynamic artificial neural network. *Expert Systems with Applications, 40*(16), 6266–6282. doi:10.1016/j.eswa.2013.05.057

Giannella, C., Han, J., Pei, J., Yan, X., & Yu, P. S. (2003). Mining frequent patterns in data streams at multiple time granularities. In H. Kargupta, A. Joshi, K. Sivakumar, & Y. Yesha (eds.), Next generation data mining, 191-212. doi:10.1.1.14.2327

Gibson, C. H. (1991). A concept analysis of empowerment. *Journal of Advanced Nursing, 16*(3), 354–361. doi:10.1111/j.1365-2648.1991.tb01660.x PMID:2037742

Gittelman, S., Lange, V., Crawford, C. A. G., Okoro, C. A., Lieb, E., Dhingra, S. S., & Trimarchi, E. (2015). A new source of data for public health surveillance: Facebook likes. *Journal of Medical Internet Research, 17*(4). doi:10.2196/jmir.3970 PMID:25895907

Glaser, F. (2017). *Pervasive decentralization of digital infrastructure: a framework for blockchain enabled system and use case analysis.* Hawaii: HICSS.

Glasgow, R. E., Kurz, D., King, D., Dickman, J. M., Faber, A. J., Halterman, E., ... Ritzwoller, D. (2012). Twelve-month outcomes of an internet-based diabetes self-management support program. *Patient Education and Counseling, 87*(1), 81–92. doi:10.1016/j.pec.2011.07.024 PMID:21924576

Gold, A. H., Malhotra, A., & Segars, A. H. (2001). Knowledge management: an organizational capabilities perspective. *Journal of Management Information Systems, 18*(1), 185–214. doi:10.1080/07421222.2001.11045669

Goldzweig, C. L., Towfigh, A., Maglione, M., & Shekelle, P. G. (2009). Costs and benefits of health information technology: New trends from the literature. *Health Affairs, 28*(2Supplement 2), w282–w293. doi:10.1377/hlthaff.28.2.w282 PMID:19174390

Gomber, P., Kauffman, R. J., Parker, C., & Weber, B. W. (2018). On the Fintech revolution: interpreting the forces of innovation, disruption, and transformation in financial services. *Journal of Management Information Systems* (35:1), pp. 220-265.

Google Play. (2019). Android apps on Google Play: Health and fitness. Retrieved from https://play.google.com/store/apps/category/HEALTH_AND_FITNESS

Gorman, P. N., Yao, P., & Seshadri, V. (2004). *Finding the answers in primary care: information seeking by rural and nonrural clinicians.* Paper presented at the Medinfo.

Graves, A., & Jaitly, N. (2014, January). Towards end-to-end speech recognition with recurrent neural networks. In *Proceedings International Conference on Machine Learning* (pp. 1764-1772).

Hagel, J. III, & Rayport, J. F. (1997). The coming battle for customer information. *Harvard Business Review*, *75*(1), 53. PMID:10174454

Hall, W. J., Chapman, M. V., Lee, K. M., Merino, Y. M., Thomas, T. W., Payne, B. K., ... Coyne-Beasley, T. (2015). Implicit racial/ethnic bias among health care professionals and its influence on health care outcomes: A systematic review. *American Journal of Public Health*, *105*(12), e60–e76. doi:10.2105/AJPH.2015.302903 PMID:26469668

Hannah, L. (2017). What it was like losing my job because of my illness. Retrieved from https://themighty.com/2017/04/losing-job-for-being-sick/

Haughton, J., Wadsworth, J., Falk, L. H., & Horstmeier, P. (2014). *The changing role of healthcare data analysts—how our most successful clients are embracing healthcare transformation (Executive report).* HealthCatalyst.

Hedegaard, H. B., Johnson, R. L., & Ballesteros, M. F. (2017). Proposed ICD-10-CM surveillance case definitions for injury hospitalizations and emergency department visits. *National Health Statistics Reports*, (100): 1–8. PMID:28135183

Heintzman, N. D. (2016). A digital ecosystem of diabetes data and technology: Services, systems, and tools enabled by wearables, sensors, and apps. *Journal of Diabetes Science and Technology*, *10*(1), 35–41. doi:10.1177/1932296815622453 PMID:26685994

He, K., Zhang, X., Ren, S., & Sun, J. (2016). Deep residual learning for image recognition. In *Proceedings of the IEEE conference on computer vision and pattern recognition* (pp. 770-778).

Henderson, R., & Divett, M. J. (2003). Perceived usefulness, ease of use and electronic supermarket use. *International Journal of Human-Computer Studies*, *59*(3), 383–395. doi:10.1016/S1071-5819(03)00079-X

Henderson, T., Shepheard, J., & Sundararajan, V. (2006). Quality of diagnosis and procedure coding in ICD-10 administrative data. *Medical Care*, *44*(11), 1011–1019. doi:10.1097/01.mlr.0000228018.48783.34 PMID:17063133

Hennington, A., & Janz, B. D. (2007). Information systems and healthcare XVI: physician adoption of electronic medical records: applying the UTAUT model in a healthcare context. *Communications of the Association for Information Systems*, *19*(1), 5.

Hersh, W. R., Weiner, M. G., Embi, P. J., Logan, J. R., Payne, P. R., Bernstam, E. V., ... Saltz, J. H. (2013). Caveats for the use of operational electronic health record data in comparative effectiveness research. *Medical care, 51*(8 0 3), S30.

Hersh, W. (2008). Information retrieval in literature-based discovery. In *Literature-Based Discovery* (pp. 153–172). Springer. doi:10.1007/978-3-540-68690-3_10

Herskovic, J. R., Tanaka, L. Y., Hersh, W., & Bernstam, E. V. (2007). A day in the life of PubMed: Analysis of a typical day's query log. *Journal of the American Medical Informatics Association*, *14*(2), 212–220. doi:10.1197/jamia.M2191 PMID:17213501

Herzig, S. J., Schnipper, J. L., Doctoroff, L., Kim, C. S., Flanders, S. A., Robinson, E. J., ... Williams, M. V. (2016). Physician perspectives on factors contributing to readmissions and potential prevention strategies: a multicenter survey. *Journal of General Internal Medicine*, *31*(11), 1287–1293. doi:10.100711606-016-3764-5 PMID:27282857

Hevner, A. R., March, S. T., Park, J., & Ram, S. (2004). Design science in information systems research. *Management Information Systems Quarterly*, *28*(1), 75. doi:10.2307/25148625

Hillestad, R., Bigelow, J., Bower, A., Girosi, F., Meili, R., Scoville, R., & Taylor, R. (2005). Can electronic medical record systems transform health care? potential health benefits, savings, and costs. *Health Affairs*, *24*(4), 1103–1117. doi:10.1377/hlthaff.24.5.1103 PMID:16162551

Hinton, G. E., Osindero, S., & Teh, Y. W. (2006). A fast learning algorithm for deep belief nets. *Neural Computation*, *18*(7), 1527–1554. doi:10.1162/neco.2006.18.7.1527 PMID:16764513

Hinton, G., Deng, L., Yu, D., Dahl, G. E., Mohamed, A. R., Jaitly, N., ... Kingsbury, B. (2012). Deep neural networks for acoustic modeling in speech recognition: The shared views of four research groups. *IEEE Signal Processing Magazine*, *29*(6), 82–97. doi:10.1109/MSP.2012.2205597

Hisham, M., Yaakob, S. N., Raof, R. A., Nazren, A. A., & Embedded, N. W. (2015). Template matching using sum of squared difference and normalized cross correlation. In *Proceedings 2015 IEEE Student Conference on Research and Development (SCOReD)*. 10.1109/SCORED.2015.7449303

Hoffer, J., Venkataraman, R., & Topi, H. (2018). *Modern database management* (13th ed.). US: Pearson.

Hore, S., Chakraborty, S., Chatterjee, S., Dey, N., Ashour, A. S., Van Chung, L., & Le, D.-N. (2016). An integrated interactive technique for image segmentation using stack based seeded region growing and thresholding. *International Journal of Electrical & Computer Engineering (2088-8708), 6*(6).

Hripcsak, G., Duke, J. D., Shah, N. H., Reich, C. G., Huser, V., Schuemie, M. J., ... Van Der Lei, J. (2015). Observational health data sciences and informatics (OHDSI): Opportunities for observational researchers. *Studies in Health Technology and Informatics*, *216*, 574. PMID:26262116

https://jln1.pressbooks.com/chapter/3-introducing-the-key-stakeholders-patients-providers-payors-and-policymakers-the-four-ps/

https://www.cms.gov/Research-Statistics-Data-and-Systems/Downloadable-Public-Use-Files/SynPUFs/DE_Syn_PUF.htmlCMS Linkable 2008–2010 medicare data entrepreneurs' synthetic public use file (DE-SynPUF) –

Hu, J.-X., Chen, C.-L., Fan, C.-L., & Wang, K.-H. (2017). An intelligent and secure health monitoring scheme using IoT sensor based on cloud computing. *Journal of Sensors*, 2017.

Ibrahim, A., Gannapathy, V., Chong, L., & Isa, I. (2016). Analysis of electromyography (EMG) signal for human arm muscle: A review. In Advanced Computer and Communication Engineering Technology (pp. 567-575): Springer.

Im, K. C., Choi, I. S., Ryu, J.-S., Eo, G. S., Kim, J. S., & Moon, D. H. (2010). PET/CT fusion viewing software for use with picture archiving and communication systems. *Journal of Digital Imaging*, *23*(6), 732–743. doi:10.100710278-009-9227-3 PMID:19657696

Inupakutika, D., Natarajan, G. V., Kaghyan, S., Akopian, D., Evans, M., Zenong, Y., & Parra-Medina, D. (2018). An integration of health tracking sensor applications and elearning environments for cloud-based health promotion campaigns. *Electronic Imaging, 2018*(6), 1-8.

Isik, O., Jones, M. C., & Sidorova, A. (2013). Business intelligence success: the role of BI capabilities and decision environment. *Information & Management*, *50*(1), 13–23. doi:10.1016/j.im.2012.12.001

Islam, M. S., Hasan, M. M., Wang, X., Germack, H. D., & Noor-E-Alam, M. (2018). A systematic review on healthcare analytics. *Application and Theoretical Perspective of Data Mining Healthcare (Basel, Switzerland)*, *6*(2), 54. doi:10.3390/healthcare6020054 PMID:29882866

Jarvis, P. A., Lunt, T. F., & Myers, K. L. (2005). Terrorist activity with AI plan- recognition technology. *AI Magazine*, *26*, 73–81. doi:10.1609/AIMAG.V26I3.1827

Johnston, M. E., Langton, K. B., Haynes, R. B., & Mathieu, A. (1994). Effects of computer-based clinical decision support systems on clinician performance and patient outcome: A critical appraisal of research. *Annals of Internal Medicine*, *120*(2), 135–142. doi:10.7326/0003-4819-120-2-199401150-00007 PMID:8256973

Jordan, K., Porcheret, M., & Croft, P. (2004). Quality of morbidity coding in general practice computerized medical records: A systematic review. *Family Practice*, *21*(4), 396–412. doi:10.1093/fampra/cmh409 PMID:15249528

Kaçar, S., & Sakoğlu, Ü. (2016). Design of a novel biomedical signal processing and analysis tool for functional neuroimaging. *Computer Methods and Programs in Biomedicine*, *125*, 46–57. doi:10.1016/j.cmpb.2015.11.011 PMID:26679001

Kaisler, S., Armour, F., Espinosa, J. A., & Money, W. (2013). Big data: Issues and challenges moving forward. In *Proceedings the 2013 46th Hawaii International Conference on System Sciences.* 10.1109/HICSS.2013.645

Kallinikos, J., & Tempini, N. (2014). Patient data as medical facts: social media practices as a foundation for medical knowledge creation. *Information Systems Research, 25*(4), 817–833. doi:10.1287/isre.2014.0544

Kao, H.-Y., Yu, M.-C., Masud, M., Wu, W.-H., Chen, L.-J., & Wu, Y.-C. J. (2016). Design and evaluation of hospital-based business intelligence system (HBIS): a foundation for design science research methodology. *Computers in Human Behavior, 62*, 495–505. doi:10.1016/j.chb.2016.04.021

Kargupta, H., Bhargava, R., Liu, K., Powers, M., Blair, P., Bushra, S., ... Vasa, M. (2004). Vedas: A mobile and distributed data stream mining system for real-time vehicle monitoring. *Proceedings of the SIAM International Data Mining Conference, Orlando, FL.* 10.1137/1.9781611972740.28

Kathuria, A., Mann, A., Khuntia, J., Saldanha, T. J., & Kauffman, R. J. (2018b). A strategic value appropriation path for cloud computing. *Journal of Management Information Systems, 35*(3), 740–775. doi:10.1080/07421222.2018.1481635

Kathuria, A., Saldanha, T. J. V., Khuntia, J., & Andrade Rojas, M. G. (2016). How information management capability affects innovation capability and firm performance under turbulence: evidence from India. In *Proceedings of the Thirty Seventh International Conference on Information Systems*, Dublin.

Kathuria, R., Kathuria, N. N., & Kathuria, A. (2018a). Mutually supportive or trade-offs: An analysis of competitive priorities in the emerging economy of India. *The Journal of High Technology Management Research, 29*(2), 227–236. doi:10.1016/j.hitech.2018.09.003

Kaur, H., & Rajni, R. (2017). Electrocardiogram signal analysis for R-peak detection and denoising with hybrid linearization and principal component analysis. *Turkish Journal of Electrical Engineering and Computer Sciences, 25*(3), 2163–2175. doi:10.3906/elk-1604-84

Khan, N., Yaqoob, I., Hashem, I. A. T., Inayat, Z., Ali, M., Kamaleldin, W., ... Gani, A. (2014). Big data: Survey, technologies, opportunities, and challenges. *The Scientific World Journal*, 2014. PMID:25136682

Khosla, V. (2014). 20-percent doctor included: Speculations & musings of a technology optimist.

Khuntia, J., Tanniru, M., Fragoli, F., & Nawrocki, M. (2016). Mindfulness differences in hospital unit operations: analysis of response to nurse call systems [PAJAIS]. *Pacific Asia Journal of the Association for Information Systems, 8*(1), 33–64. doi:10.17705/1pais.08102

Khuntia, J., Tanniru, M., & Weiner, J. (2015). Juggling digitization and technostress: the case of alert fatigues due to intelligent care system implementation at a hospital. *Health Policy and Technology, 4*, 364–377. doi:10.1016/j.hlpt.2015.08.005

Khuntia, J., Tanniru, M., & Weiner, J. (2017). Dimensions of patient experience and overall satisfaction in emergency units. *Journal of Patient Satisfaction, SAGE Publications, 4*(3), 95–100.

Khuntia, J., Yim, D., Tanniru, M., & Lim, S. (2017). Patient empowerment and engagement with a health infomediary. *Health Policy and Technology*, *6*(1), 40–50. doi:10.1016/j.hlpt.2016.11.003

Kifer, D., Bendavid, S., & Gehrke, J. (2004). Detecting change in data streams. In *Proceedings of the International Conference on Very Large Data Bases*.

Kim, G., Shin, B., Kim, K. K., & Lee, H. G. (2011). IT capabilities, process-oriented dynamic capabilities, and firm financial performance. *Journal of AIS*, *12*(7), 487–517.

Kinsman, L., Rotter, T., James, E., Snow, P., & Willis, J. (2010). What is a clinical pathway? Development of a definition to inform the debate. *BMC Medicine*, *8*(1), 31. doi:10.1186/1741-7015-8-31 PMID:20507550

Koch-Weser, S., Bardshaw, Y. S., Gualtieri, L., & Gallagher, S. S. (2010). The Internet as a health information source: Findings from the 2007 Health Information National Trends Survey and Implications for Health Communication. *Journal of Health Communication, 15*(Sup3), 279-293.

Koh, H. C., & Tan, G. (2011). Data mining applications in healthcare. *Journal of Healthcare Information Management*, *19*(2), 64–72. PMID:15869215

Koh, K. W., Wang, W., Richards, A. M., Chan, M. Y., & Cheng, K. F. (2016). Effectiveness of advanced practice nurse-led telehealth on readmissions and health-related outcomes among patients with post-acute myocardial infarction: ALTRA Study Protocol. *Journal of Advanced Nursing*, *72*(6), 1357–1367. doi:10.1111/jan.12933 PMID:26915719

Kong, G., Xu, D.-L., & Yang, J.-B. (2008). Clinical decision support systems: A review on knowledge representation and inference under uncertainties. *International Journal of Computational Intelligence Systems*, *1*(2), 159–167.

Kreimeyer, K., Foster, M., Pandey, A., Arya, N., Halford, G., Jones, S. F., ... Botsis, T. (2017). Natural language processing systems for capturing and standardizing unstructured clinical information: A systematic review. *Journal of Biomedical Informatics*, *73*, 14–29. doi:10.1016/j.jbi.2017.07.012 PMID:28729030

Krizhevsky, A., Sutskever, I., & Hinton, G. E. (2012). Imagenet classification with deep convolutional neural networks. In Advances in Neural Information Processing Systems (pp. 1097-1105).

Kullback, S. (1997). *Information theory and statistics*. Dover Pubns.

Lafferty, J. D., McCallum, A., & Pereira, F. C. N. (2001). Conditional random fields: Probabilistic models for segmenting and labeling sequence data. *Proceedings of the Eighteenth International Conference on Machine Learning*.

Lamsweerde, A. V. (2008). *Requirements engineering: From system goals to UML models to software specifications*. Wiley.

Larochelle, H., & Bengio, Y. (2008, July). Classification using discriminative restricted Boltzmann machines. In *Proceedings of the 25th International Conference on Machine Learning* (pp. 536-543). ACM.

Lau, D. H. (2002). Patient empowerment: A Patient-centred approach to improve care. *Hong Kong Medical Journal, 8*(5), 372–374. PMID:12376717

Lebied, M. (2017). Business intelligence in healthcare: improving patient care and expenses. *Business Intelligence*, Retrieved from https://www.datapine.com/blog/business-intelligence-in-healthcare/

Lebied, M. (2018). 12 examples of big data analytics in healthcare that can save people. *Business Intelligence*. Retrieved from https://www.datapine.com/blog/big-data-examples-in-healthcare/

LeCun, Y., Bengio, Y., & Hinton, G. (2015). Deep learning. *nature, 521*(7553), 436.

Lee, B.-S., Martin, T. P., Clarke, N. P., Majeed, B., & Nauck, D. (2004). Dynamic daily-living patterns and association analyses in tele-care systems. In *Proceedings Fourth IEEE International Conference on Data Mining (ICDM'04)*. 10.1109/ICDM.2004.10023

Lee, C., Luo, Z., Ngiam, K. Y., Zhang, M., Zheng, K., Chen, G., ... Wei, L. J. Y. (2017). *Big healthcare data analytics: challenges and applications. Handbook of large-scale distributed computing in smart healthcare*. Scalable Computing and Communications. *Springer International Publishing*. doi:10.1007/978-3-319-58280-1_2

Lemaire, J. B., Schaefer, J. P., Martin, L. A., Faris, P., Ainslie, M. D., & Hull, R. D. (1999). Effectiveness of the quick medical reference as a diagnostic tool. *CMAJ, 161*(6), 725-728.

Lenhart, A., Purcell, K., Smith, A., & Zickuhr, K. (2010). Social media & mobile internet use among teens and young adults. Millennials. *Pew internet & American life project*.

Lenz, R., & Reichert, M. (2007). IT support for healthcare processes, premises, challenges, perspectives. *Data & Knowledge Engineering, 61*(1), 39–58. doi:10.1016/j.datak.2006.04.007

Leung, M. K., Delong, A., Alipanahi, B., & Frey, B. J. (2015). Machine learning in genomic medicine: A review of computational problems and data sets. *Proceedings of the IEEE, 104*(1), 176–197. doi:10.1109/JPROC.2015.2494198

Li, H., Zhang, Q., & Duan, P. (2008). *A novel one-pass neural network approach for activities recognition in intelligent environments.* Paper presented at the 2008 7th World Congress on Intelligent Control and Automation.

Li, W., Xu, Y., Tan, B., & Piechocki, R. J. (2017). Passive wireless sensing for unsupervised human activity recognition in healthcare. In *Proceedings 2017 13th International Wireless Communications and Mobile Computing Conference (IWCMC)*. 10.1109/IWCMC.2017.7986511

Liao, L., Patterson, D. J., Fox, D., & Kautz, H. (2007). Learning and inferring transportation routines. *Artificial Intelligence, 171*(5-6), 311–331. doi:10.1016/j.artint.2007.01.006

Liberati, E. G., Ruggiero, F., Galuppo, L., Gorli, M., González-Lorenzo, M., Maraldi, M., ... Vespignani, R. (2017). What hinders the uptake of computerized decision support systems in hospitals? A qualitative study and framework for implementation. *Implementation Science; IS*, *12*(1), 113. doi:10.118613012-017-0644-2 PMID:28915822

Limieux, V. (2017). Blockchain and distributed leaders as trusted record keeping systems: an archival theoretic evaluation framework. *Future Technology Conference*, Vancouver, Canada.

Li, R., Lu, B., & McDonald-Maier, K. D. (2015). Cognitive assisted living ambient system: A survey. *Digital Communications and Networks*, *1*(4), 229–252. doi:10.1016/j.dcan.2015.10.003

Lobo, P., & Guruprasad, S. (2018). Classification and segmentation techniques for detection of lung cancer from CT images. In *Proceedings 2018 International Conference on Inventive Research in Computing Applications (ICIRCA)*. 10.1109/ICIRCA.2018.8597273

Löhr, H., Sadeghi, A. R., & Winandy, M. (2010, November). Securing the e-health cloud. In *Proceedings of the 1st ACM International Health Informatics Symposium* (pp. 220-229). ACM.

LoPresti, E., Mihailidis, A., & Kirsch, N. (2004). Assistive technology for cognitive rehabilitation: State of the art. *Neuropsychological Rehabilitation*, *14*(1-2), 5–39. doi:10.1080/09602010343000101

Lu, J., Hales, A., Rew, D., & Keech, M. (2016). Timeline and episode-structured clinical data: Pre-processing for Data Mining and analytics. *IEEE 32nd International Conference on Data Engineering Workshops (ICDEW)*. doi:10.1109/ICDEW.2016.7495618

Ludwig, H., Dan, A., & Kearney, R. (2004). Crona: An architecture and library for creation and monitoring of ws-agreents. *Proceedings of the 2nd international conference on service oriented computing* (pp. 65-74). New York, NY: ACM Press. 10.1145/1035167.1035178

Lusch, R. F., & Nambisan, S. (2015). Service innovation: a service-dominant logic perspective. *Management Information Systems Quarterly*, *39*(1), 155–175. doi:10.25300/MISQ/2015/39.1.07

Lu, Y. (2017). Industry 4.0: A survey on technologies, applications and open research issues. *Journal of Industrial Information Integration*, *6*, 1–10. doi:10.1016/j.jii.2017.04.005

Lu, Y. (2019). Artificial intelligence: A survey on evolution, models, applications and future trends. *Journal of Management Analytics*, *6*(1), 1–29. doi:10.1080/23270012.2019.1570365

Mahmoud, S., Lotfi, A., & Langensiepen, C. (2013). Behavioural pattern identification and prediction in intelligent environments. *Applied Soft Computing*, *13*(4), 1813–1822. doi:10.1016/j.asoc.2012.12.012

Manafo, E., Petermann, L., Mason-Lai, P., & Vandall-Walker, V. (2018). Patient engagement in Canada: A scoping review of the 'how' and 'what' of patient engagement in health research. *Health Research Policy and Systems*, *16*(5).

Manjunath, T. N., Hegadi, R. S., & Ravikumar, G. K. (2010). Analysis of data quality aspects in datawarehouse systems. *International Journal of Computer Science and Information Technologies*, *2*(1), 477–485.

Marimuthu, R., Shivappriya, S. N., & Malarvizhi, K. (2019). Machine learning-based cognitive support system for healthcare. *Body Area Network Challenges and Solutions*. pp. 87-103. doi:10.1007/978-3-030-00865-9_5

Mariscal, G., Marban, O., & Fernandez, C. (2010). A survey of data mining and knowledge discovery process models and methodologies. *The Knowledge Engineering Review*, *25*(2), 137–166. doi:10.1017/S0269888910000032

Marr, B. (2016). Big data in healthcare: Paris hospitals predict admission rates using machine learning. *Forbes*. Retrieved from https://www.forbes.com/sites/bernardmarr/2016/12/13/big-data-in-healthcare-paris-hospitals-predict-admission-rates-using-machine-learning/#1215710e79a2

Marshall, M. (2000). *Astrid: A social and technological response to meeting the needs of individuals with dementia and their carers; a guide to using technology within dementia care.* London, UK: Hawker.

Marsland, S. (2014). Machine learning - an algorithmic perspective (2nd ed.), Chapman and Hall/CRC. Machine learning, and Pattern recognition series.

Martens, J., & Sutskever, I. (2011). Learning recurrent neural networks with hessian-free optimization. In *Proceedings of the 28th International Conference on Machine Learning (ICML-11)* (pp. 1033-1040).

Maurer, U., Smailagic, A., Siewiorek, D. P., & Deisher, M. (2006). Activity recognition and monitoring using multiple sensors on different body positions. *Proceedings - BSN 2006: International Workshop on Wearable and Implantable Body Sensor Networks*. 10.21236/ADA534437

McAllister, M., Dunn, G., Payne, K., Davies, L., & Todd, C. (2012). Patient empowerment. The need to consider it as a measurable patient-reported outcome for chronic conditions. *BMC Health Services Research*, *12*(1), 157. doi:10.1186/1472-6963-12-157 PMID:22694747

McColl, M., Carlson, P., Johnston, J., Minnes, P., Shue, K., Davies, D., & Karlovitz, T. (1998). The definition of community intergration: Perspectives of people with brain injuries. *Brain Injury: [BI]*, *12*(1), 15–30. doi:10.1080/026990598122827 PMID:9483334

McHugh, J., Wherton, J., Prendergast, D., & Lawlor, B. (2012). Identifying opportunities for supporting caregivers of persons with dementia through information and communication technology. *Gerontechnology (Valkenswaard)*, *10*(4), 220–230.

Medicare Hospital Readmissions Reduction Program. (2013, Nov. 12). Health Affairs. Retrieved from http://www.healthaffairs.org/healthpolicybriefs/brief.php?brief_id=102

Melville, N., Kraemer, K., & Gurubaxani, V. (2004). Information technology and organizational performance: an integrative model of IT business value. *Management Information Systems Quarterly*, *28*(2), 283–322. doi:10.2307/25148636

Meng, X.-Y., Zhang, H.-X., Mezei, M., & Cui, M. (2011). Molecular docking: A powerful approach for structure-based drug discovery. *Current Computer-aided Drug Design*, *7*(2), 146–157. doi:10.2174/157340911795677602 PMID:21534921

Merriam-Webster. (2019). Dictionary by Merriam-Webster. Retrieved from https://www.merriam-webster.com

Mesko, B. (2017). The role of artificial intelligence in precision medicine. *Expert Review of Precision Medicine and Drug Development*, *2*(5), 239–241. doi:10.1080/23808993.2017.1380516

Mettler, T., & Vimarlund, V. (2009). Understanding business intelligence in the context of healthcare. *Health Informatics Journal*, *15*(3), 254–264. doi:10.1177/1460458209337446 PMID:19713399

Miliard, M. (2017). How predictive analytics helped reduce readmission at UnityPoint Health. *HealthcareITNews*. Retrieved from https://www.healthcareitnews.com/news/how-predictive-analytics-helped-reduce-readmissions-unitypoint-health

Miller, R. A., Waitman, L. R., Chen, S., & Rosenbloom, S. T. (2005). The anatomy of decision support during inpatient care provider order entry (CPOE): Empirical observations from a decade of CPOE experience at Vanderbilt. *Journal of Biomedical Informatics*, *38*(6), 469–485. doi:10.1016/j.jbi.2005.08.009 PMID:16290243

Miller, R. H., & Sim, I. (2004). Physicians' use of electronic medical records: Barriers and solutions. *Health Affairs*, *23*(2), 116–126. doi:10.1377/hlthaff.23.2.116 PMID:15046136

Mining of sensor data in healthcare: A survey 91-125. (2015). CRC Press.

Mitchell, T. M. (2013) *Machine learning* (1st ed.), McGraw Hill Education.

Mitra, S., & Shankar, B. U. (2015). Medical image analysis for cancer management in natural computing framework. *Information Sciences*, *306*, 111–131. doi:10.1016/j.ins.2015.02.015

Mohamed, A. R., Dahl, G. E., & Hinton, G. (2012). Acoustic modeling using deep belief networks. *IEEE Transactions on Audio, Speech, and Language Processing*, *20*(1), 14–22. doi:10.1109/TASL.2011.2109382

Mohri, M., Rostamizadeh, A., & Talwalkar, A. (2012). *Foundations of machine learning*. Cambridge, MA: MIT Press.

Monekosso, D. N., & Remagnino, P. (2010). Behavior analysis for assisted living. *IEEE Transactions on Automation Science and Engineering*, *7*(4), 879–886. doi:10.1109/TASE.2010.2049840

Money, W. H., Kaisler, S. H., Armour, F., & Espinosa, J. A. (2017). Big data: The path to maturity. *International Journal of Systems and Service-Oriented Engineering*, *7*(2), 1–23. doi:10.4018/IJSSOE.2017040101

Monica, N., & Kumar, K. R. (2013). Survey on Big Data by coordinating mapreduce to integrate variety of data. *International Journal of Science and Research (IJSR) (Online)*, 2319-7064.

Moore, M., & Loper, K. A. (2011). An introduction to clinical decision support systems. *Journal of Electronic Resources in Medical Libraries*, *8*(4), 348–366. doi:10.1080/15424065.2011.626345

Moorfields Eye Hospital. (2016). *Moorfields Announces Research Partnership*. Retrieved from https://www.moorfields.nhs.uk/news/moorfields-announces-research-partnership

Morrisey, M. A., Alexander, J. A., & Ohsfeldt, R. L. (1990). Physician integration strategies and hospital output. *Medical Care*, *28*(7), 586–603. doi:10.1097/00005650-199007000-00005 PMID:2366600

Morton, M. E., & Wiedenbeck, S. (2009). A framework for predicting EHR adoption attitudes: a physician survey. Perspectives in health information management/AHIMA, American Health Information Management Association, 6(Fall).

Moss, L. T., & Atre, S. (2007). *Business Intelligence Roadmap*. Boston, MA: Pearson Education.

Mouton Dorey, C., Baumann, H., & Biller-Andorno, N. (2018). Patient data and patient rights: Swiss healthcare stakeholders' ethical awareness regarding large patient data sets – a qualitative study. *BMC Medical Ethics*, 19. PMID:29514635

Mueller, M., Heger, O., & Niehaves, B. (2018, Jan. 3). Investigating ethical design requirements for digitalized healthcare support: the case of ambulatory physiotherapeutic assistance systems. In *Proceedings of the Hawaii International Conference on System Sciences (HICSS)*, Waikoloa Village, HI. 10.24251/HICSS.2018.372

Nagy, P. G., Warnock, M. J., Daly, M., Toland, C., Meenan, C. D., & Mezrich, R. S. (2009). Informatics in radiology: Automated Web-based graphical dashboard for radiology operational business intelligence. *Radiographics*, *29*(7), 1897–1906. doi:10.1148/rg.297095701 PMID:19734469

Nair, V., & Hinton, G. E. (2010). Rectified linear units improve restricted Boltzmann machines. In *Proceedings of the 27th international conference on machine learning (ICML-10)* (pp. 807-814).

Nakashima, H., Aghajan, H., & Augusto, H. (2009). Handbook of ambient intelligence and smart environments. Handbook of Ambient Intelligence and Smart Environments. doi:10.1007/978-0-387-93808-0

Nambisan, P. (2014, January). EMR adoption among office-based physicians and practices: Impact of peer-to-peer interactions, peer support and online forums. In *Proceedings 2014 47th Hawaii International Conference on System Sciences (HICSS)*, (pp. 2733-2740). IEEE.

NAQC. (2018). *Adoption of best practices among state quitlines. North American Quitline Consortium*. Phoenix, AZ: Author.

National Institute of Diabetes and Digestive and Kidney Diseases database. Retrieved from https://www.kaggle.com/uciml/pima-indians-diabetes-database

Ngoepe, M., Choonara, Y., Tyagi, C., Tomar, L., Du Toit, L., Kumar, P., ... Pillay, V. (2013). Integration of biosensors and drug delivery technologies for early detection and chronic management of illness. *Sensors (Basel)*, *13*(6), 7680–7713. doi:10.3390130607680 PMID:23771157

Nguyen, H. Q., Donesky, D., Reinke, L. F., Wolpin, S., Chyall, L., Benditt, J. O., ... Carrieri-Kohlman, V. (2013). Internet-based dyspnea self-management support for patients with chronic obstructive pulmonary disease. *Journal of Pain and Symptom Management*, *46*(1), 43–55. doi:10.1016/j.jpainsymman.2012.06.015 PMID:23073395

Nie, L., Wang, M., Zhang, L., Yan, S., Zhang, B., & Chua, T.-S. (2015). Disease inference from health-related questions via sparse deep learning. *IEEE Transactions on Knowledge and Data Engineering*, *27*(8), 2107–2119. doi:10.1109/TKDE.2015.2399298

Norén, G. N., Hopstadius, J., Bate, A., Star, K., & Edwards, I. R. (2010). Temporal pattern discovery in longitudinal electronic patient records. *Data Mining and Knowledge Discovery*, *20*(3), 361–387. doi:10.100710618-009-0152-3

Normandeau, K. (2013). Beyond volume, variety and velocity is the issue of big data veracity. *Inside big data.* Retrieved from https://insidebigdata.com/2013/09/12/beyond-volume-variety-velocity-issue-big-data-veracity/

O'Riain, C., & Hlefert, M. (2005). Analysis healthcare information strategies in Europe. In *UKAIS 2005, 10th Annual Conference*, Newcastle, UK.

Odaibo, S. G. MomPremier, M., Hwang, R. Y., Yousuf, S., Williams, S., & Grant, J. (2019). Mobile artificial intelligence technology for detecting macula edema and subretinal fluid on OCT scans: Initial results from the DATUM alpha Study. *arXiv preprint arXiv:1902.02905.*

OECD Data. (2019). Health resources: Health spending. Retrieved from https://data.oecd.org/healthres/health-spending.htm

Okoro, C. A., Hollis, N. D., Cyrus, A. C., & Griffin-Blake, S. (2017). *Prevalence of disabilities and health care access by disability status and type among adults — United States, 2016.* In S. T. Peek, E. J. Wouters, J. Van Hoof, K. G. Luijkx, H. R. Boeije, & H. J. Vrijhoef. (2014). Factors influencing acceptance of technology for aging in place: A systematic review. *International Journal of Medical Informatics*, *83*(4), 235–248.

Olszak, C. M., & Ziemba, E. (2003). Business intelligence as a key to management of an enterprise. In Proceedings of Informing Science and IT Education, Santa Rosa, CA. doi:10.28945/2672

Olteanu, A., Castillo, C., Diaz, F., & Kiciman, E. (2019). Social data: Biases, methodological pitfalls, and ethical boundaries. *Frontiers in Big Data*, *2*, 13. doi:10.3389/fdata.2019.00013

Padfield, D. R., Mendonça, P. R., & Gupta, S. (2015). *Biomedical image analysis.*

Painter, M. W., & Jha, A. K. (2015). *Health information technology in the United States, 2015: Transition to a post-HITECH world (Executive summary) (No. 03f5b8d79339485f90149d875ac0b40b).* Mathematica Policy Research.

Parente, S. T. (2000). Beyond the hype: a taxonomy of e-health business models. *Health Affairs, 19*(6), 89–102. doi:10.1377/hlthaff.19.6.89 PMID:11192424

Parente, S. T., & Dunbar, J. L. (2001). Is health information technology investment related to the financial performance of US hospitals? an exploratory analysis. *International Journal of Healthcare Technology and Management, 3*(1), 48–58. doi:10.1504/IJHTM.2001.001104

Paul, M. J., & Dredze, M. (2011). *You are what you tweet: Analyzing twitter for public health.* Paper presented at the Fifth International AAAI Conference on Weblogs and Social Media.

Paul, M. J., & Dredze, M. (2014). Discovering health topics in social media using topic models. *PLoS One, 9*(8). doi:10.1371/journal.pone.0103408 PMID:25084530

Pearlson, K. E., & Saunders, C. S. (2013). *Managing & using information systems: a strategic approach.* Johnson Wiley & Sons.

Pellegrini, L. C., Rodriguez-Monguio, R., & Qian, J. (2014). The US healthcare workforce and the labor market effect on healthcare spending and health outcomes. *International Journal of Health Care Finance and Economics, 14*(2), 127–141. doi:10.100710754-014-9142-0 PMID:24652416

Permwonguswa, S., Khuntia, J., Yim, D., & Gregg, D. (2017). *Empowerment and knowledge sharing in health infomediary: empirical evidence from reconstructive surgery patients.* Paper presented at the Americas Conference on Information Systems 2017, Boston, MA.

Permwonguswa, S., Khuntia, J., Yim, D., Gregg, D., & Kathuria, A. (2018). Knowledge sharing in a health infomediary: role of self-concept, emotional empowerment, and self-esteem. *Health Systems (Basingstoke, England), 7*(3), 181–194. doi:10.1080/20476965.2017.1405875 PMID:31214347

Phillips, B., & Zhao, H. (1993). Predictors of assistive technology abandonment. *Assistive Technology, 5*(1), 36–45. doi:10.1080/10400435.1993.10132205 PMID:10171664

Piliouras, T. C., Suss, R. J., & Yu, P. L. (2015). Digital imaging & electronic health record systems: Implementation and regulatory challenges faced by healthcare providers. In *Proceedings 2015 Long Island Systems, Applications and Technology.* 10.1109/LISAT.2015.7160179

Pirpinia, K., Bosman, P. A., Loo, C. E., Winter-Warnars, G., Janssen, N. N., Scholten, A. N., ... Alderliesten, T. (2017). The feasibility of manual parameter tuning for deformable breast MR image registration from a multi-objective optimization perspective. *Physics in Medicine and Biology, 62*(14), 5723–5743. doi:10.1088/1361-6560/aa6edc PMID:28436922

Plaisant, C., Mushlin, R., Snyder, A., Li, J., Heller, D., & Shneiderman, B. (2003). LifeLines: using visualization to enhance navigation and analysis of patient records. In The craft of information visualization (pp. 308-312). doi:10.1016/B978-155860915-0/50038-X

Plaisant, C., Shneiderman, B., & Mushlin, R. (1998). An information architecture to support the visualization of personal histories. *Information Processing & Management, 34*(5), 581–597. doi:10.1016/S0306-4573(98)00024-7

Plum, A., Tanniru, M, & Khuntia, J. (2019, January) *An innovation platform for diffusing public health practices across a global network, HICSS-2019,* Hawaii. APA Dictionary of Psychology, 2015.

Pluye, P., Grad, R. M., Dawes, M., & Bartlett, J. C. (2007). Seven reasons why health professionals search clinical information-retrieval technology (CIRT): Toward an organizational model. *Journal of Evaluation in Clinical Practice, 13*(1), 39–49. doi:10.1111/j.1365-2753.2006.00646.x PMID:17286722

Porter, M. E. (2012). Redefining German health care: Moving to a value-based system. Heidelberg, Germany: Springer. doi:10.1007/978-3-642-10826-6

Posnack, S. (2015). Connecting health and care for the nation: a shared nationwide interoperability roadmap.

Prabhu, R., & Khan, A. (2017). *A study of bio-medical image registration algorithms.*

Priyanka, K., & Kulennavar, N. (2014). A survey on big data analytics in health care. *International Journal of Computer Science and Information Technologies*, *5*(4), 5865–5868.

Pugh, D. S. (1990). *Organization theory: selected readings*. Harmondsworth, UK: Penguin.

Quan, H., Li, B., Duncan Saunders, L., Parsons, G. A., Nilsson, C. I., Alibhai, A., & Ghali, W. A. (2008). Assessing validity of ICD-9-CM and ICD-10 administrative data in recording clinical conditions in a unique dually coded database. *Health Services Research*, *43*(4), 1424–1441. doi:10.1111/j.1475-6773.2007.00822.x PMID:18756617

Quan, H., Parsons, G. A., & Ghali, W. A. (2002). Validity of information on comorbidity derived from ICD-9-CCM administrative data. *Medical Care*, *40*(8), 675–685. doi:10.1097/00005650-200208000-00007 PMID:12187181

Quan, H., Sundararajan, V., Halfon, P., Fong, A., Burnand, B., Luthi, J. C., ... Ghali, W. A. (2005). Coding algorithms for defining comorbidities in ICD-9-CM and ICD-10 administrative data. *Medical Care*, *43*(11), 1130–1139. doi:10.1097/01.mlr.0000182534.19832.83 PMID:16224307

Raghupathi, W., & Raghupathi, V. (2014). Big data analytics in healthcare: promise and potential. *Health information science and systems, 2*(1), 3.

Raghupathi, W., & Raghupathi, V. (2018). An empirical study of chronic diseases in the United States: A visual analytics approach to public health. *International Journal of Environmental Research and Public Health*, *15*(3), 431. doi:10.3390/ijerph15030431 PMID:29494555

Raja, U., Mitchell, T., Day, T., & Hardin, J. M. (2008). Text mining in healthcare. Applications and opportunities. *Journal of Healthcare Information Management*, *22*(3), 52–56. PMID:19267032

Ramakrishnan, T., Jones, M. C., & Sidorova, A. (2012). Factors influencing business intelligence (BI) data collection strategies: an empirical investigation. *Decision Support Systems*, (52): 729–739.

Ramakrishnan, T., Khuntia, J., Kathuria, A., & Saldanha, J. V. (2018). Business intelligence capabilities. In A. Deokar, A. Gupta, L. Iyer, & M. Jones (Eds.), *Analytics and data science. Annals of information systems*. Cham, Switzerland: Springer. doi:10.1007/978-3-319-58097-5_3

Ramakrishnan, T., Khuntia, J., Kathuria, A., & Saldanha, T. (2016). Business intelligence capabilities and effectiveness: an integrative model. In *Proceedings of the 49th Hawaii International Conference on System Sciences*, Kuai, HI. 10.1109/HICSS.2016.623

Randeree, E. (2007). Exploring physician adoption of EMRs: A multi-case analysis. *Journal of Medical Systems*, *31*(6), 489–496. doi:10.100710916-007-9089-5 PMID:18041282

Rashidi, P., & Cook, D. J. (2010). Mining sensor streams for discovering human activity patterns over time. *Proceedings - IEEE International Conference on Data Mining, ICDM*. 10.1109/ICDM.2010.40

Real-time pervasive monitoring for postoperative care, 122-127 (2007).

Rebuge, A., & Ferreira, D. (2012). Business process analysis in healthcare environments: a methodology based on process mining. *Information Systems*, *37*(2), 99–116. doi:10.1016/j.is.2011.01.003

Reddy, C. K., & Aggarwal, C. C. (2015). *Healthcare data analytics", Chapman &Hall/CRC, Data Mining and Knowledge Discovery Series*. Boca Raton, FL: CRC Press.

ReferenceQ. M. (QMR). Retrieved from http://www.openclinical.org/aisp qmr.html

Resnik, P., Niv, M., Nossal, M., Schnitzer, G., Stoner, J., Kapit, A., & Toren, R. (2006). Using intrinsic and extrinsic metrics to evaluate accuracy and facilitation in computer-assisted coding. In *Proceedings Perspectives in Health Information Management Computer Assisted Coding Conference*.

Riegler, G., Urschler, M., Ruther, M., Bischof, H., & Stern, D. (2015). Anatomical landmark detection in medical applications driven by synthetic data. In *Proceedings of the IEEE International Conference on Computer Vision Workshops*. 10.1109/ICCVW.2015.21

Robinson, W. N., & Fickas, S. (2009). Talking designs: A case of feedback for design evolution in assistive technology. In K. Lyytinen, P. Loucopoulos, J. Mylopoulos, & W. Robinson (Eds.), Design requirements engineering: A ten-year perspective (pp. 215-237): Springer-Verlag.

Robinson, W. N., Akhlaghi, A., & Syed, A. (2011, January). *A framework for mining behaviors in clinical data streams*. Paper presented at the IEEE Draft, HI.

Robinson, W. N. (2002, Jan. 7-10). Monitoring software requirements using instrumented code. In *IEEE Proceedings of The 35th Annual Hawaii International Conference on Systems Sciences*, Hawaii.

Robinson, W. N. (2006). A requirements monitoring framework for enterprise systems. *Requirements Engineering Journal*, *11*(1), 17–41. doi:10.100700766-005-0016-3

Robinson, W. N., & Akhlaghi, A. (2010, Jan. 5-8). Monitoring behavioral transitions in cognitive rehabilitation with multi-model, multi-window stream mining. In *Proceedings Hawaii International Conference on Software Systems*, Kauai, HI. 10.1109/HICSS.2010.279

Robinson, W. N., & Akhlaghi, A. (2017). Sequential fraud detection for prepaid cards using hidden Markov model divergence. *Expert Systems with Applications.*

Robinson, W. N., Akhlaghi, A., Deng, T., & Syed, A. R. (2012a). Discovery and diagnosis of behavioral transitions in patient event streams. *ACM Transactions on Management Information Systems*, *3*(1), 1–28. doi:10.1145/2151163.2151167

Robinson, W. N., & Aria, A. (2019). Fraud detection using hidden Markov model divergence. *IEEE Security and Privacy.*

Robinson, W. N., Syed, A. R., Akhlaghi, A., & Deng, T. (2012b, Jan. 4 - 12). Pattern discovery of user interface sequencing by rehabilitation clients with cognitive impairments. In *Proceedings Hawaii International Conference on Software Systems*, Hawaii. 10.1109/HICSS.2012.467

Rockmann, R., Weeger, A., & Gewald, H. (2014). Identifying organizational capabilities for the enterprise-wide usage of cloud computing. In *Proceedings of the Pacific Asia Conference on Information Systems.*

Rumbold, J. M. M., & Pierscionek, B. K. (2017). A critique of the regulation of data science in healthcare research in the European Union. *BMC Medical Ethics*, *18*(1), 27. doi:10.118612910-017-0184-y PMID:28388916

Ruotsalainen, M., Ala-Kleemola, T., & Visa, A. (2007). Gais: A method for detecting interleaved sequential patterns from imperfect data. *Proceedings of the 2007 IEEE Symposium on Computational Intelligence and Data Mining, CIDM 2007.* 10.1109/CIDM.2007.368920

Russakoff, D. B., Tomasi, C., Rohlfing, T., & Maurer, C. R. (2004). Image similarity using mutual information of regions. In *Proceedings European Conference on Computer Vision.* 10.1007/978-3-540-24672-5_47

Sabherwal, R., & Kris, P. (1994). The alignment between organizational critical success factors and information technology capability in academic institutions. *Decision Sciences*, *25*(2), 301–330. doi:10.1111/j.1540-5915.1994.tb01844.x

Safdar, S., Zafar, S., Zafar, N., & Khan, N. F. (2018). Machine learning based decision support systems (DSS) for heart disease diagnosis: A review. *Artificial Intelligence Review*, *50*(4), 597–623. doi:10.100710462-017-9552-8

Sahraeian, S. M. E., & Yoon, B.-J. (2011). A novel low-complexity hmm similarity measure. *IEEE Signal Processing Letters*, *18*(2), 87–90. doi:10.1109/LSP.2010.2096417

Saif, K. F., Nawaz, A., Jan, A., & Khan, M. I. (2012). Synthesizing the theories of job-satisfaction across the cultural/attitudinal dimensions. *Interdisciplinary Journal of Contemporary Research in Business*, 1382–1396.

Sainath, T. N., Kingsbury, B., & Ramabhadran, B. (2012, March). Auto-encoder bottleneck features using deep belief networks. In *Proceedings 2012 IEEE International Conference on Acoustics, Speech, and Signal Processing (ICASSP),* (pp. 4153-4156). IEEE. 10.1109/ICASSP.2012.6288833

Sak, H., Senior, A., & Beaufays, F. (2014). *Long short-term memory recurrent neural network architectures for large scale acoustic modeling.* Paper presented at the Fifteenth Annual Conference of the International Speech Communication Association.

Salakhutdinov, R., & Larochelle, H. (2010, March). Efficient learning of deep Boltzmann machines. In *Proceedings of the Thirteenth International Conference on Artificial Intelligence and Statistics* (pp. 693-700).

Sambamurthy, V., & Zmud, R. (1997). At the heart of success: organizational wide management competencies. In C. Sauer, P. Yetton, & L. Alexander (Eds.), *Steps to the future: fresh thinking on the management of IT-based organizational information* (pp. 143–163). San Francisco, CA: Jossey-Bass.

Samoocha, D., Bruinvels, D. J., Elbers, N. A., Anema, J. R., & van der Beek, A. J. (2010). Effectiveness of web-based interventions on patient empowerment: a systematic review and meta-analysis. *Journal of Medical Internet Research, 12*(2). doi:10.2196/jmir.1286 PMID:20581001

Sanders, D., Burton, D. A., & Protti, D. (2013). The healthcare analytics adoption model: a framework and roadmap.

Savova, G. K., Masanz, J. J., Ogren, P. V., Zheng, J., Sohn, S., Kipper-Schuler, K. C., & Chute, C. G. (2010). Mayo clinical text analysis and knowledge extraction system (cTAKES): Architecture, component evaluation and applications. *Journal of the American Medical Informatics Association, 17*(5), 507–513. doi:10.1136/jamia.2009.001560 PMID:20819853

Schaefferling, A. (2013). Determinants and consequences of IT capability: review and synthesis of the literature. In *Proceedings of the 19th American Conference on Information Systems,* Chicago, IL.

Schindelin, J., Rueden, C. T., Hiner, M. C., & Eliceiri, K. W. (2015). The ImageJ ecosystem: An open platform for biomedical image analysis. *Molecular Reproduction and Development, 82*(7-8), 518–529. doi:10.1002/mrd.22489 PMID:26153368

Schobel, J., Pryss, R., Schickler, M., & Reichert, M. (2016). Towards flexible mobile data collection in healthcare. *IEEE 29th International Symposium on Computer-Based Medical Systems (CBMS),* doi:10.1109/CBMS.2016.43

Schulman-Green, D., Jaser, S., Martin, F., Alonzo, A., Grey, M., McCorkle, R., ... Whittemore, R. (2012). Processes of self-management in chronic illness. *Journal of Nursing Scholarship, 44*(2), 136–144. doi:10.1111/j.1547-5069.2012.01444.x PMID:22551013

Schwartz, H. A., Eichstaedt, J. C., Kern, M. L., Dziurzynski, L., Lucas, R. E., Agrawal, M., . . . Seligman, M. E. (2013). *Characterizing geographic variation in well-being using tweets.* Paper presented at the Seventh International AAAI Conference on Weblogs and Social Media.

Schwartz, K. L., Roe, T., Northrup, J., Meza, J., Seifeldin, R., & Neale, A. V. (2006). Family medicine patients' use of the internet for health information: a metronet study. *Journal of the American Board of Family Medicine*, *19*(1), 39–45. doi:10.3122/jabfm.19.1.39 PMID:16492004

Senthilkumaran, N., & Vaithegi, S. (2016). Image segmentation by using thresholding techniques for medical images. *Computer Science & Engineering: An International Journal*, *6*(1), 1–13.

Services, U. S. D. O. H. A. H. (2002). *Add fact sheet*. Retrieved from http://www.acf.dhhs.gov/programs/add/Factsheet.htm

Sharma, G., & Kumar, K. (2017). Acceleration of images via software and hardware using proprietary tools & open sources for healthcare industry. *International Journal of Image, Graphics, and Signal Processing*, *9*(7), 10–22. doi:10.5815/ijigsp.2017.07.02

Sharma, S. K., Xu, H., Wickramasinghe, N., & Ahmed, N. (2006). Electronic healthcare: issues and challenges. *International Journal of Electronic Healthcare*, *2*(1), 50–65. doi:10.1504/IJEH.2006.008693 PMID:18048234

Shen, D., Wu, G., & Suk, H.-I. (2017). Deep learning in medical image analysis. *Annual Review of Biomedical Engineering*, *19*(1), 221–248. doi:10.1146/annurev-bioeng-071516-044442 PMID:28301734

Sherman, E. (2019). *U.S. health care costs skyrocketed to $3.65 trillion in 2018*. Retrieved from https://fortune.com/2019/02/21/us-health-care-costs-2/

Shi, J., Jiang, Q., Zhang, Q., Huang, Q., & Li, X. (2015). Sparse kernel entropy component analysis for dimensionality reduction of biomedical data. *Neurocomputing*, *168*, 930–940. doi:10.1016/j.neucom.2015.05.032

Shiver, J., & Cantiello. (2016). *Managing integrated health systems*. Jones & Bartlett, Burlington, MA.

Shneiderman, B., Plaisant, C., & Hesse, B. W. (2013). Improving healthcare with interactive visualization. *Computer*, *46*(5), 58–66. doi:10.1109/MC.2013.38

Sidorova, A., Gupta, B., & Dinter, B. (2018). Introduction: research and research-in-progress. In A. Deokar, A. Gupta, L. Iyer, & M. Jones (Eds.), *Analytics and data science. annals of information systems*. Cham, Switzerland: Springer. doi:10.1007/978-3-319-58097-5_2

Siegel, C., & Dorner, T. E. (2017). Information technologies for active and assisted living—Influences to the quality of life of an ageing society. *International Journal of Medical Informatics*, *100*, 32–45. doi:10.1016/j.ijmedinf.2017.01.012 PMID:28241936

Signorini, A., Segre, A. M., & Polgreen, P. M. (2011). The use of Twitter to track levels of disease activity and public concern in the US during the influenza A H1N1 pandemic. *PLoS One*, *6*(5). doi:10.1371/journal.pone.0019467 PMID:21573238

Silbajoris, C., McDuffee, D., & Olney, C. (2007). Creating the first MedlinePlus "Go Local" service: Lessons and recommendations from the evaluation of NC Health Info. *Medical Reference Services Quarterly*, *26*(2), 75–86. doi:10.1300/J115v26n02_07 PMID:17522010

Silberschatz, A., & Tuzhilin, A. (1996). What makes patterns interesting in knowledge discovery systems. *IEEE Transactions on Knowledge and Data Engineering*, *8*(6), 970–974. doi:10.1109/69.553165

Simon, H. A. (1947). *Administrative behavior*. New York, NY: Macmillan.

Simultaneous tracking and activity recognition (star) using many anonymous, binary sensors. 62-79. (2010).

Sixsmith, A. J., Gibson, G., Orpwood, R. D., & Torrington, J. M. (2007). Developing a technology 'wish-list' to enhance the quality of life of people with dementia. *Gerontechnology (Valkenswaard)*, *6*(1), 2–19. doi:10.4017/gt.2007.06.01.002.00

Skinner, R. I. (2003). The value of information technology in healthcare/reply. *Frontiers of Health Services Management*, *19*(3), 3–15. doi:10.1097/01974520-200301000-00002 PMID:12645778

Smith, J. W., Everhart, J. E., Dickson, W. C., Knowler, W. C., & Johannes, R. S. (1988). Using the ADAP learning algorithm to forecast the onset of diabetes mellitus. In *Proceedings of the Symposium on Computer Applications and Medical Care.* (pp. 261-265). IEEE Computer Society Press.

Snijders, C., Matzat, U., & Reips, U.-D. (2012). Big data: Big gaps of knowledge in the field of internet science. *International Journal of Internet Science*, *7*(1), 1–5.

Sohlberg, M. K. M., Turkstra, L. S., & Wilson, B. A. (2011). *Optimizing cognitive rehabilitation: Effective instructional methods*. The Guilford Press.

Sohlberg, M. M., Ehlhardt, L., Fickas, S., & Todis, B. (2002). Core: comprehensive overview of requisite e-mail skills. In M. M. Sohlberg, S. Fickas, L. Ehlhardt, & B. Todis, (Eds.), *The longitudinal effects of accessible email for individuals with severe cognitive impairments. Aphasiology*, *19*(7), 651–681.

Soley, M. (2013). *Dealing with missing data: Key assumptions and methods for applied analysis, Bori, Report*. Boston University School of Public Health, Department of Health Policy and Management.

Soumerai, D., & Koppel, R. (2012, Sept. 18). A major glitch for digital health records. *The Wall Street Journal*, A17.

Sow, D., Turaga, D. S., & Schmidt, M. (2013). Mining of sensor data in healthcare: A survey. In *Managing and mining sensor data* (pp. 459–504). Springer. doi:10.1007/978-1-4614-6309-2_14

Sox, H., McNeil, B., Wheatley, B., & Eden, J. (Eds.). (2008). *Knowing what works in healthcare: a roadmap for the nation*. National Academies Press.

Spruit, M., Vroon, R., & Batenburg, R. (2014). Towards healthcare business intelligence in long-term care: an explorative case study in the Netherlands. *Computers in Human Behavior, 30*, 698–707. doi:10.1016/j.chb.2013.07.038

Srivastava, N., & Salakhutdinov, R. R. (2012). Multimodal learning with deep Boltzmann machines. In Advances in Neural Information Processing Systems (pp. 2222-2230).

Staheli, R. (2014) How to avoid the 3 most common healthcare analytics pitfalls and related inefficiencies. Retrieved from https://www.healthcatalyst.com/avoid-common-healthcare-analytics-pitfalls-related-inefficiences

Staheli, R. (2016). *4 ways healthcare data analysts can provide their full value.* Retrieved from https://www.healthcatalyst.com/insights/healthcare-analytics-best-practices

Stieglitz, S., & Dang-Xuan, L. (2013). Social media and political communication: A social media analytics framework. *Social Network Analysis and Mining, 3*(4), 1277–1291. doi:10.100713278-012-0079-3

Stikic, M., Huỳnh, T., Laerhoven, K. V., & Schiele, B. (2008). Adl recognition based on the combination of RFID and aeeelerometer sensing. *Proceedings of the 2nd International Conference on Pervasive Computing Technologies for Healthcare 2008, PervasiveHealth.* 10.1109/PCTHEALTH.2008.4571084

Stroetmann, B., & Aisenbrey, A. (2012). Medical knowledge management in healthcare industry. *International Journal of Social, Behavioral, Educational, Economic, Business and Industrial Engineering, 6*(4), 531–536.

Subramanian, H. (2018, January). Decentralized blockchain-based electronic market places. *Communications of the ACM, 61*(1), 78–84. doi:10.1145/3158333

Su, J. G., Barrett, M. A., Henderson, K., Humblet, O., Smith, T., Sublett, J. W., ... Sublett, J. L. (2016). Feasibility of deploying inhaler sensors to identify the impacts of environmental triggers and built environment factors on asthma short-acting bronchodilator use. *Environmental Health Perspectives, 125*(2), 254–261. doi:10.1289/EHP266 PMID:27340894

Sung, W.-T., & Tsai, M.-H. (2012). Data fusion of multi-sensor for IOT precise measurement based on improved PSO algorithms. *Computers & Mathematics with Applications (Oxford, England), 64*(5), 1450–146. doi:10.1016/j.camwa.2012.03.092

Sutcliffe, A., Fickas, S., & Sohlberg, M. K. M. (2006). Pc-re: A method for personal and contextual requirements engineering with some experience. *Requirements Engineering, 11*(3), 157–173. doi:10.100700766-006-0030-0

Sutskever, I., Martens, J., & Hinton, G. E. (2011). Generating text with recurrent neural networks. In *Proceedings of the 28th International Conference on Machine Learning (ICML-11)* (pp. 1017-1024).

Tanniru, M. (2019) Engagement leading to empowerment—digital innovation strategies for patient care continuity, Forthcoming in *Journal of Hospital Management and Health Policy*

Tanniru, M., Khuntia, J., & Weiner, J. (2018). Hospital leadership in support of digital transformation, *Pacific Asia Journal of Association of Information Systems, (PAJAIS), 10*(3), Article 1.

Tanniru, M., Jones, J., Kazziha, S., & Hornberger, M. (2019). Strategies to address care transition - a methodology and a case study. *Journal of Hospital Administration, 8*(3). doi:10.5430/jha.v8n3p38

Terry, A. L., Giles, G., Brown, J. B., Thind, A., & Stewart, M. (2009). Adoption of electronic medical records in family practice: The providers' perspective. *Family Medicine, 41*(7), 508. PMID:19582637

Thamir, A., & Poulis, E. (2015). Business intelligence capabilities and implementation strategies. *International Journal of Global Business, 8*(1), 34–45.

Todis, B., Sohlberg, M. M., Hood, D., & Fickas, S. (2005). Making electronic mail accessible: Perspectives of people with acquired cognitive impairments, caregivers and professionals. *Brain Injury: [BI], 19*(6), 389–401. doi:10.1080/02699050400003957 PMID:16101262

Tong, L., Song, Q., Ge, Y., & Liu, M. (2013). Hmm-based human fall detection and prediction method using tri-axial accelerometer. *IEEE Sensors Journal, 13*(5), 1849–1856. doi:10.1109/JSEN.2013.2245231

Torres, R., Sidorova, A., & Jones, M. C. (2018). Enabling firm performance through business intelligence and analytics: a dynamic capabilities perspective. *Information & Management, 55*(7), 822–839. doi:10.1016/j.im.2018.03.010

Trivedi, M. (2009). A study of search engines for health sciences. *International Journal of Library and Information Science, 62*(68), 062-073.

Trybou, J., Gemmel, P., & Annemans, L. (2011). The ties that bind: An integrative framework of physician-hospital. *BMC Health Services Research, 11*(1), 36. doi:10.1186/1472-6963-11-36 PMID:21324128

Tseng, C.-C., & Cook, D. (2006). Mining from time series human movement data. In *Proceedings 2006 IEEE International Conference on Systems, Man and Cybernetics*. 10.1109/ICSMC.2006.384617

Vail, D. L., Veloso, M. M., & Lafferty, J. D. (2008). *Conditional random fields for activity recognition. Association for Computing Machinery.*

van de Klundert, J., Gorissen, P., & Zeemering, S. (2010). Measuring clinical pathway adherence. *Journal of Biomedical Informatics, 43*(6), 861–872. doi:10.1016/j.jbi.2010.08.002 PMID:20696277

Van den Broeck, J., Cunningham, S. A., Eeckels, R., & Herbst, K. (2005). Data cleaning: Detecting, diagnosing, and editing data abnormalities. *PLoS Medicine, 2*(10), e267. doi:10.1371/journal.pmed.0020267 PMID:16138788

Van Kasteren, T. L. M., Englebienne, G., & Kröse, B. J. A. (2010). An activity monitoring system for elderly care using generative and discriminative models. *Personal and Ubiquitous Computing, 14*(6), 489–498. doi:10.100700779-009-0277-9

van Kasteren, T., & Krose, B. (2008). *Bayesian activity recognition in residence for elders. Institution of Engineering and Technology.*

van Lamsweerde, A. (2003). From system goals to software architecture. *Formal Methods for Software Architectures*, 25–43.

van Lamsweerde, A. (2004). Elaborating security requirements by construction of intentional anti-models. In *Proceedings 26th International Conference on Software Engineering, 2004. ICSE 2004.* 148-157.

van Lamsweerde, A., Darimont, R., & Massonet, P. (1995, March 27-29). Goal-directed elaboration of requirements for a meeting scheduler: Problems and lessons learnt. In *Proceedings IEEE Second International Symposium on Requirements Engineering*. 10.1109/ISRE.1995.512561

Vanhaecht, K., Witte, K. D., Depreitere, R., & Sermeus, W. (2006). Clinical pathway audit tools: A systematic review. *Journal of Nursing Management, 14*(7), 529–537. doi:10.1111/j.1365-2934.2006.00705.x PMID:17004963

Varatharajan, R., Manogaran, G., Priyan, M. K., & Sundarasekar, R. (2018). Wearable sensor devices for early detection of Alzheimer disease using dynamic time warping algorithm. *Cluster Computing, 21*(1), 681–690. doi:10.100710586-017-0977-2

Vargo, S. L., & Lusch, R. F. (2008). Service-dominant logic: continuing the evolution. *Journal of the Academy of Marketing Science, 36*(1), 1–10. doi:10.100711747-007-0069-6

Varshney, U. (2007). Pervasive healthcare and wireless health monitoring. *Mobile Networks and Applications, 12*(2-3), 113–127. doi:10.100711036-007-0017-1

Venkatesh, V., Zhang, X., & Sykes, T. A. (2011). "Doctors do too little technology": A longitudinal field study of an electronic healthcare system implementation. *Information Systems Research, 22*(3), 523–546. doi:10.1287/isre.1110.0383

Vidaurre, D., Quinn, A. J., Baker, A. P., Dupret, D., Tejero-Cantero, A., & Woolrich, M. W. (2016). Spectrally resolved fast transient brain states in electrophysiological data. *NeuroImage, 126*, 81–95. doi:10.1016/j.neuroimage.2015.11.047 PMID:26631815

Vincent, P., Larochelle, H., Bengio, Y., & Manzagol, P. A. (2008, July). Extracting and composing robust features with denoising autoencoders. In *Proceedings of the 25th International Conference on Machine Learning* (pp. 1096-1103). ACM. 10.1145/1390156.1390294

Vishwanath, A., & Scamurra, S. D. (2007). Barriers to the adoption of electronic health records: Using concept mapping to develop a comprehensive empirical model. *Health Informatics Journal, 13*(2), 119–134. doi:10.1177/1460458207076468 PMID:17510224

Wade, D. (2007). Ethics of collecting and using healthcare data. *BMJ (Clinical Research Ed.)*, *334*(7608), 1330–1331. doi:10.1136/bmj.39247.679329.80 PMID:17599978

Wadsworth, J. (2017). *The best organizational structure for healthcare analytics*. Retrieved from https://www.healthcatalyst.com/best-organizational-structure-healthcare-analytics

Walter, Z., & Lopez, M. S. (2008). Physician acceptance of information technologies: Role of perceived threat to professional autonomy. *Decision Support Systems*, *46*(1), 206–215. doi:10.1016/j.dss.2008.06.004

Wang, J., Han, J., & Pei, J. (2003). Closet+: Searching for the best strategies for mining frequent closed itemsets¤. *Proceedings of the ninth ACM SIGKDD international conference on Knowledge discovery and data mining - KDD '03*, 236. doi:10.1145/956750.956779

Wang, Y., Kung, L., & Byrd, T. A. (2018). Big data analytics: Understanding its capabilities and potential benefits for healthcare organizations. *Technological Forecasting and Social Change*, *126*, 3–13. doi:10.1016/j.techfore.2015.12.019

Wang, Y., Wang, L., Rastegar-Mojarad, M., Moon, S., Shen, F., Afzal, N., ... Sohn, S. (2018). Clinical information extraction applications: A literature review. *Journal of Biomedical Informatics*, *77*, 34 49. doi:10.1016/j.jbi.2017.11.011 PMID:29162496

Wang, Y., Yu, Y., & Mylopoulos, J. (2007). An automated approach for monitoring and diagnosing requirements. In *Proceedings the 22nd IEEE/ACM International Conference on Automated Software Engineering*, Atlanta, GA. 10.1145/1321631.1321675

Warmerdam, L., van Straten, A., Twisk, J., Riper, H., & Cuijpers, P. (2008). Internet-based treatment for adults with depressive symptoms: randomized controlled trial. *Journal of Medical Internet Research*, *10*(4), e44. doi:10.2196/jmir.1094 PMID:19033149

Weber, V., Bloom, F., Pierdon, S., & Wood, C. (2008). Employing the electronic health record to improve diabetes care: a multifacted intervention in an integrated delivery system. *Journal of General Internal Medicine*, *23*(4), 379–382. doi:10.100711606-007-0439-2 PMID:18373133

Weiner, J., Tanniru, M., Khuntia, J., Bobryk, D., Naik, M., & Page, K. L. (2016). Digital leadership in action in a hospital through a real time dashboard system implementation and experience. *Journal of Hospital Administration*, (May), 2016.

White, M. (2012). Digital workplaces: Vision and reality. *Business Information Review*, *29*(4), 205–214. doi:10.1177/0266382112470412

Wilson, B. A., Emslie, H. C., Quirk, K., & Evans, J. J. (2001a). Reducing everyday memory and planning problems by means of a paging system: A randomised control crossover study. *Journal of Neurology, Neurosurgery, and Psychiatry*, *70*(4), 477–482. doi:10.1136/jnnp.70.4.477 PMID:11254770

Wright, P., Rogers, N., Hall, C., Wilson, B., Evans, J., Emslie, H., & Bartram, C. (2001). Comparison of pocket-computer memory aids for people with brain injury. *Brain Injury: [BI]*, *15*(9), 787–800. doi:10.1080/02699050110045161 PMID:11516347

Wu, J. H., Wang, S. C., & Lin, L. M. (2007). Mobile computing acceptance factors in the healthcare industry: A structural equation model. *International Journal of Medical Informatics*, *76*(1), 66–77. doi:10.1016/j.ijmedinf.2006.06.006 PMID:16901749

Wu, L., Li, J. Y., & Fu, C. Y. (2011). The adoption of mobile healthcare by hospital's professionals: An integrative perspective. *Decision Support Systems*, *51*(3), 587–596. doi:10.1016/j.dss.2011.03.003

Wu, X., Kumar, V., Ross Quinlan, J., Ghosh, J., Yang, Q., Motoda, H., ... Yu, P. (2008). Top 10 algorithms in data mining. *Knowledge and Information Systems*, *14*(1), 1–37. doi:10.100710115-007-0114-2

Xu, H., Crossler, R. E., & Belanger, F. (2012). A value sensitive design investigation of privacy enhancing tools in web browsers. *Decision Support Systems*, *54*(1), 424–433. doi:10.1016/j.dss.2012.06.003

Yang, H., Guo, X., & Wu, T. (2015). Exploring the influence of the online physician service delivery process on patient satisfaction. [Retrieved from edselp.]. *Decision Support Systems*, *78*, 113–121. doi:10.1016/j.dss.2015.05.006

Yang, J.-J., Li, J., Mulder, J., Wang, Y., Chen, S., Wu, H., ... Pan, H. (2015). Emerging information technologies for enhanced healthcare. *Computers in Industry*, *69*, 3–11. doi:10.1016/j.compind.2015.01.012

Yan, Y., Fung, G., Dy, J. G., & Rosales, R. (2010, July). Medical coding classification by leveraging inter-code relationships. In *Proceedings of the 16th ACM SIGKDD international conference on Knowledge discovery and data mining* (pp. 193-202). ACM. 10.1145/1835804.1835831

Yao, W., & Kumar, A. (2013). Conflexflow: Integrating flexible clinical pathways into clinical decision support systems using context and rules. *Decision Support Systems*, *55*(2), 499–515. doi:10.1016/j.dss.2012.10.008

Yetim, F. (2011). Bringing discourse ethics to value sensitive design: pathways toward a deliberative future. *AIS Transactions on Human-Computer Interaction*, *3*(2), 133–155. doi:10.17705/1thci.00030

Yim, D., Khuntia, J., & Argyris, Y. (2015). Identifying bands in the knowledge exchange spectrum in an online health infomediary. [IJHISI]. *International Journal of Healthcare Information Systems and Informatics*, *10*(3), 63–84. doi:10.4018/IJHISI.2015070104

Yin, J., Yang, Q., & Pan, J. J. (2008). Sensor-based abnormal human-activity detection. *IEEE Transactions on Knowledge and Data Engineering*.

Yong, X., Ward, R. K., & Birch, G. E. (2008). *Robust common spatial patterns for EEG signal preprocessing*. Paper presented at the 2008 30th Annual International Conference of the IEEE Engineering in Medicine and Biology Society.

Yoo, S., Cho, M., Kim, S., Kim, E., Park, S. M., Kim, K., ... Song, M. (2015). Conformance analysis of clinical pathway using electronic health record data. *Healthcare Informatics Research*, *21*(3), 161–166. doi:10.4258/hir.2015.21.3.161 PMID:26279952

Young, M., Magassa, L., & Friedman, B. (2019). Toward inclusive tech policy design: A method for underrepresented voices to strengthen tech policy documents. *Ethics and Information Technology*, *21*(2), 89–103. doi:10.100710676-019-09497-z

Zahedi, F. M., & Song, J. (2008). Dynamics of trust revision: using health infomediaries. *Journal of Management Information Systems*, *24*(4), 225–248. doi:10.2753/MIS0742-1222240409

Zhang, J., Cheng, B., & Goldsby, H. (2007, Sept. 30 – Oct. 5). *Amoeba-rt: Run-time verification of adaptive software.* Paper presented at the Models@Run.Time'07 Workshop, ACM/IEEE 10th International MoDELS 2007, Nashville, TN.

Zhang, S., Breitner, S., Cascio, W. E., Devlin, R. B., Neas, L. M., Diaz-Sanchez, D., ... Peters, A. (2018). Short-term effects of fine particulate matter and ozone on the cardiac conduction system in patients undergoing cardiac catheterization. *Particle and Fibre Toxicology*, *15*(1), 38. doi:10.118612989-018-0275-z PMID:30305173

Zhang, X., Yao, L., Huang, C., Sheng, Q. Z., & Wang, X. (2017). Intent recognition in smart living through deep recurrent neural networks. In *Proceedings International Conference on Neural Information Processing*. 10.1007/978-3-319-70096-0_76

Zhao, Y., Parvinzamir, F., Wilson, S., Wei, H., Deng, Z., Portokallidis, N., ... Dong, F. (2017). Integrated visualisation of wearable sensor data and risk models for individualised health monitoring and risk assessment to promote patient empowerment. *Journal of Visualization / the Visualization Society of Japan*, *20*(2), 405–413. doi:10.100712650-016-0402-6

Zheng, J., Chapman, W. W., Crowley, R. S., & Savova, G. K. (2011). Coreference resolution: A review of general methodologies and applications in the clinical domain. *Journal of Biomedical Informatics*, *44*(6), 1113–1122. doi:10.1016/j.jbi.2011.08.006 PMID:21856441

Zhou, L., Plasek, J. M., Mahoney, L. M., Karipineni, N., Chang, F., Yan, X., ... Rocha, R. A. (2011). Using medical text extraction, reasoning and mapping system (MTERMS) to process medication information in outpatient clinical notes. In *Proceedings AMIA Annual Symposium.*

Zhu, Y., Li, H., Liao, Y., Wang, B., Guan, Z., Liu, H., & Cai, D. (2017). What to do next: Modeling user behaviors by time-LSTM. In *Proceedings IJCAI.* 10.24963/ijcai.2017/504

Zimmerman, M. A. (2000). Empowerment theory. In J. Rappaport, & E. Seidman (Eds.), *Handbook of community psychology* (pp. 43–63). New York: Springer. doi:10.1007/978-1-4615-4193-6_2

About the Contributors

Jiban Khuntia is an Assistant Professor of Information Systems and Health Administration at the Business School of the University of Colorado Denver. His research interests are in the areas of health information technology and emerging IT service innovations. His work has appeared in the Journal of Management of Information Systems, Production and Operations Management, and Decision Support Systems, amongst others. He earned in Ph.D. from the University of Maryland. Before that, he has more than a decade of experience in IT and supercomputing areas.

* * *

Andrea Aria has teaching and research interests in software development, programming languages, machine learning, and big data. He has several publications in the field of stream-mining and event-based pattern discovery in ACM Transactions on MIS, and sponsored conferences. He has taught courses in object-oriented programming, web programming, data structure and algorithm analysis and design. Since 2004 he has been working in the IT industry concentrating on software development.

David Bobryk is a graduate of Oakland University in management information systems and received his master's degree in healthcare administration. David has worked in healthcare for 13 years as director of health informatics and data analytics."

Majid Dadgar is Assistant Professor of Business Analytics and Information Systems at University of San Francisco's School of Management. He received his M.A. in industrial and product design and applied software engineering from the Ohio State University, and his Ph.D. in Management Information Systems (MIS) from Washington State University. He has published articles in Journal of Business Ethics (JBE), Journal of the Association for Information Systems (JAIS), International Journal of Electronic Healthcare (IJEH), International Journal of Information Technology and Management (IJITM), and presented his research at the conferences ICIS, HICSS, AMCIS, DSI, and DESRIST.

Tianjie Deng is an assistant professor of the Department of Business Information and Analytics at the Daniels College of Business, University of Denver. She is doing research to apply data mining techniques to derive process models and theories from event streams. She has applied this research method in various domains such as patient rehabilitation, fraud detection in financial transactions, and software development. Her work has appeared in academic journals and conference proceedings including ACM Transactions on Management Information Systems, Information and Management, Americas Conference on Information Systems, Hawaii International Conference on System Science, and International Conference on Global Perspectives on Design Science Research.

Joel Fredrickson has doctoral degree in Computer Science and Information Systems from University of Colorado Denver. Currently the Analytics and Reporting Manager at AxisPoint Health, a private health care management company. Research agenda addresses the use of medical histories in clinical decision support systems. The fundamental part of his agenda is a similarity measure to help care managers better identify patients that have strong resemblance based on their medical history. Follow-up studies evaluate the similarity measure to assess its classification performance and applicability. Longer-term plans involve integration of patient record data elements to enhance predictive performance, development of a query architecture for medical histories, and human factor studies assessing usage of the architecture by medical professionals.

K. D. Joshi is the Philip L. Kays Distinguished Professor of Information Systems and Chair of the Department of Management, Information Systems and Entrepreneurship at the University of Nevada. She received her Master of Science in Engineering from the University of Michigan and received her Doctor of Philosophy in Business Administration (Decision Sciences and Information Systems) from the University of Kentucky. Dr. Joshi's research interests focus on IT Workforce Issues, Broadening Participation in STEM, Knowledge Management, Crowdsourcing, IT-Enabled Innovation, Value Sensitive Designs, and Health IT. Her published research is cited over 4,600 times according to Google Scholar and her research has been featured in numerous media outlets such PBS NewsHour, Salon.com, Vancouver Business Journal, London School of Economic Business Review, Puget Sound Business Journal, & Military.Com. She has been a Principal Investigator or Co-Principal Investigator on grants totaling over $5M from the National Science Foundation (NSF). Her research has appeared in journals such as MIS Quarterly, Information Systems Research, Journal of the AIS, Decision Support Systems, IEEE Transactions of Engineering Management, and Communications of the ACM.

Abhishek Kathuria is an Assistant Professor of Information Systems at the Indian School of Business. He received his Ph.D. from the Goizueta Business School at Emory University. His research examines the business value of IT, focusing on innovation, digital platform strategies, and emerging economies. Dr. Kathuria's work has been published in journals such as Journal of Management Information Systems, Information Systems Research, The Journal of High Technology Management Research, among others, and received multiple best paper nominations and awards at various academic conferences. He is an advisor to and co-founder of multiple startups and consults on business transformation, organizational turnarounds, and IT strategy with public and private corporations in Hong Kong, India, and the Middle East.

Yang Lu received his B.S. degree from Jilin University, China, in 2004 and the M.S. degree from the University of Manchester, UK, in 2006. He is currently pursuing his Ph.D. degree in ICT (Information and Communication Technology) in USA. He is a member of IEEE. He has published research papers in refereed journals published by major publishers such as Elsevier, IEEE, Taylor & Francis, and World Scientific.

Ramalatha Marimuthu has been in teaching for 32 years and currently working as Professor in ECE in Kumaraguru College of Technology. She has published six technical books and over thirty research papers in international conferences and journals in the areas of Vedic Mathematics, Embedded System Design, Data Sciences and VLSI. Her interest in building assistive systems for the health care and special needs people has culminated into developing unique solutions for dyslexia, speech impaired, drop foot and autism. This earned her invitations from Google and various universities all over the world to deliver special lectures. She has won many international awards from organisations like IEEE, USA, Lions Club and Anita Borg Institute for Women and Technology, California for her work towards the community.

Mark P. Martz, PhD, serves as the Director of the Arizona Center for Tobacco Cessation and is an Assistant Professor of Practice in the Mel and Enid Zuckerman College of Public Health at the University of Arizona. Prior to joining the University of Arizona in November 2018, Dr. Martz served for five years at the Arizona Department of Health Services. While at the Arizona Department of Health Services, Mark served as a policy consultant, contract manager, and as the Office Chief for Tobacco Prevention and Cessation. Mark received his doctorate in Public Administration and Policy from Arizona State University in 2013 and his Master in Public Administration from Wichita State University in 2007. Dr. Martz's research and applied practice focus area centers on developing, implementing, and analyzing system-level interventions that improve health and well-being at an individual, community, and population level.

Matthew Nawrocki is a Database Administrator and Business Intelligence Developer for St. Joseph Mercy Oakland. He graduated with a B.S.from the University of Michigan, Ann Arbor, and an M.B.A., specializing in MIS, from Oakland University. His work involves business analytics, architecture, and development of software solutions, and technological implementations to improve operational processes and evidenced-based discovery.

Xue Ning is a Lecturer of Information Systems at the Business School of the University of Colorado Denver. Her main research interest is the economics of information systems with a focus on the IT strategy and IS/IT for sustainability. Her work has appeared in refereed conference proceedings, including the International Conference on Information Systems, Academy of Management, and others. She is pursuing Ph.D. in Computer Science and Information Systems at the University of Colorado Denver. She worked with international organizations in South Korea before moving to Denver.

Sumate Permwonguswa is a lecturer of Management Information Systems, Martin de Tours School of Management and Economics, Assumption University in Thailand. He received his Ph.D. in Computer Science and Information Systems from the Business School, University of Colorado Denver. His research areas are in health IT and ERP pre- and post-implementation. His work has appeared in journals including Health Systems and Health Management Policy and Innovation. He has prior experience in the software and web development industry.

Thiagarajan Ramakrishnan is an Associate Professor of Management Information Systems in the College of Business at Prairie View A&M University. He received his Ph.D. in Business Computer Information Systems from the University of North Texas in 2010. His research interests include Business Intelligence and Analytics (BI&A), Information Systems Discipline, Cloud Computing, and Social Media. His work appears in such journals as MIS Quarterly, Decision Support Systems, Computers in Human Behavior, and Journal of Organizational and End User Computing.

William Robinson is an associate professor in the Computer Information Systems Department at the Robinson College of Business at Georgia State University. His research is working towards the improvement of software systems understanding, design and operation. He is also exploring various approaches to providing automated support for systems analysts. Through the research of these two complimentary areas, Robinson has developed a theory of "negotiated design" as well as associated CASE tool support. His work has appeared in academic journals including Journal of Management Information Systems, ACM Transactions on Management Information Systems, IEEE Transactions on Software Engineering, ACM Computing Surveys, Information Systems, International Journal of Production Research, Communications of the ACM, International Journal of Open Source Software and Processes, and in conference proceedings such as Americas Conference on Information Systems, International Conference on Software Engineering, IEEE International Conference on Requirements Engineering, Hawaii International Conference on System Science, International Conference on Open Source Systems, and others.

Terence J. V. Saldanha is an Assistant Professor of Management Information Systems at the Terry College of Business at the University of Georgia. Before arriving at the University of Georgia, he was a faculty at Washington State University. He received his Ph.D. in Information Systems from the Stephen Ross School of Business at the University of Michigan. His research interests include the business value of IS, and the role of IS in innovation. His research has been published in journals such as MIS Quarterly, Journal of Management Information Systems, Journal of Operations Management, and Production and Operations Management, among others, and in various academic conference proceedings. Prior to his graduate studies, he worked in the software development industry.

M. N. Saroja acquired her B.E degree in Computer science and Engineering from PSNA College of Engineering and Technology, Anna University, Chennai in the year 2010 and Master's degree in Computer Science and Engineering from Mepco Schlenk Engineering College, Anna University, Chennai, in the year 2012 and she has been credited with the Best Outstanding Student of the department. She started her career as Assistant Professor in the Department of Information Technology, K.L.N. College of Engineering, Madurai, India. At present she is an Assistant Professor in the Department of Information Technology, Kumaraguru College of Technology, Coimbatore, India. Her area of interests includes IoT and Data Analytics. She has published 3 journals, 1 book chapter in Springer and 10 conference paper publications.

S. N. Shivappriya received her B.E (ECE) degree from Periyar University in 2004. She obtained her M.E (Communication System) degree from Anna university Chennai in 2006. She has completed her doctoral programme in Bio-Medical Engineering from Anna university Chennai in 2015. She has 13 years of teaching experience at college level. Currently she is working as Assistant Professor II in

Department of ECE at Kumaraguru College of Technology, Coimbatore. Her area of interest is Bio signal Processing, Soft computing, Embedded and Communication systems. She is member of ISTE, IEEE.She Published 12 papers in National and International Journals, 2 book chapters in springer and 30 conference paper publications.

Anupam A. Sule, MD, PhD, is the Chief Medical Informatics Officer and Medical Director of Outcomes at St Joseph Mercy Oakland, a large urban teaching hospital which is a member of Trinity Health (the second largest non-profit healthcare system in the US). He has worked at multiple hospitals and healthcare systems in Souteast Michigan in clinical, administrative and faculty positions. Dr Sule has published basic, clinical and translational research in the field of biomedical sciences, internal medicine, quality improvement and informatics. His current interests include population health management using informatics and data analytics.

Mohan Tanniru is the Professor in the Division of Public Health Practice and Translational Research in the Mel and Enid Zuckerman College of Public Health, U of Arizona, Tucson/Phoenix and a senior investigator in the Global Health Initiative at Henry Ford Health System in Detroit, MI. He is also an emeritus professor of MIS of Oakland University. He was the former Dean of the School of Business and the Dept. Head of MIS at U of Arizona. He has published over 90 research articles and his work has appeared in journals such as ISR, MIS Quarterly, Decision Sciences, DSS, JMIS, IEEE Transactions in Eng. Management, Expert Systems, and Applications, Information and Management, CACM, as well as Health Policy and Technology, J of Patient Satisfaction, J of Healthcare Management and J of Healthcare Administration. He worked with over 70 large and small corporations in support of research and teaching.

Dobin Yim is an Assistant Professor of Information Systems, Law, and Operations (ISLO) at the Sellinger School of Business, Loyola University Maryland. His research to date has examined the social impact of information technology in healthcare, media management, and environmental sustainability. He earned his PhD from the University of Maryland, and has more than 10 years of industry experience in IT fields, specializing in enterprise systems implementation.

Index

R

S

T

U

V

W

www.ingramcontent.com/pod-product-compliance
Lightning Source LLC
LaVergne TN
LVHW080558300926
849162LV00005B/989